CONSTRUCTION LAW

AUSTRALIA
The Law Book Company
Sydney

CANADA
The Carswell Company
Toronto, Ontario

INDIA
N.M. Tripathi Private Ltd.
Bombay
and
Eastern Law House (Private) Ltd.
Calcutta
M.P.P. House
Bangalore
Universal Book Traders
Delhi

ISRAEL
Steimatzky's Agency Ltd.
Tel-Aviv

PAKISTAN
Pakistan Law House
Karachi

CONSTRUCTION LAW

law and practice relating to the
construction industry

By

JOHN UFF

Q.C., Ph.D., B.Sc.(Eng.)
F.I.C.E., F.C.I.Arb.

Chartered Engineer, Barrister
Visiting Professor and Director,
Centre of Construction Law and Management,
Kings College, London

FIFTH EDITION

LONDON

SWEET & MAXWELL

1991

First Edition 1974
Second Edition 1978
Third Edition 1981
Fourth Edition 1985
Second Impression 1989
Fifth Edition 1991

*Sweet & Maxwell Limited of
South Quay Plaza, 183 Marsh Wall London E14 9FT.
Computerset by LBJ Enterprises Limited, Chilcompton and Tadley.
Printed in Scotland*

**A catalogue record for this book is
available from the British Library.**

ISBN 0–421–43330–2

©
John Uff
1991

PREFACE

Since its first edition, this book has been addressed to all those who make up the construction industry. It is not intended principally for lawyers, nor is it aimed at architects and engineers. Rather, it is written for those who practice in the field of construction law, from whatever background they approach the subject.

This book is written also in the belief that there is a body of principles which should govern the efficient performance and management of construction operations, which derive both from legal principles and from the construction activity itself. As the subject of construction law develops this is perhaps its most engaging aspect and its highest challenge. The subject has a dual nature, and to confine it to one aspect of this duality will always lead to inefficiency or worse. The six years since the last edition of *Construction Law* has seen the setting up of the Centre of Construction Law and Management at King's College London. Courses run at this Centre are aimed intentionally at both lawyers and non-lawyers. It is to be hoped that this approach will promote not only increasing numbers of persons working in the construction law field from both the legal and the technical sides of the industry, but also an increasing mobility between the professions which make up construction law. It may be that these objectives would be more focused if the subject were called construction management rather than construction law. Perhaps that will come.

The material in this new edition follows substantially the format of the fourth edition, with additions in a number of areas including: public law rights, international arbitration, contractual warranties and the incorporation of standard terms. The major area which has required substantial rewriting, is the law of negligence. As can now be seen, the case of *Junior Books* v. *Veitchi* represented a watershed. It was followed by a series of decisions culminating in the House of Lords' judgments in *DoE* v. *Thomas Bates* and *Murphy* v. *Brentwood DC*. It might be said that these decisions have reduced the law of tort to a backwater in the field of construction. On the other hand, sufficient exceptions have been left for tort to continue to play an important role, particularly in regard to professional liability. Two other aspects of the extraordinary rise and fall in the law of negligence are worthy of note. First, the expectations generated during the heyday of tortious negligence actions can be seen to have led directly to the current development of contractual warranties. Secondly, this great area of development of the common law has related almost exclusively to construction. Thus, instead of having to borrow its major principles from the field of commercial law, construction can be seen as a major generator of common law in its own right.

This edition also includes a review of the new ICE Conditions of Contract, 6th edition published in 1990, as well as coverage of the substantial revisions introduced to the JCT Form of Contract, 1980 edition.

As in previous editions, I remain greatly indebted to many friends and colleagues in the fields of civil engineering, construction, arbitration and law. In a subject still comparatively underdeveloped, discussion and exchange of views is essential. I am particularly indebted to my colleagues in Chambers and at the Centre of Construction Law and Management at King's College.

Finally, I thank both Thomas Telford Publications and RIBA Publications for their kind permission to reproduce the ICE Conditions of Contract and the JCT Form of Contract respectively.

May 24, 1991   **JOHN UFF**
10 Essex Street
London WC2

ACKNOWLEDGEMENTS

Grateful acknowledgment is made to the following publishers for permission to quote from their works:

ARBITRATION ACTS 1950 AND 1979: © Crown Copyright

CARSWELL LEGAL PUBLICATIONS: Business Law Review © Thomson Professional Publishing Canada, A Division of Thomson Canada Limited

THE INCORPORATED COUNCIL OF LAW REPORTING FOR ENGLAND AND WALES: Law Reports and Weekly Law Reports

LLOYD'S OF LONDON PRESS LIMITED: Lloyd's Reports

LONGMAN GROUP UK LIMITED: Solicitors' Journal and Building Law Reports

CONTENTS

ix

TABLE OF CASES

xiii

TABLE OF STATUTES

Chapter 1

CONSTRUCTION AND THE LEGAL SYSTEM

"Construction law" is neither a legal term of art nor a technical one. It is used to cover the whole field of law which, in one way or another, affects the construction industry. This book is an attempt to cover that field.

Most of the book is concerned with substantive law, that is, law which lays down rights and duties of individuals. The concern of most people is to keep well within the bounds of the law, and to avoid becoming involved in legal action unless it is unavoidable. Therefore substantive law is all that concerns the majority of persons. But the construction industry is a peculiar case. As presently constituted its methods and its structure seem inevitably to lead the parties frequently to the brink of legal action and not infrequently beyond it.

Many individuals in the construction industry will at some time in their careers become professionally involved in litigation or arbitration. And there can be few people who do not have some dealings with contractors' claims, which may be a prelude to litigation. For these reasons the contents of this book extend beyond substantive law, to give some account of the system of English law which lies behind the rights and duties. In this chapter the sources and categories of law are described.

THE NATURE OF LAW

Different types of law create different kinds of rights and duties. Some law applies only between individuals; if A behaves in a way which causes loss to B, then the civil law may allow B to recover his loss from A. Much of the law of contract and tort applies in this way, B's legal remedy being the only sanction against A. In

1

other types of law the State may be involved; if A drives his motor car negligently he may be liable not only for B's resulting loss (through injury to him or his property) but also to criminal prosecution. Some areas of law concern only the rights or duties of the individual against the State; for example planning law or tax law. Most of the principles discussed in this work relate to civil law.

The factor which connects various types of law is that they all exist in order to allow persons to regulate their lives with reasonable certainty, and in a manner which our society presently considers to be just. The law is often accused of unwarranted delay, and of being old fashioned and too complicated. All these things are at times true. But law is made by and for human beings, who today lead lives of unprecedented complexity. The fact that the law will, if called upon, provide a reasoned solution to any type of human problem is in no small degree remarkable.

Law and technology

Many readers will be familiar with scientific or technical subjects. It may therefore be informative to examine the nature of law through the ways in which law differs from technology.

First, in technical fields there are always some problems which, for the time being perhaps, cannot be solved. Until the invention of large-diameter bored piles engineers considered that tall buildings could not be built in London, because of the compressible clay sub-soil. In law such a situation never arises. No matter how complex may be the facts of a case or how confused the law, a judge must always decide which of the parties wins. This does not mean that the judge is always right. There may be an appeal against his decision; but the same problem then confronts a higher court.

The way in which the courts solve a difficult problem may be illustrated by a judicial example. In the case of *S.C.M.* v. *Whittall* (1970) the Court of Appeal had to decide whether the plaintiff's loss was excluded by a rule of law. The precise extent of the rule was a matter of uncertainty. In giving judgment, Lord Denning said:

> "Where is the line to be drawn? Lawyers are continually asking that question. But the judges are never defeated by it. We may not be able to draw the line with precision, but we can always say on which side of it any particular case falls."

Secondly, in engineering and building practice approximation and simplification play a large part: small light structures may be safely designed using approximate methods, while on large structures many more factors have to be taken into account. In law there is (or should be) no such scale effect. The law applied to a claim for £100 in the county court is the same as that applied to a claim for £10 million in the High Court. This view of the law perhaps explains the old adage that a lawyer will never give a simple answer to a simple question. Simplification of the facts of a case does not simplify the law involved, and one may need to know every factual detail before even a guess can be made at the probable legal result. There are many examples in the law reports of leading cases, often going to the House of Lords, where the sum in issue between the parties was very modest.

Thirdly, while technology proceeds upon logical induction and deduction, the development of the common law is different. General principles of law must be arrived at by induction. But when a judge seeks to extend an established principle of law he may do it in a way which does not amount to logical deduction. The common law in its practical application has been said to be more the embodiment of common sense than reason. The point was expressed judicially in the *S.C.M.* case above:

> "In the varied web of human affairs the law must abstract some consequences as relevant not perhaps on the grounds of pure logic, but simply for practical reasons."

Fourthly, although technology advances with increasing rapidity not everyone uses the latest theories and methods. Indeed, one could today build a perfectly satisfactory bridge using a design by Brunel. A modern bridge would simply be much cheaper. In law the situation is quite different. Legal rights and duties depend only upon what the law says at the relevant time.

A change in statute law can mean that a man may do an act on one day with impunity but on the next at his peril. Common law, or case precedent, is rather different. In theory the judge states what the law is and has always been, so that a restatement applies retrospectively. The practical effect as to the future is, however, the same as a change in the law. Thus, when considering the law on some point, the very latest sources must be consulted; and possible future changes may need to be considered. It is by no means unknown for a court to come to a wrong decision because

a recent change in statute law or recent case on the point was not
brought to its attention.

CATEGORIES OF LAW

English law may be categorised in a number of ways. It may be
divided into what is called substantive law and procedure.
Substantive law refers to all the branches of law which define
persons' rights and duties, such as contract, tort and crime. The
substantive law determines in a particular case what facts must be
proved to achieve a certain result, such as to establish that a
contract has been concluded. These may be called the facts in
issue, and in the example given, a fact in issue might be whether
the defendant withdrew his offer before the plaintiff accepted it
(see further page 81).

Procedure deals with the often complex rules through which
the process of law is set in motion to enforce some substantive
right or remedy. Procedure properly arises only when there is
resort to legal action, but nevertheless it can be as important in
practice as the substantive law. In the context of construction
disputes, procedure includes arbitration, which has its own procedural rules (see page 47).

A further division of law is into common law and statute law;
that is, into judge-made law and legislation. Then there is
another type of division between common law (used in a rather
different sense) and equity, which is a distinction based upon the
two great independent roots of English law. These latter two
divisions are discussed separately in the following sections
because they are fundamentally concerned with the sources of
our law. While considering each of the divisions it should be
borne in mind that they are not mutually exclusive. The statute
law deals with procedure and substantive law; judge-made law
comprises equity as well as common law, and so on.

Another division is between private law and public law,
sometimes called administrative law. Private law relates to rights
exercisable by and against individuals (including corporations and
other legal entities). Public law, however, applies in the domain
of the exercise of powers and duties by public bodies which may
affect the rights or expectations of individuals. The way in which
public law rights may be enforced is significantly different to
private rights, and consists essentially of applying to the courts
for orders to regulate the actions of public bodies. The enforce-

ment of public law rights is dealt with below (see page 33). Yet another division exists between so-called domestic and international law. And international law itself falls into two distinct categories: private international law, which applies to disputes having an international character but concerning individuals or other legal entities; and public international law, which applies between states. Private international law comprises the rules applied in a particular country to resolve conflict between the domestic law of that country and of other countries whose laws may affect a dispute (see further page 113). Public international law is not dealt with in this book.

Since 1972 a further category of law has applied throughout Great Britain. As a result of joining the European Economic Community (the Common Market) English law became subject to the instruments of the law-making institutions of the EEC. European law as such is not dealt with in this book. However, an early example of the effect of the EEC occurred in *Bulmer* v. *Bollinger S.A.* (1974), which became known as the "Champagne" case. The defendant French company claimed that the use of the word champagne to describe an English beverage contravened community law. The court was asked to refer the issue to the European Court of Justice under Article 177 of the Treaty of Rome. Lord Denning took the opportunity to expound the effect of the new law:

> "The first and fundamental point is that the Treaty concerns only those matters which have a European element, that is to say, matters which affect people or property in the nine countries of the common market besides ourselves. The Treaty does not touch any of the matters which concern solely England and the people in it. These are still governed by English law. They are not affected by the Treaty. But when we come to matters with a European element, the Treaty is like an incoming tide. It flows into the estuaries and up the rivers. It cannot be held back. Parliament has decreed that the Treaty is henceforward to be part of our law. It is equal in force to any statute. . . . In future, in transactions which cross the frontiers, we must no longer speak and think of English law as something on its own. We must speak and think of the community law, of community rights and obligations, and we must give effect to them."

It may be noted that there are far-reaching developments on foot within the EEC which will affect construction work. These relate to competition law, public procurement and to proposals for harmonisation in the field of liability and compensation.

The common law

English law is based upon the common law system. The common law means literally the law which was applied in common over all parts of the realm. It was created in the twelfth and thirteenth centuries by the King's judges and has been developed and handed down to the present day. The essential feature of the common law which distinguishes it from other systems, is that it is based entirely on evolving precedent, with no written principles from which the precedent stems. The common law has thus been found a wonderfully flexible instrument, capable of rapid adaption to wholly new circumstances without obvious strain.

One effect of the spread of the English-speaking peoples from the sixteenth century onwards, was that they took with them their laws. As a result, by the nineteenth century there was established literally throughout the world, a greater common law, subject, of course, to the effect of statute law in any particular state. Within the British Empire, and later the Commonwealth, this law was maintained as a truly common system by the establishment of the Privy Council (composed largely of members of the judicial committee of the House of Lords) as the final court of appeal. Today this still applies to a limited number of countries including New Zealand, Singapore and Malaysia. Countries which have abolished the right of appeal to the Privy Council, such as Canada and South Africa, tend inevitably to diverge from English law with the passage of time. The United States, which has developed its own law for 200 years has adopted some notable differences from English law, such as stricter liability under the law of tort. The remarkable fact remains, however, that English courts take note of and guidance from decisions from any common law country and to an often greater extent, English decisions are noted and often followed or adopted in many different countries.

Like the constitution, the common law is not written down or enshrined in any hallowed document. It is stated each time a judgment is given at the end of a case, when the judge gives reasons for the legal rules embodied in his decision. In practice, therefore, the common law is to be found in the reports of judgments, and the law on any topic is to be discovered by reading all the cases which turn on related facts. In some areas there will be only one or two cases, but in others there will be many dozens, perhaps going back several centuries. Building and engineering law is one field where authorities are often sparse, because of the specialist nature of these disputes. Much assistance can be gained from foreign decisions.

Law reports

Not every case before the courts makes new law. It is only cases which involve a point of law which can do so; that is, when the law is uncertain in its application to the particular facts. Many cases, particularly in the field of crime, depend simply upon conflicting versions of the facts. When the court has come to a decision on the facts the application of the law is clear. In construction cases, points of law are often involved, because the effect of the forms of contract is so often unclear. Although such decisions will be read with interest in the construction world, the judgments are not usually regarded as creating new law, but merely as elucidation of the contracts.

Of the cases which do lay down new law, the important ones are published in reports. A law report contains, verbatim, the essential points of the judge's decision. Subsequently, writers of textbooks and articles, and judges in later cases, will comment upon the judgments and mould them into propositions of law. This is an essential process to make the law manageable. But when a point of law arises the lawyer must go back to the reports to discover the words in which the judges have previously stated the law.

It is curious that in England there has never been an official organisation to produce law reports. Until the last century all law reporting was carried on by private enterprise and the quality of reports was not always very high. Today there is a semi-official body which produces a series called "The Law Reports," which are completely authoritative. There are also still a number of commercially produced series. Two well-known series which contain most cases of general interest are the Weekly Law Reports (W.L.R.) and the All England Law Reports (All E.R.). Building cases in the Law Reports will appear in Queen's Bench reports (Q.B.) or Chancery (Ch.) or Appeal Cases (A.C.). Commercial cases, including many important decisions in the field of arbitration and contract, appear in Lloyd's Reports (Lloyd's Rep.). The abbreviation in brackets is the citation for a particular series (the year, volume and page also being given). Frequently, cases will be reported in more than one series.

In addition to the well-established series, a new series was introduced in 1976 to deal exclusively with cases affecting the construction industry. Building Law Reports (Build. L.R.) do not follow the traditional pattern of publishing reports as they appear, but include earlier decisions not previously reported or not readily available. They also contain brief commentaries, and volumes cover particular topics. A further series, more recently introduced is the Construction Law Reports (Const.L.R.).

The common law is what is said by the judge, not merely what is reported. If, therefore, a case fails to get into the reports it may still be relied upon. This is done usually by obtaining a transcript of the judgment. In the field of building contracts there are sometimes important cases which do not find their way into the English reports. These, and many of the more important foreign decisions, may be found noted in text books such as *Hudson's Building and Engineering Contracts*, and *Keating's Building Contracts*.

A notable disadvantage of case law is that the law can only be altered or restated when a case comes before the court. Thus, if a decision is made which is thought to be wrong, this remains as the law until a similar case comes before that or a higher court, when the law can be reconsidered. Furthermore, the judges are concerned solely with stating what the common law is, and not what it should be. Both these disadvantages are overcome by augmenting the common law through the quite separate system of statute law.

Statute law

While the judges declare and apply the common law, Parliament in its legislative capacity passes enactments to change the law. Since the seventeenth century Parliament has had supreme authority so that in theory it can make or unmake any law. The passing of a Bill through Parliament and the argument at different stages in its passage can be followed in the news media. The end result is an officially printed document which states, in the words chosen by Parliament, the law on some topic or group of topics.

Once enacted, and in force, the words of the statute are themselves law. But there naturally arise situations where the words call for interpretation, and this is done by the courts. The declarations of the judges on the interpretation of statutes thus become a sub-branch of the common law, with which the statutes must be read to decide their meaning.

A notable example of this process is the Arbitration Act 1979, which was generally thought to be intended to facilitate appeals. The House of Lords, however, interpreted the Act in *The Nema* (1980), so as virtually to rule out any appeal save in the most exceptional cases (see further page 57).

Rules and regulations

In addition to statute law proper there has, principally during this century, grown up a great body of delegated or sub-legislation. This is written not by Parliament itself, but by some other body or official to whom Parliament has given authority. The sub-legislators range from ministers of the government to statutory bodies such as local authorities. This delegated legislation goes under such names as rules, regulations or by-laws. It takes effect as though it were contained in the parent Act, which sets out the delegated power. As an example, the Building Act 1984 contains authority under which the Building Regulations are made. A great deal of day-to-day activity in industry, including the construction industry, is covered by delegated legislation. In general this lays down more stringent and specific duties than those which are to be found in the common law (see Chapter 15).

Much of European Community law consists of delegated legislation. This is made, not under direct English statutory authority, but under powers in the European Treaties to which the United Kingdom has acceded. Rights and obligations so created are given effect to in English law by the surprisingly simple device of providing, by section 2 of the European Communities Act 1972, that such rights and obligations "are without further enactment to be given legal effect." These few words produced the effect described by Lord Denning in the Champagne case, above.

Equity

In the division between common law and equity, each branch comprises both judge-made law (found in case reports) and statute law. The difference arises because before 1873, when the systems began to be jointly administered, there were two separate legal systems. They operated in different courts. Equity was applied in the old Court of Chancery, which is still to be found in Lincoln's Inn. Charles Dickens found much to criticise in the courts of early nineteenth century England. He reserved the most biting condemnation for the interminable delays of Chancery in *Bleak House*. Happily, the delays in the Chancery Division are today no more than in the rest of the High Court.

The differences between law and equity are still of importance. One essential distinction is that a common law remedy is a right, whereas a remedy in equity is, theoretically, discretionary. It depends on the justice of the cause. The distinction may be illustrated by the consequences of a breach of contract. The common law remedy is damages. These will be awarded, however unjustly the plaintiff has acted, and whether or not damages will make good the loss suffered. Alternatively, in equity the plaintiff can ask for the remedy of specific performance, that is, that the defendant be compelled to fulfil his obligation. But this will be available only under certain conditions, *inter alia*, that the plaintiff has acted fairly, that he has not delayed in seeking his remedy, and that damages would not adequately compensate him (see further page 111).

Where to find the law

From the foregoing it may be said that the law proper is to be found only in law reports and in statutes, regulations and the like. However, textbooks and articles by academics, practitioners and judges play an important part in stating the law. Their role is not only to present the source material in a convenient form, but also to analyse, comment and speculate upon gaps in the law. In some fields, of which building and engineering contracts are a good example, what is said in the established textbooks can often be a valuable guide to the court in deciding a point of law. Sometimes the court cites with approval a particular passage from a textbook as being an accurate statement of the law. The status of any book depends, of course, on the standing of its author and current editor. As a general rule, it is said that the courts pay less attention to the views of an author while he is still alive.

Legal textbooks are of several different kinds. Many are written by individuals on particular topics. But some are published in series, intended to create an encyclopedia of law. The best known of these is *Halsbury's Laws of England*, first published in 31 volumes between 1907 and 1919. The current fourth edition is in 50 volumes and is periodically up-dated. The companion work *Halsbury's Statutes of England* deals with legislation. Each topic in these works is written or edited by one or more distinguished contributor. *Halsbury* is often cited in court as a convenient summary of the law.

THE COURTS

There are a number of different courts in which civil actions may be tried. A case will be heard at first instance in the High Court, or a small case, in the County Court. The High Court comprises a number of different types of court each of which can be found at different locations throughout the country. Appeals may then be brought to the Court of Appeal and finally to the House of Lords. These appeal courts sit only in London.

Courts of first instance

The High Court is divided into three divisions; The Queen's Bench, the Chancery and the Family Division. Although each division administers the common law and equity and could theoretically deal with any matter, in practice a particular case will be heard only in one division. Matters concerning the construction industry come usually before the Queen's Bench Division, but occasionally before the Chancery Division. The Queen's Bench Division deals with most common law work, such as contract and tort. The Chancery Division deals with matters such as trusts, contracts relating to land and company and partnership disputes.

Within the Queen's Bench Division of the High Court, there are two particular divisions where construction cases may be found. The first is the Commercial Court where mercantile, banking, insurance and shipping cases and the like are tried before High Court judges assigned from the Queen's Bench Division. The second is the Official Referee's Court. Here, matters specifically relating to the construction industry are tried by circuit judges appointed to deal with Official Referee's business. In each case, an action may be started in the Commercial Court or in the Official Referee's Court; or it may be started in the Queen's Bench Division and later transferred.

An alternative for a small action is trial in the county court by a circuit judge. Every district in the country has its local county court. There are proposals to transfer a substantial volume of cases from the High Court to the county courts. The principal alternative to court action in a construction dispute is arbitration. This is dealt with further in Chapter 3.

Appeals

After the hearing of a case at first instance either party may consider an appeal. From the High Court there is a general right of appeal in civil cases to the Court of Appeal, subject to some cases where leave is necessary. One important case in which leave is needed is an appeal from a finding of fact in an Official Referee's case. An important difference between an appeal and the original trial or action, is that the appeal will usually be concerned solely with argument. New evidence is very rarely admitted in the Court of Appeal. On appeal, the court will give its own decision on matters of law, but in matters of fact or the exercise of discretion, the appeal will be allowed only if it is shown that the judge was wrong in principle.

After appealing to the Court of Appeal, a further appeal may be brought to the House of Lords. But leave is always necessary and is sparingly given. House of Lords appeals are almost always on an important point of law. Where both the High Court and the Court of Appeal are bound by previous decisions it is possible to appeal direct from the High Court to the House of Lords.

Every court must apply statute law. However, with case law, courts are generally bound only by the decisions of higher courts, and to some extent by their own decisions. It is therefore usually necessary to take a case to a higher court if it is sought to avoid an adverse case precedent. It is possible for the House of Lords to reverse its own previous decisions. In practice the law laid down by the House of Lords is changed usually by explaining previous decisions.

Further Reading

Glanville Williams, *Learning the Law* (11th ed., 1982).
Kiralfy, *The English Legal System* (8th ed., 1990).

CHAPTER 2

LITIGATION

SOME disputes in the construction industry are tried in the courts by litigation; others are determined by arbitration. This chapter deals with the ways in which the courts function, in terms of procedure and the rules of evidence. To an extent, what is said about litigation applies also to arbitration, with the proviso that arbitration arises out of an agreement, so that what takes place is less predictable and less standardised. The procedure in a court action is described in this chapter. In the next chapter the rules and procedure in arbitration are described.

PROCEDURE

Procedure is a general term which covers the various steps necessary to turn a legal right into a satisfied judgment. It might appear that procedure is mostly concerned with the rituals of trial and is the concern only of lawyers. But this is far from the case. In many actions, particularly larger civil ones, the trial is only a small part of the whole case. What goes on before the trial can have a great effect on the course of the action, and often leads to a settlement. The pre-trial proceedings will usually extend over months, or even years. Matters such as appeals and the enforcement of judgments may prolong the matter further after the trial. Procedure covers all these different stages.

Procedure in the High Court is governed by statutory rules known as the Rules of the Supreme Court. These are published with extensive notes and annotations in a two volume work known as The Supreme Court Practice, or colloquially as the "White Book." The rules themselves are contained in some 114 Orders each of which is divided into rules and sub-rules. Each order covers a separate subject such as pleadings, amendments, discovery of documents, etc. Orders are cited as "R.S.C. Order 24," etc.

The basic steps involved in a civil action in the Queen's Bench Division, where most cases concerning the construction industry will be brought, are as follows. The action is begun by issuing and serving a writ. The defendant must file an acknowledgement of service to the writ and then an exchange of pleadings takes place so that the parties know the area of contention. The next stage is the preparation for trial which includes discovery and inspection of documents and the collection of evidence. Finally comes the trial itself which results in a judgment. If there is no appeal, the matter is concluded by enforcement of the judgment. The principal steps are enlarged upon below.

Very few actions proceed in such an apparently straightforward manner. At every stage there are alternative courses, and in fact the great majority of High Court actions (well in excess of 90 per cent.) are disposed of before reaching trial. The preparatory stages between the issue of the writ and trial are known as interlocutory proceedings. Where any decision may be given by the court at an interlocutory stage it is usually given by a master of the court. He is an official who has most of the powers of a judge. The powers of the master include giving judgment in cases which do not go to trial, for example, because there is no real defence. In cases before an Official Referee or in the Commercial Court, interlocutory orders are made by the trial judge, which has the advantage of ensuring familiarity with the issues before trial. The same applies in an arbitration.

Commencement

A typical action is begun by issuing a writ, which places the matter on the official record. A copy of the writ must be served on the defendant, either by delivering it to him personally, or by other means, such as service on his solicitor. The general rule is that the defendant must be made aware of the proceedings against him. But there is an important exception in respect of limited companies. The Companies Act 1985, section 725, provides that a company may be served by leaving the writ at its registered office, or sending it there by post. A company which does not trade from its registered office must therefore make arrangements to collect the post. A writ is normally valid for four months and must be served within this period (not 12 months, as applied until the recent change in the rules).

One particular advantage of litigation is that there may be two or more defendants, and the plaintiff may plead different causes of action in the same proceedings. In appropriate circumstances there may even be more than one plaintiff, for example, where there is some common question of law or fact which will arise. In contrast, arbitration proceedings are usually limited to the two parties to the arbitration agreement (see page 44).

Some actions must be begun by a different type of document such as an originating summons or a petition; for example, a petition is appropriate to wind up a company (and a marriage). After he has been served with a writ the defendant must formally show his intention to defend the action by entering an acknowledgment of service, after which the parties, through their counsel or solicitors, exchange pleadings.

Pleadings

The object of pleadings is to define the areas of dispute between the parties before the action comes to trial. A party will not normally be allowed to raise a matter at the trial unless he has pleaded it. A pleading should contain a concise statement of the facts relied upon, but not the evidence by which they will be proved; and matters of law should not normally be pleaded. In construction cases it is sometimes necessary to plead facts in considerable detail, and issues of construction arising out of the form of contract are often pleaded. The golden rule is that any matter which may take the opposing party by surprise should be pleaded expressly. The first pleading is called the statement of claim from the plaintiff; the defendant answers with a defence and if the plaintiff wishes, he may answer the defence with a reply. In larger cases there may be pleadings subsequent to the reply. In arbitrations, pleadings are subject to the arbitrator's directions. They often follow High Court practice, and are called points of claim, points of defence, etc.

With his defence, the defendant may raise any matter of complaint which he has against the plaintiff. When the complaint is in the nature of a cross-action, it is called a counterclaim. A common form of counterclaim in building disputes is that the work, for which the plaintiff claims payment, is defective. If the counterclaim has a sufficiently close connection with the claim (it need not always arise out of the same contract) it may operate as a set-off to the claim. The importance of a set-off is that it operates as a defence, and therefore defeats the claim *pro tanto* This means that, even if there is no defence to the claim, the plaintiff cannot claim judgment for the amount covered by a set-off until the counterclaim is determined. A set-off may also have consequences as to costs. Where there is a counterclaim, the plaintiff must serve a defence to it with his reply.

The statement of claim, and any counterclaim, must expressly claim the remedy sought. In contract and tort actions the remedy is usually damages, that is, the payment of a sum of money by way of compensation. But there are several other remedies, which may be more appropriate in different circumstances, such as an injunction, or specific performance, or rectification of the contract. The damages claimed may be either general or special. General damages are claimed where the plaintiff has suffered loss which cannot be quantified in terms of money, for example, damages for pain and suffering or for loss of use of a building by the plaintiff himself. General damages must be assessed by the judge and no specific sum is claimed in the pleading. Special damages are those which can be calculated in money as an actual or prospective loss. Special damages are sometimes referred to as "liquidated" sums, which should not be confused with "liquidated or ascertained" damages which may be specified in a building (or other) contract at £x per week for delay. Provided the liquidated damages are not wholly unreasonable, the employer (if it was for his benefit) may recover the sum without proof as to his actual loss.

Examples

The form of pleadings is illustrated by some examples below, concerning a dispute over delay and defective work. Note that the disputes emerging from the pleadings are two in number; first, whether the engineer's instructions justify a further extension of time and a monetary claim; secondly, who is responsible for the wearing course (if defective). This case is typical of many, brought either in the High Court or in arbitration. Often the question which party is to be plaintiff is a matter of chance. Had the contractor been paid in full (in the example) the employer would be more likely to initiate the proceedings. The courts attach no significance to the order of parties save that the task of pursuing the case rests with the plaintiff.

In the High Court of Justice
Queen's Bench Division
Between

AB CONTRACTORS LTD. *Plaintiff*

and

CD DISTRICT COUNCIL *Defendant*

STATEMENT OF CLAIM

1. By a contract dated January 1, 1988 incorporating the ICE conditions of contract the Plaintiff (as contractor) agreed to carry out road works for the Defendant (as employer).
2. The Plaintiff has carried out and completed the works but the Defendant has failed to pay the balance of the Plaintiff's final account namely £20,000, which sum has been certified by the engineer, one EF.
3. It was an implied term of the contract that the Defendant would not interrupt the regular and economic progress of the Plaintiff's work.
4. In breach of contract the Defendant, through the said EF, issued instructions in excessive and unreasonable numbers and at unreasonable times, whereby the Plaintiff has suffered loss and damage in the sum of £50,000. Particulars of the instructions relied on appear in Schedule I; particulars of the Plaintiff's loss appear in Schedule II.

AND THE PLAINTIFF CLAIMS

(1) Under paragraph 2 £20,000
(2) Under paragraph 4 £50,000
(3) Interest.

In the High Court, etc.

DEFENCE AND COUNTERCLAIM

1. The Defendant admits paragraphs 1 and 2 of the Statement of claim. Paragraphs 3 and 4 are denied. The Plaintiff's final account includes all sums to which they are entitled under the contract.
2. The contract required the Plaintiff to complete the works by December 31, 1988 and provided for liquidated damages at £2,000 per week. The Plaintiff failed to complete until March 25, 1989, *i.e.*

12 weeks late. EF has granted an extension of time of two weeks. The Defendant is, therefore, entitled to withhold the sum of £20,000.

3. In breach of contract, the wearing course laid by the Plaintiff did not comply with the specification. In consequence, it became fluid at a temperature of 25°C. The Defendant has incurred expense in replacing the wearing course in the sum of £60,000. Particulars of breaches of the specification are contained in Schedule III; particulars of the Defendant's expense are contained in Schedule IV.

4. The Defendant will set off the counterclaim against any sum due to the Plaintiff.

AND THE DEFENDANT COUNTERCLAIMS

(1) Under paragraph 2 £20,000
(2) Under paragraph 3 £60,000

In the High Court, etc.

REPLY AND DEFENCE TO COUNTERCLAIM

1. The Plaintiff admits paragraph 2 of the Defence and Counterclaim, save that EF should have granted a further extension of 10 weeks in respect of the matters particularised in Schedule I. The Defendant is therefore not entitled to liquidated damages.

2. Paragraph 3 is not admitted. EF orally instructed the Plaintiff to vary the specification for the wearing course, but wrongfully failed to confirm this in writing.

3. If (which is denied) the wearing course behaves as alleged, it did not require to be replaced.

Particulars

If either party needs more information than his opponent's pleadings give he may ask for further and better particulars of specific matters. If such particulars are not given voluntarily the court may order the information to be given. Requests for further particulars are very common. This should not be so, since the pleadings should contain all necessary information. In the above example, a request for further particulars of the engineer's instruction, relied on in paragraph 2 of the reply, would be justified. When further and better particulars are given, the request should be typed out, followed by the answer. The particulars given will form part of the pleading of that party, and will accordingly require amendment if there is any departure from the particulars given.

Other parties

If, in the course of the case, either party thinks that a third party should be liable to him for any part of the claim which is made by his opponent, he may serve a notice on the third party which has the effect of bringing him into the action. There will usually be an exchange of pleadings between the third party and the party who joined him. There may be more than one third party (called first or second third party, etc.). If a third party wishes to join a further party himself, that party becomes a fourth party. The court will give directions for the trial, indicating what part the third or fourth parties shall play at the hearing.

In the above example, it might be necessary for the contractor to join his surfacing sub-contractor as a third party to the counterclaim, and for the materials supplier to be joined as a fourth party. Similarly, if the engineer, EF is a private firm, the defendant might seek to join him as a third party to the counterclaim, in case the alleged instruction to vary the specification is correct. By these means, the parties truly at fault will all be before the court. Generally, these measures are not available in arbitration, unless the proposed third party is bound by an arbitration clause allowing joinder of disputes. This is sometimes the case with sub-contractors, but it is most unlikely that a supplier or a professional adviser could be brought into an arbitration.

Other claims

The situation frequently arises in construction disputes that a number of claims are brought between the same parties, either in the same or in different proceedings. It is not uncommon to have two or more arbitrations arising out of the same contract, and the same applies in court proceedings. Because of the complex factual interaction of different claims, it is sometimes found that there is an overlap. Where this is so, the so-called rule in *Conquer* v. *Boot* (1928) applies. This was a case in which the defendant contracted to build a bungalow for the plaintiff, who brought an action for breach of contract to complete in a good and workmanlike manner. After recovering damages in this action, the plaintiff then brought another action in identical terms alleging failure to build with proper materials. The Divisional Court held the plaintiff not entitled to bring the second action. Talbot J. held:

"The contract is an entire contract. No claim for payment could have been made by the defendant unless and until he had finished the bungalow. There is one contract and one promise to be performed at one time, although no doubt the defendant may have failed to perform it in one or in many respects. There may of course be many promises in one contract, the breach of each of which is a separate cause of action . . . here there is but one promise, to complete the bungalow."

The principle is that, where there is one cause of action, damages must be assessed once and for all, when the action is brought. The question that must be considered, therefore, is whether there are separate causes of action that may allow the plaintiff to bring separate claims. Ordinarily, under a complex construction contract, there may be different causes of action, but the plaintiff must nevertheless exercise caution in ensuring that all damages or remedies arising from the causes of action chosen are claimed, otherwise they may be lost.

The rule in *Conquer* v. *Boot* does not prevent a plaintiff from bringing successive or alternative claims in the same action. If the facts which the plaintiff alleges may support different causes of action (for example, a claim under the contract and an alternative claim for breach) the plaintiff may properly bring all claims available and rely on them in the alternative. He must still, however, claim all his remedies in that action. These rules apply equally in arbitration proceedings.

Judgments without trial

There are many circumstances in which the High Court may decide some issues in a case or may make orders which have the effect of terminating the case, without waiting for a trial. First, there are a number of instances in which one party may invoke the power of the court to terminate or strike out the case of the other party who is in default. For example, where no acknowledgement of service is filed to a writ or no defence served within the period laid down by the rules of court, judgment may be entered. Where one party is ordered to do something, for example, to serve particulars or to give discovery, the court in an appropriate case may order that the claim or defence of that party be struck out in default. Where a plaintiff (or a defendant who has a counterclaim) fails to take any action to bring the claim to trial and the other party suffers prejudice, the court has an inherent power to strike out that claim for want of prosecution.

After some judicial uncertainty, the House of Lords ruled in *Birkett* v. *James* (1978) that since a plaintiff ordinarily had the right to issue a writ at any time within the limitation period, striking out would not normally be ordered before the limitation period had expired. In regard to arbitration, it was held in *Crawford* v. *Prowting* (1973) that an arbitrator possessed no power at common law to strike out a claim for delay (but see page 51).

Summary judgment

In an appropriate case, the plaintiff may apply to the court for judgment on his claim (or the defendant for judgment on his counterclaim) on the ground that there is no sufficient defence. There are two separate rules which may be relied on. Under R.S.C., Order 14, the plaintiff may apply for judgment on the claim or some particular part of the claim, on the ground that there is no defence to it. If the defendant fails to satisfy the court that there is an issue which ought to be tried, the plaintiff will be entitled to immediate judgment on the claim or part of it. Frequently, the only dispute on an application for judgment under Order 14 is whether the defendant can establish a credible counterclaim which he is entitled to set-off against the sum otherwise due. Order 14A now expressly entitles the court to give summary judgment on a point of law which does not merit a full hearing.

In a construction dispute, where a valid certificate has been issued for payments to the contractor, the employer may counter an application for judgment under Order 14 by setting up a counterclaim, for example, on the ground of delay or defects in the work. One drawback of Order 14, from the point of view of plaintiffs, is the necessity to show that there is no defence as to a particular claim. It frequently happens that the plaintiff has a series of claims many of which are very likely to succeed, where it is difficult or impossible to identify one particular claim which is bound to succeed. In these circumstances, the plaintiff may apply for an interim payment under R.S.C., Order 29. This empowers the court to look more broadly at the merits of the claim and the defence and allows judgments to be given for the plaintiff of such amount as the court thinks just, not exceeding a reasonable proportion of the sum which is likely to be recovered after taking into account any cross-claim.

Discovery of documents

After the close of pleadings, if an action is to continue, there follows the work of preparing for trial which will be done mainly by solicitors. One important step is discovery and inspection of documents, when each side must disclose to the other all documents which relate to the matter in dispute. The Rules of the Supreme Court require a party to disclose all documents which are or *have been* in his custody or power. This includes documents which have been destroyed or which are in the physical custody of some other person. Such documents must be listed and described even though they cannot be produced. All relevant documents must be disclosed, except those for which privilege is claimed. Privileged documents include letters between the party and his solicitor, and documents which came into existence as a result of the dispute, such as experts' reports. The mere fact that documents were intended to be private, personal or confidential, does not permit a party to withhold them. Documents which come to light on discovery may have a profound effect upon the course of the action. Occasionally one party may fail to be sufficiently diligent in searching for documents in his possession. The rules of court allow orders to be made for the list of documents to be verified by affidavit, and for any further specific documents or classes of document not previously disclosed to be produced.

As part of its inherent power to make orders for the production and preservation of documents, the court may make an order empowering the plaintiff to enter the defendant's premises to search for and seize material documents and articles. This is known as an Anton Piller Order (*Anton Piller K.G.* v. *Manufacturing Processes* (1976)). Such an order may be made in circumstances where there is a real possibility that the defendant might destroy the material. The court will, if necessary, sit *in camera*, so that the defendant has no notice of what is intended. The plaintiff must make full disclosure of all material facts. The order usually requires the defendant to permit the plaintiff's representatives to enter, search for and remove to safe custody relevant documents or other evidence. Orders have been made in cases involving patent infringement and video piracy.

Witnesses

Another task for the solicitors is to interview witnesses and to take proofs of the evidence which they will give at the trial. A proof should be directed towards the issues remaining between the parties after the exchange of pleadings.

In cases with a technical or scientific element it is common for one or both sides to produce expert witnesses. These are persons, usually unconnected with the case, who are called to give their professional opinion on the matters in issue, for example, as to whether certain material is defective. While an ordinary witness of fact is paid only his expenses, an expert witness must be paid a proper fee for his work. It is curious that experts called in support of opposing cases tend often to disagree. While some divergence of opinion is inevitable in any dispute, experts should be wary of seeking to support the party by whom they are employed. An expert who over-states his case rarely benefits his client.

Judges, referees and assessors

The great majority of actions in the Queen's Bench Division take place before a single judge who decides all matters of fact and law. Civil jury cases are extremely rare and are practically confined to actions in defamation. Cases which involve prolonged investigation into technical matters, such as building disputes, are mostly tried in an Official Referee's Court. The judges in these courts were, before the Courts Act 1971, known as Official Referees. Now they are designated circuit judges appointed to deal with Official Referees' business. But the original term continues to be used. An Official Referee has practically the same powers as a High Court judge and sits in a special court building in Fetter Lane in London, although he may sit elsewhere.

In addition to the judge, the Rules of the Supreme Court provide for the appointment of a court assessor or, in an appropriate case, the appointment of a court expert. These devices are not frequently used, although the appointment of an expert to the tribunal is not uncommon in international arbitration. There have been a small number of cases in the Official Referee's Courts in which an assessor has been appointed to sit with the judge, and experience indicates that this may lead to saving in court time and costs. Consideration needs to be given in all such cases to the terms of appointment of the assessor or court expert, and also to his fees, which ordinarily must be paid by the parties.

Official Referee procedure

In Official Referees' cases the rules of evidence and procedure generally follow High Court practice and include pleadings and discovery of documents. There are, however, some distinctive features. As already noted, the Official Referee to whom a case is assigned, will deal with interlocutory matters so that, by the time the trial is reached, the judge has some familiarity with the case. Arising from this procedure, the Official Referees now regularly order the holding of a pre-trial summons or meeting at which the parties, often represented by junior and leading counsel, will discuss with the judge the form which the trial should take. It is now common for the Referees to order the delivery and exchange of written notes of opening speeches, lists of relevant documents, and other relevant summaries of the issues. This can greatly facilitate the progress of the hearing.

The practice of exchanging experts' reports, now enshrined in the Rules of the Supreme Court and applicable to all types of action, originated in the Official Referee's Courts. This has been found to be of great use in informing each party of the case to be advanced by the other side, and often facilitating the narrowing of issues. Orders are also frequently made for experts to meet and discuss their differences on a without prejudice basis and there is now statutory authority for such an order.

A further feature of Official Referees' business is the use of schedules as a method of collecting into a convenient form all relevant particulars from each side. Where detailed particulars are not given in the pleadings, the Official Referee may order a schedule, to be completed by each side. Where there is a dispute, for example, over rates for work, the schedule might show, for each item, the plaintiff's rate and comments and the defendant's rate and comments. Such documents are known as Official Referee's, or Scott schedules, so named after a former Senior Official Referee.

The above developments are part of a wider reforming movement which has been felt in many branches of litigation, including particularly construction disputes. The aims of this are to cut down delay and excessive cost, thereby providing a more efficient legal service to the public. Similar developments which have been occurring in the field of arbitration are described in the next chapter.

The trial

English law is based on the adversary system. The court has no duty and very little power itself to investigate the issues. It is limited to making a decision on the basis of the case presented by the parties. Consequently, unless a party is an individual who can represent himself, the parties must have their cases presented by an advocate. The right of a party to represent himself includes non-corporate bodies; but a company must act through a solicitor. The right of audience in the High Court is presently limited to barristers. Solicitors have some rights of audience in the Crown Court, and in lower courts.

The proceedings at a trial usually start with the plaintiff's representative opening the case by outlining the issues involved. If there is a counterclaim, the plaintiff will usually open his case as to this. In the course of opening, the pleadings and relevant documents will be read or referred to. In a substantial case, much time can be taken up reading out the relevant documents. To save time and costs the Official Referees (and also arbitrators) will often attempt to read the documents in advance. There may also be a written summary of the relevant documents. After opening, the plaintiff calls his witnesses, including experts, to give evidence about the matters in dispute. At the end of his evidence the plaintiff's case is "closed" and the defendant's counsel then opens his case and calls evidence for the defence. It is important for the plaintiff to ensure that he has called all necessary evidence before closing, since he will not ordinarily have an opportunity of calling further evidence should it appear that some issue has not been proved. After the close of all the evidence, there are the closing speeches and submissions on the law, first from the defendant's and then from the plaintiff's counsel. In addressing the court it is the duty of counsel to put forward all the relevant facts and law, not just those favourable to his client, although he will endeavour to present the matters in the most favourable light. This is particularly important when legally qualified advocates appear before a lay arbitrator.

Judgment and costs

Finally, the judge must come to his decision on the facts (if there is no jury) and on the law. He gives his decision in the form of a reasoned judgment. This is sometimes delivered immediately the case is concluded, but more usually reserved to a later date so that the judge can consider the case. The successful party is entitled to judgment, and his costs are usually ordered to be paid by the loser, although the award of costs is discretionary. An award of "costs" or "taxed costs" means that the successful party will recover such of his outlay in costs as were strictly necessary, in some cases subject to scales of allowable charges. In practice, a successful party is likely to recover not more than about two-thirds of what he must pay to his solicitor. This is a further reason why cases tend to settle before trial.

The award of costs becomes less clear when, in addition to (or in lieu of) a defence, the defendant has a counterclaim. If both claim and counterclaim succeed then each party is prima facie entitled to costs on his claim. This is so even where the defence operates as a set-off. The court, in awarding costs, will look at the issues which had to be litigated, not at the sums in dispute. In order to save the laborious process of taxing items of cost as between claim and counter claim, the court will often make a global order whereby one side is to pay a proportion of the costs of the other side, and also to pay his own costs. However, it must be said that the award of costs is not an exact science. The sums involved can often be very large, even in relation to the substantial sums often in dispute in construction cases. This has always to be borne in mind by those entering upon litigation.

Interest

A further matter which should be dealt with in a judgment is interest. The court is empowered to give interest under section 35A of the Supreme Court Act 1981, on any part of a claim for debt or damages which is either included in a judgment or which is paid before judgment. This section now prevents a defendant from paying the sum in issue just before the trial and thereby avoiding the payment of interest. The power is limited to awarding simple interest. The amount awarded should normally represent a realistic rate for the time during which the successful party has been wrongfully deprived of the sum awarded. In inflationary times and with the long delays of litigation, interest has become an important topic. An alternative to the recovery of statutory interest, is to claim interest as damages. In *Wadsworth* v. *Lydell* (1981) the defendant had failed to pay an agreed sum which the plaintiff required to finance the purchase of a property. The plaintiff raised the necessary sum by borrowing on mortgage and claimed the interest payments from the defendant as special damages. The Court of Appeal held that the sum was recoverable, and the House of Lords have approved the decision. Accordingly, by pleading the actual outlay of interest incurred, it is possible to recover the actual sum lost. As a further alternative, some forms of contract provide expressly for the payment of interest on overdue certificates: see ICE form, clause 60(7), Chapter 12.

Where a contract provides for the reimbursement of cost or loss there may be a right, expressly or by necessary inference, to include interest or "financing charges" in the amounts payable. The Court of Appeal so held in *Minter* v. *W.H.T.S.O.* (1980), where the formula "direct loss and/or expense" under the JCT form of contract was held to include interest. This case should, in principle, apply to other forms of contract which provide for the recovery of claims based on actual loss or cost, including the ICE Conditions of Contract.

Settlement and offers

Frequently the parties, having started an action, make attempts to settle before or during the trial. The longer the action has continued the more significant will be the impact of costs and interest, which must be taken into account in any agreed terms. Sometimes the parties will agree that the settlement terms should be embodied into a judgment of the court (or an award of an arbitrator). Alternatively, the parties may enter into a simple contract in the terms agreed, and the court or arbitrator will then be asked to stay all further proceedings. In this case, the rights of the parties which were in issue will be transferred into the agreed terms, which may be sued upon should they not be performed.

Should a case not settle but nevertheless the defendant considers he is likely to be found liable in some degree, he may protect himself against future costs by making a *payment into court*. The plaintiff will be notified of the payment in, and may within a limited period of time accept the money in settlement of his claim, together with his costs on the claim. If the plaintiff chooses not to accept the payment in and fails to obtain judgment for more than that sum, he will normally be ordered to pay the defendant's costs after the date of notification of the payment, even though he has won the action. The judge must not be told of the payment in until he has determined how much money the plaintiff is to recover. The calculation of how much to pay into court and the decision whether or not to accept the payment in settlement may require very careful consideration in view of the large sums for costs which may be at risk. Where there is a counterclaim the plaintiff may pay into court, but any payment in must state whether it takes into account the claim of the party making the payment. This has further important consequences as to costs.

Enforcement

The final stage in the action is enforcement of the judgment. If the judgment debtor does not pay, there are a number of methods available to the judgment creditor by which he may obtain at least some payment from the debtor. The most important of these are that the sheriff, who is a court officer, may seize and sell the debtor's goods; the debtor's land may be charged for the payment, or a receiver may be appointed to receive the rents and profits; if the debtor has a bank account or has debts owed to him, his banker or debtors (if they can be identified) may be ordered to pay over the sums owed to satisfy the judgment.

A further weapon available to the judgment creditor, where the debtor is a limited company, is winding up. The Companies Act 1985, sections 517 and 518, allows the creditor to petition for winding up, *inter alia*, if a debt for more than £750 has not been paid within three weeks of demand. However, if the threat does not produce payment, winding up is unlikely to improve the judgment creditor's position, since he will then rank equally with other unsecured creditors (see further Chapter 4).

It is a fundamental principle of English law that a plaintiff bringing proceedings takes his chance as to whether there will be assets against which to enforce a judgment. However, in recent years the courts have evolved an important procedural device which, while it does not improve the plaintiff's position, prevents the defendant from worsening it. This is the "Mareva" injunction (*Mareva Compania* v. *International Bulk Carriers* (1975)), which prohibits the party against whom it is directed from disposing of or otherwise dealing with assets within the jurisdiction. Initially, this form of relief was granted against foreign defendants who might remove their assets, but developments in case law and additional statutory backing now allow such injunctions to be granted against any party where the plaintiff can show that he has a good arguable case against the defendant, and that there is a real risk that a judgment will be unsatisfied because the defendant will dispose of his assets in advance unless restrained from doing so.

Applications for Mareva injunctions are now frequent, and the courts tend to take a more restrictive attitude. As with other forms of injunction, an order may be granted *ex parte*, if necessary on very short notice; but the matter will be reconsidered on an *inter partes* hearing. The plaintiff must make full disclosure of all material facts. A Mareva injunction does not give the plaintiff any preferential right over the assets restrained. However, a defendant will sometimes offer to put up security in lieu of the injunction, so as to permit him to use the assets in question. A Mareva injunction may be obtained in aid of arbitration proceedings (Arbitration Act 1950, section 12(6)(*h*)).

EVIDENCE

Every fact in dispute which is necessary to establish a claim must be proved to the judge or to the arbitrator by admissible evidence whether oral, documentary or of other kind. The evidence must normally be given by a person who heard or saw what took place.

In a civil action the facts in dispute must be proved on a balance of probabilities, unlike criminal cases where proof beyond reasonable doubt is required. The burden of proving a fact usually lies upon the party asserting the fact. When deciding how much evidence must be adduced in a case, it must be considered that a judge, unlike an arbitrator, cannot draw upon his own knowledge, except in very obvious matters, and therefore every fact relied on must be proved. In practice some of the facts of the case will usually be admitted by the other side and they will not then need to be proved. Admissions may be made in the pleadings, or in any other appropriate manner, for instance, in open correspondence between solicitors. If party A refuses to admit some fact which, while likely to be true would be expensive to prove formally (for example, that the clerk of works signed hundreds of day-work sheets purporting to bear his signature), party B may serve him with a *notice to admit facts*. If the facts are not then admitted, the court may order party A to pay the costs of proof, whoever wins the action. A similar procedure may be adopted in arbitration by analogy.

Admissibility

The main body of the law of evidence is concerned with which matters are admissible as evidence; that is, which matters a party is entitled to try to prove in order to establish his case. For example, matters which are subject to privilege are not admissible. It is a matter for the opposing party to raise, if he wishes to challenge the admissibility of certain evidence. If there is no such objection, the evidence will be adduced in the ordinary way. Sometimes, the parties may agree to waive privilege attaching to documents. Note, however, that privilege binds both parties, and accordingly cannot be waived by one party only.

Normally a witness may relate only what he himself has perceived. Facts which another person has told him are hearsay and are admissible only under special circumstances. Here again, it is up to the party objecting to hearsay evidence to raise the point, but a judge or arbitrator may also object to such evidence.

Certain hearsay evidence is admissible under the Civil Evidence Act 1968 and Rules of Court, which apply equally to an arbitration. Under these provisions, a party may put in evidence a statement (usually contained in a document) made by a third party on a previous occasion, by serving notice on the other party. The grounds on which such evidence may be called include the maker of the statement being overseas, unfit, untraceable or dead. In long construction cases, it is often prudent to take statements from elderly or infirm witnesses in case they do not survive the trial, so that their evidence may be used.

A witness may not normally give his opinion; although an expert may do so, and is usually introduced solely to give his professional opinion on matters in dispute. In almost every case there is, in addition to oral testimony, documentary evidence. The documents, if admissible, must either be admitted as authentic by the other side, for example, on discovery; or if they are not admitted, they must be proved.

Giving evidence

The law of evidence also deals with the way in which oral testimony may be given. The normal practice, which still applies in some civil actions and in criminal cases, is that evidence must be given orally from memory. However, it has been found that this process is very time-consuming and costly, and in many civil actions (and particularly in arbitration) the practice is frequently adopted of exchanging witness statements and taking the contents of such statements as read. This practice is now enshrined in the Rules of the Supreme Court (Order 38, rule 2A) which applies (*inter alia*) to proceedings in the Commercial Court and to

Official Referees' business. There are various procedures for dealing with contentious parts of statements. In the Commercial Court, the practice is to require particular parts of the statement objected to by the opposing party to be adduced by conventional question and answer. In arbitration, particularly in international cases, there is a strong trend towards putting all evidence in writing and dispensing with oral evidence as far as possible.

Where evidence is adduced orally in support of a party's case, this is normally done by his advocate putting questions to the witness. This is known as examination-in-chief, and there is a fairly strict rule that the advocate must not "lead" by asking questions which suggest an answer. This is not merely to avoid unfair advantage: leading questions in-chief may succeed in giving quite misleading evidence, because witnesses often try to be helpful. After a witness has given his evidence in-chief (whether orally or simply by putting in a signed statement) it is an important requirement that a witness must be offered for cross-examination by the opposing party or his advocate. Cross-examination is not restricted to the matters which the witness has given evidence in-chief about. A witness may be questioned on any matter relevant to the case, including his own truthfulness. Some people take the view that cross-examination is of doubtful value. However, it is a fundamental part of the English adversarial system, and many lawyers will have experience of the process having a material or dramatic effect on exposing the truth in a case. Cross-examination is the more important when written statements are used, because there is a constant temptation for witnesses to include material which is not properly within their knowledge, and it is clearly right that this should be challenged.

A party may compel the attendance at the trial of any person whom he wishes to give evidence for him. Attendance is enforced by serving a *subpoena* on the witness and paying his expenses. In an arbitration the High Court has a specific power under the Arbitration Act 1950, section 12, to issue subpoenas. Witnesses may be compelled to attend either to give oral evidence or to produce relevant documents in their possession. Discovery cannot normally be ordered against a person who is not a party to the action.

There is no right or property in witnesses. Any person may be called by either side. The potential witness is, however, entitled to refuse to give a statement in advance to one side (or both). A party may even compel his opponent to give evidence. But it is unwise to call a person who may be hostile because he cannot be cross-examined by the party calling him. There is therefore no means of challenging what such a witness says in evidence.

Expert evidence

Evidence which is proposed to be given by an expert is subject to special Rules of Court, which apply equally to an arbitration. These require leave to be obtained for the calling of such evidence, and, as noted above, it is the usual practice in all courts to make such leave conditional upon the exchange of such reports between the parties, in advance of the trial. This is to facilitate the narrowing of issues.

There is no precise definition of expert evidence. Its function depends upon the tribunal before which it is to be adduced. In the High Court, expert evidence is necessary to explain technical features of a case. Conversely, in arbitration, expert evidence should be unnecessary where the arbitrator is appropriately qualified. Despite this, it is a common practice to call such evidence. Views differ about the proper way to adduce expert evidence. Since the expert will have a written report, some advocates will ask the expert to read verbatim, and others will read the report to the expert, asking him to comment on particular sections. A more usual practice in the Official Referee's Courts, is to invite the court to adjourn to read all the expert evidence, which is then either taken as read or introduced briefly by the witness, before being cross-examined. In arbitration, it is often appropriate for the arbitrator himself to ask the questions, or even to adduce the evidence. Particular provision is made in the ICE arbitration procedure for this (see page 53).

An important distinction between an expert and a witness of fact, is that the former is entitled to be paid a proper professional fee, which may be recovered on taxation. This sometimes leads to serious argument about whether a particular witness is an expert. In the case of *James Longley* v. *S.W. Regional Health Authority* (1983) the claimant contractor in an arbitration sought to include in the bill for costs a substantial sum in respect of the fees of an unqualified "claims consultant." The respondent objected that the consultant was not qualified to give expert evidence, and that his evidence was not admissible. On a review of taxation in the High Court, it was held that such evidence was admissible, and an expert might be appropriately qualified by skill and experience. It is, however, necessary that the work undertaken should be of an expert nature: mere preparation work for a trial or arbitration (even though such work might have been done by the solicitor) will not qualify as expert work for inclusion in a bill of costs.

Until the report of an expert is exchanged, his views and opinions remain the subject of privilege. Accordingly if a party obtains an unfavourable opinion from one expert, he may go to another advisor and rely exclusively upon his opinion, should it be more favourable. A party who takes this course, however, runs a grave risk that the identity of the first expert may be discovered by the opposition, who may then subpoena him to give evidence. Parties are usually well advised to accept the first opinion they are given. An expert should, of course, always give an independent and unbiased opinion on the issues. It is, however, quite proper for the expert, both in his report and in his evidence to emphasise any technical points in his client's favour. Technical issues are often arguable in just the same way as legal issues are.

PUBLIC LAW RIGHTS

Public law concerns the exercise of powers and duties by public bodies, usually arising under statute. In some cases this may give rise to a direct right of action in civil law against the public body. For example, claims against local authorities alleging negligence in the enforcement of Building Regulations relates to such public law duties or powers. Where statutes do not provide expressly whether or not an individual who suffers damage may bring an action, it is necessary for the Courts to construe the statute. The case of *Anns* v. *London Borough of Merton* (see page 333) contains an analysis of the question whether the Building Regulations and their governing statutes create a right for individuals to sue (in that case the answer was affirmative, but see page 336.

A different aspect of public law is the right of an individual who is affected by the exercise of such a power or duty to seek an order from the courts restraining or controlling the way in which the public body acts. This involves a distinct form of civil procedure known as Judicial Review. The law and procedure have become transformed in recent years. Formerly, an aggrieved individual had the right to ask the court to make a "prerogative order" in one of three types: *certiorari*, to quash the decision of a public body or tribunal; *prohibition*, to prohibit a public body or tribunal from acting in a particular manner; and *mandamus*, to compel the public body or tribunal to act in accordance with its duty. These specific remedies have become enlarged by new statutory provisions and rules of court which now permit an individual to apply for the more general remedies of injunction or declaration, and on an application for Judicial Review the court may award damages to the applicant. The new procedure is set out in Order 53 of the Rules of the Supreme Court.

Judicial Review applies to an almost unlimited range of matters, including decisions of government ministers and local authorities, public bodies, inferior courts and tribunals, and covers all types of law, both civil and criminal, including, for example, prison regulations. Perhaps the most numerous are claims relating to immigration decisions and actions of local authorities. The procedure now laid down is simple. An applicant must first obtain leave of the court and this requires only the filing of certain papers and particulars. The decision to grant or refuse leave is now generally made by a single judge without a hearing, *i.e.* on a simple review of the papers. Where leave is refused, the application may be renewed in open court. The application for leave is *ex parte*, and if granted, a hearing then takes place with the body or authority who is the subject of the complaint appearing and being represented. The rules require applications to be made promptly and in any event normally within three months of the relevant event.

The principles of law which the courts apply on application for Judicial Review are common law principles, developed by the courts themselves, principally in a series of cases following the introduction of the new procedure. On an application for Judicial Review, the court is not concerned with deciding whether it agrees with the decision or action of the relevant authority, nor is the process an appeal. The court is concerned only with restraining the wrongful exercise of public law powers and duties, and the grounds on which the court will intervene are limited. The principal grounds are the following:

Want or excess of jurisdiction: this ground may include error of law.

Irrationality: this ground is colloquially referred to as "the Wednesbury principle" following the case of *Associated Provincial Picturehouses* v. *Wednesbury Corporation* (1948), in which a local authority granted a licence for cinema performances on a Sunday on the condition that no children under 15 years of age should be admitted. The owners challenged the decision as an unreasonable exercise of discretion. Lord Greene M.R. said in this case:

> "It is clear that the local authority are entrusted by Parliament with a decision on a matter which the knowledge and experience of that authority can best be trusted to deal with. The subject-matter with

which the condition deals is one relevant for its consideration. They have considered it and come to a decision upon it. It is true to say that if a decision on a competent matter is so unreasonable that no reasonable authority could ever come to it, then the courts can interfere . . . . It is not what the court considers unreasonable, a different thing altogether."

The principle is that the court will intervene if the decision is such that no authority properly directing itself on the relevant law and acting reasonably could have reached it.

Procedural impropriety: this ground covers failure by a body to observe its own procedural rules, but the main area of application is in breach of the rules of natural justice. These rules broadly require public bodies to act fairly in the particular circumstances. For example, a person liable to be dismissed from a public office must be given a hearing, and must be notified of the allegations against him. A particular requirement of natural justice is that the person exercising a power or giving the decision must not have an interest in it. This was demonstrated in the celebrated case of *Dimes* v. *Grand Junction Canal* (1852), where, in the course of a long dispute between the company and an adjoining landowner, the Lord Chancellor gave a decision, after which it was found that he was a substantial shareholder in the company. The House of Lords subsequently expressed their views on the situation, Lord Campbell saying:

"No one can suppose that Lord Cottenham could be, in the remotest degree, influenced by the interest that he had in this concern; but, my Lords, it is of the last importance that the maxim that no man is to be a judge in his own cause should be held sacred. And that is not to be confined to a cause in which he is a party, but applies to a cause in which he has an interest. Since I have had the honour to be Chief Justice of the Court of Queen's Bench, we have again and again set aside proceedings in inferior tribunals because an individual, who had an interest in a case, took a part in the decision. And it will have a most salutary influence on these tribunals when it is known that this high Court of last resort, in a case in which the Lord Chancellor of England had an interest, considered that his decree on that account a decree not according to law, and was set aside. This will be a lesson to all inferior tribunals to take care not only that in their decrees they are not influenced by their personal interest, but to avoid the appearance of labouring under such an influence."

There are many situations in which Judicial Review might be appropriate in the context of construction contracts, for example, decisions of local authorities regarding their tender lists. Such decisions are open to judicial review and may be set aside if appropriate grounds are proved. See, for example, *R.* v. *London Borough of Enfield* (1989), where a decision was set aside because the Borough had not complied with the appropriate procedural rules. In such a case, the decision about the tender list is that of the authority and the court will not intervene here except on the Wednesbury principle (see above).

INTERNATIONAL CASES

Many activities in the construction industry contain some foreign element, particulary since for legal purposes Scotland is a foreign country. Such activities may be the design of works abroad by architects or engineers based in England, or construction work abroad by an English company. Disputes arising out of such projects may entail procedural problems above those encountered in domestic actions. Whenever a dispute exists which has a foreign element, two preliminary questions must be answered before any court can determine the matter. First, which national court has jurisdiction to determine the dispute? Secondly, what law will the court apply? A third question which may arise after the dispute has been determined is how the judgment can be enforced. The resolution of these questions forms a separate branch of English law which is called conflict of laws or private international law. The second title is a misnomer, because there is in fact no international law relating to private suits, but only national laws for solving international conflicts.

In the construction industry the international problems most likely to be encountered are those involving contract or tort. In this section the problems of jurisdiction, procedure and enforcement of judgments in the English courts are discussed; the question of which law the English courts will apply is dealt with in the general chapters on contract and tort (see pages 113 and 358).

Jurisdiction and procedure

The English courts normally assume jurisdiction to hear actions in contract and tort in three cases. First, if the defendant is served with a writ while he is present in England: a foreign company is regarded as being present in England if it carries on business here. Secondly, if a defendant submits to the jurisdiction, for example, by bringing an action himself in the English courts. Thirdly, the English courts may in certain cases allow a writ to be served abroad so that the action can proceed, if necessary, in the absence of the defendant. The principal grounds on which this is allowed are: that the defendant is normally resident in England; or that the dispute arises from a tort committed in England; or that the dispute arises from a contract which was made or broken in England, or agreed to be governed by English law. But in the latter cases, relating to actions in contract, the rules of court provide exceptions where the defendant is ordinarily resident in Scotland. Actions in contract against Scottish defendants must generally be brought in Scotland.

Where there is a conflict of laws involving an arbitration clause in a contract, the validity and effect of the clause is to be determined by the proper law of the contract (see page 113), unless the contract provides otherwise. But the arbitration is not necessarily governed by the same law as the contract. The leading case of *Whitworth* v. *Miller* (1970) held that the procedure in an arbitration was governed prima facie by the law of the country in which the proceedings were conducted.

If the English courts have jurisdiction to try a case it may proceed to trial in the same way as a similar case with no foreign element, and generally English rules of procedure and evidence are applied. After establishing the facts in a case, it is necessary to decide which country's law is to be applied. If this should be English law, then the judge will treat it as an ordinary domestic case and decide upon the law himself. If the law to be applied is a foreign law, then the relevant provisions of that law must be proved to the court, usually by an expert legal witness.

Enforcement

An ancillary problem in international cases may be the enforcement of a judgment in a country other than that which gave the judgment. In every country enforcement depends solely on the internal laws. To be enforced in England, the courts here require generally to be satisfied that the foreign court had proper jurisdiction, that the judgment is final and for a fixed sum and that it was properly obtained.

If these conditions are satisfied a foreign judgment may be enforced in England under reciprocal statutory arrangements made between England and various foreign states. These arrangements allow a foreign judgment to be registered in England and enforced as an English judgment. They similarly allow English judgments to be enforced abroad. Particular arrangements which apply to enforcement of judgments throughout the member states of the European Community, are contained in the Civil Jurisdiction and Judgments Act 1982. A judgment from a country with which there is no statutory arrangement is treated in England as a simple contract debt, which may be enforced by suing in the English courts. Enforcement of English judgments abroad, without the aid of reciprocal arrangements, depends on the internal rules applied in the country where enforcement is sought. Enforcement of arbitration awards in different countries involves different considerations and is dealt with in the next chapter.

Further Reading

Odgers on High Court Pleading and Practice (23rd ed., 1991) D. B. Casson.
Cross and Wilkins, *Outline of the Law of Evidence* (5th ed., 1980).

CHAPTER 3

ARBITRATION

THE term "arbitration" has several meanings. In popular usage, it denotes the placing of a dispute before a third party to obtain a fair or equitable decision, based on discretion rather than on fixed rules. In industrial matters, it refers to a process of conciliation, where attempts are made to find a formula acceptable to two parties in disagreement. In law, arbitration has acquired a more definite and fixed meaning, as a process, subject to statutory controls, whereby formal disputes are determined finally by a private tribunal of the parties' own choosing. It is in the third sense that arbitration has become widely adopted for the resolution of disputes under construction contracts. It is thus an alternative to the determination of disputes in the courts. But, as will be seen, there are cases where arbitration is an exclusive remedy and, even where there is a theoretical choice of tribunal, one party may be able to enforce arbitration.

SETTING UP AN ARBITRATION

Three things are required before there can be an arbitration. First, there must be a dispute. This requires one party to make a claim or assertion and the other party to deny it. Thus, there can be no dispute about a claim which has not been submitted, or which has not been finally rejected. Secondly, there must be an agreement to arbitrate. Thirdly, there must be a reference of the dispute to arbitration.

In construction contracts, the agreement to arbitrate is often included as one of the clauses of a standard form of contract, such as article 5 and clause 41 of the JCT form and clause 66 of the ICE form. In such clauses the parties agree to submit specified future disputes to arbitration. There may also be an agreement to arbitrate made after the dispute has arisen.

In either case there must be a reference of specified disputes to arbitration, by one party serving notice on the other. No particular form is required for a reference but it is an important step, since it is deemed to be the commencement of the arbitration for the purpose of limitation, and is thus equivalent to the issuing of a writ. Section 34 of the Limitation Act, 1980 provides that the arbitration is to be treated as being commenced when one party serves on the other notice requiring him "to appoint an arbitrator or to agree to the appointment of an arbitrator."

No particular form is required for an arbitration agreement, whether made in advance or after a dispute has arisen. If the agreement is in writing (which is invariably the case) the arbitration will be governed by the Arbitration Act 1950. This provides that the arbitrator's authority is irrevocable except through the court (section 1) and that the arbitrator's award is final and binding (section 16) unless the parties agree otherwise. The Act also contains important provisions governing the conduct of the proceedings.

The Act provides that a reference to arbitration is deemed to be to a single arbitrator unless the contrary is expressed (section 6). Many commercial arbitrations (such as shipping disputes) employ three arbitrators who usually sit as a court of two arbitrators (one appointed by each side) with an umpire to settle any disagreement. This mode of trial has never been favoured in building and engineering disputes. The JCT and the ICE forms of contract refer specifically to one arbitrator; the international (FIDIC) conditions contemplate that there may be more than one arbitrator.

The selection and appointment of an arbitrator follows the reference to arbitration. It is unnecessary for the arbitrator to be named in the arbitration agreement (section 32). Written agreements usually provide for the arbitrator to be agreed by the parties or appointed by a specified person or body. The JCT and ICE forms provide for appointment, in default of agreement, by the presidents of the RIBA or ICE respectively. Where the parties cannot agree and there is no mechanism for the appointment, the court has power to appoint an arbitrator (section 10).

What is arbitration?

Arbitration proper is to be distinguished from various less formal processes met in construction contracts. The essentials of arbitration are that there must be a dispute, which is referred to an independent arbitrator for decision, usually after hearing the parties and receiving any evidence they wish to put forward. His decision is final, subject to review by the courts. Other analogous processes which do not constitute arbitrations include the following. *Certifying*: here there is a duty to act independently or fairly, but there is no dispute, and the decision need not be final. *Negotiation*: here there is a dispute, but no independent decision (there may be no "arbitrator") and no finality. *Conciliation*: this is sometimes done to try to reach a settlement, but the parties do not bind themselves to accept the result. *Valuation*: here the parties agree to accept an independent opinion, but there is usually no hearing or submission of evidence.

In some cases it is difficult to determine whether what has taken place is an arbitration. A party dissatisfied with the outcome may wish to appeal under the Arbitration Acts. If there is no arbitration, he cannot. An example of procedure which is difficult to categorise is the engineer's decision on a dispute under clause 66 of the ICE conditions (see page 321). The decision must be made independently and may become binding. But there is no duty to hear representations, so the process does not amount to arbitration. Arbitrators (like judges) are generally immune from action by the parties. It was suggested in the case of *Sutcliffe* v. *Thackrah* (1974) that such immunity would not extend beyond a "quasi-arbitration" that is, one to which the Acts did not apply, but which was an arbitration in all but name. Thus, certifiers, valuers and conciliators owe an equal duty of care to the parties, and may be liable for their negligent acts.

Arbitration and the courts

Arbitration is a private alternative to litigation as a means of settling disputes. Inevitably, there are many connections between the two processes. Broadly, arbitration has to be conducted within and in accordance with the law, the underlying function of the court being to support and enforce the arbitration process. The courts have a number of specific powers which can be exercised in relation to arbitration proceedings, so as to ensure that they are properly conducted (see below). Arbitration proceedings are sometimes conducted in a manner closely analogous to proceedings in the High Court, for example, with pleadings, discovery and evidence closely following the High Court Rules. This is not necessary, however, and it should always be remembered that arbitrators have a very wide discretion as to the way in which they conduct proceedings, the courts themselves being much more closely restricted by the Rules of the Supreme Court.

Some disputes may be brought in court or in arbitration and where this is so the possibility of conflict arises. Historically, the courts have been jealous of their supremacy, but the modern position is that the courts appear to encourage parties to take disputes, particularly technical ones, to arbitration. Where a conflict could arise, the courts take the view that it is a matter for the parties whether they wish to proceed with the resolution of their disputes by arbitration or in court. In the case of *Lloyd* v. *Wright* (1983) the parties commenced an arbitration but the plaintiff subsequently issued a writ repeating the same claims, and the question arose whether this brought the arbitration to an end. Eveleigh L.J. in the Court of Appeal held:

> "The principle that the court will not allow its jurisdiction to be ousted is at the root of the defendant's argument. However, the court does not claim a monopoly in deciding disputes between parties. It does not, of its own initiative, seek to interfere when citizens have recourse to other tribunals. The court exercises its jurisdiction when appealed to. Until then, the court is not conscious of ignominy if an arbitrator decides a question with which the court is competent to deal. Furthermore, the court will not refuse to allow the subject matter of an action already begun to be referred to arbitration, if the parties so agree . . . . The court, however, will not permit its assistance to be denied to a party who has invoked it except by that party's consent or by its own ruling."

Effect of an Arbitration Agreement

Since arbitration is a matter of private agreement, the arbitrator's authority depends upon the scope of that agreement. This may be completely general, such as an agreement to refer "any dispute or difference arising under or in connection with the contract"; or it may be limited to specified areas of dispute, for example, an agreement in a lease that disputes as to rent increases are to be settled by arbitration. Building and engineering contracts usually contain wide arbitration clauses, but the clauses in the JCT and ICE forms are expressed to be subject to certain time limits. Also, arbitration under some forms cannot, in respect of most disputes, usually be opened until after completion of the works (see page 274).

Until 1984 it was generally thought that arbitration and litigation were alternatives, so that where the parties took their dispute to court the judge would exercise all or any powers given to the arbitrator. In the case of *Northern RHA* v. *Derek Crouch* (1984), the Court of Appeal held this was not so. In this case, the parties had entered into a JCT form of contract which provided, by the arbitration clause, that an arbitrator should have the power to "open up, review and revise any certificate opinion decision requirement or notice" of the architect. The question arose whether the court could exercise the same powers.

In the judgment of Browne-Wilkinson L.J. it was said:

> "If this matter were to be litigated in the High Court (whether before the Official Referee or a Judge) the court would not have power to open up, review and revise certificates or opinions as it thought fit since so to do would be to modify the contractual obligations of the parties. The limit of the court's jurisdiction would be to declare inoperative any certificate or opinion given by the architect if the architect had no power to give such certificate or opinion or had otherwise erred in law in giving it. The court could not (as an arbitrator could) substitute its discretion for that of the architect."

This case has been considered in a number of subsequent actions before Official Referees. In *Finnegan* v. *Sheffield City Council* (1988) Sir William Stabb explained its effect as follows:

> "I take the view that the Court of Appeal in the *Crouch* case were of the opinion not that the arbitration clause deprived the court of jurisdiction but rather that it gave to the arbitrator a jurisdiction to open up and review certificates which the court does not possess and that accordingly, whether or not there is any arbitration clause, the court cannot go behind an architect's certificate in a contract of this kind."

While the *Crouch* case has been much criticised, and the House of Lords may not approve it, the present position is that claims which depend on challenging the decision of a third party (such as an architect) must be brought by arbitration. One way of achieving this is for the parties to agree to appoint the Official Referee as arbitrator, which is permitted under section 11 of the Arbitration Act 1950; he may then exercise all powers given to the arbitrator under the contract. An alternative approach is to abrogate or cancel the arbitration clause with the intention of permitting the parties to go to court. However, in the light of the observations in *Finnegan*, this might result in the parties being unable to challenge certain decisions at all. The logical conclusion from these cases is that if you wish to take disputes to court, there needs to be a clause expressly empowering the court (or an Official Referee) to open up, review and revise the decisions of the architect or engineer. These considerations do not appear to affect claims that one party is in breach of contract: the court retains its inherent power to adjudicate on such claims and award damages.

The Courts and Legal Services Act 1990, contains two provisions which bear on the above matters. First, the Lord Chief Justice is to regulate the availability of Official Referees to accept appointments as arbitrator under section 11 of the Arbitration Act 1950. In view of the heavy work load, this may simply have the effect of bringing such appointments to a stop. Secondly, there is a new section 11A to the Act which expressly permits the parties to confer the powers of an arbitrator on a judge, but only by agreement. The new section appears to require agreement in respect of an actual dispute, so that it may not be possible to write such a provision into arbitration clauses. Where there is no agreement, the position will remain that the arbitrator's jurisdiction is exclusive.

Multi-party proceedings

One of the recurrent difficulties of construction industry arbitration is that disputes tend to involve more than two parties. Ordinarily, an arbitration must be limited to the two parties to the contract, there being no powers available in arbitration comparable to those available in court (see page 18). In the past, a solution had been found in taking all the disputes to court so that, for example, an owner might bring parallel proceedings against the contractor and against the designer alleging alternative cases. This procedure has been seriously impeded by the *Crouch* case (see above), as the court may now not be able to adjudicate certain of the disputes. The result is that most potential multi-party actions must now be brought in arbitration.

Multi-party arbitration is subject to certain theoretical difficulties, but the main problems are practical ones. You cannot force a party into a multi-party arbitration unless he agrees to it. There is ample scope for refusing to agree, and indeed for thwarting the whole process by appointing a different arbitrator in the related dispute. There are various attempts in the standard form of contract to get round these difficulties, by the use of special arbitration clauses, particularly in main contracts and sub-contracts. The JCT 80 forms of contract contain provisions which oblige the employer, contractor, and sub-contractor to consent to the joining of disputes which are "substantially the same or connected" (see further, Chapter 11). However, there are many forms of contract and sub-contract in common use which do not provide for joinder, and it is very rare to find professional services agreements which would permit the employer to bring alternative claims against the designer and the contractor in arbitration.

There are theoretical difficulties in actually conducting two related arbitrations. Unless the parties consent, the arbitrator must continue to treat the two arbitrations as separate. Thus, he must be prepared for the possibility of reaching different and not necessarily consistent decisions in the two arbitrations, since the evidence and arguments will be different. These difficulties may be overcome by an agreement that all the relevant related disputes be dealt with in one combined hearing, but agreement on this will not always be forthcoming. The only complete solution is to avoid arbitration and to take all the disputes to the courts.

Stay of proceedings

Where a dispute is such that the court could assume jurisdiction, the question still remains whether one party is entitled to issue proceedings in court. If one party to an arbitration agreement starts an action he is technically in breach of contract. The courts will not, however, order specific performance of an arbitration agreement. Instead, the party wishing to arbitrate may apply for a stay of the court proceedings, thus leaving arbitration as the only remedy. If a stay is not granted the action will continue in court.

The court's power to order a stay of proceedings is contained in section 4(1) of the Arbitration Act 1950:

> "If any party to an arbitration agreement, or any person claiming through or under him, commences any legal proceedings in any court against any other party to the agreement, or any person claiming through or under him, in respect of any matter agreed to be referred, any party to those legal proceedings may at any time after appearance, and before delivering any pleadings or taking any other steps in the proceedings, apply to that court to stay the proceedings, and that court or a judge thereof, if satisfied that there is no sufficient reason why the matter should not be referred in

accordance with the agreement, and that the applicant was, at the time when the proceedings were commenced, and still remains, ready and willing to do all things necessary to the proper conduct of the arbitration, may make an order staying the proceedings."

Note that the section gives a discretion. The court leans in favour of granting a stay, so that the burden of persuasion falls on the party wishing to litigate. There are several grounds on which the court may refuse a stay. For example, if there are more than two parties involved in the dispute a stay may be refused on the ground it would mean the dispute being tried before two different tribunals. The Arbitration Acts do not make provision for multi-party proceedings. This problem is expressly dealt with the new JCT forms of contract (see above and page 274).

In international disputes, most countries will enforce an arbitration clause without regard to the merits or effect. Where a dispute in England has an international element, the Arbitration Act 1975 makes a similar provision, requiring the court to stay the proceedings without discretion.

In small domestic cases, the recent Consumer Arbitration Agreements Act 1988 provides for the opposite result. Section 1 of the Act provides that an arbitration agreement contained in a contract is not to be enforced against a consumer without written consent, given after the dispute has arisen, unless the court determines that arbitration would be "not detrimental to the interests of the consumer." Where the court is of this opinion, there is then a discretion to order stay. One of the factors to be considered in deciding whether arbitration is detrimental, is the availability of legal aid, which ordinarily will be available in court, but not in arbitration. These provisions have no application to the generality of substantial construction disputes.

Despite the requirements that a party applying for a stay must be "ready and willing" to arbitrate, the court will grant a stay of proceedings even though that party intends to rely on a time-bar in the contract. Thus the court will enforce any requirement for notice of arbitration to be given within a fixed period, such as that contained in clause 66 of the ICE form (see page 321). The remedy of a party who is out of time is to invoke the power of the court to enlarge time under section 27 of the Act of 1950:

"Where the terms of an agreement to refer future disputes to arbitration provide that any claims to which the agreement applies shall be barred unless notice to appoint an arbitrator is given or an arbitrator is appointed or some other step to commence arbitration proceedings is taken within a time fixed by the agreement, and a dispute arises to which the agreement applies, the High Court, if it is of opinion that in the circumstances of the case undue hardship would otherwise be caused, and notwithstanding that the time so fixed has expired may, on such terms, if any, as the justice of the case may require, but without prejudice to the provisions of any enactment limiting the time for the commencement of arbitration proceedings, extend the time for such period as it thinks proper."

This power is exercised sparingly. It is not sufficient that the applicant will otherwise lose his claim. An example of a justifiable ground under clause 66 of the ICE conditions may be genuine doubt that the engineer's decision was given under that clause.

A further hurdle which may confront a party wishing to go to court is a particular form of arbitration agreement making the award of an arbitrator a condition precedent to litigation. This will be enforced by the courts and means that no action may be brought until the amount of liability has been determined by arbitration. This form of agreement is known as *Scott* v. *Avery* clause, after the case in which it first came before the courts. Neither the JCT nor the ICE arbitration clause is in this form. Such clauses are, however, commonly found in insurance policies and in more traditional forms of commercial contract.

PROCEDURE IN ARBITRATION

The conduct of an arbitration, both in the interlocutory stages and at the hearing, is within control and discretion of the arbitrator. This is expressly provided by section 12(1) of the Arbitration Act 1950, which states:

"Unless a contrary intention is expressed therein, every arbitration agreement shall, where such a provision is applicable to the reference, be deemed to contain a provision that the parties to the reference, and all persons claiming through them respectively, shall, subject to any legal objection, submit to be examined by the arbitrator or umpire, on oath or affirmation, in relation to the matters in dispute, and shall, subject as aforesaid, produce before the arbitrator or umpire all documents within their possession or power respectively which may be required or called for, and do all other things which during the proceedings on the reference the arbitrator or umpire may require."

These provisions must be read as qualified by any agreement which the parties may make, since the arbitrator owes his authority to the agreement of the parties. However, the arbitrator must also bear in mind the duty imposed by section 13(3) of the Act which requires him to use all reasonable dispatch in the reference (see below). In practice, complaints about the excessive use of power are rare. Arbitrators should, in general, be encouraged to take positive control of procedure and to direct the parties how the dispute should be formulated and dealt with.

Arbitrators are often requested, in the absence of other applicable procedure, to follow High Court practice in ordering pleadings, discovery and other matters. While this may be a useful guide, these rules do not apply to arbitration, and the arbitrator should in every case use his discretion as to what is really required. There may be cases where, in lieu of formal pleadings, it is sufficient for the claimant to rely on an existing claim document, and for the respondent to be ordered to submit details of grounds of disagreement. This may save considerable time and cost to the parties. Similarly, there is no requirement for an arbitrator to direct a formal hearing following practice in the High Court. He might, if appropriate, direct the parties to attend on site and explain their dispute to him there. Or he might require the parties to deliver documents to him so that he may investigate the dispute before proceeding further. Or again, if he forms the view there is some issue of principle upon which the dispute will turn, he might order the parties to deal with this issue at the outset. In all such matters, the arbitrator is the master of his own procedure, and should not blindly follow what the parties suggest.

Duties of the arbitrator

In his conduct of the arbitration, the arbitrator must conform to certain minimum requirements of fairness and impartiality. This is sometimes referred to as "natural justice," but there are no fixed rules. The essential requirements are that the arbitrator should in fact be unbiased and should act so as to convey this impression to the parties; he should ordinarily act only upon the evidence presented and when he wishes to take any step which might take the parties by surprise or which might be regarded as unconventional, he should keep the parties informed of what he is doing (although not necessarily of his reasons). He should give each party an opportunity of dealing with every relevant point. This does not require the arbitrator to listen to endless speeches, but he must act fairly and properly if he wishes to cut short the argument.

The arbitrator must take a sufficient note of the evidence and argument to enable him to determine the issues and to deliver a reasoned award, if called for. The parties may agree to provide a shorthand note of the proceedings. Alternatively, some arbitrators choose to make their own tape recordings of the hearing. This should not, however, be regarded as a normal requirement; and it should never be regarded as a substitute for following the argument as it proceeds.

Misconduct

By section 23 of the Arbitration Act 1950, the court has power to remove an arbitrator who has misconducted himself or the proceedings, or to set aside his award. In some of the older cases, misconduct constituted actual bias or partiality. This is, however, not a serious problem today. The decided cases show that the courts are much more concerned with the denial of justice by incompetence. Despite the popular belief that an arbitrator should never express his opinion, misconduct is more likely to be committed by keeping silent than by an arbitrator who makes known his intentions, right or wrong.

A modern example of misconduct is the case of *Fox* v. *P. G. Wellfair* (1981). The respondent builders were in liquidation at the time of arbitration proceedings in respect of flats which contained numerous defects. The proceedings were continued to obtain the benefit of NHBC guarantees, but were effectively undefended so that the plaintiff's evidence was unchallenged. Instead of making an award in accordance with the plaintiff's evidence, the arbitrator substantially reduced the sums claimed. He relied on his own opinion about the defects, but did not disclose this to the claimants, who had no reason to suppose that their evidence was contested. It was held by the Court of Appeal that the arbitrator had committed misconduct by failing to bring his views to the attention of the claimants, so that they might deal with them. The arbitrator had thus erred by his silence.

An alternative, less drastic remedy lies under section 22, by which the court has power to remit matters to the arbitrator for reconsideration. An example of remission is where an award deals wrongly with the question of costs, such as, by awarding them to the unsuccessful party. The court has no power to substitute its own decision for that of the arbitrator. If satisfied that the award cannot stand, the court will remit the matter to the arbitrator with directions as to the court's opinion.

Power of the courts

Although arbitrators have very wide general powers of control, they lack many specific powers possessed by judges. The policy of the Arbitration Acts has been to allow the parties to go to court to obtain certain orders necessary to the conduct of the arbitration. The principal powers are contained in section 12(6) of the Arbitration Act 1950 which provides as follows:

"The High Court shall have, for the purpose of and in relation to a reference, the same power of making orders in respect of
    (*a*) security for costs;
    (*b*) ...
    (*c*) the giving of evidence by affidavit;
    (*d*) examination on oath of any witness before an officer of the High Court or any other person, and the issue of a commission or request for the examination of a witness out of jurisdiction.
    (*e*) the preservation, interim custody or sale of any goods which are the subject matter of the reference;
    (*f*) securing the amount in dispute in the reference;
    (*g*) the detention, preservation or inspection of any property or thing which is the subject of the reference or as to which any question may arise therein, and authorising for any of the purposes aforesaid any persons to enter upon or into any land or building in the possession of any party to the reference, or authorising any samples to be taken or any observation to be made or experiment to be tried which may be necessary or expedient for the purpose of obtaining full information or evidence; and
    (*h*) interim injunctions or the appointment of a receiver;
as it has for the purpose of and in relation to an action or matter in the High Court:
    Provided that nothing in this subsection shall be taken to prejudice any power which may be vested in an arbitrator or umpire of making orders with respect to any of the matters aforesaid."

All the foregoing powers may be exercised by an arbitrator where the parties agree to vest him with authority. Such powers are contained in the ICE arbitration procedure, which is dealt with below. Note that the Courts and Legal Services Act 1990 has abolished section 12(6)(*b*) of the Arbitration Act 1950, which formerly gave power to the High Court to order discovery. The question of discovery thus lies solely within the discretion of the arbitration, pursuant to section 12(1) of the Act.

The Arbitration Act 1979 provides for a possible extension of the powers of an arbitrator where one party is in default. Section 5 states:

"(1) If any party to a reference under an arbitration agreement fails within the time specified in the order or, if no time is so specified, within a reasonable time to comply with an order made by the arbitrator or umpire in the course of the reference, then, on the application of the arbitrator or umpire or any party to the reference, the High Court may make an order extending the powers of the arbitrator or umpire as mentioned in subsection (2) below.

(2) If an order is made by the High Court under this section, the arbitrator or umpire shall have power, to the extent and subject to any conditions specified in that order, to continue with the reference in default of appearance or of any other act by one of the parties in like manner as a judge of the High Court might continue with proceedings in that court where a party fails to comply with an order of that court or a requirement of rules of court."

This section, despite its potential usefulness, has not been much used, probably because of the inconvenience and expense of applying to the court. In practice, a firm arbitrator can deal effectively with most defaults.

Remedies for delay

The position in an arbitration in regard to delay is not analogous to that in the High Court. In the latter case, the court has many inherent powers and sanctions to control the conduct of the parties. Arbitration, however, is consensual, and it is necessary to consider the effect of any delay on the agreement to arbitrate. There has been considerable development in this field on the question when the court can, in effect, strike out an arbitration by declaring the parties no longer bound by the arbitration agreement. In the leading case of *Bremer Vulcan* v. *South India Shipping* (1981) the House of Lords, while recognising that the arbitration agreement could be brought to an end by frustration or repudiation, held that the obligations to proceed with the arbitration were mutual. Thus, one party was not entitled to complain that the arbitration had "gone to sleep" as both parties were bound to proceed with the reference. Other possibilities considered in the cases are that the arbitration agreement could be held to be abandoned, if this was the clear inference from the conduct of the parties; and there could be an estoppel, if one party relied to his detriment on an unequivocal representation of the other that the arbitration was at an end. The mere lapse of time of itself is not sufficient, nor is there, in arbitration, any independent right to a fair hearing, loss of which would allow the court to terminate the proceedings. The suggestion has been made that, in an appropriate case, the court could revoke the power of the arbitrator pursuant to section 1 of the Arbitration Act 1950; but this is available only in very exceptional cases, usually akin to misconduct, where no other avenue is open.

Although the question of remedies for delay has given rise to much interesting legal analysis, particularly of the nature of the arbitration agreement, the courts have produced no useful remedy. However, a solution has now been provided by the Courts and Legal Services Act 1990, which has introduced a new section 13A into the Arbitration Act 1950 empowering an arbitrator to dismiss a claim for delay in circumstances analogous to those where the High Court would possess such a power (see above, page 20). Where one party is in default, the arbitrator is not without effective powers, as was recognised in *Bremer Vulcan* by Lord Diplock who said:

> "I see no reason why an arbitrator should not have the . . . power to fix a date for the hearing and to make an award *ex parte* in favour of the respondent when the claimant failed to appear at the time and place so fixed, and likewise if he did appear, to debar, the claimant from raising any claim of which, in breach of the arbitrator's directions, he had failed to give the respondent adequate and timely notice."

Where, conversely, the default is that of the arbitrator and not of the parties, there is a clear remedy in section 13(3) of the Arbitration Act 1950 as follows:

> "The High Court may, on the application of any party to a reference, remove an arbitrator or umpire who fails to use all reasonable despatch in entering on and proceeding with the reference and making an award, and an arbitrator or umpire who is removed by the High Court by this sub-section shall not be entitled to receive any remuneration in respect of his services."

Thus, both the arbitrator and the parties in fact possess ample powers to ensure the reasonable despatch of the proceedings.

TRADE AND PROFESSIONAL RULES

There is no uniform system of procedure which applies in arbitration comparable to the Rules of the Supreme Court. It is therefore natural that various trade and professional bodies should consider creating their own rules of procedure. The modern attitude of the courts to such rules is one of support and indulgence. If the parties agree upon a mode of settlement for their disputes, then the courts will intervene only in cases of obvious miscarriage of justice.

The desirability of procedural rules is shown by the extreme diversity of arbitrations. At one extreme, there are commodity arbitrations concerning consignments of goods, where the arbitrator may be required to form an instant opinion as to the quality of perishable goods (sometimes referred to as a "look-sniff" dispute). At the other extreme there are commercial disputes involving contractual argument, many documents and lengthy evidence, which are conducted in a manner similar to disputes in the High Court. While many construction disputes tend to resemble more the latter class, there is often a substantial element of the former, and it is therefore the more important that construction arbitrators should be in a position to exercise effective control with flexibility. This is greatly assisted by appropriate rules. Those most likely to be encountered in the construction field are referred to below.

ICE Arbitration Procedure (1983)

This was the first set of rules dedicated to construction disputes. Provision was made for their incorporation in clause 66 of the ICE conditions, and the current revision of the conditions makes their use mandatory (clause 66(8)). The rules contain a number of powers not ordinarily available to arbitrators. These include power to give an interim payment, after taking into account any cross-claim (rule 14), by analogy with Orders 14 and 29 of the Rules of the Supreme Court; the power to order disclosure of proofs of evidence; and to require notice of questions for cross-examination (rule 16). The arbitrator is given specific jurisdiction over issues connected with the matters originally referred, even though the new issues may not have been referred to the engineer under clause 66 (rule 4). The arbitrator is given specific power to make orders for security for costs and to secure the amounts in dispute (rule 6). The rules contain two special procedures which may be useful in particular cases. Part F (Short Procedure) sets out the detailed procedure for a hearing essentially on documents, which should take no more than about three months to complete. Part G (Special Procedure for

Experts) is designed to facilitate the early resolution of technical disputes where each party employs an expert and the arbitrator is himself technically qualified. The intervention of lawyers is kept to a minimum. Generally, these rules have been successful in promoting the speedy resolution of engineering diputes and keeping down costs, without introducing undue procedural complication.

JCT Arbitration Rules (1988)

These rules apply to a variety of contracts and forms issued by the JCT. They set out three alternative forms of procedures with a detailed programme for each: procedure without a hearing (rule 5), full procedure with hearing (rule 6), and short procedure with hearing (rule 7). Rule 4 requires the parties initially to agree which of the procedure is to be applied. If they do not agree, then the arbitrator is required to direct that rule 5 should apply (procedure without hearing) unless he thinks rule 6 (full procedure with hearing) is more appropriate, *i.e* the alternative of a short procedure with hearing is' open to the parties only if they so agree.

In addition to these alternative procedures, there are provisions covering inspection, fees and payment to a trustee-stakeholder (rules 8, 9 and 10). Rule 12 gives the arbitrator certain additional powers including power to order security costs and to proceed in the absence of a party who has been given reasonable notice of the hearing.

ICC Rules of arbitration

The International Chamber of Commerce, located in Paris, in addition to other commercial interests, administers a substantial body of international arbitration, much of it in the field of construction. ICC arbitration is different in a number of essential respects from English domestic arbitration. Thus, the rules require the service of a "request for arbitration" and "answer" which may be accompanied by a counterclaim (articles 3, 4 and 5) before the tribunal is fully constituted, these steps being taken under the administration of the ICC Court. These initial documents are intended to contain a much fuller statement of each party's case than a conventional English pleading. They include the nomination by each party of an arbitrator. After these steps have been taken, a chairman is appointed (or in an appropriate case, a sole arbitrator). The full tribunal of three arbitrators is then required, with the parties, to draw up terms of reference (article 13). These define the jurisdiction of the tribunal, the applicable procedural rules and other matters that may be necessary or desirable. Thus, unlike English Domestic Arbitration (where the arbitrator is appointed at the outset with jurisdiction deriving from the request for arbitration), an ICC tribunal defines its jurisdiction through the terms of reference after the parties have stated their cases.

The procedure is left for the parties and the arbitural tribunal to decide. Depending on the wishes and expectation of the parties, there may be formal oral hearings, or the case may be conducted largely on documents. The question whether full or partial discovery is to be ordered will again depend on the procedural rules to be agreed or settled by the arbitrators (article 11). The applicable procedural law will to an extent be influenced by the law of the place (or seat) of the arbitration, and this is to be fixed by the court unless the parties agree (article 12). When the arbitrators make their award, it is required to be submitted to the ICC Court for scrutiny (article 21). The ICC controls the administrative costs and arbitrators' fees, by requiring deposits from the parties at the outset. The arbitrators are given power to award costs (article 20). There is no presumption under ICC procedure that costs should normally follow the event (unless the procedural law is specified as English law).

Other procedural rules

The Chartered Institute of Arbitrators, located in London, issues its own procedural rules which may be incorporated into arbitration clauses or adopted for an existing dispute. In the international field, there are a number of other contenders. The London Court of International Arbitration issues rules which are used by parties in a wide sphere from the United States to the Far East. The International Bar Association (IBA) issues rules which are frequently encountered on the continent of Europe. International arbitration world-wide has been the subject of a major United Nations initiative through the United Nations Commission on International Trade Law (UNCITRAL). They have issued both a model law on international commercial arbitration for adoption by individual states, and arbitration rules. The latter may be adopted by any parties who so agree. The model law, however, requires to be enacted, and this has been the subject of much debate in recent years. The model law is substantially different from English Arbitration Law and traditions, and the Mustill Committee (1989) has advised against its adoption in England and Wales. The model law has, however, been adopted and enacted in a number of states in Australia and Canada and in California; and it is likely to be adopted in many more countries with undeveloped or less well-developed arbitration systems.

AWARDS

No particular form is required for an award, but in a construction dispute it should ordinarily be in writing and should be carefully drafted and checked by the arbitrator, since it cannot be altered later. The essential requirements of an award are that it should decide finally every matter which it deals with, it must be certain in its effect, and it must be consistent with any other findings or awards of the arbitrator in the same matter.

Once the arbitrator has expressed a decision in an award, he ceases to have further jurisdiction over that matter and is *functus officio*. Thus, the arbitrator must be careful not to decide matters which either party may wish to argue further; he should not express decisions on matters where he may wish to alter his view; and he should never express an opinion on a matter which has not been submitted or argued. Where the arbitrator is asked to make an award, but he is in a position to deal only with some of the matters within the reference, the award will be an *interim award*. The effect of decisions within an interim award is no different from decisions in a final award: in neither case can they be reopened. An award which deals with all matters in issue save for costs or interest will also be an interim award, since the arbitrator must still deal with these matters.

Costs and interest

In dealing with costs, the arbitrator must adhere broadly to the principles adopted in the High Court, *i.e.* the successful party should have his costs unless there are proper reasons for departing from this order. Where there is a claim and counterclaim, each must be considered in relations to costs, but it is frequently found convenient to reflect all the matters argued in one global order, such as that one party should have a proportion of his costs. Curiously, despite the severe limitation on the right to bring a substantive appeal (see below) the courts will readily entertain an application to remit an award on costs on the ground that the arbitrator has applied a wrong principle in making his decision.

In awarding interest, the arbitrator should also follow similar principles to those applied in the High Court. He should normally award interest by allowing a realistic rate on the sum awarded from such date as the money ought ordinarily to have been paid, *i.e.* for the period the successful party has been deprived of the sum awarded. The right to award interest formerly existed through the application, by analogy, of the statutory power available in the High Court. Since 1983, however, there has been an express power contained now in section 19A of Arbitration Act 1950 which provides as follows:

> "(1) Unless a contrary intention is expressed therein, every arbitration agreement shall, where such a provision is applicable to the reference, be deemed to contain a provision that the arbitrator or umpire may, if he thinks fit, award simple interest at such rate as he thinks fit—
>> (*a*) on any sum which is the subject of the reference but which is paid before the award, for such period ending not later than the date of payment as he thinks fit; and
>> (*b*) on any sum which he awards, for such period ending not later than the date of the award as he thinks fit.
>
> (2) The power to award interest conferred on an arbitrator or umpire by subsection (1) above is without prejudice to any other power of an arbitrator or umpire to award interest.

Note that this section (which is to the same effect as the Act now applying in the High Court) empowers the arbitrator to award interest on any sum which was the subject of the reference, but which is paid before the award. The position remains, therefore, both in litigation and in arbitration, that there can be no statutory claim for interest alone, where the sum in issue is paid before reference to arbitration. Any such claim might, however, be brought as a claim for special damages (see page 26).

Appeals

Before 1979, points of law arising in a reference could be referred to the High Court under a procedure known as "case stated." The decision of the court could be obtained during the reference, or a case could be stated at the end, the award depending upon the opinion of the court. This procedure produced a substantial number of references to the High Court, such that the decision of the arbitrator could rarely be regarded as achieving finality. In order to remedy this position and to make London a more attractive venue for international disputes, the Commercial Court Committee promoted reforming legislation which is now embodied in the Arbitration Act 1979.

Under this Act, the case stated procedure is abolished and replaced by a limited right of appeal as follows:

> "1(2). Subject to subsection (3) below, an appeal shall lie to the High Court on any question of law arising out of an award made on an arbitration agreement; and on the determination of such an appeal the High Court may by order—
> (a) confirm, vary or set aside the award; or
> (b) remit the award to the reconsideration of the arbitrator or umpire together with the court's opinion on the question of law which was the subject of the appeal;
> and where the award is remitted under paragraph (b) above the arbitrator or umpire shall, unless the order otherwise directs, make his award within three months after the date of the order."

An appeal may be brought by either party within 21 days of the delivery of the award. Section 1(3) provides that an appeal may be brought only if the other party consents, or if the court grants leave. By section 1(4) the court will not grant leave unless the question of law could substantially affect the parties' rights. Leave may be granted on terms such as giving security for the sum in dispute or for costs.

On its face, the new Act appears to create a general right of appeal, subject to the leave of the court. However, the House of Lords have construed the Act so as to place severe restrictions upon the circumstances in which leave may be obtained. In *BTP Tioxide* v. *Pioneer Shipping* (*The Nema*) (1981) the House held that leave to appeal should be given only in the following circumstances:

(i) Where the issue was a "one off" question of construction, leave would not be given unless the award was obviously wrong.

(ii) Where the issue concerned a standard form of contract, leave might be given where there was a strong prima facie case that the arbitrator was wrong.

There has been much judicial refinement of these principles, but the broad effect remains. Thus, in place of the substantial volume of cases previously appealed under the case stated procedure, the number of awards which may be brought before the court on appeal has been reduced to a very small number. In practical terms, an arbitrator's award is to be regarded usually as conclusive of issues both of fact and law. Consequently, if parties to an arbitration foresee the possibility of an appeal, the only way of ensuring that the issue can be brought before the court is by agreement under section 1(3) of the Act.

Reasons

Under the previous law, an award could be set aside for error on the face. Consequently, arbitrators went to great length to avoid giving reasons with the award. This ground of setting aside has been abolished by the 1979 Act, and there is consequently no bar on giving reasons with an award. The 1979 Act contains provisions, under section 1(5), to allow the court to order an arbitrator to state reasons for his award sufficient for the court to consider an appeal. The exercise of this power depends, usually, upon one of the parties having given advance notice that reasons will be required. However, because of the difficulty in obtaining leave to appeal, this part of the Act is of little practical importance.

The effect of the 1979 Act is, therefore, that arbitrators may now give reasons with little fear that the award may thereby be invalidated. It is usually a matter for the discretion of the arbitrator whether he will give reasons. But where the parties agree and request reasons, the arbitrator should have good grounds for declining to do so. Reasons may be desirable on many grounds, including giving the losing party an opportunity of knowing what went wrong, and avoiding similar mistakes in the future. However, when making an interim award where other issues remain to be argued, the arbitrator should be careful not to give reasons which might prejudice the position of the parties in arguing subsequent issues.

Section 3 of the 1979 Act allows for an "exclusion agreement" which will preclude the right of appeal to the courts. This must normally be entered into after commencement of the arbitration, so that such an agreement cannot be included in the arbitration clause of a standard form. Such agreements are of limited importance, in view of the difficulty of obtaining leave to appeal. But it may be proper for an arbitrator to take into account the existence of such an agreement when deciding whether to give full reasons for his decision.

INTERNATIONAL ARBITRATION

There is no universal definition of an international arbitration; the term is used here to mean arbitrations between parties based in different states. Viewed from the United Kingdom, international arbitration has a number of different aspects. There are wholly foreign international cases (for example between a Greek company and a German company, the proceedings to take place in Rome) in which a person from the United Kingdom might be appointed as a neutral arbitrator. He will then be dealing with foreign procedure, and probably with foreign law as well. One of the reasons why such appointments are made is that many such foreign disputes are conducted in the English language. Alternatively, the same wholly foreign dispute might be heard in London sometimes with one or more English arbitrators. In this case, the parties might choose to instruct English lawyers to conduct the arbitration. There may also be arbitrations in either category in which a UK company is one of the parties.

In any international arbitration, the parties face the same procedural problem as exists in domestic cases, but the barriers of distance and language, as well as cultural and other differences, give rise to a large variety of problems, actual or potential. There will usually be an arbitration clause in the relevant contract which deals with many of the potential problems, such as the means of appointing arbitrators, the venue for the hearing and the applicable procedural law. The venue (or seat) of the arbitration, once determined, will influence the procedural law which is to be applied. Under English law (see further page 37), English procedural rules will apply, prima facie, to any arbitration conducted in England. In other countries, however, the position is not necessarily the same, nor are the same matters regarded as governed by procedural law. For example, limitation under English law is regarded as a matter of procedure, so that in an international arbitration conducted in London, the defendant would be entitled to raise English limitation rules as a defence, whatever the substantive law. In other countries, the question of limitation might be regarded as governed by the applicable substantive law, which could produce a different result.

As to the substantive law, this depends on the contract (see further page 113). Some academics argue that international disputes may or should be subject to international concepts of commercial law collectively referred to as *lex mercatoria*. This is a body of principles not deriving from the laws of any particular state. The English courts have shown no enthusiasm for adopting this approach, and adhere to the view that the substantive law must be at least a recognised and defined system. Many of the procedural and practical problems in international arbitration can be resolved by adopting some form of institutional arbitration, such as that administered by the International Chamber of Commerce (ICC) in Paris. The ICC Rules are incorporated into the arbitration clause in the international FIDIC form of contract, and other standard forms as well. The main features of the ICC Rules are referred to above (page 54).

Some states have a distinct body of domestic law which applies to international arbitration conducted in that country. This has not generally been the case in the United Kingdom. The principal exceptions are that the court has no discretion to refuse to stay proceedings where there is an international arbitration agreement (Arbitration Act 1975, section 1); and parties to an international arbitration agreement may make a valid agreement excluding the right of appeal before a dispute arises (Arbitration Act 1979, section 3).

International arbitration has a distinct advantage over litigation in that it avoids the perceived bias of selecting, as the forum, the court of one state, which is necessarily more closely connected with one of the parties. An international arbitration tribunal of three (or more) members can properly reflect the national and cultural interests of the parties as well as selecting genuinely neutral members. The record of enforcement of arbitration awards is at least as good as that of court judgments being enforced in different countries.

ENFORCEMENT OF AWARDS

An arbitration award does not of itself compel the losing party to comply with its terms. The aid of the court must be invoked, and this may be done in two ways. First, under section 26 of the Arbitration Act, the award may, by leave of the High Court, be enforced as a judgment. For the purpose of obtaining leave, an originating summons is issued in the High Court. Secondly, the award may be enforced by action, not relying on the Arbitration Act. If the award is for a sum of money, the claimant may seek to enter summary judgment for the amount awarded. In either case the losing party is entitled to object to enforcement, for example, on the ground that the arbitrator had no jurisdiction.

Where enforcement of a foreign award is sought, either in England or abroad, the right of enforcement depends upon international conventions. Their effect is to limit the grounds on which an award may be challenged. But their application depends on whether they have been ratified by the country in which enforcement is sought. The Geneva Convention of 1927 is ratified in this country by the Arbitration Act 1950. It provides for enforcement of awards in convention countries, provided both parties are subjects of, and the award is made in, convention countries. These do not include much of the Middle East and Africa, where a great deal of international construction work is carried out.

A later convention, drawn up by the United Nations, is known as the New York Convention of 1958. It was ratified here in the Arbitration Act 1975. It provides for reciprocal enforcement where an award is obtained in a convention country. Enforcement is possible only in a convention country, but the nationality of the parties is immaterial. Thus it can be used to enforce an award against a non-convention national who has assets in a convention country. The list of states who have acceded to the New York Convention is more extensive than those to the Geneva Convention, and includes some Middle Eastern and African states.

The New York Convention is arguably the single most important instrument in the whole sphere of international arbitration, in that without it international arbitration would hardly exist, having regard to the difficulties of enforcement of awards and the variety of national concepts of arbitration. As in the United Kingdom, the Convention takes effects in other states by incorporation into their domestic law. The Convention defines the concept of an arbitration agreement, and further provides an exhaustive definition of the grounds upon which enforcement may be refused. The principal grounds are that (Arbitration Act 1975, section 5):

(a) a party to the arbitration was under some incapacity;
(b) the arbitration agreement was not valid under the applicable law;
(c) the party against whom enforcement is sought had no proper notice of the proceedings;
(d) the award is outside the terms of the submission;
(e) the composition of the arbitral authority is not in accordance with the agreement or with law;
(f) the award is not technically binding.

The effecting of enacting the New York Convention into English law is illustrated by the case of *Kuwait Ministry of Public Works* v. *Snow* (1984), in which enforcement was sought in England of an award made in Kuwait in 1973. The United Kingdom acceded to the Convention by the 1975 Arbitration Act, and Kuwait acceded in 1978. The House of Lords held that this later accession nevertheless had the effect of making the existing award "a convention award" so that direct enforcement in the United Kingdom was then available.

Enforcement without the benefit of either convention depends on the internal laws of the country where enforcement is sought. Generally, common law countries accept and enforce awards which are apparently valid under the law of the country in which they were obtained. But the presence of the party against whom enforcement is sought is usually required. The carrying on of business is usually sufficient. Conversely, in civil law countries (notably France and Italy), an award may be re-opened to ensure that the law applied does not conflict with their own rules. But the presence of assets may be sufficient to give jurisdiction.

Further Reading

Mustill and Boyd, *Commercial Arbitration* (2nd ed., 1989).
Russell, *The Law of Arbitration* (21st ed., 1989).

CHAPTER 4

SPECIAL PARTIES

THE principles of substantive law apply to an individual of full age and legal capacity. While most persons involved in the construction industry will have attained the age of majority (now 18) they will usually be involved as employees or representatives of some larger body whose legal capacity and liability is limited. In this chapter the position and status of the different parties who make up the construction industry is examined. Then the legal capacities and liabilities of those bodies most commonly encountered is discussed.

PARTIES IN THE CONSTRUCTION INDUSTRY

The most essential person is the client, who is to pay for the building or works. He may be referred to as the building owner or promoter, but the term "employer" is used in the JCT and ICE forms of contract. The employer may have practically any status. He may be a private individual, partnership, limited liability company, part of local or central government or any other incorporated or unincorporated body. Contractors are not usually concerned with the status of the client, and assume that someone will be held liable to pay for the work. This is not always true.

Contractors

The person who carries out the works is the contractor, sometimes called the builder, building contractor, civil engineering contractor, etc. The employer and the contractor are the two parties to the main contract, which may also be called the construction contract, or the building or engineering contract according to the nature of the works. Although there are other persons connected with the main contract, who may even be named in it, such as the architect, these are not parties to the main contract. Their relationship is by separate contract either with the employer (as in the case of the architect or engineer) or with the contractor (as in the case of a sub-contractor) or even with both, as when the sub-contractor gives a direct warranty to the employer before entering into the sub-contract (see page 178).

The contractor, in all but the smallest jobs, sub-contracts (or sub-lets) parts of the work to one or more sub-contractors. Main contracts commonly provide for certain sub-contractors to be chosen by the employer. They may then be called "nominated" sub-contractors. Main contracts usually contain special provisions governing the rights of the parties in regard to nominated sub-contract work (see JCT form, clauses 35, 36, ICE form, clause 59). Sub-contractors who are not nominated are sometimes called domestic sub-contractors. Both the contractor and the sub-contractor will usually be a limited liability company although small concerns may be partnerships or even sole traders. A practical problem often met is that the contracting "company" is a group consisting of a "holding" company and several "subsidiary" companies. The holding company owns the shares in the subsidiaries, and often has most of the assets of the group. This arrangement has taxation advantages, but means also that a subsidiary can be allowed to be wound up to the detriment of creditors, without financial harm to the group.

The professional team

The task of designing and of supervising the construction of the works is usually carried out by the same person or body. Under a building contract he is the architect, and under a civil engineering contract, the engineer. The title "architect" is, in England, reserved by statute for those professionally entitled to it (under the Architects Registration Act 1938). Unfortunately the same is not true for engineers, although in some countries, such as Italy and Germany, the title is protected. Statutory registration for engineers was recommended by the Finniston Committee, but was not accepted by government. Instead a uniform system of qualification has been created for all professional engineers, by award of the title "Chartered Engineer," abbreviated as

"C.Eng." Usually a specific person or firm is designated as the architect or the engineer under the main contract. The person so designated will be given certain powers and duties by the contract which he must exercise as the construction work proceeds.

The architect or engineer is not a party to the main contract or to any sub-contract, but is engaged under his own contract with the employer. In building contracts where the employer engages an architect, a civil or structural engineer may be required to carry out part of the design work. He may be engaged directly by the employer or by the architect (see page 177). Similarly, an architect may be brought in to assist in the design of civil engineering works. Engineers (who professionally call themselves Consulting or Chartered Engineers, to avoid confusion with engine drivers) and architects practise mostly in partnerships. More recently, however, many firms of engineers and architects have set up as limited liability companies.

A quantity surveyor is often found on larger contracts. His principal function is to take off quantities from the drawings and other technical descriptions of the work and to prepare from them bills of quantities; and to carry out measurements and valuations. In the JCT form a quantity surveyor is named and given certain duties. He does not appear in the ICE form. His duties there are placed on the engineer (see page 313), but are usually carried out by a surveyor. The surveyor may be engaged by the employer or by the architect or engineer under a separate contract. Again, surveyors have traditionally practiced as individuals or partnerships; but more recently many have turned into limited companies. This is particularly so among surveyors who carry out post-contract work, who are often known as "claims consultants."

In his capacity under the main contract, the architect or engineer is required to carry out functions as the employer's agent (see page 126), when he must represent the interest of his employer. In addition, the architect or engineer is usually required to carry out certain duties in an independent capacity, such as certification. In such cases while he remains the employer's agent, he is under a duty to hold the scales fairly between the two parties (see page 169).

In recent years a new role has appeared in many construction projects, that of the project manager. Although his position may be precisely defined in a particular case, he does not fulfil a fixed role in the way that the designer or supervisor does. Project management can be a separate professional role, dedicated to the achievement of cost, time and performance requirements, using sophisticated programming and monitoring techniques. This type of service will be performed under a separate contract of engagement with the employer. A project manager will also be found appointed by the contractor under a management contract. Equally, one may find a project manager appointed under more conventional construction contracts, carrying out the work normally ascribed to the contractor's agent. It is, therefore, not possible to give a single definition of the role and status of the project manager.

In addition to these major participants, there is a group of persons who appear in building and engineering contracts with certain functions and powers. These include the engineer's representative, the clerk of works, the agent and the foreman. All these persons are individuals who represent one or other of the major parties; thus, the engineer's representative and the agent represent on site, respectively, the engineer and the contractor.

Effect of status

The differing legal capacities and liabilities of those bodies most often encountered in the construction industry are discussed below. It will be seen that the most common is the limited company, while many of the professional bodies will be partnerships. One significant aspect of the different legal status of parties lies in the ability to enforce debts against them. For example, where a building owner has a claim against his contractor (a limited company) for bad workmanship, and alternatively against his architect (a partnership) for bad supervision, unless the contractor has assets, the claim may force the company into liquidation so that nothing is recoverable. This is so even though the directors may personally be well off. The architect's firm however will have no such protection. Even if the firm as such is insolvent, the partners may be liable to the limit of their personal possessions.

A practical consequence of this is that professional firms must maintain professional indemnity insurance. This is ostensibly for the protection of the partners, but in practice it represents insurance available to the client, should anything go wrong either during or after completion of the project. Conversely, insurances provided by a contractor are for the most part maintained in force only during the course of the work, so that claims for latent defects will usually be dependent on the contractor's own assets (see further page 201).

LIMITED COMPANIES

The word "company" embraces any body of persons combined for a common object, whether incorporated or not, for instance, the company of heaven. But it can be used, as it is here, in the narrower sense of an incorporated company, as opposed to a partnership. A company may be limited by shares or by guarantee, or it may be unlimited. This section is concerned only with companies limited by shares. This will include the great majority of incorporated companies likely to be connected with the construction industry.

The essential feature of a limited share company is that it exists as a separate entity, distinct from its shareholders (members). The assets and debts belong to the company, which has perpetual existence, until it is dissolved. Changes of the directors or the members (shareholders) do not change the company. When a company contracts only the company can sue or be sued on the contract. If a wrong is done by or to a company, the proper party in any action is the company itself. A shareholder is generally not entitled to conduct an action even if he holds a majority of the shares. Reference is often made in the financial press to companies being taken over or bought and sold. These rather loose terms mean only that the purchaser has acquired a majority of the shares in the company. Companies are taken over because of their assets (including such intangibles as goodwill). But they also take with them all debts and liabilities.

Ownership of companies

The assets of any company are contributed initially by the members, who purchase the shares. Perhaps the main advantage of a limited company, as opposed to a partnership lies in the ability to acquire a financial interest in a commercial venture while not participating in the risks: the liability of shareholders is ordinarily limited to the value of the share held, unlike a partnership, where the partners are liable for the whole of the debts, without limitation.

Companies owe their existence to and are closely regulated by statute. Most of this law is now consolidated into a single statute, the Companies Act 1985. Under this Act, there are two types of company limited by shares. These are known as public and private companies. Private companies are usually much the smaller and are often family businesses, although they comprise by far the greater number of registered companies. In a private company the number of members is limited, and the shares cannot be freely transferred. But a private company enjoys certain privileges which make its operation simpler. In a public company the membership is unlimited; shares are quoted on the stock exchange and are freely transferable. Both private and public companies must file annual accounts which are open to public inspection. Only unlimited companies are not required to file accounts. The Companies Act 1989 has amended the Act of 1985 and contains extensive new provisions relating to company accounts.

Any legal person, including another company, can buy shares. Subject to certain restrictions, a company may even purchase its own shares. The capital of a company has a nominal or authorised limit, which in a small private company is often £100. Some or all of this will be sold or "issued" by dividing it into shares of, say, £1 each. The proceeds of sale become the initial assets. Thereafter the company, according to its fortunes, may prosper so that its assets go up in value, or founder so that they go down. This rise or fall is reflected in the price for which the shares would sell. Thus the initial value of the shares and the value of the issued capital may bear no relation at all to the financial state of the company. A £100 company may have assets worth many thousands of pounds so that a £1 share is worth perhaps £100; whereas a company with issued capital of £1 million might be insolvent so that its shares are worthless. Shareholders are paid an annual dividend out of the company's profits. Additional capital can be raised by selling unissued shares, or, more usually, by a fresh issue of shares for some specified new venture. Companies may also borrow money. This may be done by issuing a debenture as security.

Public companies must distinguish themselves by ending their name with "public limited company," or with the abbreviation "plc." Private companies must use the term "limited" or the more familiar "Ltd." Some companies, principally those who are non-profit making, may omit any such title.

The company's business

Every company must have written rules for its operation, set out in formal documents. These are known as the articles and memorandum of association. The articles regulate the internal management of the company, including the appointment and powers of directors. The memorandum sets out, *inter alia*, the objects for which the company was formed. A company is entitled to do only those things set out in the memorandum, and anything reasonably incidental to them. An act outside the company's objects is *ultra vires* and void.

The effect of the *ultra vires* rule on a person dealing with a company is substantially amended by the European Communities Act 1972, section 9. This provides that in favour of a person dealing with a company in good faith, a transaction is deemed to be one which is within the capacity of the company to enter into. Such a person is not bound to inquire into the capacity of the company to contract. The modern practice is to draft the objects clauses of commercial companies very widely so that a building company, for example, may if it wishes, carry on business in property development or plant hire or financing. There will, however, always be some activities which are *ultra vires*, such as (in one reported case) pig breeding.

Management of companies

A company is run jointly by its board of directors and by the members in general meeting. Prima facie, only the board has power to act for the company. But subject to the articles, it may delegate powers to a managing director and to other directors, who frequently hold paid employment in the company. Directors who are not employed by the company are sometimes called "non-executive" directors. Subject to the *ultra vires* rule a company can contract in the same way as an individual and will be equally bound by written or oral contracts provided they are entered into by an agent with authority (see page 122). A company may be liable for torts, although they must necessarily be committed through its servants. A question which may arise is whether the company is vicariously liable for the particular act of its servant (see page 350).

The primary duty of a director is to the company rather than to the shareholders. He must act in the best interests of the company, and must disclose his personal interest in any contract made. A director must act with reasonable skill and care, although he may delegate his duties to employees of the company. Although the liability of members is limited, a director may become personally liable, if he commits breach of duty, or fraud. A company must have a secretary who is responsible for putting into effect the decisions of the board and for keeping records.

The members exercise their powers by voting in general meetings. It is obligatory to hold an annual general meeting at which the usual business includes dividends, accounts and reports, and the election of directors. Any other meeting is called an extraordinary general meeting, and may be held to consider business such as the removal of a director or amalgamation with another company. Meetings must be conducted strictly in accordance with statutory procedure.

Company management has recently become more closely controlled by statute. Particular matters covered include regulation of the conduct of directors who have personal interests. "Insider" share dealings are now unlawful. Directors are also required to have regard to the interests of employees in carrying out their functions.

Winding up

When a company is wound up its business is concluded by a liquidator who takes over the powers of the board. He collects in the debts which are owed to the company and, so far as he is able, pays off the creditors. He may have to decide whether an alleged liability should be settled, such as a pending action for damages against the company. When the debts are paid, any money left is distributed among the members. Finally the company is dissolved and ceases to exist.

Winding up may be compulsory or voluntary. Compulsory winding up is by order of the court, upon the petition, usually, of a creditor. In most cases the ground for winding up is that the company is unable to pay its debts. This is an incentive to a solvent company to pay its debts promptly or to risk a winding up petition from a creditor. A company may be wound up voluntarily for any reason by the passing of a resolution in general meeting. This may be done, for example, to amalgamate with another company, or because its liabilities prevent it from carrying on business. If the company is insolvent the creditors control the winding up. For the consequences of insolvency, see Chapter 9.

If a company is insolvent, secured debts such as debentures will be paid first upon winding up, and they may consume all or most of the assets. Ordinary debts include an unsatisfied judgment against the company. Thus, if a creditor is owed an undisputed ordinary debt, a judgment for the debt is of no advantage if the company goes into liquidation before it can be executed. Often, debenture holders will pre-empt a winding up by appointing a receiver to protect their security (see page 201). The subsequent liquidation is then more of a formality.

PARTNERSHIPS

As opposed to a limited company, a partnership or firm is an unincorporated body of persons combined for a common object. While the incorporation or dissolution of a company is an unequivocal act, it can be difficult to determine whether or not a partnership exists. There is often a written partnership agreement or articles of association, which may be in the form of a deed. Professional firms such as architects or consulting engineers will invariably have their constitution set out in such a document. However, a partnership agreement may be oral or even inferred from the course of dealing between the parties. The essential feature which distinguishes a partnership is the carrying on of a business in common with a view to profit. There must be a sharing of net profits, although the shares need not be equal and it is unnecessary for all the partners to take part in running the firm. They may make whatever arrangements they wish among themselves.

A partnership is not a separate legal entity. It is owned by the partners in common, and each partner, except a limited partner, is liable for the firm's debts. The capital of the firm is contributed by the partners in any proportions they agree, so that one partner may contribute only capital and another only his expertise. They may agree to share profits in any proportions and prima facie losses must be shared in the same proportions. The question whether a partnership exists or not may have important consequences, for instance, in relation to loans. If A lends £100 to B to help finance B's business, then depending on the circumstances, there may be a partnership between A and B so that A might, in addition to losing his £100, become liable for B's business debts.

In the absence of a special agreement, a partnership ceases on the death, bankruptcy or retirement of a partner and must be dissolved. A partnership agreement therefore usually provides for the firm to be carried on by the surviving or remaining partners. Much of partnership law is codified in the Partnership Act 1890.

A partnership may be formed for any legal purpose. A partnership agreement usually specifies the nature of the business so as to limit the partners' powers to bind each other. But they are always free to vary the agreement so that the *ultra vires* principle has no application. Neither the partnership agreement nor the accounts are ever open to public inspection. A partnership agreement may specify the duration of the firm but if no time is stipulated it lasts during the will of the partners. A partnership created to carry out a specific project is sometimes called a syndicate. Partnerships have traditionally been found to be a suitable mode of association for professional persons, such as consulting engineers, architects and solicitors. Partners are liable to income tax but not to corporation tax.

Management of a firm

Partners, between themselves, must act with the utmost good faith. No partner may make a private profit from the firm's business. Subject to agreement to the contrary, every partner may take part in the management of the partnership. Ordinary business matters are decided by a majority of partners, but changes in the constitution of the firm, such as taking in a new partner, must be agreed unanimously. Every partner is prima facie the agent of the firm and can make binding contracts on its behalf. If a partner commits a tort in the course of the firm's business, the firm will be liable.

When a firm is liable in contract or debt the partners are jointly liable so that they should all be sued, either in their own names or in the name of the firm. A judgment may be enforced against any of the partners sued, but if they cannot satisfy the judgment and another partner is discovered who was not joined in the action he cannot subsequently be sued. It is therefore important to sue all the partners in contract. In tort, however, partners are jointly *and* severally liable so that they may all be sued together, or sued separately until a judgment is satisfied.

Dissolution

Partnerships, like marriages, are made until death or dissolution. But partnerships have the added advantage that they may be dissolved without the help of the courts. A partnership is dissolved automatically upon the expiry of a fixed term for which it was formed; or if it was formed for an indefinite period, by one partner merely giving notice to the other of his intention to dissolve it. If the partnership is for a fixed and unexpired term it can only be dissolved by a decree of the court on the grounds, for example, that one of the partners is guilty of prejudicial conduct, or that the business can only be carried on at a loss.

Unlike the dissolution of a company, which can take place only after winding up and distribution of assets, dissolution of a partnership is the first act. This is followed by the winding up of the firm's affairs, for which purpose the partner's authority continues but may be limited by the appointment of a receiver.

OTHER CORPORATE BODIES

Local authorities

Local authorities are corporate bodies whose constitution and powers derive directly or indirectly from statutes. Constitutional and general matters are found principally in the Local Government Act 1972. The powers and duties of local authorities are laid down in many statutes. Examples of particular importance are the Public Health Acts 1936 and 1961, the Education Act 1944, the Highways Act 1980 and the Town and Country Planning Act 1990. Every part of the country is within the jurisdiction of one or more authority. The distribution of functions between different local authorities and between the authorities and central government varies according to district and according to the service in question. Different local authorities may combine to provide services by setting up joint committees or a permanent joint board.

The Local Government Act 1972, brought about a massive reorganisation of local government. In addition to the re-drawing of boundaries, the Act created a two-tier structure of local government throughout England and Wales. In any area, the primary local authority is now either a county or a metropolitan borough council. Below this are district councils, many of which have as their base the former county boroughs or boroughs.

London has traditionally occupied a special position. Its local authority system was laid down in the London Government Act 1963. It consists of 32 London Borough Councils, including the City. The Greater London Council, which formerly presided over the London Boroughs has now been abolished, together with the metropolitan county councils, thereby reducing the number of tiers of local government.

The powers of a local authority to enter into contracts are similar to those of an incorporated company. A local authority will be bound by a contract whether written or oral, provided it is made by an agent acting with authority. However, since the powers of all local authorities derive directly or indirectly from statute, their capacity to contract is limited by these powers in the same way that an incorporated company is limited by its objects. Any contract which a local authority purports to make for a purpose beyond such powers is *ultra vires* and void.

In entering into a contract a local authority must also comply with its own standing orders, unless they have been suspended for the purpose. In the case of *R. v. Hereford Corporation, ex p. Harrower* (1970), the Council sought to negotiate a contract with the Electricity Board and failed to invite tenders in accordance with the standing orders, because the Board were to prepare the design. The Court of Appeal rejected this as a ground for non-compliance, holding that there was a statutory duty to observe the standing orders. The question then arose whether the applicants had the right to apply to the court. Lord Parker C.J. held:

> "The mere fact that these applicants were electrical contractors does not, in my judgment, of itself give them a sufficient right. But if, as I understand they or some of them are rate payers as well, then, as it seems to me, there would be a sufficient right to enable them to apply for mandamus."

However, a contract once entered into is valid despite any breach of standing orders. Any member of a local authority having an interest in a contract made or proposed must disclose the fact in the same way as a director of a company. Such a member may not, however, take part in discussion or voting connected with the contract.

As an alternative to using commercial contractors for construction work, many local authorities have set up "direct labour" organisations whereby they employ their own workforce to carry out construction work. In some cases this has led to major projects being undertaken by Councils acting, in effect, as their own main contractor. Direct labour organisations also carry out work for bodies other than their parent authorities. The practice is now controlled by the Local Government Planning and Land Act 1980, which restricts the power of local authorities to enter into agreements to carry out work for other bodies and regulates the way in which direct labour organisations carry out work for their parent authorities. In certain circumstances, competitive tenders must be obtained, and authorities are required to publish accounts and to show a return on capital employed.

The Crown

The word "Crown" has several different meanings. It is used here to denote the sum of governmental powers exercised through the civil service, that is, central government as opposed to local government. It is not synonymous with the monarch. But historically, governments have found it convenient to invest themselves and their executive departments with the privileges and immunities attaching personally to the monarch, and so the term "Crown" is an apt metaphor. Formerly the Crown enjoyed general immunity in tort and could only be sued in contract by a special process. The situation was radically changed by the Crown Proceedings Act 1947, which now allows the appropriate government department, or the Attorney-General, to be sued by ordinary process of law.

In contract the Crown is bound by any agreement made on its behalf by an agent having authority. But if a contract provides for funds to be voted by Parliament, an affirmative vote is a condition precedent to liability. With some exceptions, principally relating to the armed forces, the Crown is liable in tort as if it were a private person of full age and capacity, and it can be made liable for the acts of its servants or agents. By virtue of its residuary immunities the Crown cannot be restrained by injunction, nor can it be deprived of property. The Crown also has a far-reaching privilege to restrain disclosure of documents in legal proceedings, whether or not it is a party to the proceedings.

Building and engineering contracts in which the employer is a government department are often subject to a standard form known as GC/Works/1. This gives the Crown (or "the authority") very wide powers of control (see page 211). However, some departments favour the use of the standard forms used in the private sector, such as the ICE form.

The above discussion concerns the position of British government departments being sued in England and Wales. Where it is sought to bring an action against a foreign government, whether the action is brought here or abroad, the position may be very different. As a general rule a foreign sovereign state is immune from action brought in this country, whether in civil or criminal law. Further, if there is no local equivalent to the Crown Proceedings Act, it may not be possible to bring proceedings in the country in question. Parties contracting with foreign states should therefore give serious consideration to the question of guarantees or performance bonds.

Public corporations

Public corporations, which operate the nationalised industries, are essentially companies which are owned by and run for the benefit of the state. They have almost all been created by statute since 1945. Most of the corporations have a complete monopoly, although there are exceptions. There is no fixed pattern for the constitution of a public corporation, but each constituent Act provides for a minister to be answerable to Parliament for the industry, and he will have powers to appoint and dismiss members of the board and to give general directives in the national interest. Some nationalised industries function principally through centralised control, such as the National Coal Board, while others have regional units which are relatively free from central control. During the 1980s the government has operated a policy of privatisation, which has involved converting public corporations into private companies and selling their shares to the public.

The powers of a public corporation to make contracts and to conduct legal proceedings are substantially the same as those of an incorporated company. A public corporation could theoretically be restrained from an *ultra vires* act, but the objects set out in the constituent Acts are expressed in such general terms that in practice it is unlikely. The corporations do not in general enjoy the privileges and immunities of the Crown, and their employees are not classed as civil servants.

Further Reading

Underhill and Ivamy, *Principles of The Law of Partnership* (12th ed., 1986).

Wade and Bradley, *Wade and Phillips* (*Constitutional Law*) (10th ed., 1985).

Charlesworth and Cain, *Company Law* (13th ed., 1991).

CHAPTER 5

CONTRACT: GENERAL PRINCIPLES

ENGLISH law of contract is contained principally in case law. It is only during the present century that statutes have begun to play any significant part. Historically the law of contract has been built up by the judges as a coherent whole so that there exists a body of principles which apply generally to all contracts including building and engineering contracts. In this chapter the general principles are discussed under three headings: first, the formation of a contract; secondly, contracts which though validly formed may not be binding; thirdly, the discharge of contracts. In later chapters there are considered some particular types of contract including building and engineering contracts. These particular contracts, in addition to the general principles set out in this chapter, have their own characteristics, and some are governed by individual statutes.

The law of contract is based on the concept of bargain, in that each side must contribute something to the agreement to make it binding. The only exception to this principle is a contract made by deed. Such contracts were formerly referred to as "under seal," but seals are abolished by the Law of Property (Miscellaneous Provisions) Act 1989 and replaced by the simpler requirement for signature in the presence of a witness. It may be that references to contracts under seal will continue for some time in views of their long history. A contract by deed binds its maker without need of any bargain. Contracts other than those made by deed are called simple contracts, whether made orally or in writing. Although the practice is not universal, some lawyers use the term *agreement* to denote a mutual understanding between the parties and reserve the term *contract* for an agreement which is binding in law. In such terms there can be an agreement without a contract, but every contract must embody an agreement, except perhaps a contract by deed. This terminology is used in the following pages.

In general the parties to a contract are free to make any terms they choose, but certain limits may be placed upon them by the common law and by statute. For example, terms may be implied into a contract which will mitigate the severity of an agreement; or one party may have relief against the other for a misrepresentation outside the terms of the contract itself. Apart from such limits, the courts will attempt to implement contracts according to the terms agreed. However unjust the terms are, or however unjust they may become the courts have no power to rewrite the terms of an agreement. Thus, if a contractor has contracted to carry out works at such prices that he is bound to make a loss, he must still carry out the works or pay damages for breach of contract.

FORMATION OF CONTRACT

If a simple contract is to be legally binding, there must be an offer from one party which is accepted by the other, and each party must contribute something to the bargain. The contribution is called consideration. If a contract exists the courts will determine what its terms are, for instance, when part of the agreement is in writing and part oral, or when there are implied terms. These points are considered in order.

Offer and acceptance

An offer must consist of a definite promise to be bound on specified terms, and it may be made to a particular person or class of persons, or even the public at large. The exhibition of goods for sale is not an offer but an invitation to make an offer. Thus, a shopkeeper may accept or reject an offer from a customer to buy. He is not bound to sell the goods at the price shown. The same applies to an invitation to tender for the construction of building works. The invitation to tender, whether to the public or to an individual builder, is no more than an offer to negotiate. The contractor's tender constitutes an offer which the client may accept or not. Once accepted it forms a binding contract. This is so despite any provisions as to subsequent execution of formal documents (see ICE form, clause 9).

A proviso that the client is not bound to accept the lowest or any tender is generally unnecessary as the contractor, whether the successful tenderer or not, must bear the costs of tendering. However, where the contractor at the employer's request does work outside the normal scope of tendering (such as design work) there may be an implied promise to pay a reasonable sum for such work. Thus, where a contractor was led to believe he would get the work and prepared calculations and other particulars which the employer used for obtaining a war damage claim, it was held that the employer must pay a reasonable sum for the work done: *William Lacey* v. *Davis* (1957). In this case, Barry J. observed:

> "In my judgment, the proper inference from the facts proved in this case is not that the work was done in the hope that this building might possibly be reconstructed and that the plaintiff company might obtain the contract, but that it was done under a mutual belief and understanding that this building was being reconstructed and that the plaintiff company was obtaining the contract. . . . The court should imply a condition or imply a promise that the defendant should pay a reasonable sum to the plaintiff for the whole of these services which were rendered by them."

The offer and the acceptance may be in writing or oral, or may even be inferred from the parties' conduct. Thus, a person who goes into a barber's shop and sits down in the chair is bound to pay for the ensuing haircut. However, if a particular method for communicating acceptance is prescribed, it must be adopted; although an equally expeditious method may be sufficient. For example, if an offer requires acceptance by return of post, a telegram would be sufficient. When the post is used the rule is that the acceptance is effective and the contract made at the moment of posting. Generally silence cannot constitute acceptance. If an offerer says "I will consider my offer accepted unless I hear to the contrary by Friday," the offeree is not bound if he refrains from replying, unless he has agreed to be bound by his silence. But there is an exception when goods are taken on a sale or return basis. There will be an implied acceptance if they are not returned within a reasonable time.

An acceptance must be unqualified. A conditional acceptance or a counter offer may destroy the original offer so that it cannot be accepted later. The traditional form of acceptance "subject to contract" is not binding at all. Acceptance of a contract may have retrospective effect if this is the intention of the parties. Thus where a contractor was instructed to proceed and started work while the contract for the works was still under negotiation, it was held that the parties had intended such works to be governed by the contract as eventually made: *Trollope & Colls* v. *Atomic Power Construction* (1963). The judgment of Megaw J. included the following:

"Frequently, in large transactions a written contract is expressed to have retrospective effect, sometimes lengthy retrospective effect; and this in cases where the negotiations on some of the terms have continued up to almost, if not quite, the date of the signature of the contract. The parties have meanwhile been conducting their transactions with one another, it may be for many months, on the assumption that a contract would ultimately be agreed on lines known to both the parties, though with the final form of various constituent terms of the proposed contract still under discussion. The parties have assumed that when the contract is made—when all the terms have been agreed in their final form—the contract will apply retrospectively to the preceding transactions . . . I can see no reason why, if the parties so intend and agree, such a stipulation should be denied legal effect."

In some types of building contract (and many other commercial transactions) the principles of implied or retrospective acceptance need often to be applied to discover the legal basis of contracts which neither party has ever doubted were binding. A problem which frequently occurs is where the parties enter into correspondence as to the precise terms on which they are to contract. This happens often between main contractor and sub-contractor. The contractor places an "order" on his standard terms and the sub-contractor "accepts" on his standard terms, which are inconsistent with the order. Correspondence follows in which some terms are agreed and others not. At some point the sub-contractor starts the work. The principles to be applied to such problems are that the last letter is deemed to be accepted if the recipient then starts or continues the work (or permits the other party to do so). But if the parties show by their continuing negotiation that they do not regard themselves as bound, there may be no contract. Further, if the parties are not agreed as to some important term there will be no contract. The party who has carried out work at the request of the other will then be entitled to payment of a reasonable sum or *quantum meruit.*

Revocation of an offer is effective only when it reaches the offeree. A promise to keep an offer open for a certain period does not prevent the offer from being revoked prematurely, unless the promise is itself a binding contract, such as an option to purchase shares in a company. An agreement for the periodic supply of goods to order has the legal effect of a standing offer from the supplier which creates a binding contract each time goods are ordered. The offer may accordingly be revoked by the supplier except in respect of orders already placed. If there is no period fixed an unaccepted offer may lapse after a reasonable time.

Standard terms of business

Most main contract work is undertaken through competitive or organised tendering on the employers' pre-stated conditions. Questions that arise regarding formation of the contract are usually limited to whether other documents (such as qualifying letters) have been incorporated, in addition to the employers' standard terms. In other types of transaction, typified by orders for sub-contract work and materials, more fundamental questions arise where standard terms of business are produced by one or both parties. These may be incorporated by reference or printed on the back of order forms or "acceptance" forms. Such terms may compete with each other, for example, each purporting to exclude the other; and there may be particularly onerous provisions hidden within such standard clauses.

The attitude of the courts to such problems has a long history, covering many types of transaction involving tickets, receipts and the like which contain or refer to standard conditions. The courts have evolved principles applicable in certain cases which require that the conditions or particular onerous clauses should have been fairly brought to the attention of the party adversely affected. This branch of the law is now fundamentally affected by the Unfair Contract Terms Act (see below), which refers to the question whether the "customer" knew or ought reasonably to have known about the terms being relied on. Despite this, where necessary, the common law principles will still be applied, in effect, permitting the court to refuse to enforce onerous conditions. In a case decided before the Unfair Contract Terms Act (*Spurling* v. *Bradshaw* (1956)), Lord Denning made the celebrated remark:

> "Some clauses which I have seen would need to be printed in red ink on the face of the document with a red hand pointing to it before the notice could be held to be sufficient."

The notice principles were applied more recently in the case of *Interfoto* v. *Stiletto* (1988), in which the defendant hired 47 transparencies from a lending library, the transaction being subject to printed conditions which required return within 14 days or a fee of £5 a day plus V.A.T. for each one retained. The defendant, who had not read the conditions, returned the transparencies four weeks later and was given a bill for £3783.50. Judgment was given for the plaintiff in the County Court, but the Court of Appeal held that the plaintiff had failed to show that the relevant clause had been brought fairly and reasonably to the defendant's attention, and therefore substituted a reasonable charge of £3.50 per transparency per week. Dillon L.J. in giving judgment said:

> "In the ticket cases the courts held that the common law required that reasonable steps be taken to draw the other party's attention to the printed conditions or they would not be part of the contract. It is, in my judgment, a logical development of the common law into modern conditions that it should be held . . . that if one condition in a set of printed conditions is particularly onerous or unusual, the party seeking to enforce it must show that that particular condition was fairly brought to the attention of the other party. In the present case, nothing whatever was done by the plaintiffs to draw the defendant's attention particularly to condition 2; it was merely one of four columns' width of conditions printed across the foot of the delivery note. Consequently condition 2 never, in my judgment, became part of the contract between the parties."

These principles have as their basis the assumption that ordinary members of the public are not to be taken as anticipating the type of harsh conditions often imposed by standard terms. Where both parties are in the same position and each trying to impose its terms on the other, then the question of notice is unlikely to be relevant. This exchange of standard conditions is sometimes referred to as "the battle of the forms" and the principles which are applied here are simply those of offer and acceptance which, however, may be complicated by the conditions themselves.

The general principle applicable was stated in *Butler Machine Tools Co.* v. *Ex-cell-o Corp* (1979), where the plaintiff gave a quotation providing that orders were accepted only on terms of the quotation, which included a price variation clause. The defendant gave an order subject to their own terms and conditions, having no price variation clause, but having a tear-off acknowledgment for signature and return which accepted the order "on the terms and conditions thereon." The plaintiff signed and returned the acknowledgment but with a covering letter stating that delivery was to be "in accordance with our revised quotation." The Court of Appeal construed the acknowledgment as an acceptance which did not bring back the plaintiff's price variation clause. Lord Denning M.R. explained the law as follows:

> "It will be found that in most cases where there is a 'battle of the forms' there is a contract as soon as the last of the forms is sent and received without objection being taken to it . . . the difficulty is to

decide which form, or which part of which form, is a term or condition of the contract. In some cases the battle is won by the man who fires the last shot. He is the man who puts forward the latest terms and conditions: and if they are not objected to by the other party, he may be taken to have agreed to them . . . in some cases the battle is won by the man who gets the blow in first. If he offers to sell at a named price on the terms and conditions stated on the back: and the buyer orders the goods purporting to accept the offer—on an order form with his own different terms and conditions on the back—then if the difference is so material that it would affect the price, the buyer ought not to be allowed to take advantage of the difference unless he draws it specifically to the attention of the seller. There are yet other cases where the battle depends on the shots fired on both sides. There is a concluded contract but the forms vary. The terms and conditions of both parties are to be construed together.''

An alternative approach was suggested by Lord Wilberforce in *New Zealand Shipping Co.* v. *Satterthwaite & Co.* (1975), a case concerning the question whether a negligent stevedore could rely on the terms of a bill of lading issued by agents of the carrier for whom the stevedore carried out unloading. The question was, therefore, who were the relevant parties to the transaction. Lord Wilberforce observed:

"It is only the precise analysis of this complex of relations into the classical offer and acceptance, with identifiable consideration, that seems to present difficulty, but this same difficulty exists in many situations of daily life, *e.g.* sales at auctions; supermarket purchases; boarding an omnibus; purchasing a train ticket; tenders for the supplies or goods; offers of rewards; acceptance by post; warranties of authority by agents; manufacturers' guarantees; gratuitous bailments; bankers' commercial credits. These are all examples which show that English law, having committed itself to a rather technical and schematic doctrine of contract, in application takes a practical approach, often at the cost of forcing the facts to fit uneasily into the marked slots of offer, acceptance and consideration."

A further matter that can create difficulty is in clauses or provisions which are inconsistent with or repugnant to the remainder of the document. The leading case is *Glynn* v. *Margetson* (1893), which concerned the shipment of oranges from Malaga to Liverpool. The bill of lading provided for liberty to proceed to a variety of other ports for any purpose. The port of shipment was left blank and was filled up in writing. The ship deviated to another Spanish port and as a result, when the oranges were delivered to Liverpool, they were damaged. The case is authority on the question of a written clause prevailing over printed clauses. But the House of Lords also dealt with the question of clauses inconsistent with the main purpose of the contract. Lord Halsbury said:

> "It seems to me that in construing this document, which is a contract of carriage between the parties, one must in the first instance look at the whole of the instrument and not at one part of it only. Looking at the whole of the instrument, and seeing what one must regard . . . as its main purpose, one must reject words, indeed whole provisions, if they are inconsistent with what one assumes to be the main purpose of the contract. The main purpose of the contract was to take on board at one port and to deliver to another port a perishable cargo."

The repugnancy principle is not to be applied lightly, but does provide authority for enforcing the main purpose of a contract where other provisions are inconsistent.

Consideration

Each party to a contract not by deed must give consideration if the contract is to be binding. The most common forms of consideration are payment of money, provision of goods, or performance of work. But it may also consist in any benefit accruing to one party or detriment to the other. For example, A may promise to release B from a debt if he will dig A's garden. The courts are not concerned with whether the bargain was a good one. If B's debt was £1,000 and the garden takes 10 minutes to dig, there is still good consideration.

There are, however, certain acts and promises which constitute no consideration at all. Anything which has already been done is no consideration. If B voluntarily dug A's garden yesterday, today's promise of reward is not binding because B gives no fresh consideration. Further, if a party promises to do nothing more than he is already bound to do he provides no consideration. If B is A's gardener, A's promise of additional reward is not binding.

The courts have, however, on many occasions shown a highly liberal attitude towards what may constitute consideration. In *Williams* v. *Roffey Bros.* (1989) the defendant, the main contractor, concerned that the plaintiff, a carpentry sub-contractor, might not be able to complete on time, orally promised additional payments if the work was completed on time. The Court of

Appeal upheld the decision of the trial judge that this promise was enforceable, the consideration being the benefit, or the avoidance of detriment to the defendant. In any such case, the defendant may argue that the plaintiff has done nothing more that he was already bound to do. But if the sub-contractor agrees, for example, to accelerate (which he may have no obligation to do) this could amount to valuable consideration, and the court would not thereafter be concerned with the adequacy or fairness of the bargain.

Intention to be legally bound

Sometimes, despite the undoubted existence of offer, acceptance and consideration, one party alleges that the contract is not binding because there was no intention to create legal relations. This is not uncommon in family arrangements and it is presumed that domestic agreements are not intended to create legal relations. It is therefore up to the party seeking to enforce such a contract to rebut the presumption. But even where there is no enforceable contract at law, equity may affect the situation. In *Hussey* v. *Palmer* (1972) a mother-in-law who lived with the family paid for building work to the house. Although there was no enforceable loan, it was held that the value of the work done was held on trust for the mother-in-law. In giving judgment, Lord Denning observed:

> "By whatever name it is described, it is a trust imposed by law whenever justice and good conscience require it. It is a liberal process founded upon large principles of equity, to be applied in cases where the legal owner cannot conscientiously keep the property for himself alone, but ought to allow another to have the property or the benefit of it or a share in it. The trust arises at the outset when the property is acquired, or later on, as the circumstances may require. It is an equitable remedy by which the court can enable an aggrieved party to obtain restitution."

In commercial agreements there is naturally a strong presumption that there was an intention to create legal relations. Nevertheless, the intention may be rebutted. The parties may go further and make it an express condition that the contract is not to be binding in law. This is invariably a condition under which football pool companies accept entries, and the effect is that no enforceable contract exists. A similar result is achieved by a clause purporting to exclude the parties' rights to bring actions in the courts upon the contract. Such a clause will be treated as of no effect by the courts, but may make the contract void and unenforceable.

Terms of a contract

The final step in the formation of a contract is the identification of the terms and their effect. If the contract is wholly in writing, the problem is one of construction. But often there are additional terms. Statements made by the parties during their negotiations may have contractual effect. There may also be terms implied in the contract. An express term purporting to exclude or limit liability may raise special problems of interpretation. These points are discussed below.

A statement made during the negotiation of a contract may be a mere representation (see below page 97) or it may become a term and have full contractual effect. There is no decisive test, but a statement is more likely to become a binding term if it is made immediately before agreement is reached, or if the maker of the statement had special knowledge as against the other party, or if the agreement was not reduced to writing.

Implied terms

In addition to the express terms there may be other terms implied into a contract which, although not specified by the parties either in writing or orally, are nevertheless as binding as express terms. The leading case on the general implication of terms into contracts is *Liverpool C.C.* v. *Irwin* (1977), in which tenants in a multi-storey council block sought to establish against the local authority a duty to repair and maintain common parts, including lifts and staircases, which were frequently unusable because of vandalism and defects. The House of Lords, in holding that the Council was under a duty, albeit only to take reasonable care, considered the contractual basis of the arrangement, which was on a tenancy agreement which was silent as to the matters in issue. Lord Wilberforce dealt with the question of implication of terms as follows:

> "To say that the construction of a complete contract out of these elements involves a process of 'implication' may be correct; it would be so if implication means the supplying of what is not expressed. But there are varieties of implications which the courts think fit to make and they do not necessarily involve the same process. Where

there is, on the face of it, a complete bilateral contract, the courts
are sometimes willing to add terms to it, as implied terms: this is
very common in mercantile contracts where there is an established
usage: in that case the courts are spelling out what both parties
know and would, if asked, unhesitatingly agree to be part of the
bargain. In other cases, where there is an apparently complete
bargain, the courts are willing to add a term on the ground that
without it the contract will not work . . . . There is a third variety of
implication, that which I think Lord Denning M.R. favours, or at
least did favour in this case, and that is the implication of reasonable
terms. But though I agree with many of his instances, which in fact
fall under one or other of the preceding heads, I cannot go so far as
to endorse his principle; indeed, it seems to me, with respect, to
extend a long and undesirable way beyond sound authority. The
present case, in my opinion, represents a fourth category or I would
rather say a fourth shade on a continous spectrum. The court here is
simply concerned to establish what the contract is, the parties not
having themselves fully stated the terms. In this sense the court is
searching for what must be implied."

An example of an attempt to imply a term in the third
category, namely one that would be reasonable, occurred in the
case of *Trollope and Colls* v. *N.W. Met. Hospital Board* (1973),
where the parties had made a contract for construction work to
be carried out in phases, but had omitted to make any provisions
for the consequences of the first phase overrunning. It would
doubtless have been reasonable to introduce a term which
regulated the timing of subsequent phases, but the contract made
no such provision and the judgment of the House of Lords
illustrates the limitations on the power of the court to do what is
reasonable. Lord Pearson expressed himself thus:

"The court does not make a contract for the parties. The court will
not even improve the contract which the parties have made for
themselves, however desirable the improvement might be. The
court's function is to interpret and apply the contract which the
parties have made for themselves. If the express terms are perfectly
clear and free from ambiguity, there is no choice to be made
between different possible meanings: the clear terms must be
applied even if the court thinks some other terms would have been
more suitable. An unexpressed term can be implied if and only if
the court finds that the parties must have intended that term to form
part of their contract: it is not enough for the court to find that such
a term would have been adopted by the parties as reasonable men if
it had been suggested to them; it must have been a term that went
without saying, a term *necessary* to give business efficacy to the
contract, a term which, though tacit, formed part of the contract
which the parties made for themselves."

An example of the application of established usage or trade custom occurred in the case of *William Lacey* v. *Davis* (see above) where, in relation to the contractor's claims for costs of tendering work, the judge said:

> "Mr. Daniel rightly conceded that if a builder is invited to tender for certain work, either in competition or otherwise, there is no implication that he would be paid for the work—sometimes the very considerable amount of work—involved in arriving at his price: he undertakes this work as a gamble, and its cost is part of the overhead expenses of his business which he hopes will be met out of the profits of contracts as are made as a result of tenders which prove to be successful. This generally accepted usage may also—and I think does also—apply to amendments of the original tender necessitated by bona fide alterations in the specification and plans."

There are certain types of contract into which terms are implied by statute, such as under the Sale of Goods Act (see below page 115). The principles of this Act have been extended to contracts for the supply of services, by the Supply of Goods and Services Act 1982 which applies, whether or not goods are also transferred, so that it will govern ordinary construction contracts. Sections 13, 14 and 15 of the Act provide that such contracts are subject to implied terms that the supplier will carry out a service with reasonable care and skill and that, in the absence of agreement, the service will be carried out within a reasonable time and for a reasonable charge. These terms may be negatived or varied by express agreement subject, however, to the effect of the Unfair Contract Terms Act (see below).

Implied terms in building contracts

Terms which have been implied in decided cases may act as precedents for similar contracts and therefore give rise to what is sometimes called a common law contractual duty, beyond the express terms of the contract. There are some important terms which are usually to be implied into building and engineering contracts. Such terms require that the building owner shall give possession of the site within a reasonable time, and give instructions and information at reasonable times. Similarly the contractor must carry out his work with proper skill and care or, as sometimes expressed, in a workmanlike manner. Goods and materials must normally be of good quality and reasonably fit for their purpose (as to the effect of sub-contracts, see page 195).

However, there will be no implied term where the matter in question is dealt with by express terms. The matters just mentioned are often covered by express provisions in building contracts, so that there may be no case for further implication.

There are some notable terms which are normally not to be implied into building and engineering contracts. The employer gives no implied warranty of the nature or suitability of the site or subsoil, or as to the practicability of the design. Thus, where a contractor agreed to build a new bridge over the Thames using caissons, it was found they could not be used and the work proved much more expensive. There was held to be no implied warranty that the bridge could be built according to the engineer's design: *Thorn* v. *London Corporation* (1876). In giving judgment the Lord Chancellor, Lord Cairns, observed:

"Can it be supposed for a moment, that the Defendants intended to imply any such warranty? My Lords, if the contractor in this case had gone to the Bridge Committee, then engaged in superintending the work, and had said: You want *Blackfriars Bridge* to be rebuilt; you have got specifications prepared by Mr. *Cubitt*; you ask me to tender for the contract; will you engage and warrant to me that the bridge can be built by caissons in this way which Mr. *Cubitt* thinks feasible, but which I have never seen before put in practice. What would the committee have answered? Can any person for a moment entertain any reasonable doubt as to the answer he would have received? He would have been told: You know Mr. *Cubitt* as well as we do; we, like you, rely on him—we must rely on him; we do not warrant Mr. *Cubitt* or his plans; you are as able to judge as we are whether his plans can be carried into effect or not; if you like to rely on them, well and good; if you do not, you can either have them tested by an engineer of your own, or you need not undertake the work; others will do it.

My Lords, it is really contrary to every kind of probability to suppose that any warranty could have been intended or implied between the parties; and if there is no express warranty, your Lordships cannot imply a warranty, unless from the circumstances of the work some warranty must have been necessary, which clearly is not the case here, or, unless the probability is so strong that the parties intended a warranty, that you cannot resist the application of the doctrine of implied warranty."

The other side of the coin is that where a contractor builds in accordance with detailed instructions, he will give no implied warranty as to the fitness of the finished product. Thus, where a builder constructed, as specified, a solid brick wall without rendering which allowed rain to enter the house, it was held that the builder was not liable for the defect: *Lynch* v. *Thorne* (1956). In giving judgment, Lord Evershed held:

> "If a skilled person promises to do a job, that is, to produce a particular thing, whether a house or a motor car or a piece of machinery, and he makes no provision, as a matter of bargain, as to the precise structure or article which he will create, then it may well be that the buyer of the structure or article relies on the judgment and skill of the other party to produce that which he says he will produce. That, however, is only another way of formulating the existence in such circumstances of an implied warranty. On the other hand, if two parties elect to make a bargain which specifies in precise detail what one of them will do, then, in the absence of some other express provision, it would appear to me to follow that the bargain is that which they have made; and so long as the party doing the work does that which he has contracted to do, that is the extent of his obligation."

Where the builder, in similar circumstances, is under an obligation to comply with the Building Regulations, it may be contended that there is an express obligation to ensure that the works are adequate. However, this is a matter of construction of each contract (see page 387).

Exclusion clauses

It is common practice, particularly in standard form contracts, for one party to insert a term excluding or limiting his liability to the other. This is often done by suppliers of goods or services to exclude or limit liability for defective materials or work. Such clauses may be wholly or partly unenforceable by virtue of recent statutes. However the courts have always been ready to find grounds on which exclusion clauses could be avoided. It is therefore necessary to consider first the position at common law.

An exclusion clause must be carefully drafted since it will be construed against the party seeking to rely upon it (see page 143). General words are unlikely to exclude specific liability. If the term is contained in a document forming part of the contract then the party assenting to such a document is bound by its terms, whether or not he reads them and whether or not he signs the document. But a written exclusion clause may be over-ridden by an oral statement. Thus, where a customer took a dress to be dry cleaned, she was asked to sign a document excluding all liability; the assistant, however, said that the exclusion covered only

damage to buttons. It was held that the cleaners could not rely on
the clause to exclude liability: *Curtis* v. *Chemical Cleaning Co.*
(1951). Denning L.J. in the Court of Appeal held:

> "By failing to draw attention to the width of the exemption clause,
> the assistant created the false impression that the exemption related
> to the beads and sequins only, and that it did not extend to the
> material of which the dress was made. It was done perfectly
> innocently, but nevertheless, a false impression was created. . . . It
> was a sufficient misrepresentation to disentitle the cleaners from
> relying on the exemption, except in regard to the beads and sequins.
> In the present case the misrepresentation was as to the extent of the
> exemption. In other cases it may be as to its existence. For instance,
> if nothing was said by the assistant, this document might reasonably
> be understood to be, like a boot repairer's receipt, only a voucher
> for the customer to produce when collecting the goods, and not to
> contain conditions exempting the cleaners from their common law
> liability for negligence."

Standard terms often try to avoid this result by providing that
no statement is to affect the conditions unless confirmed in
writing. But such a term is likely to be effective only where the
parties communicate primarily in writing; it would be unlikely to
affect the decision in the *Curtis* case above.

Where an exclusion clause is exhibited in an hotel or a garage
stating "The management accepts no responsibility . . ." the term
is not binding unless the party must be taken to have known of,
and agreed to it, before entering into the contract. Even when
such a term is effective, it can normally protect only the parties to
the contract, so that the negligence of servants, agents or sub-
contractors may not be excluded. Nevertheless, the terms of the
contract may be relevant to duties in tort undertaken both by the
immediate parties to the contract and by others (see page 327).

It should be noted that while liability may be limited or
excluded, it can generally be done only by contract or in
situations akin to that of contract. The exhibition on a motor car
of a sign saying "no liability for negligent driving" would not
prejudice the rights of the public at large. But where liability in
tort would arise, for example, from free advice which is given
negligently, such liability may be excluded or limited by an
appropriate written or oral statement (see further page 341).
While clauses excluding all liability are construed most strictly by
the courts, clauses which seek only to limit liability to some
specified or determinable sum, (for example, the contract price)
will be construed more liberally and given their natural meaning.

Thus, a party is more likely to be protected by limitation than by exclusion.

Statutory alteration of contract terms

The above represents the common law position on exclusion and limitation clauses. The fundamental principle of freedom and enforceability of contract terms has been the subject of statutory intervention. Provisions introduced in 1973 (now re-enacted in the Sale of Goods Act 1979) required that clauses excluding or restricting the implied rights of the buyer of goods in regard to their conformity with description or sample, quality or fitness, should be void in a consumer sale; and in a non-consumer sale, *i.e.* one between commercial parties, such terms were to be enforceable only in so far as fair and reasonable (see further page 118).

By the Unfair Contract Terms Act 1977 these provisions were extended in their application to other contracts involving the provision of goods (section 7), which include building contracts. The Act contains other far-reaching provisions governing exclusion clauses and notices. Liability for death or personal injury may not be excluded where resulting from negligence, which includes an obligation to exercise care or skill in contract or tort (section 2(1)). Liability for other loss resulting from negligence may be excluded only so far as fair and reasonable (section 2(2)). The effect of a contractual term excluding or restricting liability for breach of contract depends on the relative position of the parties. Where the innocent party deals as a consumer or on the other party's written standard terms of business, such a term is enforceable only so far as it is fair and reasonable (section 3). A private employer under a building contract may deal as a consumer, and therefore be entitled to the protection of section 3. It is not clear to what extent other employers under building contracts would be regarded as dealing on the contractor's standard terms where, for example, these are the JCT or ICE conditions.

Where an exclusion clause is required to be fair and reasonable, it is to be given effect even when the contract has been terminated by acceptance of repudiation (section 9). The application of the Act is restricted in regard to certain types of contract, including contracts of insurance, and contracts having a foreign element. The Act is not to apply where English law applies merely as a choice of proper law in a foreign contract (see page

113). However the Act cannot be excluded by stipulating a foreign proper law in an otherwise English contract.

An example of the application of the test of fairness occurred in the case of *George Mitchell* v. *Finney Lock Seeds* (1983), where similar provisions contained in the Sale of Goods Act (see page 115) were considered in relation to a contract for sale of late cabbage seed. The seed delivered was of the wrong variety, and had to be ploughed in, after 60 acres had been planted and had germinated. The buyer claimed loss of profit. The contract limited the right of the buyer to replacement or refund of the price paid. It was shown in evidence that the sellers could have insured against the risk of crop failure at little additional cost, and that it was the practice of seed merchants to attempt to negotiate and settle claims by farmers. The buyers had no opportunity to negotiate the terms offered, which were common to all seed suppliers. In those circumstances, the Court of Appeal and the House of Lords held the clause limiting liability to be unfair and consequently unenforceable. Lord Bridge also observed:

> "The only other question of construction debated in the course of the argument was the meaning to be attached to the words 'to the extent that' in sub-section (4) and, in particular, whether they permit the court to hold that it would be fair and reasonable to allow partial reliance on a limitation clause and, for example, to decide in the instant case that the respondents should recover, say, half their consequential damage. I incline to the view that, in their context, the words are equivalent to 'in so far as' or 'in the circumstances in which' and do not permit the kind of judgment of Solomon illustrated by the example."

An application of the Unfair Contract Terms Act in the context of construction occurred in *Smith* v. *E. S. Bush* (1989), a case concerning the purported exclusion of liability by surveyors acting for a building society, whose report was shown to, and relied on, by the house purchaser. Both the Court of Appeal and the House of Lords held that it would not be fair and reasonable to allow reliance on the disclaimer included in the report. Lord Griffiths in the House of Lords observed that while it was impossible to draw up an exhaustive list of factors to be taken into account, the following matters should always be considered:

1. Where the parties are of equal bargaining power the requirement of reasonableness will be more easily discharged than in a case where the purchaser has no effective power to object;
2. In the case of advice, it is relevant to consider whether it is reasonably practicable to obtain advice from an alternative source;

3. Where the task undertaken is difficult or dangerous, with a high risk of failure, that is a pointer towards exclusion of liability being reasonable;
4. The practical consequences of excluding liability should be considered, including the question whether either party can insure, and at what difficulty and cost.

Form of contract

Simple contracts may, in general, be in any form and are enforceable despite a complete absence of documentation. But a few special types of contract are unenforceable unless evidenced in writing. These are, principally, contracts for the sale or disposition of land or an interest in land, and some others such as a contract of guarantee. Such a contract need not be made in writing, but some written evidence is necessary which must be signed by or on behalf of the defendant and which states the material terms. However, a contract which does not comply with these requirements may sometimes be enforceable in equity if there has been a part performance of the contract by the person seeking to enforce it, such as a buyer who has entered into possession of a house.

CONTRACTS WHICH ARE NOT BINDING

The law recognises a number of situations where although a contract has been formed one or both parties are unable to enforce the agreement. The most common of these situations are: when one or both parties make a mistake of fact; and when the contract is induced by misrepresentation. Other contracts which may not bind the parties include those which involve illegality, and contracts where one party is under some legal incapacity. These various categories are discussed below.

Mistake

There are two distinct legal categories of mistake. First, where both parties make the same common mistake, the existence of agreement is undisputed, but one party may say that the mistake has deprived the contract of its efficacy. Where the mistake relates to the existence of the subject matter the contract is void, as in the case of a sale of goods which have perished at the time of sale, or which never existed. But less fundamental mistakes may not be sufficient. Thus, the sale of a painting by Constable was held not to be void when the picture turned out to be by a lesser artist: *Leaf* v. *International Galleries* (1950). Denning L.J. in the Court of Appeal observed:

> "There was a mistake about the quality of the subject-matter because both parties believed the picture to be a Constable; and that mistake was in one essential or fundamental. But such a mistake does not avoid the contract: there was no mistake at all about the subject-matter of the sale. It was a specific picture 'Salisbury Cathedral.' The parties were agreed in the same terms on the same subject-matter and that is sufficient to make a contract."

The second category of mistake arises when the parties have different intentions. Whether they are both mistaken or whether the mistake is unilateral (one party merely acquiescing in the other's mistake) the law considers this as a question of offer and acceptance. The contract is void only if the mistake prevents one party from appreciating the fundamental character of what he is offering or accepting. A mistake which affects only motives, as when one party thinks he had a much better bargain than was the case, cannot affect the validity of the contract.

If the parties had different intentions the court will, if possible, ascertain the true meaning of the contract. If this cannot be done the contract is void. Thus, where parties contracted for the sale of cotton *ex Peerless* from Bombay, there were two ships called Peerless; the buyer intended one and the seller the other. It was held there was no binding contract: *Raffles* v. *Wichelhaus* (1864). The difference in the *Leaf* case above was that the parties there were agreed on one picture as the subject-matter of the contract. Where one party only was mistaken the question is whether there was an acceptance of what was offered. If there was such acceptance the contract is not void, but may still be voidable for misrepresentation (see below).

In addition to common law remedies for mistake, other relief may be available in equity. Principally, if both parties, or even one party, intended something different from what the documents record, the contract may be rectified (see page 148).

Misrepresentation

A representation is a statement relating to a contract made by one party which is not a term of the contract. If it is untrue, whether fraudulent or innocent, it is a misrepresentation and the general effect is to render the contract voidable. A voidable contract may be renounced by the injured party, but until such time it is valid. Only when a misrepresentation has induced mistake can the contract be automatically void.

In order to constitute a representation, the statement must be made before or at the time of contracting; and it must be a statement of fact, not opinion or mere "puff." An estate agent's description of a second rate house as a desirable residence is not to be taken as a statement of fact. Silence may amount to a misrepresentation, as when a previous statement becomes false before the contract is concluded. Further, a misrepresentation does not make a contract voidable unless it induced the contract. Thus, the injured party must have relied on the statement and it must have been a material cause of his entering into the contract.

The rights and remedies which flow from a misrepresentation depend upon whether it was fraudulent or innocent. If the person who made the representation did not honestly believe it to be true then, whatever his motive, it is fraudulent. This gives the other party a right in tort to damages for deceit, and a further right to elect either to affirm the contract (when it will continue for both parties) or to rescind it. Rescission involves cancellation of the contract and restoration of the parties to the state they were in before the contract was made.

A misrepresentation is innocent if the maker honestly, although carelessly, believed it to be true. The principal remedy for the other party is then under the Misrepresentation Act 1967 whereby damages can be recovered unless the maker proves that he had reasonable grounds for believing that the facts represented were true. The person to whom the innocent misrepresentation is made may also sue for rescission, as well as for damages. However, under the Misrepresentation Act the court may in its discretion award damages in lieu of rescission.

The right to rescind a contract for misrepresentation, innocent or fraudulent, is available only if restoration of the parties to their former positions is possible, and if no innocent third party would suffer. A party who affirms the contract loses the right to rescind. An alternative remedy for misrepresentation may be available under the law of tort for negligent misstatement (see page 341). Further, a representation which has become a term of the contract will give rise to the usual remedies for breach of contract if it proves untrue (see page 106).

Illegal contracts

Contracts which contravene the law are in general void and no action may be brought upon them. The illegality may involve doing an act prohibited by statute, such as building contrary to the Building Regulations; or it may consist in a project not as such prohibited, for example, an agreement to commit a crime or a tort or some immoral act. Such contracts cannot be enforced by either party.

The law draws a distinction between a contract which is illegal in its inception and one which is merely performed in an unlawful way. A contract illegal in its inception is totally void and no action can be brought by either party. Property transferred under the contract cannot generally be recovered. But when a contract is illegal only as performed, the effect depends upon the extent of the illegality. If this goes to the core of the contract then a guilty party will have no remedy, while an innocent party may have the usual contractual remedies. If, however, the illegality is not essential to the performance of the contract, both parties may have their normal remedies. Thus, where a ship was illegally overloaded in the course of a voyage, it was held that the owners could still recover the freight charges since the overloading was not an essential incident of the contract: *St. John Shipping* v. *Rank* (1957). Devlin J. in giving judgment held:

> "There is . . . a distinction between the contract which has as its object the doing of the very act forbidden by the statute and the contract whose performance involves an illegality only incidentally . . . . There is no doubt that the plaintiffs cannot succeed if their claim for freight involves showing that they carried the goods in an overloaded ship. But in my judgment, the plaintiffs need show no more in order to recover their freight than that they delivered to the defendants the goods they received in the same good order and condition as that in which they received them."

Where building work is carried out in contravention of statutory provisions, such as the Building Regulations or Planning Acts, the above principles apply in determining whether the builder can recover the price of the work (apart from the question of statutory powers as to enforcement and penalties). Thus where on the face of the contract the work must contravene the law, the contractor cannot recover payment. In *Townsend* v. *Cinema News* (1958) building work which was specified so as to comply with the law was carried out in contravention of a building by-law. It was held that the contractor could recover payment for the work since there was no fundamental illegality. But in such circumstances the building owner will usually be entitled to set off a counterclaim in respect of any work necessary to make the original work comply with statutory requirements.

Difficulties arise, for instance, where the fault lies in the foundations, which can be cured only by demolition and rebuilding of parts which are properly built. Such problems depend upon whether the local authority seek to enforce compliance, whether the building owner has acquiesced in the breach and also on the express terms of the contract.

Incapacity of parties

Certain parties are restricted in their contractual capacity and liability. The most important of these are corporate bodies and infants. A corporate body (such as a limited company or a local authority) can make contracts only within its specific powers; any contract outside these powers is void (see page 69).

An infant occupies a privileged position under the law of contract. He is, in general, bound only by contracts which are substantially for his benefit. Thus, if an infant contracts to purchase goods, he is only liable to pay for them if they are necessary and suitable for his requirements, and he is liable to pay only a reasonable price. An acquisition of property such as land or shares is binding, but may be avoided by an infant before or within a reasonable time after reaching majority (*i.e.* 18 years). The fact that the infant himself may not be bound does not mean that he cannot take advantage of the contract, such as, by suing the supplier of defective (though non-necessary) goods, it has also been held that a guarantee by an adult of an infant's unenforceable contract was itself void. Contracts with infants should therefore be approached with caution. For even greater privileges which may be enjoyed by a foreign government, (see page 76).

Privity

The common law rule of privity is that a contract cannot be enforced by or against a person who is not a party to that contract. For example, a clause in a building contract enabling the employer to pay money direct to a sub-contractor may be used by the employer, but cannot be enforced by the sub-contractor, who is not a party to the main contract. There are, however, exceptions both general and specific. The law of agency is a general exception, for the principal may sue and be sued on contracts made by his agent (see page 122). Specific contracts on which a stranger may sue include (by statute) a contract under seal respecting land or other property, and a third party insurance policy (see page 133). Contracts which can be enforced against a stranger are practically limited to restrictive covenants over land, which on certain conditions are enforceable against a person who subsequently acquires the land (see page 368).

An important aspect of the law of privity is whether, and in what circumstances, a third party can take advantage of an exempting or limiting clause in a contract which binds the parties seeking to make the claim. The leading case is *Scruttons* v. *Midland Silicones* (1962), in which the House of Lords held that a negligent stevedore was not entitled to rely on a limitation clause in the bill of lading. The House left open the possibility that the head contract containing the relevant clause could be expressed in such terms as to permit the third party, in effect, to set up a contract directly with the party suffering the loss. Such an argument was advanced, unsuccessfully, in relation to the taking-over certificate in the Model Form A contract (clause 30), which states that for the purpose of the clause, the contractor contracts "on his own behalf and on behalf of and as trustee for his sub-contractors." In *Southern Water Authority* v. *Lewis and Duvivier* (1984), Judge Smout said:

> "I must be cautious before extending into a wider field those decisions insofar as they apply the principle of unilateral contract to the specialised practice of carriers and stevedores in mercantile law. To my mind, the principle of unilateral contract does not, taken by itself, fit easily on to the accepted facts in the instant case and it strikes me as uncomfortably artificial."

Judge Smout found that the conditions laid down in the *Midland Silicones* case were not satisfied, but nevertheless held that the contract certificate could be relied on as a defence in tort (see further page 328).

DISCHARGE OF CONTRACTS

Discharge of contract is a general term for release of contractual obligations, when the parties become freed from obligation to do anything further under the contract. This must generally be brought about by some act of the parties. Contracts do not end automatically, unless perhaps by becoming statute barred (see page 112). Once a contract is discharged neither party can rely on its terms but can only enforce whatever rights may arise from the discharge. It is therefore important to know whether or not a contract is discharged (this may well be an issue between the parties). Determination of the contractor's employment under a provision in a building contract does not generally determine the contract, so that the parties remain bound by all its terms (see ICE, clause 63, JCT, clauses 27 and 28).

Discharge of a contract may be brought about in four ways. First, if the parties perform all their obligations the contract is said to be discharged by performance. Secondly, if an event during the course of the contract renders performance impossible or sterile, it may be frustrated. Thirdly, in certain circumstances a breach by one party may render the contract discharged; and whether or not the contract is discharged by a breach, the innocent party can always sue for damages. These methods of discharge and also the wider topic of recovery of damages for breach of contract are discussed below. The fourth category of discharge is by express agreement; this is discussed elsewhere under variation of contracts, (see page 149).

Performance

In general only exact and complete performance of contractual obligations can discharge the contract and a party who has only partially performed his obligations cannot recover payment. This rule is mitigated in a number of cases. Where a contract has been substantially performed, payment may be due with an allowance for deficiencies. Further, when a contract is divisible, either expressly or impliedly, payment will be due for parts which have been completed (as to performance of building contracts, see page 154).

A building or engineering contract will be discharged by performance when the contractor has completed all the work, including his obligations as to maintenance, the architect or engineer has issued all requisite certificates and the employer has paid all sums due. If undisclosed defects are later discovered it is sometimes, wrongly, suggested that the contractor is not liable since the contract has been discharged by performance. The contract has not been performed if there are hidden defects. The employer will retain his rights to sue for breach during the period of limitation, subject to the effect of any certificates (such as the JCT final certificate) under the contract.

Frustration

As a general rule contractual obligations are absolute in that a party is not absolved merely because performance becomes more expensive or even proves to be impossible. A party who contracts to do the impossible is liable for failing to do it, unless he excludes such liability: see ICE, clause 13. If, however, without default of either party, the circumstances change so that performance of a contractual obligation becomes radically different from that undertaken, the contract may be frustrated and thereby automatically discharged.

Examples of situations which have constituted frustration are: where a building in which one party is to carry out work for the other is accidentally destroyed by fire; where seats are sold to view a public event which does not take place; and where government action prohibits performance of contract for a substantial period. If a term of the contract provides for the contingency which has occurred, it is a question of construction whether it covers the particular circumstances, and thus keeps the contract in being. In *Metropolitan Water Board* v. *Dick Kerr* (1918) the contractor had agreed in 1914 to construct a reservoir in six years, with a provision for extensions of time for various delays. In 1916, due to the war, the Ministry ordered the work to cease. It was held that the interruption was likely to be so long that the contract would be radically different, and the extension of time provision did not prevent frustration. Lord Dunedin, giving judgment in the House of Lords observed:

> "The order pronounced under the Defence of the Realm Act not only debarred the respondents from proceeding with the contract, but also compulsorily dispersed and sold the plant. It is admitted that an interruption may be so long as to destroy the identity of the work or service, when resumed, with the work or service when interrupted. But quite apart from mere delay it seems to me that the action as to the plant prevents this contract ever being the same as it was."

Examples of building or engineering contracts being frustrated are extremely rare. It may be stated with some certainty that such contracts are not frustrated by the work proving more difficult than could have been anticipated, in any degree, unless the difficulty arises from some change of circumstance or supervening event. In the case of *Thorn* v. *London Corporation* (1876), the contract was not frustrated when the engineer's design for a new bridge over the Thames, with piers constructed inside caissons, proved impossible to construct. The contractor had taken the risk as to the method of construction and remained liable to carry out the work by whatever means were necessary, at no extra cost (see page 168).

The legal effect of frustration is that the contract is discharged as to the future. Money paid before frustration is recoverable and money payable ceases to be payable. But the court may permit a party to retain or recover a sum to compensate him for any expense incurred, or for any benefit to the other party before the time of frustration. A contractor whose contract becomes frustrated may therefore be unable to recover any payment if the employer gets no benefit from what work has been completed. These rules are, however, subject to the provisions of the contract, and will usually be mitigated by insurances.

Breach of contract

Breach of contract occurs when a party fails to perform some primary obligation under the contract, for example, when goods are not delivered on the date fixed, or when materials or workmanship do not conform to contractual requirements. Under normal building and engineering contracts defective work will not necessarily be a breach of contract if the contractor is not bound to execute particular work at a specified time. A breach would, however, occur if the contractor refused to obey a proper instruction to remove defective work or if work were not completed according to the contract by the date when it should have been completed.

It is important, particularly in dealing with claims under a building or engineering contract, to appreciate the distinction between a claim for *breach* of contract and a claim *under* the contract. A claim under the contract arises when some event occurs (which may or may not be a breach of contract) for which the contract provides some remedy. The remedy is usually the payment of a sum of money to or by the contractor, or it may be some other benefit such as an extension of time. Often the same event will give rise to claims both under and in breach of contract. But the consequences of the two heads of claim are different. For example, consequential damages may be recovered for a breach; but under the contract only such remedies as are provided can be recovered. A claim under a contract is a way of enforcing its provisions. This section is concerned only with breach.

A breach of contract may have two principal consequences. First, every breach entitles the innocent party to sue for damages. Secondly, if the breach is sufficiently serious it gives the innocent party an option to treat the party in breach as having repudiated the whole contract. In such a case the innocent party may bring the contract to an end by accepting the repudiation; or he may at his option treat the contract as subsisting, when it will continue to bind both parties.

Repudiation

A repudiation may consist in an express or an implied refusal by one party to perform the contract; or it may be a serious breach which goes to the root of the contract. The latter type of breach may be called a fundamental breach, or breach of a fundamental obligation. Fundamental breach of a building contract might consist in building a house without foundations, or perhaps constructing a bridge in the wrong place. But in each case the question whether the breach is to be taken as a repudiation depends upon the importance of the breach in relation to the contract as a whole. In practice, breaches such as those given as examples are very unlikely to occur if the works are properly specified and supervised. In other words, such errors are likely to be discovered and rectified before the work is so far advanced that they become fundamental breaches.

One type of repudiation which may occur in a building contract is where a contractor carries out defective work and fails or refuses to comply with a proper instruction to rectify it. This constitutes a refusal to perform the contract rather than a fundamental breach. In such circumstances the employer has various remedies available including the right to refuse to pay for the work and to claim damages for delay until the work is properly completed. But he has, in addition, an option to accept the contractor's repudiation as terminating the contract, and expel the contractor from the site. The employer will then be entitled to sue the contractor for all loss arising from the original breach and from the termination, including the additional costs of completing the contract works. In addition to the above remedies most building contracts provide, in such a situation, for determination of the contractor's employment *under* the contract. In such a case the contract is not determined and the parties remain bound by its provisions.

One method of describing the relative importance and effect of the obligations under a contract is to call a particular term a *condition* if a breach will amount to repudiation, and a *warranty* if a breach will give a right to damages only. This sharp distinction is inadequate for complex contractual terms and it would be impossible to distinguish the terms of a building contract in this way. But under the Sale of Goods Act the terms of contracts of sale are so classified (see page 118). Thus, the delivery of goods which do not correspond to a sample amounts to repudiation of the contract of sale, and gives the buyer a right to terminate the contract and reject the goods.

Where the innocent party elects to treat the contract as discharged he must expressly or impliedly tell the other party. His choice is binding and will terminate the contract as from the election. Alternatively, if the innocent party chooses to treat the contract as subsisting, it will continue to bind both parties.

Effect on exclusion clauses

When a contract is terminated by acceptance of repudiation, the question arises whether the party in breach may nevertheless rely on an exclusion or limitation clause. In a number of cases it was held that such clauses were destroyed with the contract. But it is now settled that this is not so. In the case of *Photo Productions* v. *Securicor* (1980) the defendant's employees, who were meant to guard the plaintiff's premises, entered their factory and lit a fire which destroyed the premises. It was held by the House of Lords that *Securicor* were entitled to rely on the clear words of an exclusion clause which exempted them from responsibility for default of their employee unless due to want of care on their part. In giving judgment, Lord Diplock distinguished between the "primary obligation" of a contract, being the services to be provided, and the "secondary obligations" which arose upon breach of the primary obligations. Every failure to perform a primary obligation would be a breach of contract, and this would give rise to secondary obligations such as the payment of monetary compensation for loss sustained. The termination or rescisson of a contract for repudiation brings to an end the primary obligations but leaves intact the secondary obligations. Lord Diplock went on to hold that exclusion clauses were to be applied according to their proper construction:

> "In commercial contracts negotiated between businessmen capable of looking after their own interests and of deciding how risks inherent in the performance of various kinds of contract can be most economically borne (generally by insurance), it is, in my view,

wrong to place a strained construction upon words in an exclusion clause which are clear and fairly susceptible of one meaning only even after due allowance has been made for the presumption in favour of the implied primary and secondary obligations."

The continued existence of a relevant exclusion clause is also supported by statutory authority. Under the Unfair Contract Terms Act 1977, where an exclusion clause is required to be fair and reasonable, the clause is to be given effect even when the contract is terminated by acceptance of repudiation (see above, page 93).

REMEDIES FOR BREACH

If the innocent party has the right to treat the contract as discharged, and does so, he is relieved from further liability. He may then sue for damages which may include both loss flowing from the breach and loss flowing from the termination of the contract. The latter will usually include the additional cost of completing the contract. If the contract is not discharged, either because the innocent party elects to treat it as still subsisting or because the breach was not one which could discharge the contract, the innocent party may recover damages, subject to a number of rules which restrict the monetary loss recoverable. These are dealt with below. Alternatively, in very limited circumstances, the court will sometimes order specific performance (see below), that is, it will compel the defendant to do what he has contracted to do. This remedy is very rare in construction cases.

Damages recoverable

Not every loss which stems from a breach of contract is recoverable in damages. A claim can succeed only in respect of damage which is, in law, not too remote. Further, the innocent party must take all reasonable steps to mitigate his loss.

Damage is not too remote if the parties must reasonably have contemplated it at the time the contract was entered into. The common law has, however, developed two separate "limbs," which derive from the leading case of *Hadley* v. *Baxendale* (1854). In this case, the plaintiffs, who were mill owners, contracted with the defendant to carry a broken crankshaft to the makers at Greenwich. There was delay in transit which resulted in the mill remaining idle so that the plaintiffs claimed loss of profit. In giving judgment Baron Alderson held:

> "Where two parties have made a contract which one of them has broken, the damages which the other party ought to receive in respect of such breach of contract should be such as may fairly and reasonably be considered either arising naturally, *i.e.* according to the usual course of things, from such breach of contract itself *or* such as may reasonably be supposed to have been in the contemplation of both parties, at the time they made the contract, as the probable result of the breach of it."

This classic formulation led to the two possible grounds of claiming damages becoming known as the first and second "limb" of *Hadley* v. *Baxendale*. Thus, the first limb covers such loss as will arise from the natural course of events, each party being deemed to be aware of such natural matters. The second limb (separated by the word *or* in the quotation) covers such additional or special consequences which may arise from the actual events, provided, however, that the parties, at the time of the contract, were aware of such consequences. The second limb is further illustrated by the more modern case of *Victoria Laundry* v. *Newman* (1949), where the plaintiff ordered a new boiler from the defendant for the purpose of taking on new work of an exceptionally profitable nature. The boiler was not delivered and the work was lost. It was held that the plaintiff could recover only the normal profit to be expected, since the defendant had no actual knowledge, at the time the contract was entered into, of the proposed new work.

The rules of remoteness have no application to a claim under a contract as opposed to a claim for breach. Thus if a dealer warrants that a motor car is in good condition and it breaks down, the purchaser may recover as damages for *breach* of contract the cost of repairs and the cost of hiring an alternative vehicle. If, however, the dealer promises only to replace defective parts, the purchaser's entitlement *under* the contract is to the cost of repairs, and no question of consequential damage arises. In contracts of sale, an undertaking to replace defective items is often given in lieu of any warranty as to quality or fitness, so that the supplier is not in *breach* if the article is defective. In building contracts the position may be different. Defect liability clauses, which oblige the builder to put right defects, do not normally prevent the builder also being in *breach* so that consequential loss may be recoverable even though the builder has repaired the work (see also page 190).

Remoteness and causation

The party claiming damages for breach of contract must also prove that the damage was caused by the breach. Similar problems may occur as under the law of tort (see page 353). In *The Wilhelm* (1866), the master of a ship, at the onset of winter, delayed departure from port with the effect that the ship became frozen in until the spring. The defendant was held liable for the whole of the delay since the possibility was apparent and reasonably to have been contemplated. Conversely, in *Associated Portland Cement* v. *Houlder* (1917), another shipping case, the defendant was late on a voyage during wartime to load the plaintiff's goods. The day after the due date, the ship was sunk *en route* by a submarine. The plaintiff recovered damages in respect of the one day's delay; the event which caused the remainder of the damage was not reasonable to be contemplated. The question of causation in a construction case is illustrated by *Quinn* v. *Burch Bros.* (1966), where the plaintiff, an independent plastering sub-contractor, was carrying out work for the defendant who was to supply necessary equipment. The defendant failed to supply a stepladder, as a result of which the plaintiff improvised a trestle, which collapsed causing him injury. Although the defendant was in breach of contract, Sellers L.J. in the Court of Appeal held:

> "This cannot be said to be an accident which was caused by the defendant's breach of contract. No doubt that circumstance was the occasion which brought about this conduct of the plaintiff, but it in no way caused it. It was in no way something flowing probably and naturally from the breach of contract."

Measure of damages

The measure of damages awarded is usually the actual monetary loss. The principle is that the innocent party should be restored to the position he would have been in had the other party performed his obligation. Thus where the plaintiff's factory was burnt down as a result of the defendant's breach and there was no reasonable alternative to rebuilding the factory, the plaintiff recovered the full cost of rebuilding: *Harbutts Plasticine* v. *Wayne Tank* (1970). Lord Denning held, in this case:

> "When this mill was destroyed the plasticine company had no choice. They were bound to replace it as soon as they could, not

only to keep their business going, but also to mitigate the loss of profit. They replaced it in the only possible way, without adding any extras. I think they should be allowed the cost of replacement. True it is that they got new for old; but I do not think the wrong-doer can diminish the claim on that account. If they had added extra accommodation or made extra improvements, they would have to give credit. But that is not this case."

Where a contractor in breach of contract puts up defective work, the normal measure of damages is the actual or estimated cost of re-instatement; and where the breach consists of not doing work the damages will normally be the extra cost of completing the work at the earliest reasonable time. Additional damages such as loss of rents and profits will depend upon the rules of remoteness set out above. Where the cost of remedial work is disproportionate or where other circumstances dictate that remedial cost is not the true measure of loss, the plaintiff may be compensated for the loss in value to the property.

Inflation in building costs often results in argument as to the date at which repair costs should be assessed for the purpose of an award of damages. The position was recently clarified by the Court of Appeal in *Dodd Properties* v. *Canterbury C.C.* (1980). The defendants were liable for damaging the plaintiff's garage premises in 1968. There was delay in carrying out repairs until 1978, which resulted in a considerable increase in cost, for which the defendants disputed liability. The plaintiffs delayed doing the work because the cost would have resulted in financial stringency, and they were reluctant to lay out money before being sure of recovering it. It was held that the plaintiffs could recover the 1978 price of the work. The general position was re-stated as follows:

"The general object underlying the rules for the assessment of damages is, so far as is possible by means of a monetary award, to place the plaintiff in the position which he would have occupied if he had not suffered the wrong complained of, be that wrong a tort or a breach of contract. In the case of a tort causing damage to real property, this object is achieved by the application of one or other of two quite different measures of damage, or, occasionally, a combination of the two. The first is to take the capital value of the property in an undamaged state and to compare it with its value in a damaged state. The second is to take the cost of repair or reinstatement. Which is appropriate will depend upon a number of factors, such as the plaintiff's future intentions as to the use of the property and the reasonableness of those intentions. If he reasonably intends to sell the property in its damaged state, clearly the diminution in capital value is the true measure of damage. If he reasonably intends to continue to occupy it and to repair the damage, clearly the cost of repairs is the true measure. And there may be in-between situations.

. . . In a case in which the plaintiff has reinstated his property before the hearing, the costs prevailing at the date of that operation which were reasonably incurred by him are prima facie those which are relevant. Equally in a case in which a plaintiff has *not* effected reinstatement by the time of the hearing, there is a prima facie presumption that the costs then prevailing are those which should be adopted in ascertaining the cost of reinstatement. There may indeed be cases in which the court has to estimate costs at some future time as being the reasonable time at which to reinstate."

This case concerned a claim in tort, but the principles are equally applicable in contract.

There is an apparent exception to the rule of reinstatement of the plaintiff's loss where a surveyor gives an erroneous report on the condition of the property. The purchaser relying on the report can recover, not the cost of repairing the undisclosed defects, but the difference in value between the property as reported and as it actually was: *Phillips* v. *Ward* (1956). This case is not a true exception to the rule, however. The purchaser's position, had the surveyor performed his contract properly, would be that he knew the true value of the property, and would not pay more than this figure. The surveyor could be liable for the cost of rectifying defects only if he had given a warranty that the house was free of such defects.

Joint liability

Where more than one person is liable in respect of the plaintiff's damage, this does not affect the plaintiff's right to recover the full loss from any one of the defendants. However, as between the defendants who are each liable, the court has power to apportion liability. Formerly, this power was available only in respect of joint tortfeasors (see page 354). But it now applies whatever the legal basis of liability (including breach of contract) by virtue of the Civil Liability (Contribution) Act 1978. A defendant may bring another person who may be liable into an action as a third party; or separate proceedings may be brought against the other person later, to recover a contribution. The way in which the law of contribution applies in construction cases has, rightly, been criticised in the DTI Report on Professional Liability (HMSO, 1989). The application of the rules is illustrated in the case of *Eckersley* v. *Binnie* (the facts of which are given on page 184). The trial judge in that case apportioned liability 55 per cent. to Binnie, 30 per cent. to the Water Authority and 15 per cent. to the contractor. On appeal, the second and third defendants were found not liable at all, so that Binnie had to take a 100 per cent. of the responsibility. The same result would have obtained if other defendants had been unable to pay their share of the damages: the plaintiff would have been entitled to recover in full from any of them.

Where the fault lies partly with the plaintiff himself the damages recoverable may be reduced by the court if the claim is brought in tort (see page 340) under the Law Reform (Contributory Negligence) Act 1945. What has not been clear for many years, is whether this Act also applies where the plaintiff sues only in contract, and it is shown that the plaintiff's negligence contributes to the damage. In the case of *Basildon* v. *Lesser* (1984), it was held by an Official Referee that the Act did not apply at all to claims in contract. However, *Basildon* and other cases touching on this question were considered by the Court of Appeal recently in *Forsikringsaktienselskapet Vesta* v. *Butcher* (1989), where it was held that the 1945 Act did apply where the defendant's liability in contract was the same as his liability in the tort of negligence. Thus, in such a case, the plaintiff cannot avoid a reduction in the damages recoverable by pleading the claim in contract rather than in tort.

Specific performance

Specific performance is an equitable remedy and is discretionary. It is not normally awarded if damages would be an adequate remedy, or if performance would require supervision by the court. Therefore, as a general rule, specific performance will not be ordered of a contract to build. The remedy may be available, however, in exceptional circumstances, such as when the plaintiff sells or leases land to be built upon. Specific performance may be ordered if the following conditions are satisfied: the plaintiff has a substantial interest such that damages would not compensate him; the defendant is in possession of the land so that the plaintiff cannot do the work without committing trespass; and the work is sufficiently particularised. Specific performance may be granted of a landlord's repairing covenant in a lease, when the tenant himself has no right to carry out the work.

LIMITATION PERIODS

A final condition which must be satisfied is that the claim must ordinarily be brought within the period of limitation. The effect of the limitation acts is to bar the remedy rather than the right of action. Accordingly, limitation will be relevant only if raised by the defendant in his defence.

The present law of limitation is set out principally in the Limitation Act 1980, which provides that an action founded on simple contract must be brought within six years of the date on which the cause of action accrued (section 5) and a claim upon a contract by deed within 12 years (section 8). In contract, the cause of action accrues on the date of the breach of contract. The fact that damage is suffered later does not give the plaintiff any further or other cause of action. In the case of a building contract, however, the date upon which a breach occurs may not be limited to the date upon which the acts complained of were carried out. For example, although defective work may create one cause of action when carried out, a further breach and a further cause of action may arise when a builder fails to comply with an instruction to rectify the defects. The final date of breach may be as late as the end of the maintenance period. Thus, it is necessary to construe the contract and to consider the facts to ascertain the latest date upon which the plaintiff is entitled to commence proceedings.

An exception to the ordinary limitation periods is provided by section 32 of the Limitation Act 1980 which provides for postponement of the limitation period where any fact relevant to the plaintiff's right of action has been deliberately concealed from him by the defendant. The period of limitation is not to begin until the plaintiff has discovered the concealment or could with reasonable diligence have discovered it. The section provides that deliberate commission of a breach in circumstances in which it is unlikely to be discovered for some time amounts to deliberate concealment of facts. The section codifies previous decisions of the court, which are illustrated by the case of *King* v. *Victor Parsons* (1973):

> In 1962 the plaintiff purchased from developers a plot of land on which the foundations and concrete oversite had already been laid with two courses of brickwork completed. The developers undertook to complete the house to the plaintiff's reasonable satisfaction. The plaintiff went into occupation in 1962. In 1968 large cracks developed and the plaintiff brought an action in breach of contract.

The house had been built over a rubbish tip, and the developer had disregarded advice as to the type of foundation needed. It was held that the developer, or the builder as his agent, knew of these facts, and the failure to inform the plaintiff amounted to deliberate concealment so that the plaintiff's action was not statute barred.

INTERNATIONAL CASES

In Chapter 2 (page 36) the effect of a foreign element was considered upon procedure in a case. In this section it is assumed that the English courts are proceeding to hear a case in contract containing a foreign element. The question arising is which national law to apply.

The law to be applied in determining a dispute arising out of a contract depends upon the nature of the dispute. But most aspects are governed by one particular national law, known as the proper law of the contract. This can be chosen by the parties, expressly or impliedly. If there is no choice the courts will determine it.

The parties to a contract are generally free to choose as the proper law, the law of any nation, even if it has no connection with the contract (but subject now to the Unfair Contract Terms Act 1977: see page 94). Thus, if a Scottish company contracts in England to build a pipeline in Egypt for an American company the parties may, if they wish, stipulate that the contract is to be governed by French law. In the event of a dispute an English court, if it accepted jurisdiction, would determine the dispute according to the law of France. The choice of French law does not mean that the dispute must be taken to a French court. If an English court has jurisdiction, even a express choice of a foreign tribunal to settle disputes cannot oust that jurisdiction. A stipulation that disputes were to be settled in Paris would, however, probably take effect as implied choice of French law as the proper law of the contract.

The International Conditions of Contract for civil engineering work (FIDIC) contain a clause in which the national law to be applied to the contract is to be specified. Before agreeing to a foreign law a party should, of course, ascertain the effects of that law, for instance, as to whether clauses in the contract for his benefit will be enforceable. In past years it was customary to stipulate English law to govern these contracts, where either the engineer or the contractor was British. In more recent times it has become common to specify the national law of the employer, which is usually where the works are sited. This can pose difficult problems where the country in question is part of the developing world. It may be found that areas of law assumed by the draftsmen of the contract do not exist, or are found only in a rudimentary form.

Where there is no express or implied choice of law, the proper law is determined by the court as the law of the country having the closest connection with the contract. This may be decided by considering, *inter alia*, in which country the contract was made, where it was performed and the place and currency of the payment, although none of these factors is conclusive.

When the proper law has been identified it will determine such matters as whether a binding contract has been made, how the provisions of the contract are to be construed, what is the effect of a misrepresentation, and whether a clause excluding liability is valid. If a contract is illegal by the proper law it is unenforceable in England. However, there are some topics which are governed by a different law. For example, a transfer of land is governed generally by the law of the place where the land is situated. Further, in a building case, a Scottish company had contracted in the standard JCT form to carry out works in Scotland for an English company. The House of Lords held that the proper law of the contract was English, but that the arbitration proceedings were not necessarily governed by the same law. The House held that the parties had accepted Scottish law as governing the proceedings, so that there was no right to use the English case stated procedure: *Whitworth* v. *Miller* (1970). Lord Wilberforce observed in giving judgment:

> "It is a matter of experience that numerous arbitrations are conducted by English arbitrators in England on matters governed by contracts whose proper law is or may be that of another country, and I should be surprised if it had ever been held that such arbitrations were not governed by the English Arbitration Act in procedural matters."

One of the most important factors in deciding the procedural law will be the location of the arbitration, but this is not decisive, particularly in a case which is conducted at different locations.

Further Reading

Chitty on Contracts (Guest *et al.* (26th ed., 1989), Vol. 1
Cheshire and Fifoot's *Law of Contract* (11th ed., 1986), Cheshire, Fifoot and Furmston.

CHAPTER 6

SPECIAL CONTRACTS

THIS chapter deals with special types of contract which are likely to be encountered in the construction industry, and which are governed by their own special rules in addition to the general principles set out in Chapter 5.

The topics covered are the sale of goods, which is perhaps the most universal form of legal transaction; the law of agency, which defines the position of architects and many other persons who act on behalf of another; and contracts of insurance, which are an incident to most building and engineering contracts. Finally, the section on sale of dwellings covers a combination of contractual and other relationships which may be encountered when a recently built house or flat is acquired.

In addition to the matters covered in this chapter, reference should be made to Chapter 4, which deals with the legal status of parties involved in the construction industry. These may also embody a special type of contract; for example, that between a company and its members or directors, and between the partners of a firm. Chapter 8 should be consulted for the special features of building and engineering contracts.

SALE OF GOODS

Contracts for the sale of goods are governed by the Sale of Goods Act 1979. This field covers a multitude of transactions ranging from retail purchases in shops to the sale of articles of great value or rarity, and may include contracts under which the goods are to be specially made. The Act does not apply, *inter alia*, to contracts which are in substance to carry out work or which relate to hire-purchase, or the sale of land or "things in action" such as shares or debts. The law applicable to transactions which involve "sale" of articles under a contract which also includes work or design, is considered at the end of this section.

The Act does not displace the ordinary principles of the law of contract except where they are inconsistent with its provisions. Thus, the formation of contract and the effects of misrepresentation and mistake are the same as for any other contract. The Sale of Goods Act is a codification of the common law, so that its principles can apply outside the limited sphere to which the Act strictly applies. The most important part of the Sale of Goods Act lays down a series of terms which, unless excluded or modified, are to be implied into all contracts to which the Act applies. These consist of four terms relating to description and quality and one relating to title. This legislation was originally contained in the Sale of Goods Act 1893, which was substantially amended by the Supply of Goods (Implied Terms) Act 1973. Both Acts are now consolidated in the Act of 1979.

Implied terms as to quality

Where goods are sold by description, the goods must *correspond with the description*. And if the sale is by sample as well as by description, it is not sufficient if the goods correspond only with the sample; they must also correspond with the description (section 13). Even a small deviation from description, providing it is not absolutely trifling, will constitute a breach of the term. Where a variation can be permitted it is therefore in the interests of the seller to stipulate a specific tolerance or margin. Description may extend not only to the goods but also to their packing. Thus, where a contract of sale stipulated for tins to be packed in cartons of 30, the buyer was held to be entitled to reject a delivery in which some of the cartons contained 24 tins: *Re Moore and Landauer* (1921). In this case Atkin L.J. held, in the Court of Appeal:

> "It appears to me to be clear that the stipulation in the contract that there shall be two and a half dozen tins in a case is part of the description of the goods. There is, therefore, an implied condition that the goods when tendered shall correspond with the description. That condition was broken, and there was a right to reject."

Although in a construction contract there would be no such right of rejection, this case illustrates the importance of ensuring that only such terms as are considered relevant and necessary are incorporated into a contract.

Where there is a sale by sample, the goods must *correspond with the sample in quality*, and the buyer must be given a reasonable opportunity for comparison. Further, despite correspondence with the sample, the goods must also be free from latent defects rendering them unmerchantable (section 15). The use of a sample does not therefore protect the seller from hidden defects in the goods. Sections 13 and 15 apply to all contracts of sale, but section 14 (see below) applies only to sales which are made in the normal course of business by a dealer. Thus, in private sales, the only terms to be implied are those relating to correspondence with description and with sample. Dealers are additionally bound by two important terms which relate to fitness for purpose and to merchantability (or quality).

If a dealer is expressly or impliedly informed of a particular purpose for which the goods are wanted, they must be reasonably fit for that purpose. However, such an obligation is not to be implied where the circumstances show that the buyer does not rely, or that it is unreasonable for him to rely, on the seller's skill and judgment (section 14(3)). Fitness for purpose may extend to the container as well as the goods. Where the condition applies, the dealer's liability is strict. It is no defence that all reasonable care was taken if the goods are still unfit.

In addition to being fit for their purpose, the goods purchased from a dealer must be of merchantable quality. The buyer is under no duty to examine the goods but if he does, however superficially, the dealer is not liable for defects which examination ought to have revealed. Nor is he liable for defects drawn to the buyer's attention before the contract is made (section 14(2)). Goods are of merchantable quality if they are as fit for the purpose or purposes for which such goods are commonly bought as it is reasonable to expect having regard, *inter alia*, to their description and price (section 14(6)).

The type of defect which can render goods unmerchantable or unfit for their purpose will generally be a much more substantial defect than is necessary for a breach of section 13 or 15. However, the fact that goods are substantially defective does not mean there must be a breach of both sections 14(3) and 14(2). In the *Hardwicke Game Farm* case (1969), feeding stuff was supplied to the plaintiffs who bred pheasants. It contained a substance which killed the pheasants. When the supplier sought an indemnity from his supplier it was held that there was a breach of section 14(3) as the goods were unfit for their particular purpose. However, the evidence established that the contaminated feeding stuff was acceptable for the manufacture of cattle foods, and consequently it was held that the goods supplied could not be said to be unmerchantable. There was, thus, no breach of section 14(2) of the Act.

Right to sell

In any sale, unless a different intention is shown, the seller must always have a right to sell the goods at the time of sale (section 12). The right to sell applies usually to the ability to pass good title to the goods, but it may also cover any other matter which affects the right to deal in the goods. Thus, in the case of *Niblett* v. *Confectioners' Materials* (1921), the contract was for the supply of tins of condensed milk. Certain of the cases supplied were labelled "Nissly Brand," which was considered to be an infringement of the "Nestlé" trade mark, and as a result the purchasers were forced to resell the goods unlabelled. Scrutton L.J. held, in the Court of Appeal:

> "The respondents impliedly warranted that they had then a right to sell (the goods). In fact they could have been restrained by injunction from selling them, because they were infringing the right of third persons. If a vendor can be stopped by proceed of law from selling, he has not the right to sell. Therefore the purchasers . . . have made out a cause of action for breach of section 12(1)."

The more usual application of the section is where the seller cannot pass title, for example because he holds the goods on hire purchase. Where there is a breach of the section, the buyer can recover the whole price even though he may have used the goods.

Until 1973, all the implied conditions described above could in principle be excluded from the contract of sale by an appropriately worded clause (see page 91). This situation was radically altered by the Supply of Goods (Implied Terms) Act 1973. This Act provided that any clause excluding or restricting the operation of sections 13, 14 or 15 of the Sale of Goods Act was void in the case of a consumer sale, and in any other case it was unenforceable so far as it was not fair or reasonable to allow reliance upon it. Any exclusion or restriction of section 12 was void. These provisions are now substantially re-enacted by the Unfair Contract Terms Act 1977, which also applies the same principles to other types of contract (see page 93).

Other rights and remedies

Remedies of the buyer under the Sale of Goods Act for breach of contract depend on whether the term broken is to be construed as a condition or as a warranty. These words are used in a technical and rather artificial way in the law of sale of goods. In construction contracts, they are used more loosely, and care must be exercised when making comparisons. The essential difference between sale of goods and construction (or work and materials) contracts is that in the former case, the law insists on precise performance, and allows rejection for anything less; while in construction, the client is bound to accept the work (since it is attached to his land) and must usually rely on damages as a remedy. Thus, in sale of goods, breach of a condition gives the buyer a right to treat the contract as repudiated (as well as the right to sue for damages). Breach of a warranty gives only a right to damages, and the buyer remains liable for the price.

The buyer may at his option treat the breach of a condition as a breach of a warranty. If he has accepted the goods the buyer must so treat the breach, so that he cannot reject the goods after accepting them and can only sue for damages. The five implied terms set out above are stated in the Act to be conditions so that a breach of any one of them, subject to the effect of any exclusion clause, gives the buyer a right to refuse to accept the goods. Which other terms are conditions and which are warranties depends on the construction of the contract. Time of delivery or performance is another matter in which sale of goods and other commercial transactions differ from construction contracts. In many commercial transactions, time of delivery is a "condition" so that the buyer may refuse to accept delivery and may cancel the transaction if the goods are not delivered on time. Such contracts sometimes use the expression "time to be of the essence." In such a case, the only risk of the seller is that there may be a loss in reselling the goods elsewhere. In construction, however, the "goods" are attached to the land and must be in the ownership of the buyer, so that rejection would have catastrophic consequences for the seller. Thus, time is not usually regarded as a condition in a construction contract. Where such a contract provides that time is to be of the essence, the parties usually mean no more than that the contractor will be held liable in damages for late completion.

Contracts which include design or work

Contracts for the sale of goods are essentially simple transactions, compared to construction contracts. The subject matter of a "sale" is usually ascertained at the date of the contract, and compliance with the terms of the contract can be ascertained with reasonable certainty. Thus, it has been possible for the law to prescribe simple direct sanctions, such as the right of rejection and cancellation of the contract. In contracts where the supplier has to carry out design or work as part of the obligation, the situation is more complex: you cannot tell whether the goods conform to the contract until the design has been implemented or work carried out, so that the supplier has virtually performed his obligations. Where the contract concerns construction work on the purchaser's land, the goods become fixed and simple rejection is no longer possible.

In these circumstances it is necessary to revert to common law principles which underlie the Sale of Goods Act. Since the Act codified the common law in regard to particular types of contract, it follows that contracts outside the ambit of the Act continue to be governed by the same principles.

One of the leading cases concerned a contract for making false teeth. In *Samuels* v. *Davis* (1943) the plaintiff alleged that the goods were not reasonably fit for their purpose. It was argued for the dentist, the defendant, that the Sale of Goods Act did not apply, and the defendant's obligation was only to use materials of good quality and reasonable skill and care. The judge at first instance had acquitted the defendant of negligence. In the Court of Appeal, Scott L.J. said:

> "In my view, it is a matter of legal indifference whether the contract was one for the sale of goods or one for services to do work and supply materials. In either case, the contract must necessarily, by reason of the relationship between the parties and the purpose for which the contract was entered into, import a term that, given reasonable co-operation by the patient, the dentist would achieve reasonable success in his work."

A similar point arose in relation to construction work in *Young & Martin* v. *McManus Childs* (1969), where roofing tiles were purchased by a sub-contractor and installed during the construction of a number of houses. The question then arose whether the main contractor was responsible for latent manufacturing defects in the tiles (see also page 195). In the House of

Lords, Lord Wilberforce considered the question of the application of warranties in the main contract:

> "Before the Sale of Goods Act 1893, the courts had to consider questions of implied warranty under the common law and they did so, both in relation to sales, and to analogous contracts, not strictly or at least not purely sales, in precisely the same way. Their conclusions as to sales were taken into the Act, but the pre-existing principles remained and continued to be applied . . . since the Sale of Goods Act 1893, it has been fully accepted by the courts that suitable warranties, adapted to the nature of the contract, ought to be applied in contracts where there are mixed elements of supply of goods and work to be done."

More recently, further areas of the common law have been codified. The Supply of Goods and Services Act 1982, by analogy with the Sale of Goods Act 1979, creates implied terms, *inter alia*, of quality and fitness for purpose in a variety of contracts which involve the transfer of property in goods (see further page 89). It seems that the 1982 Act has not brought about any substantive change in those areas which would previously have been covered by the common law. In regard to quality, therefore, the Acts of 1979 and 1982, and the underlying common law, may be seen as achieving the same result, overlapping in many cases. In addition, where materials are supplied as part of a contract to carry out work on a dwelling, the Defective Premises Act 1972 requires the supply of "proper materials" and that the work be carried out so that the dwelling will be fit for habitation when completed. The purchaser thus has a further alternative in the event of complaint.

Property in goods

Much may depend upon precisely when the property in goods passes from the seller to the buyer if, for example, the goods are damaged or stolen or one party becomes insolvent before physical delivery of the goods. No property can pass until the goods are ascertained, such as, by separating the number to be sold from a bulk. Once the goods are ascertained or specified the property passes when the parties intend it to pass. But if no intention is expressed or to be implied, the Sale of Goods Act defines when the property is to pass. In the simplest case where the sale is unconditional and the goods are in a deliverable state, property passes when the contract is made (sections 17 and 18).

Unless otherwise agreed, risk passes with the property. Thus, if a contract is made to sell specific goods, delivery to be suspended until payment, the risk passes to the buyer on making the contract. If the goods are damaged or destroyed before delivery, the buyer remains liable for the price.

In building and engineering contracts these problems can occur under supply sub-contracts. The construction industry operates on credit. Suppliers have naturally tried to retain some security over their goods until they are paid for. In the case of *Aluminium Industrie Vaassen* v. *Romalpa* (1976) the Court of Appeal upheld a clause which prevented the passing of property in goods until paid for. The argument in this case was as to the effect of the clause where the goods had been used in the defendant's manufacturing processes, and then sold on to third parties. The Court of Appeal held that there was no objection to the creation, as between seller and buyer, of a fiduciary relationship which entitled the unpaid seller to claim the proceeds of sale in full, despite the insolvency of the buyer. The effect of the clause was, therefore, to place the buyer in the position of an agent. Roskill L.J. held, in the Court of Appeal:

> "If an agent lawfully sells his principal's goods, he stands in a fiduciary relationship to his principal and remains accountable to his principal for those goods and their proceeds. A bailee is in like position in relation to his bailor's goods. What, then, is there here to relieve the defendants from their obligation to account to the plaintiffs for those goods of the plaintiffs which they lawfully sell to sub-purchasers?"

Since this decision many contracts of sale have incorporated so-called Romalpa clauses to seek to protect the unpaid seller. The ICE conditions (see page 309) stipulate the opposite effect, namely that all goods when on the site are deemed to be the property of the employer. This provision may run into difficulties when the property in the goods has never passed to the main contractor, since no-one can pass a better title to goods than he has himself. There is, however, a further overriding principle that anything attached to land (or to buildings) belongs to the owner of the land (see page 366). Thus, once goods or materials are built into the works the unpaid seller will be reduced to the rank of an unsecured creditor (see page 201), whatever his contract says.

AGENCY

Agency is a broad term describing the relationship between two parties whereby one, the agent, acts on behalf of the other, the principal. Common situations when this arises are when a person is appointed to buy or sell goods, or to conduct business on behalf of the principal. Examples of agents are brokers, auctioneers, architects and engineers. An agency may be either special, that is limited to a particular transaction, or it may be general. An agent may represent his principal in many different ways. He may conduct legal proceedings, or even commit a tort on behalf of his principal. This section is concerned only with the ways in which an agent may affect the contractual position of his principal.

An agency may arise under a contract, whereby the agent is appointed by his principal to carry out certain duties. Engineers and architects are frequently so appointed to act for promoters of building schemes. The appointment may be to act expressly on behalf of the employer, as when the engineer is appointed to act as supervisor under a contract. An agency will also arise where the engineer is appointed to carry out design work, where this involves acting on behalf of the client, for example, dealing with the planning authority, the public health inspector and with other necessary bodies. In all such cases the engineer will act as the agent of the employer. An agency may also arise not under contract but because of the relationship between the principal and the agent. A director of a company or a partner of a firm may hold such an agency. This section applies generally to both types of agency.

When an agent acting on behalf of his principal makes a contract with a third party the usual result is that the agent drops out, leaving the contract enforceable only between the principal and the third party. Agency is thus a substantial exception to the rule of privity of contract (see page 99). There may be two or three distinct contracts involved in an agency transaction. First, there is the relationship between principal and agent creating the agency. Secondly, there is the contract with the third party which the agent makes on behalf of the principal. There may also be an implied promise by the agent to the third party that he has authority to contract for the principal; this is referred to as a warranty of authority.

Formation of agency

Agency can arise in many ways. The most common is by an agreement under which the principal expressly authorises an agent to perform certain duties for him usually in return for a fee or other payment. The agent will have, in addition to his express authority, the implied authority to do things reasonably incidental to his express powers. Implied authority depends upon the circumstances of the agency and is discussed below in relation to architects and engineers.

Alternatively there are three ways in which an agency may arise without actual authority. First, if the principal acts so as to clothe a person with ostensible authority, the principal will be bound by acts within such authority. For example, an estate agent instructed to find a purchaser may have ostensible authority to accept a deposit. If this is so and the agent defaults, the principal will be liable for repayment. Secondly, an agency may arise when it becomes an urgent necessity to perform some action on behalf of another person whose instructions cannot be obtained, such as where a person is in charge of goods in transit which are in danger of perishing. In such a situation the person in charge of the goods may lawfully sell them on behalf of the owner. Thirdly, if a person without authority purports to act as agent for an identified principal, that principal may within a reasonable time ratify the agent's act and become bound by it. Ratification of a contract relates back to the date when the agent purported to make it. But the principal must be competent to make the contract both at the date of the agent's act and at the date of ratification. Thus for example, a fire insurance policy made by a broker without the owner's authority may not be ratified by the owner after his premises have burnt down.

Rights of parties

The position of the third party, that is, the person with whom the agent makes the contract, depends upon whether the third party knows that he is dealing with an agent. If an agent with authority discloses his agency, the third party can in general sue and be sued by only the principal. But if an agent with authority does not disclose his agency, in general either the agent or the undisclosed principal can sue on the contract. The third party, after discovering the principal, may choose whether to sue the principal or the agent on the contract. But his choice is binding, and if a judgment obtained against one is unsatisfied, he cannot then sue the other. These rules will apply to a person dealing with an individual builder who is in fact acting on behalf of a company: either the individual or the company may sue for payment, and the client has the option of suing either of them if he is dissatisfied with the work, but cannot obtain judgment against both.

Where an agent purports to act as agent but acts without authority, or in excess of his actual authority, the principal will be bound only if he has clothed the agent with ostensible authority or if he ratifies the contract. Otherwise the agent himself will be liable to the third party, not on the contract which he has purported to make (which is of no effect) but for breach of warranty of authority. The agent is so liable whether he has acted fraudulently or innocently.

The relationship arising out of a contract of agency is akin to that of employment, in that an agent has certain legal rights and duties. His rights are: to an indemnity against all liabilities properly incurred; to a lien over the principal's goods in his possession; and to payment. If the contract of agency makes no express provision for payment, an agent is entitled to receive what is customary or reasonable. Disputes may arise as to when payment becomes due. This is a matter of construction of the contract of agency, but in the case of an estate agent there is a presumption that his commission is payable out of the purchase money, so that it is not normally due unless and until the property is sold. If, however, the terms required the estate agent only to produce a ready and willing purchaser, the fee would be payable whether or not the sale took place.

The duties of an agent are to act honestly and obediently, and to exercise reasonable skill and care. The agent must generally himself carry out the duties entrusted to him. However, there are circumstances in which an agent may delegate his duties. These arise when there is an express or implied agreement to permit delegation, or where it is necessary for the proper performance of the work. In the construction industry, an architect has no power to delegate his duty without express authority. If an architect agrees to design a building but is unable to perform the structural design work, there are two courses open to him. He may request the client to employ a specialist; or he may, while remaining liable to the client, himself seek advice and assistance (see page 177). In either event the client will have a remedy for negligent design work.

An agent must not take any secret profit from his transactions, nor must his own interest conflict with his duty. Thus, where an agent who arranged coal supplies received secret commission from suppliers, it was held that the employer was entitled to recover damages jointly and severally from the agent and from the suppliers, and in addition to recover from the agent the secret commission: *Mayor of Salford* v. *Lever* (1891). Lord Esher in the Court of Appeal observed:

> "Hunter (the agent) had received money from the defendant for the performance of a duty which he was bound to perform without any such payment. Nothing could in law be more fraudulent, dangerous or disgraceful and therefore the law has struck at such conduct in this way. It says that, if an agent takes a bribe from a third person, whether he calls it a commission or by any other name, for the performance of a duty which he is bound to perform for his principal, he must give up to his principal whatever he has by reason of the fraud received beyond his due. It is a separate distinct fraud of the agent."

Termination

A contract of agency may be brought to an end by the parties themselves, or by operation of law. Architects and engineers are normally employed, expressly or impliedly, until the completion of the works, although such an appointment may be limited to separate stages of the work. An agency may at any time be terminated by agreement, and there is frequently a provision for termination upon reasonable notice. A contract of agency may be terminated automatically by the death of either party (not being a corporate body) or by the bankruptcy of the principal. It may also be terminated by frustration, such as by destruction of the subject matter, or by the contract becoming illegal.

Architects and engineers as agents

An agency between the promoter of a building scheme and his architect or engineer will arise as soon as there is an appointment to carry out design or investigation work. The extent of the agency will initially be limited, but will be enlarged by subsequent instructions, such as to obtain planning consent and then to obtain tenders for the work. The agency will not normally embrace entering into contracts on behalf of the promoter. Building contracts are almost invariably made directly between the contractor and the promoter. The role of the architect or engineer is usually to represent the interests of the promoter during the course of the works, in addition to his duties as independent certifier under the building contract (see page 169).

Architects and engineers are frequently employed under standard conditions of engagement, such as those of the RIBA or the Association of Consulting Engineers (see further Chapter 10). Under such conditions, the work is usually divided into phases, and the authority of the client is necessary before each new phase is commenced. The conditions usually deal expressly with particular duties required to be carried out, such as supervision of the works. However, such appointments rarely deal fully with the authority of the agent, and it is necessary to consider what implied or ostensible authority will exist, where not expressly given.

An express duty to certify payments to the contractor will usually carry with it an implied authority to supervise the works. There is no implied authority to vary the terms of the contract nor to warrant the accuracy of information in the contract documents. There is further no implied authority to order variations or extra works. However, standard building contracts invariably give express powers to the architect or engineer. He will always have an ostensible authority to exercise such powers under the building contract, unless the contractor has been expressly informed of any limitation of authority. Thus, the employer or promoter will not be able to deny the architect's or engineer's authority when sued by the contractor. Where the architect or engineer is an employee of the promoter his ostensible (or actual) authority is likely to be more extensive and may cover negotiation of the contract terms with the builder. This applies particularly to local government officers, such as the Borough Engineer. This may allow the contractor to sue the employer directly on an oral variation order, if the contract requires an order in writing.

As an exception to the normal position, when an architect or engineer negotiates with a nominated sub-contractor he is no longer the agent of the employer, who is not a party to the sub-contract. He must therefore exercise caution when conducting such negotiations, especially before the appointment of the main contractor, since he may become personally liable for breach of warranty of authority.

The remuneration due to an architect or engineer under standard conditions of engagement is usually based upon a percentage of the cost of the works. One important function of the conditions of engagement is to define with precision the cost upon which the percentage fee is to be calculated. This method of remuneration is somewhat artificial, and often results in payment being made (apparently) for items not carried out by the person receiving payment. An alternative method is to calculate payment on a time basis; this is often used for partial services. Where there is no express agreement as to the means of payment, the engineer or architect will be entitled to a reasonable fee, which may be calculated either by reference to the standard conditions, or to the time spent.

A question which frequently gives rise to disputes is the ownership of work produced by architects and engineers. The formal documents which are prepared for the purposes of a building project, such as the drawings or specification, become the property of the client; but if there is a dispute about payment of fees, the architect or engineer has a lien over such documents in his possession, against the payment of money due.

Documents such as working papers, calculations and correspondence, will normally not become the property of the employer.

The ownership of the designs produced by the engineer or architect is known as the copyright. This remains vested in the designer, and may be transferred or sold like other property. The person who employs an architect or engineer has an implied right to make use of the designs produced in constructing the project. But this does not extend to repeating the design. This was held in the case of *Meikle* v. *Maufe* (1941), which concerned the design of premises in Tottenham Court Road for Heals. The original premises were designed and built in 1912. Using another architect Heals, in 1935, embarked upon extensions based substantially on the original design. It was held that there was no implied right to reproduce the original design in an extension, and the copyright remained vested in the original architect.

INSURANCE

The nature of a contract of insurance is that one party (the insurer) undertakes to make payments to or for the benefit of the other party (the assured) on the happening of some event. The contract may generally be in any form, even oral; but it is usually contained in a document called a policy. The consideration provided by the assured is referred to as the premium.

Insurance and assurance

There are two different types of insurance. The more common is where the insurer agrees to compensate for losses which the assured may suffer in certain events. This type is called an indemnity insurance. The other type provides for the payment of a specified sum on the happening of some event, such as the death of the assured. This may be referred to as non-indemnity insurance, or sometimes as assurance. In many ways the two types are governed by the same rules. But there is one essential difference. On an indemnity insurance the insurer pays out only the actual financial loss. The essence of a non-indemnity policy is that the fixed sum should be paid when the event occurs. Common examples of indemnity policies are fire, motor and third party liability insurance. Non-indemnity policies include life and personal accident insurances. Life Assurance policies are often used as a vehicle for investment, with provision for accumulation and repayment of premiums. The only additional benefit likely under an indemnity policy is a "no claims" bonus.

Formation of contracts

An essential feature of practically every insurance contract is that the assured must have an *insurable interest*. This usually means a foreseeable financial loss or liability resulting from the event insured against. But there is no complete definition. A person has an insurable interest in his own life even though his loss will hardly be a financial one.

A person need not own the thing he seeks to insure in order to have an insurable interest. For example a carrier or custodian of goods has a sufficient interest to insure them himself. Works under construction may be insured against loss either by the contractor or by the employer, or by both. The parties to an action or arbitration have an insurable interest in the life of the judge or arbitrator, since his death may result in loss of the costs incurred. But there are cases in which no insurable interest exists. Thus, in *Macaura* v. *Northern Assurance Co.* (1925) the plaintiff, who owned the shares in a timber company, insured the timber in his own name. When the timber was destroyed by fire it was held that he could not recover under the policy. Lord Sumner in the House of Lords said, of the appellant:

> "He owned almost all the shares in the company, and the company owed him a good deal of money, but neither as creditor nor as

shareholder could he insure the company's assets. The debt was not exposed to fire nor were the shares, and the fact that he was virtually the company's only creditor, while the timber was its only asset, seems to me to make no difference. He stood in no legal or equitable relation to the timber at all. He had no concern in the subject insured. His relation was to the company, not to its goods."

Insurance is often effected through an agent or broker. Generally, such a person has no authority to make a binding contract on behalf of the insurer. His duties are limited to issuing and receiving proposals, although a broker may be authorised to issue temporary cover as a separate contract. The broker is, in law, the agent of the assured.

Duration of cover

Because the obligation to pay is dependent upon the happening of an event, it is important for any policy to define the time limits between which it is to apply. If the event occurs outside the time limit, for example, if the proposed assured dies before the policy is effected, there can be no liability.

Cover will usually run from the date of the original policy, or from such later date or time as may be specified in the policy. An accident or indemnity policy may be arranged to run for a specified period. Thus, a specific policy covering building works may be expressed to extend to a date which is the anticipated completion date plus a reasonable margin. At the other extreme, a life assurance policy will usually extend during the life of the assured, although such policies may be taken out for a specific and limited period. Most indemnity policies including professional indemnity, are periodic, usually annual. Although such policies have the appearance of being perpetual, the need for annual renewal means that the insurer annually has the opportunity of increasing the premium or of altering the terms of the policy, or of declining to accept a further renewal.

In professional indemnity insurance, it is often important to know in which year a particular claim must be accounted for. In all such policies, the insured is covered not against negligent acts as such, but against claims being made arising from such acts. Consequently, the claim will apply normally during the year in which it is notified to the insurer, irrespective of the fact that the negligent act complained of may have occurred several years earlier. This arrangement is of benefit to the insured person, and to the party making the claim, because they have the advantage of any increased level of cover available under the later policy. There will be a considerable disadvantage, however, to any person who was insured at the time of the event complained of but who ceased to be insured under the policy before the claim was made, for example because he retired from the practice. Such a person will be uninsured against subsequent claims, and must therefore make appropriate arrangements for protection with the remaining partners. A further consequence of annual renewal is that all claims within a particular year must be satisfied out of the indemnity available for that year. Thus, if a professional is insured for £1 million, and three claims arise in the same year for £0·5 million, the liability of the insurer is limited to £1 million, even though there may be no claims at all in the preceeding and succeeding years.

Voidable policies

Any insurance contract is said to be *uberrimae fidei*, that is, based upon utmost good faith. Thus, the assured must make full disclosure of every material fact known to him. A fact is material if it would influence the judgment of a prudent insurer. The duty of disclosure continues after filling in the proposal form, up to the making of the contract. Non-disclosure of a material fact makes a policy voidable by the insurer. Thus, where diamond merchants insured their diamonds without disclosing that their sales manager had a previous conviction for diamond smuggling, it was held this was a material fact and the policy was therefore voidable: *Roselodge* v. *Castle* (1966). Under a policy which is annually renewable, the duty of disclosure arises upon every renewal. Thus, where a consulting engineer becomes aware of a defect in a structure which could ultimately result in a claim being made, he will be under a duty of disclosure, and failure to bring this to the attention of the insurer may render the next annual policy voidable.

The policy

Policies such as life insurance tend to be neatly printed on thick paper, relatively easy to follow, and of little interest other than financial. Conversely, indemnity policies, particularly annually renewable ones, tend to exist on many different pieces of paper, sometimes physically attached to a standard policy document, and sometimes not. There are often separate endorsements, exclusions and memoranda all of which have to be identified and construed together.

Despite this, there are certain provisions common to most forms of insurance. There must be a definition of the events upon which the insurer agrees to pay, and this may be accompanied by certain exclusions of liability. In an indemnity policy, such as a house insurance policy, the right to payment will be defined by specifying the property or item insured (the house and contents) and the risks insured against (such as fire, flood, subsidence, etc.). There may be a term requiring notice of an event which may lead to a claim. Some policies, especially motor insurances, contain an "excess clause" requiring the assured to bear the first £x of any claim. Such a term does not, however, prevent the assured himself suing the third party to recover the excess. If goods or property are insured for a sum less than their full value, an "average clause" may be inserted to reduce the sum payable by the proportion of their under-insurance. Where there is more than one indemnity policy covering the same risk there may be provisions which prevent full recovery, or even any recovery, on one or other of the policies.

Rights of parties

Upon the happening of an event insured against, the assured has a right to sue for payment under the policy, irrespective of any rights which may exist against a third party. But under an indemnity policy the sum payable is limited to the actual loss, and subject to any excess clause. The right of the assured is a claim *under* the contract, and accordingly there can be no claim for losses consequential to the insured risk, such as delay in building works occasioned by an insured accident on the site. Consequential loss may itself be insured by a suitable policy.

When the insurer pays out on the policy a right of subrogation arises. This is a right to sue, in the name of the assured, any person who could have been sued by the assured in respect of the loss. Thus, a house insurer who has paid on the policy in respect of a subsidence claim may, in the name of the assured, sue the builder or architect in respect of defective foundations, to recover the sum paid. Where the party insured is legally liable for the loss, the insurer may nevertheless seek, under his right of subrogation, indemnity or contribution from any other party who caused or contributed to the loss (see further page 354).

The attitude of the courts is, therefore, that the existence of insurance policies available to one of the parties, or even to both, is legally irrelevant. The courts used once to avoid even mentioning insurance, on the footing that it might be seen as prejudicial to a party's case if he was known to be insured. This attitude has now changed, and the availability of insurance is now recognised as relevant in the application of the Unfair Contract Terms Act (see page 93). In this context, in the case of *Smith* v. *Eric Bush* (1989) Lord Griffiths said:

> "There was once a time when it was considered improper even to mention the possible existence of insurance cover in a law suit. Those days are long passed. Everyone knows that all prudent professional men carry insurance, and the availability and cost of insurance must be a relevant factor when considering which of two parties should be required to bear the risk of a loss (under the Unfair Contract Terms Act)."

The assured is under a duty not to prejudice the insurer's right. He must not release a third party from any liability he may be under in respect of the insured loss. Thus, he must not admit the claim, but must preserve the right of the insurer to dispute it. If the insurer pays out a sum on the policy less than the actual loss, and the assured then receives some other payment in respect of the loss, the assured must repay to the insurer anything received in excess of the actual loss. The assured may not recoup more than he has lost.

Third party rights

There are statutory provisions which enable a third party, who is not a party to the insurance contract, to obtain the benefit of the policy despite the common law rule of privity of contract (see page 99). The Third Parties (Rights against Insurers) Act 1930 applies when the insured person or company becomes insolvent. If liability is incurred to a third party, either before or after the insolvency, the right against the insurer vests in the third party. The Act also imposes duties on the insured person and on the insurer to give information to the third party. Apart from these provisions, either the insurer would escape liability or the insurance money would go to the creditors and not to the injured party. Under a motor insurance policy a third party, having obtained judgment against the assured, may claim against the insurer irrespective of the solvency of the assured.

INSURANCE IN CONSTRUCTION PROJECTS

There are a variety of provisions and practices in construction work which usually result in there being a considerable variety of policies applying to different aspects of the work, covering different parties and providing different types of cover. Some of these are compulsory, being required by conditions of contract, while others are discretionary and taken out for the protection of individual parties. The result is often that, when a loss occurs, the disputes between the parties turns into a dispute between those who have insured the parties against their loss or liability. This can have the unintended effect that the parties effectively lose control of the dispute, and the decision whether to fight or settle is that of the insurers. A number of alternatives to this situation have been suggested, which are mentioned further below.

Construction contracts invariably make a number of express requirements for insurance. Particular cover required under the JCT and ICE contracts is dealt with later (see pages 237 and 290). In general, construction contracts require two different types of cover. First, insurance is required on the works themselves. This is often a policy which is to be taken out in joint names (of the contractor and the employer) but the terms and the risks to be insured, depend on the wording of the particular contract. Thus, the ICE form (clause 21) requires insurance against loss or damage "from whatsoever cause arising" except for the "excepted risks," which include faulty design, war, radioactivity and like perils. The JCT form, conversely (by clause 22), requires insurance against specified perils only (fire, storm and the like). The JCT contract provides, alternatively, for the employer to take these risks, in which case the contractor is not required to insure.

The other, separate type of cover, is insurance against third party claims. This is a quite different type of cover in that insurance of the works is insurance of "property," whether the cover is against all risks or specified perils. Third party insurance is against "liability." Thus, the ICE conditions (clause 23) require the contractor to insure against damage to any property or person arising out of the works; and the JCT contract (clause 21) makes similar provision. One of the reasons for the difference in these two types of cover is that, while the contractor (and the employer) have an insurable interest (see above) in the works, they have no such interest in third party property other than through their potential liability for damage to it.

The insurances just mentioned are specific to the contracts in question, although they may be taken out pursuant to standing arrangements with insurers. In addition to these policies, contractors invariably maintain a continuing policy covering a variety of matters, called a Contractors' All-Risks (CAR) Policy. The type of cover provided tends to vary, but a CAR policy typically provides some cover against liability for design work, and to some extent, against defects in material or workmanship. The usual procedure is for contracts to be noted on the policy, which continues upon annual renewals. The insurances required under construction contracts are usually released at or shortly after completion. The importance of a CAR policy is that it will continue in force, so that claims made, perhaps long after completion, may be covered. In practice, this is often the only cover which the contractor has against latent defects.

The other major insurance cover under construction projects, is the professional indemnity (PI) cover taken out by engineers and architects. These are continuing annual policies which cover the professional against legal liability, which will usually arise through negligence (see page 174). PI cover operates on a "claims made" basis. That is, each annual policy covers claims arising during the year of its currency. In addition to terms concerning matters such as notification of claims, there will always be a limit of cover, which may be expressed in terms of each claim or the aggregate of claims during the year. This limit will tend to increase with inflation and with expansion of the professional's business, so that the person making the claim will get the advantage of a higher limit being available in subsequent years. The importance of PI cover is that, unlike the contractors' policies under the contract, it will continue (subject to renewals) after completion of the project. Thus, in regard to latent defects, the insurance position is often that the professional's PI cover is the major insurance available, supplemented by the contractor's CAR policy, if applicable to the claim.

The effect of "liability" insurance is illustrated by the case of *Wimpey* v. *Poole* (1984), where the contractor undertook a design and construct contract for a new anchored quay wall. The wall suffered partial failure which was found to be due to softening of the clay at the toe. The contractor had a PI policy which covered claims arising from "any omission error or negligent act in respect of design or specification of work." The contractor carried out remedial work at his own expense and sought to recover the cost from the insurer, contending that it had carried out the design negligently. The commercial court held that the plaintiff had failed to establish his own negligence, but nevertheless, the failure of the design to make sufficient provision for softening of the clay amounted to an omission or error in respect of that design, and was therefore prima facie covered by the policy. For other reasons, the plaintiff failed to recover the bulk of its loss. The case illustrates the legal contortions that may arise from insurance of liability rather than property.

The availability of insurance has no effect on the ability of a claimant to pursue a claim against a defendant who is held liable. In regard to claims against contractors, if the company is actively trading, there will usually be sufficient assets to meet uninsured claims. As regards professionals trading as partnerships, the individual partners are liable, and any judgment may be enforced against their personal assets, including bankruptcy. For this reason, many professional organisations have turned themselves into limited companies, although this does not rule out the possibility of tort action being brought against individuals. In addition to the contractor and the professional team, sub-contractors and others involved in disputes may have their own insurance arrangements. These may consist either of property-based insurance (for example, sub-contractors will insure their goods and materials) or, more usually, liability-based insurance.

The availability of different insurances essentially covering the same type of loss creates many procedural problems, as the cover under different policies will overlap. Another problem is that, where cover is based on liability, it is necessay to establish that liability before the insurer becomes bound to pay. This explains why disputes about latent defects can be so protracted and costly. A number of solutions have been put forward to deal with these problems. As regards the overlapping cover provided during the currency of the contract, it is possible to take out a "project" insurance policy which is designed to supersede all the different levels of cover otherwise provided, in theory at a lower cost. The more difficult problem is that of latent defects, *i.e.* those arising or appearing after completion. Here, the problem is even more complicated because employers, particularly developers of commercial buildings, tend to sell on or lease the premies at or soon after completion, often on terms which place liability for latent defects on the purchaser or lessee (see further page 361). These arrangements have in past years led to tort claims against designers and contractors by purchasers or lessees. With the demise of such claims (see page 335), contractual and assignable warranties have been created giving other rights of action (see page 178). Such complicated arrangements inevitably lead to lengthy and costly litigation, in which the damaged owner receives no compensation until the claims are settled or resolved through the courts.

This unsatisfactory state of affairs was considered in a government committee set up through the National Economic Development Office (NEDO), which in 1988 produced the BUILD (Building Users Insurance against Latent Defects) Report. This recommends a new type of insurance based on the French decennial system whereby the owner takes out a policy effective from completion of the work, which insures the property (not merely liability) against latent defects. The report recommends surrender of the right of subrogation (see above) so that litigation will not automatically follow any claim. Policies of this type are now available and many have been effected. It is to be expected that the insurer will need to be identified at the outset, and will take an active interest in the design and construction of the building, as well as its subsequent maintenance, in order to protect his liability. BUILD policies are recommended to run for 10 years and to be assignable or otherwise to cover the interests of subsequent owners and occupiers. The major limitation on these policies is that they cannot cover all aspects of buildings, and cover is usually limited to major elements such as the structure and weathershield.

SALE OF DWELLINGS

The term "dwelling" is used to cover any form of residential accommodation. The purchase of a dwelling often forms the most important economic transaction which many individuals enter into during their lives. It may involve complex problems relating to the title of the property sold, and to the means of raising finance. This section is concerned solely with problems relating to the quality of the building and the rights of parties where there is a dispute. It is further limited to the sale of new or recently built dwellings, where the sale is of the land and building together. When builders are employed to build a house on a person's own land, the rights of the owner will be governed primarily by the building contract.

The term "sale" is used here loosely. The essential feature of the transaction is that the property should be transferred or conveyed from vendor to purchaser. In the case of a house this is usually done by a conveyance by which the title of the land is vested in the purchaser. In the case of flats and maisonettes, and sometimes houses also, the vesting of title may be by a lease, usually for a fixed (but long) period. In either case all that needs to be transferred is the physical *space* in which the building stands (or is to stand, if not completed). The law automatically transfers with the land everything attached to it, including buildings, paths, walls, trees, etc. The conveyance or lease may therefore create no rights in respect of the building itself.

The conveyance or lease is, however, almost invariably preceded by the contract of sale. This needs to be in writing or at least evidenced in writing (see page 361). The contract may contain (in addition to the agreement of sale) terms relating to the building, such as, that the work has been or will be carried out in accordance with an identified plan or specification, or in a good and workmanlike manner. But contracts of sale are sometimes entirely silent as to the building itself. In the absence of contractual terms, and until certain recent developments, the law was expressed by the maxim *caveat emptor*: let the buyer beware. He had no redress if the building proved to be defective.

Substantially, this remains the law in respect of the sale of old houses. Where the building is new or of recent construction, a number of developments in the law have changed the position radically. In *Hancock* v. *Brazier* (1966) the Court of Appeal held a purchaser entitled to damages in respect of defective hardcore which had been incorporated into the foundation of a house before the date of the contract of purchase. Lord Denning summarised the law as follows:

> "When a purchaser buys a house from a builder who contracts to build it, there is a three-fold implication: that the builder will do his work in a good and workmanlike manner; that he will supply good and proper materials; and that it will be reasonably fit for human habitation."

However, this did not protect the purchaser of a completed house, nor subsequent purchasers of newly built houses. An important further measure of protection was introduced by a private body now known as the National House Building Council (the NHBC).

The NHBC publish forms of agreement relating to the quality of the building (see page 218 for a review of the principal features of the forms). They operate a scheme of registration under which builders and developers must undertake to comply with NHBC Rules and Requirements. This gives a wide measure of protection to the first purchaser, which is intended also to protect subsequent purchasers. The scheme is backed by extensive insurance provisions so that purchasers will have a considerable degree of protection in the event of the vendor's insolvency. However, there remains the possibility of purchasers being unprotected, for example if necessary notices are not given, or because a subsequent purchaser fails to acquire the right to enforce the agreement. In such cases the purchaser may have further rights under statute.

In 1972 Parliament passed an Act to impose duties on all persons taking on work for or in connection with the provision of dwellings. The Defective Premises Act, which came into force on January 1, 1974, creates a general duty on such persons to see that the work is done in a workmanlike or professional manner, with proper materials and so that the dwelling will be fit for habitation (section 1). The duty applies to builders and to professional persons such as architects. It may be enforced independently of any contract which may exist, by any person acquiring an interest in the dwelling. Purchasers' rights under the Act cannot be excluded by contract (section 6(3)).

During the 1970s and 1980s the courts developed alternative remedies under the law of negligence. As a result of recent decisions of the House of Lords (see page 338), these remedies apply only to damage occurring to other property (*i.e.* not the building itself) or to personal injury. The law of tort now affords no effective remedy for a defective dwelling.

Further Reading

Chitty on Contracts Guest *et al.*, (26th ed., 1989), Vol. II.
Schmitthoff and Dobson, *Charlesworth's Mercantile Law* (15th ed., 1991).
Robert Lowe, *Commercial Law* (6th ed., 1983).

CHAPTER 7

DOCUMENTS

ALTHOUGH in most cases an oral contract is as good in law as a written contract there are obvious practical differences. When the parties to an oral contract are in dispute they often disagree over the terms of the contract. It is therefore an advantage to put agreements into writing. This is almost invariably done with building and engineering contracts. The principal problem which then arises is to construe the contract, that is, to decide the meaning of the words used. This can be difficult where the circumstances which have arisen were not foreseen by the drafts-man, or when the full implications of the terms were not properly considered.

In addition to their construction, written documents can give rise to other problems. One of the parties may claim that a document does not record what was agreed. If this is so he may, in certain circumstances, obtain rectification of the contract through the courts. If the parties agree that they intended something different from the written agreement, or if they subsequently change their intentions, they may themselves alter the contract. It may then be necessary to determine the legal effect of the alterations. These problems are discussed in this chapter.

CONSTRUCTION

As a general rule a written document is interpreted as the sole declaration of the parties' intention and it is from the words used that the intention must be discovered. It is therefore important to ensure that what is written truly records what the parties have agreed. One way to do this is to use words and phrases which have acquired accepted meanings through precedent. These may make a contract sound archaic but they are more likely to cover an unexpected situation. This is one advantage of using a standard form of contract. A contract will generally be construed as a whole so that no words can have an absolute meaning out of context. But the meaning of similar words in another document is often a guide to construction, and previous decisions of the courts on the meaning of the standard forms of contract are treated as binding precedents.

Evidence admissible

The general rule that intention is to be inferred from the words alone has several exceptions, when extrinsic evidence (that is, evidence outside the document) is admissible to interpret the terms. Thus, evidence may be admitted to establish a special trade usage (for example the proverbial baker's dozen) or to show the meaning of a technical term. The principal exception is in the admission of evidence to prove the surrounding circumstances. The precise extent of this exception may be a matter of dispute, since the "circumstances" relied on by one side may be much wider than the other side is prepared to admit. In the case of *Prenn* v. *Simmonds* (1971) the House of Lords considered the amount of evidence admissible to construe a share option, the exercise of which was dependent upon the available profits. The issue was whether "profits" meant the separate profits of one company or the group profits. In giving judgment, Lord Wilberforce observed that there had been prolonged negotiations between solicitors leading ultimately to the ambiguous clause. The judgment continued:

> "The reason for not admitting evidence of these exchanges is not a technical one or even mainly one of convenience . . . it is simply that such evidence is unhelpful. By the nature of things, where negotiations are difficult, the parties' positions with each passing letter, are changing and until a final agreement, though converging, still divergent. It is only the final document which records a concensus. . . . It may be said that previous documents may be looked at to explain the aims of the parties. In a limited sense this is true: the commercial or business object of the transaction, objectively ascertained, may be a surrounding fact. . . . But beyond that it may be difficult to go: it may be a matter of degree or judgement how far one interpretation or another gives effect to a common intention: the parties indeed may be pursuing that intention with differing emphasis and hoping to achieve it to an extent which may differ, and in different ways. The words may, and often do,

represent a formula which means different things to each side, yet may be accepted because that is the only way to get 'agreement' and in the hope that disputes will not arise. The only course then can be to try to establish the 'natural' meaning. . . . In my opinion, then, evidence of negotiations, or of the parties intentions, and *a fortiori* of Dr Simmonds' intentions, ought not to be received, and evidence should be restricted to evidence of the factual background known to the parties at or before the date of the contract, including evidence of the 'genesis' and objectively the 'aim' of the transaction."

The application of these principles to ambiguities is often difficult. The safer course is to define any terms which may give rise to dispute. This is often done by incorporating a "definitions" clause such as that often found at the beginning of the standard forms of contract.

Sometimes the body or operative part of the document is preceded by a recital relating what has led up to executing the document. For example, the JCT forms of contract commence with a number of recitals beginning "Whereas . . . " which give a brief description of the works with the name of the architect, and a list of contract drawings. In the absence of doubt as to construction, the body of the document alone is effective. But where there is an ambiguity in the body, the recital, if clear, may give the true meaning. Recitals can also be useful in setting out the surrounding circumstances so as to provide an agreed background for the construction of any phrases which may later appear ambiguous.

Where a contract is partly in a printed standard form and partly in terms specially written, the latter will usually prevail in the event of an inconsistency, on the basis that they represent the parties' true intention, rather than a document which was prepared by others (see page 158). Thus, provisions of a standard form may be over-ridden by an inserted clause, or by a contrary provision in the specification or bill of quantities. This is subject, however, to the terms of the contract itself: *see* JCT form, clause 2.2.1 and ICE, clause 5.

Maxims of construction

Where doubt as to the precise meaning of a document remains after allowing for such extrinsic evidence as may be admissible, and after giving due weight to the different parts of the document, there are a number of maxims of construction which may assist in arriving at a definite meaning. They are often quoted in Latin but, for the most part, an English rendering is offered here:

The law prefers a reasonable to an unreasonable meaning. This is part of a wider legal principle by which many things are judged against an objective standard of reasonableness. Thus, if a document can be read as having a sensible meaning or an absurd meaning, it is taken to have the sensible meaning. Further, if there is either a lawful or unlawful meaning, the lawful meaning will be adopted.

An erroneous description can be given effect as it should have been stated, provided it is clear what was meant. This maxim can be used to correct an obvious error in a document. It may apply for example to the statement of a price in pounds when pence was obviously meant, and vice versa. If there is genuine doubt, however, the contract will be enforced as written.

Where there is express mention of some things, others of the same class not mentioned will be excluded. This may assist where it is not clear what is to be included in a list of items. Thus, a contract to sell a house and a factory with the fixtures of the house will be taken to exclude the fixtures of the factory. Further, a contract to supply and lay bricks and to supply paving slabs would not include laying the paving slabs. In most building and engineering contracts such matters are put beyond doubt by the contract documents.

The meaning of a doubtful word may be ascertained from the words associated with it. For example, the term "general contractors" might include almost any commercial activity; but in the context "engineers and general contractors" it must be limited to the field of engineering. This is part of a wider rule that words are to be construed in their context, which may include looking at the whole document.

Where a series of words comprises a class and is followed by general words, the general words cover only things of that class. This is known as the *ejusdem generis* rule, and an example is probably simpler than a statement of the rule. Thus, the words "iron, steel, brass, lead and other materials" could include copper since the class is one of metals; but stone or wood could not be included. However, if the words had been " . . . and other materials of whatsoever kind" they would preclude the operation of the rule and include any other materials. Further, a list reading "steel, bricks, plywood and other materials" forms no particular class, so that again the rule is excluded.

Contra Proferentum

The words of a document are to be construed against a person seeking to rely on them. This is another maxim of construction, but its importance is such as to deserve separate treatment. The effect of the rule is that a clause purporting to exclude liability must be drafted precisely and must cover the particular matters to be excluded, as any loophole will be interpreted against the "*proferens*," and in favour of the party against whom the clause is applied. As an example, there are a series of cases in which exclusion clauses have been held not to cover negligence where the clause could be construed as covering other events. Exactly the same principle is applied to an indemnity clause (which is the obverse of an exemption clause). In the case of *Smith* v. *South Wales Switchgear* (1978) the plaintiff motor manufacturer employed the defendant, an electrical company, to carry out maintenance work upon the plaintiff's standard conditions of contract, which provided that the defendant should indemnify the plaintiff against "any liability, loss or claim or proceedings whatsoever under statute or common law in respect of personal injury to, or death of any person whomsoever . . . ." One of the defendant's employees suffered injury as a result of the plaintiff's negligence and breach of statutory duty. The plaintiff claimed to be indemnified under its standard conditions. The House of Lords held that the clause did not afford indemnity against the plaintiff's own negligence because there was no express provision, and the clause could not be construed as covering negligence by the plaintiff's own servants. Lord Dilhorne said:

> "When considering the meaning of such a clause one must, I think, regard it as even more inherently improbable that one party should agree to discharge the liability of the other for acts for which he is responsible. In my opinion, it is the case that the imposition by the *proferens* on the other party of liability to indemnify him against the consequences of his own negligence must be imposed by very clear words. It cannot be said, in my opinion, that it has been in the present case."

This very strict approach to exemption clauses has been modified by a number of factors. First, the law concerning fundamental breach, much of which involved construing exclusion clauses so as not to cover supposed flagrant breaches of contract, has been transformed by the House of Lords' decision in *Photo Production* v. *Securicor* (1980) (see page 105). Secondly, the advent of a series of statutes culminating in the Unfair Contract Terms Act 1977, which permit the courts to override "unfair" exempting provisions, has removed the need for the application of strained methods of construction. Thirdly, the courts have recognised the need to apply less exacting standards where the parties have entered into an arrangement which limits, but does not entirely exclude, the right of the injured party to compensation. Thus, in *Ailsa Craig Fishing* v. *Securicor* (1981) the House of Lords held that a security company was entitled to rely on a clause which clearly limited its liability to £1000 even though it was admitted that the loss had been caused by their negligence. Lord Wilberforce held:

> "Whether a clause limiting liability is effective or not is a question of construction of that clause in the context of the contract as a whole. If it is to exclude liability for negligence, it must be most clearly and unambiguously expressed and in such a contract as this must be construed *contra proferentum*. I do not think that there is any doubt so far. But I venture to add one further qualification, or at least clarification: one must not strive to create ambiguities by strained construction, as I think the appellants have striven to do. The relevant words must be given, if possible, their natural, plain meaning. Clauses of limitation are not regarded by the courts with the same hostility as clauses of exclusion: this is because they must be related to other contractual terms, in particular to the risks to which the defending party may be exposed, the remuneration which he receives and possibly also the opportunity of the other party to insure."

A further example of the application of the *contra preferentum* rule in building and engineering contracts, is in the construction of the extension of time clauses. These are regarded as benefitting the employer, who is, therefore, seen as the *proferens*, because the clause protects his right to recover liquidated damages (see further page 189).

Ambiguity

This is a term which is often used loosely: it is frequently taken to be synonymous with doubt or uncertainty. In law, however, an ambiguity is a provision which has two (or more) possible meanings, which cannot be resolved by the rules of construction set out above. Much of the law concerning ambiguity relates to wills and trusts, but the same principles apply to any type of written instrument which has to be construed by the courts. Where construction cannot produce an answer, evidence will be admitted going beyond that which is ordinarily admitted to establish surrounding circumstances (see above). An example of this principle occurred in a case concerning a will in which the testator left £100 "to my grand-nephew Robert." There was no such grand-nephew, but there were four of other names. Evidence was therefore admitted which showed that the testator in fact thought that one of his grand-nephews, Richard, was called Robert, and he was held entitled to the bequest: *re Offner* (1909).

Clause 5 of the ICE conditions (see page 282) refers to "ambiguities or discrepancies" which are to be explained or adjusted by the engineer. Strictly, these two concepts are different, the former implying two (or more) meanings which cannot be resolved, but the latter not necessarily being incapable of resolution by means of construction. The purpose of this provision, clearly, is to permit the work to proceed by resolving "uncertainty" but in regard to the question of payment (see clause 13 of the conditions) the difference could be relevant.

Building and engineering contracts, particularly the latter, are not noted for their clarity and consistency of drafting. Problems often arise because "the contract" is contained in several long and complex documents, often written by different persons at different times. In addition, contract documents are often prepared from standard drafts which are adapted to the particular circumstances. These processes can easily lead to inconsistencies appearing between different parts of the contract. In drafting documents, the contents remain only as good as the thought which went into them. Where uncertainties arise, it may be impossible to ascribe a definite meaning. If sufficient turns upon a particular issue of construction, the parties may bring the issue before the court or before an arbitrator as appropriate for resolution. It may be necessary to apply any or all of the above rules and then to balance the competing results.

DRAFTING

The opposite process to construing is drafting. Logically it precedes construing, but if properly done there should be no room for doubt and therefore nothing which needs to be construed. Also the rules of construction must be kept in mind when putting together a document. The draftsman must constantly ask himself what his words and sentences mean, but with this added fillip: they will ultimately be construed by others, who can be relied on to search out any loopholes he may leave.

There are no rules or maxims of drafting. The writer must use his common sense and proceed in an orderly way. He may be assisted by the following considerations, the order of which is not significant.

What is the object of the document? It may be of assistance to set out in a concise form what is to be achieved by the exercise. This may involve selecting key words or phrases to be incorporated in the full draft. The object may also be expressed in diagrammatic or symbolic form. For example, a variation of price clause can usually be written as a simple algebraic formula. The many lines of prose needed to express the formula in words are a purely mechanical exercise.

Is the document dependent on other documents? If it is to stand by itself, it will need to contain or incorporate all necessary material; for example, if the document is to constitute an agreement it must encompass the terms agreed and show the assent of the parties. If the document forms part of another, such as an additional term of a contract, it must be drawn so as to effect all necessary alterations or to prevail over any inconsistency. Examples of the care and thoroughness needed to make effective amendments can be seen in statutes which amend earlier Acts, often by way of detailed schedules.

What is the most appropriate form of document? A formal contract may seem appropriate, containing recitals, articles of agreement, standard conditions, special conditions and other incorporated material. But other ends call for simpler means. If notice is required to be given under a contract, one way is to draw up a formal document stating "WHEREAS . . . NOW WE HEREBY, in exercise of the said. . . . " But it may be equally effective (and clearer) to write: "Dear Sir, We give you notice under clause. . . . " The appropriate form of document is that which will achieve the object with certainty and efficiency.

What form of drafting is called for? Where the brief is to achieve a stated object the draftsman usually has no difficulty and can indulge in a welter of "heretofore" and "notwithstanding," to arrive at certainty. But there may be objection to this approach. First, the document may be the subject of negotiation and compromise. The other party may not accept language which seems heavily weighted against him (consider the drafting of the standard forms of contract). Secondly, the document may need to be expressed in simple, direct language to fulfil its purpose. A form of contract which places duties on a supervising officer does not fulfil its purpose if the supervising officer cannot understand what is required of him without taking legal advice (consider the JCT form of contract, Chapter 11).

What formal requirements are necessary? A contract should incorporate evidence of the parties' agreement to the terms set out. Formal signature and dating are unnecessary but desirable in the interests of clarity. The most important practical consideration is the identity of the contracting party. Where one party uses a trading name, the true identity of the proprietor should be discovered; and where groups of companies are in evidence, their relationship should be ascertained. In case of suspicion, a clause prohibiting assignment or sub-contracting may be added to the contract.

Good drafting is an amalgam of clarity, style and choice of appropriate language. Its object is to achieve a result, rather than to hold the interest of the reader. Short sentences are clearer than long ones. They can be more easily adapted if provisos or further clauses need to be added. Where there is doubt in the draftsman's mind there are devices which may assist. Thus, where a clause is to be added to an existing document of less than perfect clarity, the draftsman may add words such as: "For the avoidance of doubt it is agreed that . . ." and add for good measure "notwithstanding anything to the contrary."

Care should be taken to use consistent language where a consistent meaning is intended. This may produce a stilted impression, especially when coupled with over-use of "the said . . . ." But greater clarity may result. The legal draftsman has one great advantage over the ordinary user of the English Language. As Humpty Dumpty said: "When I use a word it means just what I choose it to mean—neither more nor less" (*Through the Looking-Glass*). Thus, documents may expressly define (often in a separate clause) particular words used. This can be a considerable aid to brevity and clarity, provided the defined meaning is adhered to. If it is not, confusion will result. Where the draftsman is in doubt he may take refuge in the formula ". . . save where the context otherwise requires" (see ICE conditions, clause 1(1)).

These difficulties, both of drafting and construing, lead to the frequent use of precedents, whose meaning and effect is reasonably certain. This applies both to individual clauses and to whole documents (such as contracts, leases, notices, pleadings, etc.) This has become even more prevalent since the advent of the word processor. The problem is then to ensure that the various standard and special parts are consistent.

RECTIFICATION

If, by mistake, a document does not record the true agreement between the parties, the courts have power to rectify or alter the document so as to give effect to the true agreement. There can be no rectification of a mistake in the transaction (see page 95), but only of the way in which the transaction was put into writing. Rectification is an equitable remedy, and it is therefore not available as of right, but is discretionary. One consequence of this is that rectification will not be granted if relief can be obtained by other means. The court itself will correct an obvious mistake such as a clerical slip or even an errroneous "not," without recourse to formal rectification. It should be added that while rectification may appear to be a universal panacea for badly written contracts, it is a remedy which is rarely granted in practice.

A claim for rectification must establish that the document was intended to carry out the parties' prior agreement, and not to vary it. If the opposing party says that the prior agreement was intended to be varied by the subsequent document, a heavier burden of proof falls upon the claimant. However, it is not necessary to prove that a prior concluded agreement was reached before drawing up the document. It is sufficient to show that the parties had a common intention, and that the written contract failed to conform to that intention. Usually the mistake to be rectified is one of fact, but it may also be as to the legal effect of the words used.

Generally the mistake must be common to both parties, but in a few situations a unilateral mistake may be rectified. These situations include the case where one party is mistaken but the other is fraudulent, and also where one party is mistaken and the other party knows of his mistake. Thus, where a building contractor tendered to build a school in 18 months, the employer, after accepting the tender, inserted a period of 30 months into the formal contract without the contractor's knowledge. It was held that the employer knew of the contractor's mistaken belief as to the term, and that the contractor was entitled to have the contract rectified by insertion of a completion period of 18 months: *Roberts* v. *Leicestershire C.C.* (1961).

VARIATION OF CONTRACTS

This section refers only to variations of the terms of a contract and not to variations made pursuant to an express power in the contract, such as the usual provisions for the variation of the work found in building and engineering contracts.

An agreement to vary a contract is like any other contract in that it requires either to be for consideration or under seal in order to be binding. A variation may take the form of an alteration of some of the terms of the contract, or its replacement by a new contract, or even its complete discharge. If the original contract is one which is not required to be evidenced in writing (see page 361), it can be varied by an oral agreement even if the original is in writing or under seal. An example of a variation is where each side surrenders some outstanding obligation. Each surrender constitutes consideration and the agreement will be binding. Thus, if the employer (without express power) wishes to omit a piece of work and the contractor agrees to the omission, the variation is binding and no action will lie for breach of contract by either party.

When only one party agrees to waive or not to insist on some right under a contract, the other party gives no consideration for the waiver. Nevertheless, if the other party has acted on a waiver, the court may treat it as binding. Where a waiver is binding, it remains effective until reasonable notice of withdrawal has been given. Waiver is a principle which parties in litigation frequently seek to rely on or to hide behind; its effect may be that where a party has not insisted on his legal rights, he may be unable to claim the benefit retrospectively. In the case of *Rickards* v. *Oppenheim* (1950) the defendant ordered a Rolls Royce from the plaintiff, to be completed by a certain date. It was not finished on time, but the defendant continued to press for delivery. Eventually the defendant stated that if the car was not completed by a specified date he would not accept it; the car was not finished in the time. It was held that the defendant had waived the original completion date. Denning L.J. giving judgment in the Court of Appeal went on to hold:

> "It would be most unreasonable if, having been lenient and having waived the initial expressed time, he should thereby have prevented himself from ever thereafter insisting on reasonably quick delivery. In my judgment, he was entitled to give a reasonable notice making time of the essence of the matter. Adequate protection to the suppliers is given by the requirement that the notice should be reasonable."

There are however certain rights which, once waived, cannot subsequently be relied on. This applies, for example, to the right to written notice of a claim within a specified period. If oral notice is received within the period and is acted on, the recipient cannot, after expiry of the period, insist on written notice.

Where one party has completely performed his obligations under a contract any variation or release of the obligations of the other party will be binding only if made under seal or if the party being released provides some new consideration, since he has no rights under the contract to give up. The consideration may take any form, and what is commonly surrendered is a potential claim. Thus, where a contractor has completed his work and agrees to accept a sum less than the full amount due in return for the surrender by the employer of a claim for bad workmanship, the agreement is binding. Such an arrangement is called an "accord and satisfaction" and the surrender constitutes good consideration provided the claim is bona fide, even though in fact not sustainable.

Further Reading

Odgers' *Construction of Deeds and Statutes* (5th ed., 1967), Dworkin.
Bead, Bishop and Furmston *Contract-Cases and Materials* (2nd ed., 1990).

CHAPTER 8

CONSTRUCTION CONTRACTS

THE essence of a construction contract is that the contractor agrees to supply work and materials for the erection of a building or other works for the benefit of the employer. The design of the work to be carried out is often supplied by or on behalf of the employer, but may also be supplied in whole or in part by the contractor. In legal terms there is no difference between a building and an engineering contract, and the term Construction Contract is adopted to cover both.

Almost invariably there will be other parties involved in a construction contract in addition to the contractor and the employer. There may be an architect or engineer who provides the design and supervises the work; and there are likely to be sub-contractors employed to carry out part of the work. The status and capacity of these parties is considered in Chapter 4. This chapter deals with those particular areas of the common law which help to define the rights and duties of the parties and which regulate the performance of construction contracts.

The number of statutory provisions which directly affect construction contracts (as opposed to construction operations) is small. Similarly the number of decided cases which apply directly to construction contracts is not great compared to the amount of case law in other fields. There are some areas of construction law in which there is no direct authority. In such a situation assistance may be obtained from the standard textbooks. These are often consulted by, and sometimes expressly approved by the courts in deciding new points of building law.

In Chapter 6 a number of special types of contracts are considered. Each of these contracts has its own special features; for example, a sale of goods is governed by extensive statutory provisions. The special nature of construction contracts arises from the form which most contracts take and from features such as the functions assigned to the architect or engineer and the

152

provisions for payment as the work proceeds. These matters are dealt with in this chapter. The following chapter covers factors outside the contract itself which affect the parties' rights. The particular provisions of common forms of building and engineering contracts are considered in Chapters 10, 11 and 12.

New forms of contract

While the majority of construction work in the UK and abroad is carried out under conventional arrangements, with a main contractor, sub-contractors and a professional team, a number of potentially radical departures have appeared in recent years. The "prime cost" contract (see below) has developed into the management contract, in which there is a main contractor ostensibly responsible for the whole of the work. But his legal liability is substantially restricted in regard to the performance of sub-contractors, who normally perform the entirety of the physical work. The role of the main contractor then becomes essentially that of a manager, charged with organising and co-ordinating the work of the sub-contractors. A major feature of management contracts is that the design is evolved as the work proceeds, with the main contractor participating in or advising on design decisions. This arrangement offers the opportunity of commencing work at an early stage, without waiting for the design to be finalised, and it also permits more financial control, to the extent that this depends on design choices.

A further, logical development from management contract is the "construction management" contract (sometimes called a project management contract) in which the party filling the role of management contractor does not enter into contracts with those who carry out different elements of the work, but supplies only management and other professional services. The work is carried out under a series of direct "trade contracts," and the construction management contract contains obligation limited to managing and co-ordinating these individual direct contracts. These new forms of contract tend to involve certain common drafting difficulties in the definition of the work being taken on, the provision of workable sanctions and the residual responsibility of the contractor. Further, many of the forms of contract utilised tend to be individual or in-house forms (that is, offered by one contractor or construction group). It is, therefore, difficult to identify the principles that apply to these new forms of contract, and further development will inevitably occur.

PERFORMANCE AND PAYMENT

In a construction contract, the contractor agrees to carry out the works. The employer's side of the bargain is a payment of money. Problems may arise in deciding when the contractor's obligation is discharged, and when and what amount of money is payable. In each case the answer depends first on construction of the contract, since the parties may make whatever contractual provisions they choose. There are, however, some general principles which may amplify the parties' intentions.

Where the contract is to carry out and complete a specific piece of work, the general rule is that only complete performance can discharge the contractor's obligation and no payment is due until the work is substantially complete. Thus, where a builder contracted to erect two houses and stables on the defendant's land for a lump sum and abandoned the contract part-completed, it was held that in the absence of entitlement under the contract, the builder was not entitled to further payment for the unfinished work, despite the fact that the employer retained the benefit: *Sumpter* v. *Hedges* (1898). A. L. Smith L.J. giving judgment in the Court of Appeal held:

> "The learned Judge had found as a fact that he abandoned the contract. Under such circumstances, what is the building owner to do? He cannot keep the buildings on his land in an unfinished state forever. The law is that, where there is a contract to do work for a lump sum, until the work is completed the price of it cannot be recovered. Therefore the plaintiff could not recover on the original contract. It is suggested, however, that the plaintiff was entitled to recover for the work he did on a *quantum meruit* but, in order that that may be so, there must be evidence of a fresh contract to pay for the work already done."

The contractor in such a situation is not, however, always without a remedy. He may recover if he can show that completion was prevented by the employer, or that a fresh agreement to pay for the partially completed work is to be implied.

The contract price

Construction contracts usually state a price for which the work is to be completed. This is invariably subject to modification as the work proceeds on account of ordered variations, allowable price fluctuations, re-valuation of prime cost or provisional sums, claims, etc. In addition, the original stated price may not itself be fixed. If it is fixed the contract may be called a "lump sum" contract. But if the sum is based on quantities which are to be recalculated when the work is done, the contract is called a "re-measurement" contract. This is so when there is an express right to have the work re-measured; or where the bills are stated to be provisional or approximate. The JCT form of contract is a lump sum contract, whether or not it is based on quantities (see Chapter 11). The ICE form creates a re-measurement contract; this is emphasised by the fact that the price of the work is referred to as the "tender total" (see Chapter 12). A further term sometimes used is "fixed price." This is generally taken to mean a contract where the sum payable is not adjustable by reason of price increases (fluctuations). The price may, however, be adjustable on many other grounds. Where the employer wishes to know the exact price of the work in advance, none of the common forms of contract is appropriate. While possible, an "invariable price" contract would be difficult to draft and uneconomic.

Stage payment

In most construction contracts of any substance there are express provisions for interim or stage payments to be made as the work proceeds. The usual provision is for the contractor to be paid the value of the estimated quantities of work done and materials supplied less a retention which the employer holds as security for completion of the works. In such cases the rule of payment on substantial completion (see above) may still apply to each payment, but subject also to the provisions as to certificates (see page 169). Even where there is no express provision for interim payments there may be, in the absence of express agreement to the contrary, an implied term for interim payments as the work proceeds.

No price agreed

In most cases the sums payable to the contractor are expressly provided in, or to be ascertained from the contract. Where this is not so, the contractor's claim for payment is called a *quantum meruit*. This is a claim for payment of a reasonable sum. The question of what sum is reasonable is for the court to decide, if the parties cannot agree. Such a claim is appropriate where there is an express agreement to pay a reasonable sum or where such an agreement is to be implied, for example, because no sum was agreed. *Quantum meruit* is also the proper claim where work is done under a contract which proves to be void. A *quantum meruit* claim will not, however, assist a contractor who has not completed work, the completion of which was a condition precedent to payment, unless the employer has waived the condition. In assessing what is a reasonable sum for work done the parties may use various means, such as cost of materials and labour plus profit, or measurement and assessment of reasonable rates. The courts do not lay down rules as to this (see also page 168).

CONTRACT DOCUMENTS

It is a common feature of construction contracts that they incorporate a variety of different types of document, which are not limited to those expressed in words: drawings appear in most contracts and have to be interpreted and given legal meaning and significance. Typically, a construction contract of any importance will contain a set of conditions of contract, a specification, a bill of quantities, a set of drawings, and other documents of varying sorts. There may also be a separate "agreement" in which the parties formally bind themselves to execute the work. The question necessarily arises, how these documents fit together, which (if any) are to have precedence, and what is to happen if they conflict.

A further related question, is the definition of "the works" to be performed. Is this governed by all the contract documents, or some of them only, or is there an independent definition? These questions need to be addressed to decide, for example, what is a variation, and whether completion has been achieved. Every contract is unique, and therefore the definition of what is to be performed depends upon the particular contract provisions. However, there are two distinctly different approaches to the question. The first, and simplest, is to make all contract documents of equal weight and significance. This is the solution adopted in the ICE Conditions of Contract: see clause 5 (page 282). The problem that is then thrown up is, what happens in the event of discrepancies? The ICE conditions provide that these are to be "explained and adjusted" by the engineer. Another solution sometimes found, is to provide that the contract documents shall have an order of precedence, *i.e.* a conflicting requirement in two documents is to be resolved in favour of that having the higher priority.

The second type of solution is that adopted in the JCT forms, which typically provide that the quality and quantity of the work to be carried out is that contained in the contract bills (or in the case of a contract without quantities, in the specification): see clauses 14.1 and 2.2.1 (page 232). The effect of these provisions is that the bill (or specification) is given a limited function, and may not override the contract conditions. This type of provision has given rise to some unusual results. For example, a sectional completion provision written into the bills is likely to be ineffective if there is no corresponding amendment to the conditions of contract and the appendix providing for one over-all completion date. The principle was applied in *English Industrial Estates* v. *Wimpey* (1973), where, under a JCT form of contract, the contract bills provided for the employer to take possession and occupy parts of a factory being constructed by the defendant. But there had been no relevant amendment to the conditions of contract, which laid down a procedure for the employer to take possession of completed parts, and to become responsible for such parts. The employer in fact took over part of the works which were then destroyed by fire, and the question arose who was responsible. The Court of Appeal (relying on clauses equivalent to those given above) held that, despite the provisions in the bill, the contractor remained responsible for the parts taken over, because the procedure under the conditions had not been followed. Stephenson L.J. said:

> "It follows from the literal interpretation of clause 12 (now clause 2.1.2) that the court must disregard—or even reverse—the ordinary and sensible rules of construction and that the first of the documents (the conditions of contract) . . . expressly prevents the court from looking at the second of those documents (the bills) to see what the first of them means. But that is because the second document is . . . a hybrid document and part of it deals with matters which should have been incorporated in the first."

Contract conditions

Most contracts incorporate a set of conditions whose primary purpose is to lay down procedures of general application to a variety of types of work. It is often convenient to use a set of standard conditions, such as those dealt with in more detail in Chapters 10, 11 and 12. There is no rule as to what may or may not be included in conditions of contract. Typically, such conditions deal with the position and authority of any third party supervisor or certifier (the architect or engineer), with apportionment of risks and insurance requirements, with sanctions regarding the quality of the work, with provision for completion and delays, and with machinery for assessment and payment of sums due under the contract. One of the main objects of the conditions of contract is to facilitate the efficient control and administration of the work, while at the same time providing certainty, so that, for example, queries as to the nature of the work to be done are dealt with timeously.

Frequently, there are additional conditions variously described as "special conditions" or "conditions of particular application." Such conditions will generally be construed on an equal footing with "general" conditions, but there is a rule of construction that greater weight should be given to conditions which have been particularly drafted against those which are of a standard nature. The principle is sometimes expressed as "type" prevailing over "print" and it can also be applied to handwriting prevailing over typescript. Lord Denning, giving a dissenting judgment in the *English Industrial Estates* case, above, described the principle thus:

> "In construing this contract we should have regard to provisions C and D (of the bills). They were carefully drafted and inserted in type in the bills of quantities. They were put in specially so as to enable the contractors to make their calculations. It was on the basis of these that the contractors made their tender and the employers accepted it. They were incorporated into the formal contract just as much as the conditions in the RIBA form. In contrast, conditions 12 and 16 were not specially inserted at all. They were two printed conditions in the middle of 23 pages of small print. It was in quite general terms. On settled principles they should have taken second place to the special insertion."

However, the other two Lords Justices did not agree that, by this means, the bills could be allowed to override the conditions. Had it not been for the express provision that the conditions were to prevail, however, the typed bill would have decided the meaning of the contract.

Specification

This is the document which describes the work to be carried out, often in great technical detail. There are, however, many ways in which work may be specified without such detail. For example, reference may be made to appropriate British standards or codes of practice. Alternatively, the specification may describe the performance required, leaving the details to the contractor. However, in this case it should be noted that, when used with a JCT form of contract, a performance specification is in danger of being held ineffective in seeking to override the conditions of contract (see above). This was the case in *Mowlem* v. *British Insulated Callenders Pension Trust* (1978), where the bills required "waterproof concrete;" but this was held insufficient to impose a design liability on the contractor (see above page 185). In a JCT contract without quantities, the specification is the overriding description of the quality and quantity of the work required.

The specification may make requirements for the method of working to be adopted. In such a case, where it has full contractual effect, a change in the specified method may require a variation order, with the contractual consequences that that entails (see further below).

In a design-and-build contract, the specification acquires particular significance, because it must set out the employer's requirements to which the contractor's design, or detailed design, must comply. There are often, also, "contractor's proposals" as submitted with the tender, and these will also need to be incorporated into the specification (see further below).

Bill of quantities

These documents originated historically as non-contractual measurements, taken off drawings to assist tenderers in quoting lump sum prices. The practice developed for tendering contractors to retain a quantity surveyor to draw up a bill which all tenderers could use as the common basis for their pricing. Bills subsequently acquired another use, namely for assessing interim payments by approximate measure under a lump sum contract. This remains the primary use of bills under a JCT form of contract. Under engineering contracts, conversely, a different practice developed of using the rates quoted, but recalculating (or remeasuring) the actual quantities of work carried out for the purpose of the final payment. A refinement of this process, effectively limited to civil engineering contracts, is the provision for adjustment to the quoted rates, where the actual quantity of any item of work of itself makes the quoted rate unreasonable or inapplicable (see page 313).

A further refinement in the use of bills of quantities is in standardising the descriptions of work and what the descriptions are deemed to include. The applicable rules are set out in a separate document known as a standard method of measurement, separate versions of which exist for different types of work. For JCT contracts, the RICS method is generally used; while ICE contracts use either the ICE method or, for some government contracts, the method of measurement for road and bridgeworks. These documents are not part of the contract, but it is provided that the bill of quantities is "deemed to have been prepared in accordance with" the appropriate standard method; and any error or omission in relation to the standard method becomes a "deemed variation" (see pages 233 and 313).

The substantive effect of the RICS and ICE standard methods may be quite different, reflecting the contrasts between building and civil engineering work. Civil engineering bills tend to be much shorter and often include many complex and difficult operations rolled up into one simply described item. For example, construction of a tunnel may be measured as a single item, per metre of length. Under the RICS method, although the JCT form of contract does not permit or recognise claims for unforeseen ground conditions, the method of measurement requires separate items to be provided for "excavating in rock" and "excavating in running silt or running sand." Thus, if such material is encountered, and has not been billed, the contractor is entitled to payment for such work as an extra. Under both methods, the normal way of describing work items is in terms of the work or the product, for example, concrete or brickwork. An alternative way of producing bills, sometimes used in civil engineering work, is to use "method related" items, which are not to be paid by measured quantity, but by fixed charge or time-related charge.

Drawings

All construction contracts have some drawings. It is ususaly necessary to distinguish between those which have been incorporated into the contract (the contract drawings) and those which follow, which may be amendments of the contract drawings or further details necessary for the construction of the work. For example, in a contract for the construction of a building with a reinforced concrete frame, the contract drawings may show the dimensions of the structural frame, and the bill of quantities will record the quantities of concrete and reinforcing steel. The details of the design, including drawings showing the placement of reinforcing bars, and bending schedules showing the shapes of individual bars, will usually be issued at a later stage, when the contractor is approaching the point at which these details are required. In practice, this type of detailing will often lead to large numbers of drawings coming into existence after the work has started. This situation sometimes leads to contractors claiming that the details are more complex than had been envisaged or that they are not issued in sufficient time, in either case giving rise to claims for additional payment. In an ideal world, all drawings and details would be issued at the date of the contract (except in the case of design-and-build, or management contracts).

Drawings often contain notes and other written material, which is to be construed as part of the drawing. Difficult questions of construction can sometimes arise from such notes where they conflict with provisions elsewhere in the bill or in the specification. A particular problem for designers in large complex buildings is the interaction between the different elements of the design, for example, the services and the structure. Modern building services, particularly heating, ventilating and air-conditioning (HVAC), often require the provision of physically large ducts, which may interact with the structure and with other services and components. Design work is often carried out by different specialist teams; for example, HVAC design may be undertaken in part by a prospective nominated sub-contractor. The problems of integration may not always appear until the work is put in hand. These problems are typical of those which give rise to major construction disputes.

Method statement

In recent years a practice has grown up, particularly under civil engineering contracts, of requiring contractors to specify their intended method of construction (see further page 291). This was originally regarded as affording protection to the employer, by ensuring that he would have the benefit of the contractor's particular method (which could otherwise be changed at the contractor's option). However, in two recent cases, this principle has been applied in reverse, by contractors contending that a specified method has become impossible, leading to a requirement for the engineer to order a variation, so that the employer is required to pay the additional cost of changing the method. In the case of *Yorkshire Water Authority* v. *McAlpine* (1985) the contractor gave a method statement, which was approved by the engineer, and incorporated into the contract. The method statement provided for pipe jacking to be carried out working upstream. The contractor maintained that the work was impossible within the meaning of clause 13 of the ICE conditions (see page 288). It was held that, on the assumption that the work was impossible, the contractor was entitled to a variation order to carry out the work by some other method. This case was followed by the Court of Appeal in *Holland Dredging* v. *Dredging and Construction Co.* (1987), where the plaintiffs were dredging sub-contractors to the defendant, the main contractor, for the construction of a sea outfall pipeline under conditions of contract substantially the same as the ICE 5th edition. The sub-contract incorporated a method statement which defined the area from which material could be excavated for backfilling. There proved to be insufficient material within the specified area, and the plaintiffs incurred extra cost in winning additional material from elsewhere. The Court of Appeal held that the method statement was to be given full weight as a contract document. Purchas L.J. concluded:

> "The occurrence of the shortfall and the consequential necessity to look elsewhere for material necessary to backfill the trench to the pre-existing levels disclosed an omission in the specification and bill, unless it is to be accepted that the sub-contract is impossible to complete on its terms as agreed."

Employers should, therefore, be clear as to the effect of a method statement if they wish to have such a document incorporated into a contract. While these cases were decided under the ICE conditions, the same principles could apply under a JCT or other lump sum contract on the basis that the bills and other description of the work restrict the means by which the contractor may carry out the work.

Other documents

The contract itself is likely to be formed by signing a specially prepared "form of agreement" or "articles of agreement" which may be provided with the printed form of contract, or drawn up specially. This gives the opportunity of having the contract executed under seal, thereby increasing the limitation period (see page 112). Another function of a formal contract is to list the contract documents themselves, and this gives the opportunity of including any other documents to be incorporated. Additional documents may include the contractor's tender and correspondence in which the parties have negotiated the final agreement (this may qualify the tender or the conditions of contract). Many contracts contain "conditions of tendering" or like documents which set out matters which may become relevant to contractual disputes. These are usually not incorporated, but each contract depends on its own terms.

A document frequently referred to, but usually not incorporated, is the site investigation or other data concerning soil conditions. These are usually provided for the contractor's information, and frequently contain a statement disclaiming responsibility or requiring the contractor to form his own judgment. Such documents will still be relevant to a claim for unforeseen ground conditions (see page 316) and it is unnecessary for this purpose for the investigation to be a full contract document. Indeed, if it is incorporated, it usually adds little to the contractor's protection: a typical ground investigation consists of factual statements which are highly specific to the particular probes or tests that have been carried out, and any interpretation that may be offered will be no more than a statement of opinion.

The works

This expression appears in most construction contracts as part of the stated obligation undertaken by the contractor. It is always a matter of construing the contract to discover the meaning of the expression, and whether the term contains the whole of the contractor's obligation. For example, the contractor may be obliged to carry out "the works" as defined, but also liable for their performance, in which case the contractor will be bound to carry out any other work necessary to comply with such requirements. Each contract depends on its own terms.

Under civil engineering contracts, there is a potentially important distinction between "permanent works" and "temporary works," both expressions being included within the overall term "works." The precise distinction between the two expressions is often unclear, and there may be an overlap, for example, in relation to steel sheet piling intended to facilitate the construction process, which then becomes incorporated and left in as part of the permanent works. The importance of the distinction relates to the placing of responsibilities for different categories of work (see page 285). Also, under the standard method of measurement, it is usually the case that temporary works are not included or priced in the bill, unless they are designed by the engineer or are otherwise of sufficient importance to justify inclusion in the bill. Temporary works are not included at all in building contracts, it being assumed that the contractor will carry out all such necessary works within the prices quoted for the measured work.

VARIATIONS

One of the common features of contracts in the construction industry is that the design of the work contracted for may require variation as the work proceeds. The magnitude of variations tends to be greater in engineering works, reflecting the greater element of the unknown in such operations. But it is still a rare event for even the smallest of building jobs to be completed exactly according to the original contract provisions. Strictly the contractor is not bound, without express provision, to execute more than the contract work; and the employer will be in breach of contract if he omits a part of the work included in the contract without a contractual provision enabling him to do so. Modern Construction contracts, therefore, provide a clause stating that the employer (or his agent) may require alterations, additions or omissions to the contract work and that the contractor is bound to carry them out; see JCT form, clause 13 and ICE form, clause 51.

When there has been a departure from the work specified in the contract, it is necessary to decide whether there is, in law, a variation under the contract; if there is a variation, whether the contractor is entitled to be paid extra; and if so, the amount of the extra payment. These questions are considered below.

Contractual variations

It is pertinent to state first what is not a contractual variation. Contractors sometimes make claims on the basis that the contract work has cost more than was anticipated. This is not a variation and the contractor is entitled to no extra payment unless he can make a claim under the contract, such as for unforeseen conditions (see ICE form, clause 12). When the contractor has undertaken to carry out and complete the work for a stated price he is bound to do so, however expensive it may prove to be. Thus, where a contractor undertook to build sewerage works in unknown ground which turned out to be marshy, he abandoned the works when the engineer refused to authorise additional payment. It was held that since there was no express warranty as to the nature of the site, the contractor was not entitled to additional payment: *Bottoms* v. *Mayor of York* (1982). In giving judgment in the Court of Appeal Lord Esher held:

> "It seems to me that nobody can suggest for a moment but that it was the plaintiff who threw out the contract at a time when he had no right to throw it out, and for reasons which he had no right to act upon, and the corporation insisted upon his observing the contract and going on with it. But he resisted and refused to have anything more to do with it. If that be true, he brought himself into a very difficult position, and was not able to enforce any payment whatever. ... I take it that the real reason why he has come to this misfortune, indeed, is that he would go and tender when there was no guarantee given to him as to the kind of soil, and when there was no information given to him as to what the soil was—when there was no contract entered into by the people who asked him to tender as to what the nature of the soil was, and that he either too eagerly or too carelessly tendered and entered into the contract without any such guarantee or representation on their part, and without due examination and enquiry by himself. That is what has produced the difficulty."

These words still have an authentic ring, although the position of a modern contractor is likely to be improved under the standard forms of contract.

The contract work

Extra work for which the contractor is *prima facie* entitled to be paid must constitute something additional to what has been contracted for. It is, therefore, necessary to construe the contract to ascertain whether work claimed as extra is covered by the contract. Broadly speaking, the shorter and simpler the description of the work to be carried out, the more difficult it will be for the contractor to contend that work is extra. Thus, in a contract to construct "a three bedroomed house," the scope for variations may be limited to extra bedrooms. Most contracts are much more specific, and even where there is no variation from the contract description, there may be an obligation to pay for instructions to do anything which the contractor was not obliged to do: see, for example, the case of *Simplex* v. *St. Pancras B.C.* (page 182, below). However, where the contractor is not given additional instructions, and the work is within the contract description, there will be no right to extra payment. Thus, where the contractor agreed to build a railway in Brazil for a fixed sum, and redesign became necessary as a result of difficulties in completing the work, there was no extra to the contract, and the contractor was entitled to no additional payment: *Sharpe* v. *San Paulo Railway Co.* (1873). In this case James L.J. observed:

> "Then there was a considerable item as to the inclines up the Serra (mountain) but every statement in the bill, it seems to me, puts the plaintiffs completely out of court as to that. The bill says that the original specification was not sufficient to make a complete railway and that it became obvious that something more would be required to be done in order to make the line. But their business, and what they had contracted to do for a lump sum, was to make the line from terminus to terminus complete, and both these items seem to me to be on the face of them entirely included in the contract. They are not in any sense of the word extra works."

Where the contract is to carry out itemised works without an overall obligation to deliver a finished product, the contractor may then contend that any items omitted from the contract description are extras. In each case, this depends upon the construction of the documents and upon the application of common sense, for many items will be taken as necessarily included even though not specifically mentioned. In the case of *Williams* v. *Fitzmaurice* (1858), where the contract was to build a house for a fixed sum, the specification omitted to mention the floorboards, and the contractor claimed the boards were an extra. It was held that they must be taken to be included in the contract. Pollock C.B. said, in giving judgment:

> "It is clearly to be inferred from the language of the specification that the plaintiff was to do the flooring, for he was to provide the whole of the material necessary for the completion of the work; and unless it can be supposed that a house is habitable without any flooring, it must be inferred that the flooring was to be supplied by him. In my opinion the flooring of a house cannot be considered an extra any more than the doors or windows."

Where the contractor is obliged to carry out the whole project, he may nevertheless be entitled to payment for additional items under the terms of the contract, as automatic or "deemed" variations. This is usually the case where there is a bill of quantities drawn up by reference to a standard method of measurement. Items which should have been included in the bill, so that they would have been priced by the contractor, are to be paid for as extra work: see for example JCT Form of Contract, clauses 14.1, 2.2 and ICE Form of Contract, clause 55(2). In addition, under the ICE conditions, increases or decreases in the actual quantities of work required are to be treated, for the purpose of payment, virtually as variations (clause 56(2)).

Cost-plus contracts

In addition to these traditional forms of contract, there are many alternative forms where the concept of a "variation" may be of less importance. The simplest type is an agreement to pay the contractor the cost of the work (usually by some specified means of calculation) plus a further sum which may be called profit, or overheads, or a fee. The statement of quantities or a contract sum will be of little significance. An example of this type of contract is the JCT Fixed Fee Form of prime cost contract. An alternative form is the "target" contract under which the contractor is paid the cost of the work together with an additional sum which varies according to how close the final cost is to the pre-stated "target." This is intended to give the contractor an incentive to adhere to a particular figure, there being no such incentive under the "fixed fee" form.

Payment for extras

If the contractor carries out work which is an extra to the contract, he will be able to recover payment for that work only if he can show that the employer is bound under contract to pay. The mere doing of extra work, or doing work in a way different from that specified, does not, without more, bind the employer to pay for extras. If the building contract provides for the ordering of and payment for extras, the contractor may claim payment under the contract, provided that any condition precedent to payment is satisfied. Most contracts provide that a written order is necessary. However, there may be an implied promise to pay if an appropriate order is refused. Thus, where a building contract provided that no payment for extras would be made without a written order, it was held that there was an implied promise to pay for the works as extras if they were extras: *Molloy* v. *Leibe* (1910). Lord Macnaughten held in this case:

> "As Molloy insisted on the works being done, in spite of what the contractor told him, the umpire naturally inferred . . . that the employer impliedly promised that the works would be paid for either as included in the contract price or, if he were wrong in his view, by extra payment to be assessed by the architect. It is difficult to see how the umpire could have drawn any other inference from the facts as found by him, without attributing dishonesty to Molloy."

As an alternative, the question whether a variation order should be given for work which the employer insists on having done, will usually be within the powers of an arbitrator appointed under the contract.

If a promise is made to pay for extra works, that promise may be enforceable as a separate contract whether or not the extras are claimable under the construction contract. However, this will not avail the contractor if the "extras" are in fact no more than he was bound to do under the building contract, since the promise is then unsupported by consideration (but see page 86).

Most contracts which make provision for extras also lay down means of valuation and these will determine what the contractor is entitled to be paid. In the absence of such provision, extra work will be paid for at the contract rates or at reasonable rates. In addition, it is common for building contracts to provide for some additional payment (or a "claim") if the ordering of variations causes expense beyond the payments allowed. The JCT form allows recovery of loss or expense not recoverable elsewhere in the contract (clause 26). The ICE form permits a refixing of the rates for any items of work in addition to those varied (clause 52(2)). The International (FIDIC) form allows the contractor to recover additional payment if variations exceed 15 per cent., of the net contract sum.

Contracts do not usually place any limit on the permissible extent of variations. The usual provision that no variation is to vitiate or invalidate the contract, makes it difficult to imply any particular limit. However, it is thought there will always be some limit to what may be added to a contract. If work exceeding such limit is ordered, the contractor may be entitled to be paid for the whole of the works on a *quantum meruit* (that is, at reasonable rates) on the basis that the original contract has ceased to bind the parties. The question of entitlement to a reasonable sum was considered in the case of *Thorn* v. *London Corporation* (see page 90). In that case, the Lord Chancellor observed:

> "Either the additional and varied work which was thus occasioned is the kind of additional and varied work contemplated by the

contract, or it is not. If it is the kind of additional or varied work contemplated by the contract, he must be paid for it, and will be paid for it, according to the prices regulated by the contract. If, on the other hand, it was additional or varied work, so peculiar, so unexpected, and so different from what any person reckoned or calculated upon, that it is not within the contract at all; then, it appears to me, one of two courses might have been open to him; he might have said: I entirely refuse to go on with the contract—*Non hæc in fœdera veni*: I never intended to construct this work upon this new and unexpected footing. Or he might have said, I will go on with this, but this is not the kind of extra work contemplated by the contract, and if I do it, I must be paid a *quantum meruit* for it."

CERTIFICATES

A common feature of construction contracts is a provision for the architect or engineer to issue certificates. This is such a well-established practice that one may find certificates issued under contracts which do not provide for their issue. It should be noted that a certificate is merely a manifestation of the parties' private agreement and its effect is no more than the parties to the contract have agreed that it shall be.

The duty of issuing certificates is usually given to the architect or engineer in the contract. In this section such person is referred to as the certifier. In modern building contracts the role of the certifier is invariably to act impartially between the employer and the contractor. This is distinct from the other role of the engineer or architect as the employer's agent, when he must act in the best interests of his principal (see page 126). The role of the certifier was clarified in the case of *Sutcliffe* v. *Thackrah* (see page 174), where Lord Reid said:

"The building owner and the contractor make their contract on the understanding that in all such matters the architect will act in a fair and unbiased manner and it must therefore be implicit in the owner's contract with the architect that he shall not only exercise due care and skill but also reach such decisions fairly, holding the balance between his client and the contractor."

The fact that the law recognises and requires a fair and unbiased decision from the certifier, who is in other instances bound to act only in the employer's interest, is remarkable. This is particularly so when the certifier is an employee of the building owner, as is often the case in local authority contracts. The fact that this type of contract has continued in use for so long is a tribute to the professions whose members perform such offices.

The function of the certifier, and of the certificate, depends upon the provisions of the contract. In the great majority of building contracts the function is to record the certifier's satisfaction that the work complies with the contract. But in some cases he can impose his own standard, such as where particular items of work are required to be "to the approval of the engineer." Where the certifier is required to state his satisfaction or approval, it may be necessary to decide whether this can supersede the contract requirements.

Whether or not a certificate is conclusive as to what it purports to certify is again a matter of construction of the contract, but subject also to the possibility of avoiding the certificate (see below). A requirement for any certificate is that it must be properly made in order to have effect as provided in the contract. Thus, a certificate which is not in the correct form or which is given by the wrong person is invalid. Subject to this the courts will uphold the parties' agreement as to the effect of a certificate. Thus under the JCT form the House of Lords have held that the courts are bound by a final certificate which is to be conclusive evidence that the work has been properly carried out: *Kaye* v. *Hosier & Dickinson* (1972). In this case the architect gave his final certificate during the course of proceedings in court concerning defects. The effect of the certificate was that the employer was no longer entitled to contend that the work had been executed defectively. Lord Pearson, in the House of Lords, held:

> "The architect's function is not primarily or essentially an arbitral function. The works have to be carried out to his satisfaction, and accordingly he must give or withhold his expression of satisfaction. He may notify defects and require them to be made good. He has to issue certificates showing how much money is owing. Incidentally, his certificates and instructions may resolve some controversial points, and he has to act fairly, but he is not primarily or characteristically adjudicating on disputes. If in a contract such as this the parties agree that the architect's final certificate shall be conclusive evidence of certain matters, I do not think that there is any invasion of the court's jurisdiction or any affront to its dignity. The court's function in a civil case is to adjudicate between the parties, and if they have agreed that a certain certificate shall be conclusive evidence the court can admit the evidence and treat it as conclusive."

Types of certificate

Certificates may be of many kinds. They are usually categorised into three types. First, interim or progress certificates are those which are issued periodically during the course of the work to ascertain the amount of work carried out and the payment due to the contractor. The most usual contractual provision is for monthly interim certificates and such payments form a vital part of the economics of contracting.

An interim certificate, properly given, creates a debt due from the employer. In a series of cases, starting with *Dawnays* v. *Minter* (1971), the Court of Appeal held that the employer must pay the contractor the amount due on an interim certificate without any set-off save for liquidated or established claims. The contractor must similarly pay his sub-contractor. These cases were disapproved by the House of Lords in *Gilbert Ash* v. *Modern Engineering* (1973), which held that the general right of set-off was available against sums certified in favour of the contractor or a sub-contractor. In this case, the main contractor had refused payment due to a sub-contractor upon an architect's certificate, on the ground of a cross-claim. Lord Dilhorne in the House of Lords held:

> "Consideration of the terms of the main contract leads me to the following conclusions: There is nothing in it to justify the conclusion that it excludes the contractor's right to counter-claim and set-off under the common law and in equity. . . . An interim certificate does not create a debt of a special nature. It is a certificate of the value of work properly executed and it is only for the work properly executed . . . , less any deduction that may properly be made, that the employer has to pay the contractor and the contractor to pay the portion attributed to the sub-contractor. . . . I see no ground for holding that . . . the contractor cannot seek to deduct from the amount claimed from him the amounts bona fide claimed by him from the sub-contractor. Even if the sub-contract does not give, as it does, an express right to make such deduction, I can see nothing in it to exclude the contractor's common law and equitable rights to set off and counter-claim."

Thus, where there has been delay or defective work, the employer may generally withhold the amount of his cross-claim from certified sums due to the contractor, and the contractor may similarly withhold from a sub-contractor. In addition to a set-off, the employer is entitled to challenge the certificate, for instance, if the work has been over-valued.

The second type of certificate is the final certificate which may be issued after completion of the works. A final certificate may fulfil either or both of two functions: it may state what is finally payable to the contractor and it may certify approval of the works. The final certificate issued under the JCT form (clause 30) fulfils both functions; under the ICE conditions, the final certificate is merely a document of account (clause 60(4)) and the maintenance certificate signifies final completion of the work (clause 61).

The third type of certificate is that which records some event for the purposes of the contract. Examples of this type are certificates of substantial completion (ICE, clause 48) or practical completion (JCT, clause 17) of the works; and a certificate of non-completion where the work is delayed (JCT, clause 24). An extension of time given by the architect or engineer, although not so called, is a form of certificate given under the contract.

Recovery without a certificate

Much of the case law concerning certificates relates to recovery of money for which a certificate is required, where no certificate has been given. This situation properly arises only when, on construction of the contract, the certificate is a condition precedent to recovery. An arbitration clause in the contract may have the effect of removing the condition precedent, and permitting recovery without a certificate, if the arbitration has power to give the certificate. It is uncertain whether an interim certificate, under the common forms of contract, is a condition precedent to recovery of payment. But the better view is that a certificate is necessary to recovery. If the certificate is a condition precedent, then the contractor may nevertheless recover without a certificate if he can show that the certifier or the employer has acted improperly.

What constitutes behaviour sufficiently improper to dispense with the requirements of a certificate is illustrated by the following examples. First, fraud or collusion will disqualify the certifier and permit recovery of sums without a certificate. As a principle of civil law it is generally true that a defendant can never rely upon his own wrongful act. Secondly, a certificate may be dispensed with where the certifier has acted without fraud but improperly in some other way. Such improper conduct may consist in a failure to act independently. Thus, where an architect acceded to the employer's instructions not to issue further certificates, it was held that the contractor could recover the sums in question without certificates: *Hickman* v. *Roberts* (1913). It is also improper for the certifier to consider extraneous matters in making a decision. Where the certifier's function was to certify that work was satisfactory, but he refused to issue his certificate until satisfied that the work had also been done economically, it was held that the employer could not rely on the absence of a certificate: *Panamena Europa* v. *Leyland* (1947). In giving judgment in the House of Lords, Lord Thankerton held:

> "The respondents have done everything which was necessary for them to do in order to require (the surveyor) to proceed to consider the granting of a certificate under clause 7, but (the surveyor) declined to proceed with the matter unless he was provided with the information to which on his erroneous view of the contract he held himself entitled; in this view (the employers) concurred and this position was maintained up to and after the issue of the writ. This means that an illegitimate condition precedent to any consideration of the granting of the certificate was insisted on by (the surveyor) and by (the employer). It is almost unnecessary to cite authority to establish that such conduct on (the employers') part absolved (the contractor) from the necessity of obtaining such a certificate and that (the contractors) are entitled to recover the amount claimed in the action. . . . If (the employer) had taken the contrary view of their surveyor's function under clause 7, it would have been their duty to appoint another surveyor to discharge that function, and if they had refused to appoint another surveyor, (the contractor) would clearly have been absolved from the necessity of obtaining the surveyor's certificate; (the contractors) are equally so absolved when (the employers') wrongful view of their surveyor's function under clause 7 prevents (the contractors) from obtaining the certificate."

Thirdly, the certifier may be disqualified if there is some interest or other factor which may influence his mind and which is unknown to the contractor. Thus, where an architect, before the signing of a contract for the rebuilding of a church promised the employer that the cost would not exceed a certain figure, it was held that the architect's decision was not binding: *Kemp* v. *Rose* (1858). The Vice Chancellor said, in giving judgment:

> "Without imputing corruption to Mr. Lamb, it is enough if there was a circumstance tending to bias his judgment which was unknown to the plaintiff. The power of Mr. Lamb as the architect and engineer, to whose judgment almost everything, both as to quantity and price, was left, was in this contract, as in most others of the same kind, nearly unbounded; and that being so, if there was the smallest speck of circumstance which might unfairly bias his judgment, his decision cannot be absolutely binding upon the contracting party. Therefore, the plaintiff is entitled to have the decision of Mr. Lamb reviewed by this Court."

Negligent certification

It has long been settled that judges and those performing judicial functions, including arbitrators, are generally immune from actions in negligence. It has also been held that such immunity applied to an architect giving a final certificate. This remained the law until over-ruled by the House of Lords in *Sutcliffe* v. *Thackrah* (1974).

In *Sutcliffe's* case the architect gave an interim certificate, including work not properly done. The builder, having been overpaid for the work, became insolvent so that the employer could not recover the loss. The architect contended that, even though negligent, he was immune from action. In holding the architect liable for negligence, the court found no inconsistency in owing a duty to the employer to act with due care and skill, while being under a duty to hold the balance fairly between his client (the employer) and the contractor. The rule giving immunity applied only where there was a dispute which called for a judicial decision. Such immunity is not confined to formal arbitration proceedings, and may include the engineer when acting under clause 66 of the ICE conditions, when he is required to adjudicate on a dispute.

ENGINEERS AND ARCHITECTS

A novel feature of construction contracts is the position in law of the engineer or architect. This varies according to the function being performed. It is important for him, and for those affected by his decisions, to know his status. The engineer or architect may perform functions as the agent, or as the independent contractor of the employer, or as an impartial certifier. He may also do things which incur a duty under the law of tort to other persons. The position of the certifier (see above) and the relationship between principal and agent generally (see page 126) have already been discussed. In this section specific duties and liabilities to the employer and to others are considered.

Duties to the employer

The scope of the work normally performed by the engineer or architect may be divided broadly into pre-contract duties and duties which arise under or by virtue of the construction contract. In the pre-contract stage, the duty is to prepare skilful and economic designs for the works, acting as an independent contractor for the employer (unless the designer happens to be the employee of the building owner). When the work is in progress, the duties arising under or by virtue of the contract are to supervise and administer the carrying out of the works in the best interests of the employer. Such functions will generally be performed as the agent of the employer. In each case the duty is owed in contract and the common law requires such duties to be exercised with reasonable skill and care. Whether particular conduct will incur liability for its consequences depends primarily upon established practice, that is, whether or not others would do the same. This is ultimately a question for the judge to decide. But in practice unless the failure is gross and obvious it is usually necessary to call a person practising in the same technical field to give expert evidence as to the breach of duty complained of.

There may, however, be occasions on which the court will find that the parties intended a different standard of duty. Where the engineer or architect is employed as an expert in some field, the court may impose a higher duty. In *Greaves Contractors v. Baynham Meikle* (1975) an engineer was employed to design the structure of a building known to be subject to vibrating loads. The floors were not adequately designed to resist the vibrations. The court accepted that the engineer had not failed to exercise reasonable skill and care, but found there to be an implied term of his engagement that the building would be fit for its purpose. The engineer was therefore held liable. In this case, Lord Denning held, in the Court of Appeal:

> "The law does not usually imply a warranty that (a professional man) will achieve the desired result, but only a term that he will use reasonable care and skill. The surgeon does not warrant that he will cure the patient. Nor does the solicitor warrant that he will win the case. But when a dentist agrees to make a set of false teeth for a patient, there is an implied warranty that they will fit his gums. What then is the position when an architect or an engineer is employed to design a house or a bridge? Is he under an implied warranty that, if the work is carried out to his design, it will be reasonably fit for the purpose? Or is he only under a duty to use reasonable care and skill? This question may require to be answered some day as a matter of law. But in the present case I do not think we need answer it. For the evidence shows that both parties were of one mind on the matter. Their common intention was that the engineer should design a warehouse which would be fit for the

purpose for which it was required. That common intention gives rise
to a term implied in fact."

Design duties

What constitutes reasonable skill and care in the design of
work depends upon the circumstances of each case. The duty
may normally be discharged by following established practice,
but there is no rule that doing what others do cannot give rise to
liability. There may be situations where there is no established
practice, such as where a new construction technique is used. In
such cases the duty of reasonable skill and care may be discharged by taking the best advice available and by warning the
employer of any risks involved. In *Turner* v. *Garland & Christo-
pher* (1853) the employer instructed his architect to use a new
patent concrete roofing which proved to be a failure. It was held
that where an untried process was used, failure might still be
consistent with reasonable skill. This case (unlike modern building cases) was tried with a jury. The judge, Earle J. said, in
summing up to the jury:

> "The plaintiff will merit your verdict if the defendant was found to
> be wanting in the competent skill of an ordinary architect. If he
> possesses competent skill and was guilty of gross negligence,
> although of competent skill, he might become liable. If of compe-
> tent skill, he had paid careful attention to what he undertook, he
> would not be liable. You should bear in mind that if the building is
> of an ordinary description in which he had had abundance of
> experience, and it proved a failure, this is an evidence of want of
> skill or attention. But if out of ordinary course, and you employ him
> about a novel thing, about which he has had little experience, if it
> has not had the test of experience, failure may be consistent with
> skill. The history of all great improvements shows failure of those
> who embark on them; this may account for the defect of roof."

However, it must be emphasised that when a novel design is to
be undertaken, or where tried and traditional methods are to be
superseded by novel and cheaper processes, any risk involved
must be brought to the attention of the employer, who is being
asked to bear such risk. It is the employer, who must decide the
course to adopt, and he must be given all necessary information
to enable him to reach a proper and considered decision.

When dealing with the liabilities of the parties and with
insurances, the standard forms of contract often use the criterion
of whether or not some fault or mishap is caused by the design of

the works; see ICE form, clause 20, and JCT form, clause 21. Such a criterion does not necessarily coincide with that of whether the designer has exercised sufficient skill and care. Thus, in *Queensland Railways* v. *Manufacturers Insurance* (1969) a river bridge failed during erection because the piers were subjected to forces beyond those which could be predicted by existing knowledge. It was held that the failure was in fact due to faulty design, although there might be no fault attributable by the employer to the designer.

Delegation of design

There may be many situations where design work is undertaken by persons other than the engineer or architect named in the building contract. Problems may then arise as to who can be sued for a design defect. If the employer directly employs a consultant, or even the contractor, to do design work, he will have a remedy for design defects, depending upon the terms of the contract. Where the engineer or architect himself delegates design work, there is no contract between the employer and the designer. As a general rule the engineer or architect will remain liable for the design unless the employer concurs in a delegation of responsibility. Thus, where an architect delegated the design of reinforced concrete to the contractor and the design proved to be defective, it was held that the architect was liable; *Moresk Cleaners* v. *Hicks* (1966). The Official Referee in his judgment said:

> "If the defendant was not able, because this form of reinforced concrete was a comparatively new form of construction, to design it himself, he had three courses open to him. One was to say: 'This is not my field.' The second was to go to the client, the building owner, and say: 'This reinforced concrete is out of my line. I would like you to employ a structural engineer to deal with this aspect of the matter.' Or he can, while retaining responsibility for the design himself seek the advice and assistance of a structural engineer, paying for his service out of his own pocket but having at any rate the satisfaction of knowing that if he acts upon that advice and it turns out to be wrong, the person whom he employed to give the advice will owe the same duty to him as he, the architect, owes to the building owner."

In the case of *Merton* v. *Lowe* (1981) an architect was held to have a design responsibility in respect of a proprietory plaster system used for a swimming pool ceiling, but was found not to be in breach because he was entitled to rely on the manufacturer's expertise, when details of the design were not revealed by the specialist. The decision of the Official Referee was approved by the Court of Appeal, where Waller L.J. observed:

> "It was submitted (by the plaintiffs) that the fact that Pyrok (the sub-contractor) maintained secrecy was immaterial, and reliance was placed on the case of *Moresk Cleaners* v. *Hicks*. I entirely agree with the judgment in that case. There the architect had literally handed over to another the whole task of design. The architect could not escape responsibility for the work which he was supposed to do by handing it over to another. This case was different. Pyroc were nominated sub-contractors employed for a specialist task of making a ceiling with their own proprietory material. It was the defendant's duty to use reasonable care as architects. In view of successful work done elsewhere, they decided that to employ Pyrok was reasonable. No witness called suggested that it was not at the beginning."

The architects were, however, held liable under their general design responsibility, for failing to take adequate steps to remedy the design deficiency which subsequently became apparent.

Direct warranty

If the design work is done by a nominated sub-contractor, the employer may protect himself by obtaining a direct (or collateral) warranty from the sub-contractor. This is, in effect, a separate contract under which the sub-contractor warrants his work, usually in consideration of his nomination by the employer. It is thus essential that the warranty is obtained before the sub-contract is entered into, otherwise there is no consideration for the warranty and it may be unenforceable. The principle was first applied to a construction contract in *Shanklin Pier* v. *Detel Products* (1951). In this case a supplier stated to the employer that his paint had a life of seven to 10 years. The particular paint was specified by the employer and duly used by the contractor. The paint in fact lasted for about three months. It was held that the statement made concerning the quality of the paint con-stituted a warranty so that the employer was entitled to sue the supplier for breach. Payment of a fee will be equally effective as consideration to support any such warranty.

Standard forms of warranty have been issued by the RIBA and now the Joint Contracts Tribunal (see further page 228). The general subject of warranties has become more important since the retrenchment that has occurred in the law of tort. Developers and purchasers who hitherto relied on tort claims against those with whom they had no contract are now, in general, unable to advance such claims. Lawyers have responded by producing a new generation of warranties intended to replace such rights by creating directly enforceable contractual obligations. No new principle of law is involved in these documents, but the following points should be noted:

Who is to give the warranty: warranties are frequently requested from a variety of parties involved in a construction project, sometimes from all parties. Where professional organisations take on work as a partnership or limited company, care should be taken not to allow individuals to sign warranties, so losing any corporate protection.

Terms of the warranty: the warranty may be made to cover any part of the work, not limited to that which is the responsibility of the person giving the warranty. The party signing should be careful to understand what it is taking on.

Standard of duty: warranties requested from professionals sometimes require a promise that the work will be reasonably fit for its purpose, going beyond the ordinary duty of reasonable skill and care.

Limitation period: warranties may be expressed so as to extend the ordinary limitation period in contract, either by requiring the warranty to run for a stated period or by requiring an indemnity.

Assignment of rights: warranties frequently provide that the recipient (usually the developer) may assign the warranty or rights in it to third parties who acquire an interest in the building or works. This is a substantial enlargement of potential responsibility and the terms should be checked carefully (see further page 197).

Contribution rights: a party who gives a warranty has a right to expect that those who may share responsibility for any loss will be capable of being sued for contribution, on the basis that they are also liable. The most convenient way of ensuring this is to provide that the warranty is not to become effective unless and until other (identified) parties involved in the project have also given similar warranties.

Indemnity insurance: professionals in particular must check with their insurers whether they are covered in respect of the wider responsibility created by the warranty; many insurers will not cover duties beyond reasonable skill and care.

Fee: there is no reason why the person giving the warranty should not charge a realistic fee, although some developers will offer design commissions only on condition that the professional will agree to give warranties.

A number of standard forms of warranty have evolved, issued by professional bodies and by insurers. There are, however, many ad hoc forms in circulation, often drafted for individual projects or clients.

The effect of a contractual warranty on a claim in tort was considered in two cases. In *Greater Nottingham Co-operative Society* v. *Cementation Piling and Foundations* (1988) the Court of Appeal held that the taking of a warranty from a sub-contractor covering design but not performance of the work, prevented there being a duty in tort relating to the performance of the work, on the footing the parties had had the opportunity to create a direct duty and had not done so. Conversely, however, in *Warwick University* v. *McAlpine* (1988) Garland J. held that the failure to place any direct duty in contract on a sub-contractor did not prevent the existence of a duty of care in tort. Further clarification of this area of law can be expected in future.

Supervision

The purpose of supervision is to ensure that the works are carried out by the contractor in accordance with the requirements of the construction contract; and the engineer or architect must provide reasonable supervision for this purpose. The amount of supervision required depends on the nature of the works. The building of a house may require visits every two weeks; while engineering operations may require constant attention from a resident staff. The duty of supervision was discussed in the case of *East Ham* v. *Bernard Sunley* (1965), a case concerning the meaning of "reasonable examination" under the JCT form of contract. Lord Upjohn observed:

> "As is well known, the architect is not permanently on the site but appears at intervals, it may be of a week or a fortnight, and he has, of course, to inspect the progress of the work. When he arrives on the site there may be many very important matters with which he has to deal: the work may be getting behind-hand through labour troubles; some of the suppliers of materials or the sub-contractors may be lagging; there may be physical trouble on the site itself, such as, for example, finding an unexpected amount of underground water. All these are matters which may call for important decisions by the architect. He may in such circumstances think that he knows the builder sufficiently well and can trust him to carry out a good

job; that it is more important that he should deal with urgent matters on the site than that he should make a minute inspection on the site to see that the builder is complying with the specifications laid down by him. . . . It by no means follows that, in failing to discover a defect which a reasonable examination would have disclosed, in fact the architect was necessarily thereby in breach of his duty to the building owner so as to be liable in an action for negligence. It may well be that the omission of the architect to find the defects was due to no more that an error of judgment, or was a deliberately calculated risk which, in all the circumstances of the case, was reasonable and proper."

But whatever the frequency of inspections, they must be sufficient to check important items, especially those which will be covered up by later work. Thus, where the architect made weekly visits to a house under construction but failed to inspect the bottoming of floors, which was defective, it was held that he was liable to the employer: *Jameson* v. *Simon* (1899). In this case, the Lord Justice Clerk said:

"There may, of course, be many things which the architect cannot be expected to observe while they are being done—minute matters that nothing that daily or even hourly watching could keep a check upon. But as regards so substantial and important a matter as the bottoming of a cement floor of considerable area, such as this is shown by the plans to have been, I cannot hold that he is not chargeable with negligence if he fails before the bottoming is hid from view by the cement to make sure that unsuitable rubbish of a kind that will rot when covered up with wet cement has not been thrown in in quantities as bottoming contrary to the specification."

Administration

The term is here used compendiously to describe the various functions which the engineer or architect may or must perform under a construction contract. Administration is part of the duty normally included under the umbrella description "supervision." But it includes many matters not related directly to superintendence on the site. The most important of these are: issuing certificates and ordering variations, which are considered above; and issuing instructions and drawings. In each case the scope of the particular powers or duties depends on the express or implied terms of the contract.

In the absence of express terms (see clause 7, ICE and clause 5.4, JCT forms) the contractor is entitled to have instructions and drawing supplied in reasonable time. Whether the express or implied obligation has been complied with is often difficult to determine, for example when instructions are needed to enable a sub-contract to be placed so as to permit completion on time. This is often a source of contention between contractor and employer. But under the standard forms the contractor is usually required to give notice of any instruction which he considers necessary.

During the course of carrying out construction work the engineer or architect may sometimes issue instructions permitting a deviation from the contract to assist the contractor, when strictly the employer is entitled to rely upon the contract. In such a case the instruction should be carefully distinguished from a true variation order. In *Simplex* v. *St. Pancras B.C.* (1958), the contractor undertook to install piles of specified capacity. This proved impracticable and the contractor offered alternative, differently priced, schemes. The architect accepted one of these "in accordance with quotations submitted." It was held that although the contractor would have been liable for the failure of the first scheme, the architect's acceptance of the alternative amounted to a variation. The contractor was therefore entitled to be paid the price of the alternative scheme and not the (lower) price originally tendered. In giving judgment, Edmund-Davies J. held:

> "The architect's letter of 30th July contained an instruction involving a variation in the design or quality (or both design and quality) of the works which the plaintiffs were being instructed to perform, and I have already indicated my view that he did so in circumstances in which he was accepting on the employers' behalf that they would be responsible for the extra cost involved. Such an action fell, in my judgment, within the 'absolute discretion' vested in him by clause 1 and was motivated by his great desire 'to get the job moving' as he put it, and regardless of the legal position of the plaintiffs under their contract. It was an action which led to the plaintiffs doing something different from that which they were obliged to do under their contract, and it was an action which involved the defendants in responsibility for the extra expense which it entailed."

One way of avoiding such a problem is to add to the instruction words to the effect "provided this is at no extra cost."

Quantity surveyors

The duties of a quantity surveyor include taking off quantities from drawings, preparing bills of quantities and measuring the works. The quantity surveyor is named in the JCT forms of contract, where he is engaged by the employer. In the ICE form such duties are placed on the engineer, but in practice are usually carried out by the quantity surveyors employed by the engineer. On most construction works of any substance there will, in addition to those employed by or on behalf of the employer, be quantity surveyors employed by the contractor.

In some construction contracts, usually smaller ones, a surveyor alone may be appointed as certifier, and may also be given the functions of supervising and administering the contract. The position of the surveyor will then correspond to that of the engineer or architect under larger construction contracts.

Other liability

The duties of engineers and architects to the building owner arise by virtue of their employment under contract. Acts performed for or on behalf of the employer may, however, at the same time give rise to duties and liabilities to other persons. This may arise by virtue of the position as agent for the employer, when there may be personal liability on a contract or liability for acting without authority (see page 124). In addition, architects and engineers are subject to the Defective Premises Act 1972. Under section 1, they owe a duty to any present or future owner of a dwelling, to see that their work is done in a professional manner.

The question of liability in tort is subject to the recent retrenchment indicated in a number of decisions of the House of Lords and Court of Appeal (see further page 335). However, there are many circumstances in which professionals may still be under tortious liability in relation to construction work. Thus, where an architect failed to examine a dangerous wall and allowed it to remain in the belief that it was safe, it was held that he was liable in negligence to a workman who was injured when the wall collapsed; the contractor who employed the man and the demolition contractor were also liable: *Clay* v. *Crump* (1963). In this case Ormerod L.J. in the Court of Appeal held:

> "It may be that there was negligence in some degree on the part both of the demolition contractors and builders. If there was such negligence, it may be that it was a contributory cause of the accident. It cannot however, in my judgment, absolve the architect from a share in the blame. To hold otherwise would be to hold that an architect, or indeed anyone in a similar position, could behave

negligently by delegating to others duties he was under an obligation to perform and escape liability by the plea that the injuries caused were caused by the negligence of that other person and not of himself. I do not accept that as being the true position in law."

While this case is of interest as regards the type of duty which may be owed, there will be difficulty in recovering loss not resulting from physical damage to person or property, unless the case is brought within the principles of *Hedley Byrne* v. *Heller* (1963) (see page 341).

A more recent and disturbing case concerning tortious liability is *Eckersley and Others* v. *Binnie & Partners* (1988), the Abbeystead case. Owing to the undetected presence of methane gas in an undergound pumphouse, an explosion occurred, killing and injuring many visitors who had been invited to a view by the Water Authority. The trial judge found fault on behalf of the designer (Binnie), the contractor and the Water Authority and the loss was apportioned between them. The Court of Appeal found no liability on the part of the contractor and the authority, but by a majority held Binnie alone liable. The trial judge suggested that the designer might be under a continuing duty, after completion of the project, to advise on new information which might indicate a danger. Bingham L.J., while not prepared to rule out any possibility of such a continuing duty, said:

"What is plain is that if any such duty at all is to be imposed, the nature, scope and limits of such a duty require to be very carefully and cautiously defined. The development of the law on this point, if it ever occurs, will be gradual and analogical. But this is not a suitable case in which to launch or embark on the process of development because no facts have been found to support a conclusion that ordinarily competent engineers in the position of (Binnie) would . . . have been alerted to any risk of which they were reasonably unaware at the time of handover."

The duty owed in regard to the carrying out of the works will be more limited. In the case of *Oldschool* v. *Gleeson* (1976) it was contended that consulting engineers were liable to contractors who suffered loss through the collapse of a party wall. Sir William Stabb, the Senior Official Referee, held:

"The duty of care of an architect or of a consulting engineer in no way extends into the area of how the work is carried out. Not only has he no duty to instruct the builder how to do the work or what safety precautions to take but he has no right to do so, nor is he under any duty to the builder to detect faults during the progress of the work. The architect, in that respect, may be in breach of his duty to his client, the building owner, but this does not excuse the builder for faulty work.

I take the view that the duty of care which an architect or a consulting engineer owes to a third party is limited by the assumption that the contractor who executes the works acts at all times as a competent contractor. The contractor cannot seek to pass the blame for incompetent work onto the consulting engineer on the grounds that he failed to intervene to prevent it.

. . . The responsibility of the consulting engineer is for the design of the engineering components of the works and his supervisory responsibility is to his client to ensure that the works are carried out in accordance with that design. But if, as was suggested here, the design was so faulty that a competent contractor in the course of executing the works could not have avoided the resulting damage, then on principle it seems to me that the consulting engineer responsible for that design should bear the loss."

DESIGN CONTRACTS

In traditional construction contract practice there is a more or less rigid distinction between design and construction. Design is the task of the engineer or architect and is taken to be excluded from the contractor's function. This distinction is entirely removed in certain modern forms of contract, sometimes described as "package" or "turnkey" contracts. Before dealing with the particular difficulties of these forms, it is necessary to examine the extent to which the contractor's traditional responsibility does exclude design.

First, the word "design" has no precise meaning in building contracts. It certainly encompasses the planning of the form of the finished works. The ICE conditions (clause 8(2)) draw a distinction between design of permanent and temporary works, the latter normally being the contractor's responsibility. Under the JCT forms, temporary works are entirely the contractor's responsibility unless otherwise provided for. In regard to the permanent works, no contract can lay down every detail of the "design," for example, the precise positioning of screws or the mixing of mortar. Each such operation involves an element of design, which is left to the contractor. In simpler forms of contract, this design element may be extensive and important. It is generally accepted that, in addition to a term of good workmanship, there will be an implied term that the work and materials will be reasonably fit for their purpose, to the extent they are not fully specified. Or, in other words, the contractor is to be responsible for elements of "design" left to him.

This principle may be limited by the form of the contract. Both the ICE and JCT forms entitle the contractor expressly to be given instructions necessary to complete the works (clauses 7(1), ICE, 5.4, JCT). The ICE conditions require any design responsibility for the permanent works to be expressly stated (clauses 8(2), 58(3)). Under the JCT form, the contractor's obligation is limited to the work shown in the contract drawings and bills (clause 2.1). Where in a building contract the bills stipulated "waterproof concrete," leaving the means of achieving the result unspecified and unpriced, this was held insufficient to make the contractor responsible when the concrete (otherwise constructed in accordance with the contract) leaked: *Mowlem* v. *B.I.C.C.* (1978). In this case, Sir William Stabb held:

> "I should require the clearest possible contractual condition before I should feel driven to find a contractor liable for a fault in the design, design being a matter which a structural engineer is alone qualified to carry out and which he is paid to undertake, and over which the contractor has no control. I agree that the construction for which (Counsel for the employer) contends places the contractor in an impossible position. He cannot alter the faulty design without being in breach of contract, for this fault in the design is not, in my view, a discrepancy or divergence between the contract drawings and/or the bill of quantities, and yet if he complies with the design he would still be in breach. I decline to hold that the specification in the bill of quantities makes the contractor liable for the mistakes of the engineer and, in so far as they may purport to do so, I think that it is ineffective by reason of clause 12(1) of the (JCT form of) contract."

Drafting a design contract

Where it is desired to make the contractor fully responsible for the design, the standard forms require substantial amendment, beginning with the clauses mentioned above. A simple and effective design-and-build contract could be written in the form "Build a house with six bedrooms." Difficulties will arise when the owner seeks to elaborate the contract to retain control over the appearance, lay-out and cost of the work. One method of overcoming these problems is to invite tenderers to submit their own designs with a lump sum price. Further difficulties arise if, having selected a design, the employer wishes to vary it. Package deal contracts usually contain extensive provisions which allow the contractor to object to a variation which affects his design responsibility.

A clause expressly making the contractor responsible for the design is desirable. It should make clear that responsibility is for the adequacy (and not mere provision) of the design. Where possible, performance requirements should be specified. An effective provision in regard to dwellings is to incorporate the NHBC requirements (see page 218). In the absence of express or clear provision the courts have resolved doubts in favour of the building owner where it was clear that the design had been carried out by the contractor, or his sub-contractors. This was the case in *L.B. Newham* v. *Taylor Woodrow* (1979), where the contractor disputed liability arising from the partial collapse of a tower block known as Ronan Point. A modified JCT form of contract had been used, which was nevertheless held sufficient to put the contractor under an absolute responsibility to comply with Building Regulations. The contractor was therefore liable despite being absolved of negligence. Conversely, in *Independent Broadcasting Authority* v. *E.M.I. and B.I.C.* (1980), the sub-contractor who designed the Emley Moor T.V. mast (B.I.C) was held liable in negligence for its collapse. The House of Lords, however, expressed their view on the result had there been no negligence. They held that the main contract included design responsibility, although this was to be carried out by the sub-contractor alone. Lord Fraser went on to say:

"If the terms of the contract alone had left room for doubt about that, I think that in a contract of this nature a condition would have been implied to the effect that E.M.I. had accepted some responsibility for the quality of the mast, including its design, and possibly also for its fitness for the purpose for which it was intended. . . . It is now well recognised that in a building contract for work and materials a term is normally implied that the main contractor will accept responsibility to his employer for materials provided by nominated sub-contractors. The reason for the presumption is the practical convenience of having a chain of contractual liability from the employer to the main contractor and from the main contractor to the sub-contractor—see *Young & Marten Ltd.* v. *McManus Childs Ltd.* (1969). . . . In the present case it is accepted by B.I.C. that, if E.M.I. are liable in damages to I.B.A. for the design of the mast, then B.I.C. will be liable in turn to E.M.I. Accordingly, the principle that was applied in *Young & Marten Ltd.* in respect of materials, ought in my opinion to be applied here in respect of the complete structure, including its design. Although E.M.I. had no specialist knowledge of mast design, and although I.B.A. knew that and did not rely on their skill to any extent for the design, I see nothing unreasonable in holding that E.M.I. are responsible to I.B.A. for the design seeing that they can in turn recover from B.I.C. who did the actual designing. On the other hand it would seem to be very improbable that I.B.A. would have entered into a contract of this magnitude and this degree of risk without providing for some right of recourse against the principal contractor or the sub-contractors for defects of design."

The JCT now publish a form of contract, based on the standard form of building contract, which provides for the contractor to design the works (see Chapter 10). There are also proposals for a design and build contract to be produced by the ICE.

COMPLETION

This covers the time period within which the work must be carried out and the consequences of delay; what is necessary to achieve completion of the work; and the effect of maintenance or defects liability clauses. Generally building contracts do not require the contractor to carry out individual items of work at particular times, and a programme of work is rarely made a term of the contract. Consequently the contractor will not be in breach by reason of delay during the course of the work (save possibly under terms requiring "due diligence," etc.). Similarly the contractor is not necessarily in breach by reason only of defective work, provided he can complete in accordance with the contract. Conversely when defects appear within the maintenance period, although the contractor has the duty and right to make good, he is nevertheless in breach so that the employer may sue for damages, through being deprived of use of the works. In this event, the damages recoverable will not be limited by any provision for liquidated damages, which are recoverable for delay in achieving completion.

Time for completion

The time within which the work is to be performed is a matter of economic importance both to employer and contractor. In most contracts dates will be specified for the start and completion of the work. The contractor is bound to do the work within the period set, and will be liable in damages if he fails to complete, subject to entitlement to extensions of time. He is also entitled so to carry out the work. Thus, if the employer prevents completion, for example, by failing to give possession of the site, he will be liable in damages to the contractor. Where no time period is specified, the same principles apply, save that the contractor is obliged and entitled to complete within a reasonable time.

Damages recoverable by the employer for delay are usually limited to "liquidated damages" (see JCT, clause 24, ICE, clause 47). When the delay is caused partly by the employer's default, it has been held that no liquidated damages may be recovered unless the contract allows an extension of time to be granted on the ground of the default, and such extension is granted. Thus, in *Peak* v. *McKinney* (1970) building works were suspended after the discovery of defective piles, for which the contractor was responsible. The employer caused further delay before work restarted. The contract did not provide for an extension of time for the employer's default. It was held that no liquidated damages could be recovered for any of the delay. Salmon L.J. said in his judgment:

> "The liquidated damages and extension of time clauses in printed forms of contract must be construed strictly *contra proferentum*. If the employer wishes to recover liquidated damages for failure by the contractors to complete on time in spite of the fact that some of the delay is due to the employers' own fault or breach of contract, then the extension of time clause should provide, expressly or by necessary inference, for an extension on account of such a fault or breach on the part of the employer."

The grounds of this decision were that liquidated damages may be recovered only from a date fixed under the contract. If no date can be fixed, time is "at large." For this purpose the liquidated damages and extension of time clauses are regarded as being for the employer's benefit and are construed against him, so that general words cannot be relied on. However, this appears to ignore the fact that pre-determined damages are as likely to benefit the contractor as the employer. If damages for delay are not "liquidated," the employer may sue for his actual loss.

Extension of time

Construction contracts usually provide for extensions of time to be granted by the architect or engineer on a variety of specified grounds: see JCT form, clause 25, and ICE form, clause 44. Where the ground of extension would otherwise be the contractor's risk, the extension is purely a concession, such as for inclement weather. Where the extension is based on some act or default of the employer, for example, the ordering of variations or giving late instructions, the contractor may also be entitled to extra payment. For this reason, the contractor may seek to attribute the actual delay to grounds carrying reimbursement in respect of the period granted: see JCT form, clauses 25 and 26.

While the employer may not be entitled to rely on general words to protect his right to liquidated damages, such words will benefit the contractor: see ICE conditions, clause 44(1), where the contractor is entitled to an extension on the ground of "other special circumstances of any kind whatsoever."

Meaning of completion

Generally, full and complete performance is required to discharge contractual obligations. However in construction contracts the purpose of signifying completion is not to release the contractor, but to allow him to leave the site so that the employer may take possession of the works. Contracts, therefore, use terms such as practical completion (JCT, clause 17.1) and substantial completion (ICE, clause 48(1)). While such terms do not permit the contractor to achieve completion without finishing the whole of the work (save for permitted exceptions: see ICE, clause 48(1)), it is thought they allow completion to be certified despite the existence of non-material departures from the contract.

Completion is not prevented by the existence of latent defects (see page 197). If defects are discovered after apparent completion (whether during or after the maintenance period) the employer is entitled to sue for damages, including loss of use of the works.

Defects clauses

These oblige the contractor to rectify faults appearing within a specified period, often six or 12 months following completion. They may also oblige the contractor to maintain the works and to put right defects not due to his default, the latter at the employer's expense (compare JCT, clause 17 and ICE, clause 49).

When a default is due to the contractor's failure to comply with the contract, he is in breach. The maintenance clause permits the contractor to mitigate the effect of the breach by carrying out rectification himself, but he may further be liable to the employer for damage for loss of use of the works, which will not be limited by any stipulation for liquidated damages.

A provision which entitles the employer to have defects rectified within a specified period does not absolve the contractor from liability for defects appearing after the expiry of the period. Clear words are required to make a maintenance clause operate also as an exclusion clause.

Further Reading

Keating, *Building Contracts* (5th ed., 1991).
Hudson, *Building and Engineering Contracts* (10th ed., 1970), Wallace.

CHAPTER 9

VICARIOUS PERFORMANCE AND INSOLVENCY

CHAPTER 8 deals with the operation of construction contracts and the parties' rights arising from them. This chapter covers a number of matters outside the contract itself which may affect the parties' rights. Vicarious performance refers to the carrying out of contractual obligations by a person not party to the contract. This may be either by sub-contract or assignment. Sub-contracts are found in most construction work, since very few contractors have the resources to carry out the whole of a project themselves. Particular problems arise when the sub-contractor is nominated. Assignment is the means by which a party may transfer to another the whole or part of his rights or duties under a contract. When the contractor assigns part of his obligation to perform the work, the effect is similar to a sub-contract save that the assignee is in direct contract with the employer. Finally, insolvency and bonds deals with the rights of the parties when one of them becomes unable to perform the contract by reason of financial difficulties.

SUB-CONTRACTS

In the traditional system of contracting in the construction industry the whole of the work is initially let to the main contractor. Subject to the provisions of the main contract, the contractor is entitled to sub-let portions of the work, save where the contract is let by reason of some special skill or quality of the contractor. Thus, a contract for specialist site-investigation work is likely to be one which may not be sub-let without consent of the employer. However, performance by a sub-contractor constitutes vicarious performance on behalf of the contractor, who remains fully responsible for the work, save where the main contract provides otherwise.

The standard forms usually contain terms restricting the right of sub-letting. The JCT form prohibits sub-letting without the architect's consent, which is not to be unreasonably withheld (clause 19). The withholding of consent may be referred to arbitration, if considered unreasonable. Under the ICE form sub-letting of parts of the work is permitted without the need for consent, but sub-letting the whole requires consent (clause 4). If sub-letting occurs without any necessary consent, the contract may provide express remedies, such as determination. The employer may waive his right to object, for example, by making payment for the sub-contracted work with knowledge of the sub-contract. If there has been no waiver, the employer may call on the contractor to resume performance of the work.

In engineering contracts sub-contractors tend often to be specialists who carry out limited parts of the works, such as piling. In building, it is not uncommon for the majority of the work on a substantial contract to be carried out by a large number of different sub-contractors. In recent years a novel form of main contract has been developed under which it is intended that the whole of the work is sub-contracted, the contractor's role being that of a manager. These are known as fee or management contracts. The employer pays the actual cost of the work (the prime cost) plus a fee retained by the contractor (see further page 220).

Rights and obligations

A sub-contract creates no privity of contract between the sub-contractor and the employer. Therefore the sub-contractor can sue only the main contractor for the price of the sub-contract work. The advantage of this system to the employer is that while the work may actually be performed by various specialists, the main contractor alone remains responsible for the whole operation and, perhaps most important, for the co-ordination of his own work and that of sub-contractors. It is common to find sums included in the tender figure which are designated as "provisional" or "prime cost" (P.C.). The former usually represent work, the scope of which is not entirely foreseen. A P.C. sum often represents an important part of the work which has not been designed in any detail, and which is proposed to be sub-let to a specialist to carry out the construction, and often to furnish the design. Prime cost work is the subject of special provisions in the standard forms of contract, which are dealt with further below.

One common feature of main contracts is for the employer to retain the right to make direct payments to a nominated sub-contractor: see JCT, clause 35.13 and ICE, clause 59C. These provisions recognise that payments due to a nominated sub-contractor are generally fixed by the architect or engineer, so that the contractor acts merely as a channel for payment in this regard. However, neither nomination nor direct payment to sub-contractors gives a sub-contractor the right to sue the employer and no privity of contract is created. The only exception to this principle is where the employer obtains a collateral warranty from the sub-contractor (see page 178). The warranty itself gives the sub-contractor no right to sue for payment. The RIBA forms of warranty (see page 228) oblige the employer to operate the direct payment provisions; but such rights are generally subject to any cross-claim against the contractor which the employer may have.

One problem arising out of sub-contracts is that of incorporation of the terms of the main contract. This is often done in an attempt to pass on the contractor's obligations to the sub-contractor. A common device adopted is a general incorporation clause such as "the sub-contractor shall perform all obligations of the main contract." But this is often inadequate and may produce complete ambiguity. For example, in the above clause, is the sub-contractor bound to perform the obligations of the contractor or those of the sub-contractor set out in the main contract? And if the former, do these include the obligations of the contractor to the sub-contractor? Such clauses may not be susceptible of any rational construction and to avoid such problems it is advisable to set out precisely what the sub-contractor's obligations are intended to be. A more useful device, adopted by the standard forms of sub-contract, is to require the sub-contractor to perform so as not to render the contractor in breach of the main contract.

Nomination

The usual procedure for letting a nominated sub-contract is for the architect or engineer to obtain quotations for the work in question direct from prospective sub-contractors, and to instruct the contractor to place an order with the chosen tenderer. The terms of the sub-contract will largely be settled before the nomination, but both contractor and sub-contractor may seek to amend or alter the terms. The main contract usually gives the contractor some protection by entitling him to object to a nomination which does not contain certain beneficial terms: see ICE form, clause 59(1); the JCT form requires the sub-contractor's tender to be subject to form NSC/4 (see Chapter 11).

Liability for defects

One of the problems relating to sub-contracts is that of determining the obligations of the main contractor in respect of materials and work of nominated sub-contractors, and thus determining the rights of the employer in the event of default by a nominated sub-contractor. There is generally no problem in regard to the express description of the work. This will become incorporated in the main contract by virtue of the nomination. The problem arises when the sub-contractor's work, while complying with the express terms of main and sub-contract, is not of good quality or not fit for its purpose.

Generally, where the employer relies on the skill and judgment of the main contractor, he will be responsible both for the quality and for the fitness of materials used. Where there is a nomination, the choice of materials will be made by the architect or engineer, so that the main contractor will not be responsible for their fitness or suitability. Is he, nevertheless, responsible for their quality? In the case of *Young & Martin* v. *McManus Childs* (1968), the House of Lords held that the specification of tiles made by one manufacturer only was not sufficient to exclude the implication of a warranty of quality, so that the main contractor was held liable for latent defects in the tiles. Lord Pearce expressed his view thus:

> "It is frequent for builders to fit baths, sanitary equipment, central heating and the like, encouraging their clients to choose from the wholesalers' display rooms the bath or sanitary fittings which they prefer. It would, I think, surprise the average householder if it were suggested that simply by exercising a choice he had lost all right of recourse in respect of quality of the fittings against the builder who normally has a better knowledge of these matters. Of course, if a builder warned him against a particular fitting or manufacturer and he persisted in his choice, he would obviously be doing so at his own risk. And a builder can always make it clear that he is not prepared to take responsibility for a particular kind of fitting or material."

Conversely, in the case of *Gloucestershire County Council* v. *Richardson* (1968), a main contractor discovered, during the course of construction works, defects in pre-cast concrete columns provided by a nominated supplier. Here, it was held that the main contractor was not liable for the quality of the components, and was not therefore in breach of contract. Lord Wilberforce held:

> "The design, materials, specification, quality and price were fixed between the employer and the sub-supplier without any reference to the contractor: and so far from being expected to secure conditions or warranties from the sub-supplier, he had imposed upon him special conditions which severely restricted the extent of his remedy. Moreover, as reference to the main contract shows, he had no right to object to the nominated supplier . . . . In these circumstances, so far from there being a good reason to imply in the contract . . . a condition or warranty binding the contractor in respect of latently defective goods, the indications drawn from the conduct of the contracting parties are strongly against any such thing."

See also the case of *Independent Broadcasting Authority* v. *E.M.I.* (page 187).

A further problem arises if a nominated sub-contractor repudiates. Is the contractor himself obliged to complete the work at his own expense, so far as this exceeds the agreed sub-contract price, or must the employer pay the additional cost of finding an alternative sub-contractor? In *N.W. Metropolitan Hospital Board* v. *Bickerton* (1970) it was held that under the 1963 JCT form the architect was obliged to re-nominate, so that the employer must bear the loss. The decision was based on the fact that the contract contemplated that prime cost work would be carried out only by a nominated sub-contractor. The decision may therefore apply to other forms of main contract such as the ICE 4th edition. The ICE 5th edition contains extensive provisions dealing with parties' rights upon the default of a nominated sub-contractor, so that there is little application for the *Bickerton* principle. The 1980 JCT form now deals expressly with re-nomination in respect of sub-contractors but not nominated suppliers (see page 256).

A combination of the above problems occurs if a nominated sub-contractor repudiates leaving defects in partly completed work. If the facts are similar to the *Richardson* case above, the main contractor would not be liable for the quality of the sub-contractor's work. In the case of *Fairclough* v. *Rhuddlan B.C.* (1983), the main contractor was *prima facie* liable for the work of the sub-contractor, but was held not to be under any responsibility for defects discovered after the sub-contractor had repudiated, relying on the principle established in the *Bickerton* case, that the main contractor had neither the right nor the duty to carry out work within a P.C. sum.

Liability for delay

If a nominated sub-contractor causes delay, without repudiating, the contractor generally remains liable, and may pass on the employer's claim to the sub-contractor in default. However the JCT form provides expressly for an extension of time on the grounds of delay by a nominated sub-contractor (clause 25.3.7). This effectively deprives the employer of remedy, save under any direct warranty.

Where the nominated sub-contractor repudiates, it appeared to follow from the *Bickerton* case that the employer would remain responsible for the delay in providing a replacement sub-contractor. However, it was held by the House of Lords in *Percy Bilton v. GLC* (1982) that such delay was not the responsibility of the employer. Lord Frazer held:

> "Withdrawal of a nominated sub-contractor is not caused by the fault of the employer, nor is it covered by any of the express provisions of clause 23 . . . accordingly, withdrawal falls under the general rule and the main contractor takes the risk of any delay directly caused thereby."

Where a nominated sub-contractor has achieved apparent completion and defects are thereafter discovered in the work the question arises, under the JCT forms of contract, whether this can constitute "delay on the part of nominated sub-contractors." These facts occurred in the case of *Jarvis v. Westminster Corporation* (1970), where defects were discovered in bored piles after the sub-contractor had withdrawn from the site. The necessary remedial work resulted in substantial delays to the main contract. It was held by Lord Dilhorne in the House of Lords that:

> "A practical completion certificate can be issued when owing to latent defects the works do not fulfil the contract requirements and . . . under the contract works can be completed despite the presence of such defects. Completion under the contract is not postponed until defects which became apparent only after the work had been finished had been remedied . . . . I conclude that the (sub-contractor) had completed the sub-contract works to the reasonable satisfaction of the architects and the (main contractor) and so were not guilty of delay."

Accordingly, as in the *Percy Bilton* case, the subsequent delay was not covered by the extension of time clause, and the main contractor remained responsible for the delay.

ASSIGNMENT

An assignment is a transfer, recognised by the law, of a right or obligation of one person to another. Most rights and obligations are capable of assignment. This may be achieved in a number of ways. Assignments are sometimes brought about by operation of law. This section is concerned primarily with assignment of rights and obligations under building contracts, but the principles involved cover many other things.

An assignment, in common with other legal transactions, is distinct from a contract to make an assignment. An assignment does not generally require consideration (see page 85). But a contract to assign, in order to be enforceable, must comply with the same requirements as any other contract, including the need for consideration. An assignment of a right or obligation arising under a contract is a further exception to the doctrine of privity (see page 99) in that rights or burdens are conferred upon persons who are not party to the contract.

Assignments not permitted

Building contracts and sub-contracts often contain terms restricting or prohibiting assignments: see JCT form, clause 19, ICE, clause 3. Such terms have the effect of making any purported assignment invalid as against the other party to the contract. However the right to prevent an assignment may be lost by waiver. Thus, if the contractor assigns his right to receive payment, the employer will waive his right to object if payment is made to the assignee.

There are some rights which may not be assigned. Debts may be assigned; indeed most assignments are of money due. It is a fundamental principle of English law that a "bare" right to sue for damages cannot be assigned. Thus, a party who has suffered personal injury must pursue the claim for compensation himself: he cannot sell that right to another. However, in commercial transactions, there may be a good reason for transferring a right of action. The law on this topic was reviewed by the House of Lords in *Trendtex* v. *Credit Suisse* (1981), where a bank sought to uphold the validity of an assignment of a claim for damages arising out of a transaction financed by the bank. Lord Roskill stated the law as follows:

> "The Court should look at the totality of the transaction. If the assignment is of a property right or interest and the cause of action is ancillary to that right or interest, or if the assignee has a genuine commercial interest in taking the assignment and in enforcing it for his own benefit, I see no reason why the assignment should be struck down as an assignment of a bare cause of action or as savouring of maintenance."

In the result, it may now be possible for commercial claims under construction disputes to be transferred. For example, it may be possible for a sub-contractor who has suffered loss to take over the rights of the main contractor to enforce claims under the main contract, including his own claim. Further developments in this branch of the law, however, are awaited.

Methods of assignment

A legal assignment is one which complies with section 136 of the Law of Property Act 1925. This requires that the assignment is in writing and is absolute, and that notice in writing is given to the other party. No particular form is needed and the document need not be under seal. An assignment which is conditional, for example, until a loan is repaid, is not absolute. The assignment takes effect and becomes enforceable against the other party only on receipt of notice.

A transfer which does not comply with the requirements of a legal assignment, such as one made orally, may be enforceable as an equitable assignment. But an equitable assignment will require to be evidenced in writing if it relates to an interest in land (see page 361).

In either type of assignment it is necessary to draw a distinction between a benefit and a burden. In a construction contract the benefit to the contractor is the right to be paid and the burden is the obligation to do the work. A benefit may be assigned irrespective of the wishes of the other party (subject to rights under the contract). The burden may be assigned only with the consent of the other party. Thus the contractor may not assign the obligation to carry out the work without the employer's consent; and the employer may not assign the duty to make payments without the contractor's consent.

Apart from the above methods, the assignment of certain rights are governed by statutory provision. These include transfers of shares and debentures in companies, and assignment of life insurance policies. In addition to transfers brought about by act of the parties some assignments take place by operation of law. Thus on death, the rights of the deceased person vest generally in his personal representative. Upon bankruptcy, the rights of the bankrupt vest in the official receiver and, upon appointment, in his trustee in bankruptcy.

Effects of assignment

Upon a valid assignment, the assignor loses his rights in the things assigned. The assignee acquires the right to sue, in his own name. However, if the assignment is equitable, the assignor may need to be made a party to the action. The right acquired is subject to any rights of the other party against the assignor, including the right of set-off. Thus if a contractor assigns money payable under a certificate, the employer may set off against the assignee any claim for defects or delay. He cannot counterclaim, but the set-off may reduce or extinguish the debt.

Assignment does not generally discharge the party assigning from his own contractual obligation. Thus when a lease is assigned the landlord is entitled to look to the assignee or to the original tenant for payment of rent. Similarly if the contractor assigns the obligation to carry out work, he may still be liable to the employer for breaches, such as defective work. From the contractor's point of view, a more satisfactory arrangement is that there should be a substitution of the new contractor. This is referred to as a novation. Where both the benefit and the burden of a contract are assigned, the latter requiring express consent, this may operate as a novation. Where a new contractor is substituted in the course of a construction contract, difficulties may arise as to existing matters which may later give rise to disputes, as for example, where the work is behind programme or there are grounds for a claim. These matters are best dealt with by express agreement.

Assignment of warranties

This topic has acquired currency through the creation of contractual warranties intended to replace claims previously available in tort. The assignees are those subsequently acquiring an interest in construction works. Thus, parties involved in carrying out a construction project, particularly the designers and other professionals, may be asked to give forms of warranty (see page 178) with the intention that these may be assigned to subsequent owners or leasees. In accordance with the principles discussed above, the benefit of such a warranty is generally assignable without need of express provision or consent. However, an assignment can do no more than to transfer rights available to the assignor; it is not capable of creating new rights in favour of an assignee. Thus, while the client can in theory assign the right to have a building adequately designed, it is unclear what right would be transferred to sue for damages in the event of breach: if the developer assignor has sold the building or created a full-repairing lease, then his right would be to nominal damages only. A further difficulty would arise where a building is sold or leased to a number of different purchasers. The assignment to each of a right to have the building properly designed creates a number of problems as to what enforceable right (if any) has been transferred to each purchaser.

These problems are capable of resolution, in principle, by the terms of the document to be assigned, particularly if created by deed (so as to avoid problems of consideration). Thus, the nature and extent of rights to be transferred may be defined, as well as the damage that may be claimed in the event of a breach. A solution which avoids these problems is to draft the document in the form of a novation, whereby the assignee third party may take over the full contractual rights of the developer, as though named as an original party to the transaction.

INSOLVENCY

Insolvency is not a term of art, but means, in practical terms, inability to pay debts. The effects of this depend on whether the debtor is an individual or a company; but in either case the consequences are severe, both for the debtor and for the creditor who is unpaid. The laws of bankruptcy and of winding up companies provide for the realisation and distribution of assets, with certain debts having priority for payment. In construction contracts the insolvency of one party will usually bring the work to an end. The law on both bankruptcy and winding up are contained mainly in the Insolvency Act 1986 and the Insolvency Rules.

The fact that an individual or a company is insolvent does not mean that there will be a bankruptcy or winding up. This depends on the action of the creditors (and of the debtor). The creditors may simply defer the enforcement of their rights; or they may agree to a formal arrangement by which the debtor attempts to pay off or reduce the debts. This shows that the concept of insolvency is rather uncertain. Insolvency is often brought about not by the loss of assets but by the loss of credit facilities or, particularly in the building industry, by adverse cash-flow. This reflects the fact that construction companies often have a large cash turnover compared to small assets.

Bankruptcy proceedings

Bankruptcy applies to individuals and not to incorporated companies. Bankruptcy is a process under which possession of the debtor's property is taken for the benefit of his creditors. The debtor obtains release from his debts and liabilities, but is subject to certain restrictions.

Bankruptcy proceedings are set in train by a bankruptcy petition. The procedure to be followed is set out in Part IX of the Insolvency Act 1986. In the most usual case of a petition by a creditor, it must be shown that there is no reasonable prospect of the debt being paid. The debt must also exceed a minimum "bankruptcy level," currently £750. The debtor may himself present a petition. Where the court makes a Bankruptcy Order, the assets and affairs of the bankrupt pass, usually, to the Official Receiver initially and then to a trustee in bankruptcy, for the purpose of realising and distributing the assets of the bankrupt person. Essentially, all his assets including future earnings are taken for the benefit of creditors. The bankrupt person is allowed to retain tools, vehicles and equipment necessary for use in his employment or business, and basic household equipment and provisions needed by his family. These provisions are harsh, but it should be remembered that the statutory bankruptcy process has evolved as the alternative to imprisonment for civil debt (graphically described in a number of the novels of Charles Dickens). The bankrupt person can usually obtain discharge after two years, but this may be extended in various circumstances.

The Insolvency Act of 1986 contains new provisions designed to encourage individuals who are in financial difficulties to make binding arrangements with creditors in order to stave off bankruptcy proceedings. In such a case, the individual may apply for an "Interim Order" from the court to obtain a short period of protection against bankruptcy. The effect of such an order is that no bankruptcy petition, or other proceedings or execution, may be commenced against the debtor without leave of the court.

Where a Bankruptcy Order is made and the process of realising and distributing assets commences, the trustee has an important statutory power (now section 315 of the Insolvency Act 1986) to disclaim "onerous property." This is defined as including:

> any unprofitable contract; or
> any other property that may give rise to liability to pay money or perform any other onerous act.

This provision will operate to the serious disadvantage of any person in contract with the bankrupt, since the trustee is enabled to retain and realise any benefit which may accrue under a contract, but effectively cannot be held liable.

Assets available to trustee

The assets available for realisation include all property belonging to the bankrupt at the date of the bankruptcy, which vests automatically in the trustee. Property acquired after the commencement of bankruptcy may, with certain exceptions, be claimed by the trustee. Where debts or claims are available, the trustee is empowered to enforce these by bringing claims, which may be settled in the trustee's discretion. The defendant in such proceedings is not wholly without protection. Even though the bankrupt cannot be held liable for cross-claims, they may still be raised as a defence of set-off. Further, the trustee may be required to give security for costs, so that the defendant has some protection in the event that the action fails.

The trustee cannot override charges on property so that, as in the case of the winding-up of companies, the secured creditors will be entitled to realise their debts, leaving the trustee to realise and distribute the remaining assets to unsecured creditors.

Winding up companies

Winding up procedure is dealt with in Chapter 4. While bankruptcy is always conducted through the courts, voluntary winding up may be initiated by the company itself resolving to wind up. The company may then appoint its own liquidator. If the company is insolvent, the voluntary winding up will be controlled by the creditors who may have their own liquidator appointed. Winding up which is not voluntary is conducted by the court, in most cases being on the ground of insolvency and at the suit of the creditors. In winding up by the court, the Official Receiver initially acts as liquidator, and continues unless replaced by order of the court.

The liquidator's duty is to collect in the assets and apply them in discharge of the company's liabilities. Unlike the trustee in bankruptcy, the assets do not vest in the liquidator, unless by specific order of the court. The liquidator has powers to carry on the company's business, to sell the assets and to compromise claims. A Winding up Order operates to discharge all the directors of the company, so that only the liquidator retains the power to act for the company.

As an alternative to winding up by the court, the Insolvency Act 1986 contains a new interim procedure which empowers the court to make an "Administration Order." The purpose of this is to protect the company from the ordinary consequences of insolvency, where there is a possibility that such a temporary arrangement may save the company or at least improve the realisation of its assets. This procedure has the same intention as the Interim Order in relation to personal bankruptcy proceedings (see above). An administrator of the company is appointed who has wide powers to control the company, investigate its affairs and to make proposals for consideration by the creditors. The administration will lead either to a scheme allowing the company to continue or to winding up.

Assets available to liquidator

The liquidator must collect all assets belonging to the company which includes contributions due from members on shares which are not fully paid-up. Since the winding up is followed by dissolution, no assets are retained by the company (unlike a bankrupt individual). A liquidator is given power to disclaim unprofitable contracts (Insolvency Act 1986, section 178). As in bankruptcy, an important limitation on the company's assets arises when they are used as security. The mortgagee or debenture holder may exercise his security, and may prove in the winding up for any unsatisfied balance, including unpaid interest.

Receivers

A receiver is a person appointed to collect and preserve property. The courts have wide jurisdiction to appoint receivers, such as in pending actions to protect the subject matter of the dispute. However, this section is concerned with a receiver appointed by a party under an instrument, for example, a mortgage or debenture. The receiver's duty in such a case is to take possession of the assets mortgaged or charged in order to protect and realise the security. Such an appointment is usually indicative of the debtor's insolvency or financial difficulty. The appointment and exercise of the receiver's powers may have an important effect on the debtor's ability to perform a subsisting contract.

Receivers appointed under mortgages or charges may exercise certain powers under statute (Law of Property Act 1925, sections 101 and 109). But these are invariably enlarged by the terms of the instrument itself. This may provide for powers of management and for the receiver to be the agent of the debtor company. The instrument under which the receiver is appointed will also specify when the right to appoint arises. When the company is being wound up, a receiver may be appointed either before or after the appointment of a liquidator.

When a liquidator is appointed after a receiver, any powers as agent of the company will be terminated, since the liquidator takes precedence in managing and winding up the company. But in other matters concerning the right to the company's assets, the liquidator and the receiver may be in conflict.

The Insolvency Act 1986, following recommendations of the Review Committee on Insolvency Law and Practice, introduced the new title of "administrative receiver." This means a person appointed as receiver or manager of the whole or substantially the whole of the company's property. Such an appointment will occur under a "floating charge" by which the whole or substantially the whole of the company's assets are charged. The effect of such an appointment is to place the receiver virtually in control of the company, and the new procedure is designed to create powers and duties enabling the administrative receiver to obtain information and make reports about the affairs of the company. The administrative receiver is required to make his report available to unsecured creditors.

Effects of insolvency on a construction contract

The first effect is usually that the work is brought to a stop by the inability of the builder to continue financing the work, if he is the insolvent party. If the employer is the insolvent party, his inability to meet interim payments will stop the work. This invariably produces a serious financial loss for the innocent party, which will not be satisfied by the insolvent party. Such loss may be reduced or even avoided by an employer appropriating retention money or the contractor's plant and goods or by enforcing a bond. A contractor is likely to fare less well. His work and materials, whether paid for or not, pass to the employer and to his trustee or liquidator on insolvency, when they become attached to the land. Thereafter they cannot be removed.

The parties' rights are usually regulated by provisions of the contract which operate upon various events indicative of insolvency. When one party intimates that he cannot continue with a contract by reason of insolvency, he will repudiate the contract and the other party has no real choice but to accept. However, standard forms of contract usually provide that the innocent party may terminate the contractor's employment without ending the contract, so that advantage may be taken of contractual terms applying after such termination, for example, as to the rights in goods and plant, and claims.

The ICE form does not give the contractor any right of determination under the contract for insolvency, so that he must rely on common law repudiation as above. The employer is given the right to terminate the contractor's employment in the event (*inter alia*) of the contractor becoming bankrupt or having a receiving order or administration order made against him or going into liquidation. The employer then has the right to complete the contract by other contractors and to claim or set off the additional cost of completion (clause 63). To fortify these rights the contractor's plant and unfixed goods and materials are deemed to be the property of the employer when brought to site, so that these are available as security in the event of determination (clause 53).

The JCT form gives rights of determination to both employer and contractor. The contractor may determine for non-payment of certificates, whether or not due to insolvency (clause 28). The contractor may then claim his loss from the employer. But such claim is not secured since goods and materials, when paid for, become the employer's property (clause 16). The employer has similar rights if the contractor, *inter alia*, becomes bankrupt or has a winding up order made or a receiver of his business appointed. In such cases the contractor's employment is automatically ended, subject to reinstatement. The employer may claim the additional costs of completion from the contractor (clause 27), but the only security for such claim is the retention money and any performance bond (see below).

All the above provisions take effect subject to the laws of insolvency. The principles which may conflict with such contractual rights are: first, that provisions which vest the debtor's property, upon insolvency, in a particular creditor may be void; and secondly, the statutory right of disclaimer of a trustee in bankruptcy or liquidator cannot be excluded.

Clause 53 of the ICE form vests the contractor's property in the employer when brought to site, and it is thought this remains enforceable on determination for insolvency. The effect of the clause depends also on property in goods and materials having passed to the contractor: see page 121. As to the validity of determination upon insolvency, this is not contrary to the insolvency laws; and it is thought that a determination correctly carrried out under the above clauses cannot be challenged. But doubt has been expressed as to the validity of such determination where the trustee or liquidator seeks to complete the contract. It is thought that the provisions entitling the employer to claim his loss would not be enforceable where the trustee or liquidator seeks to exercise the right of disclaimer.

BONDS

When the contractor fails to complete the contract, whether by reason of his own default or the employer's determination, and the employer is unable to recover his loss from the contractor, the employer may have some further protection if the contractor has provided a bond.

A bond is an undertaking by a surety to make payment upon the contractor's default. The usual form of bond guarantees the contractor's performance of the contract with an undertaking to be bound in a specified sum until (and unless) such performance is achieved. Upon the contractor's failure to perform in full, the employer is entitled to call on the surety (or bondholder) to make good the loss, up to the maximum amount of the bond. Since a bond is a contract of guarantee, it requires to be evidenced in writing. Further, since the employer gives no consideration (save that the contractor must include the cost of the bond in his price for the work) the bond must be made by deed.

Subject to the terms of the bond, a surety may be discharged from liability by a material alteration in the contractor's obligation which has been guaranteed, such as extra works being ordered or an extension of the contract period being granted. The employer is also under a duty to mitigate his loss, since otherwise it may be said the loss is not caused by the contractor's non-performance. The ICE form of contract incorporates a form of bond which provides:

> "no alteration in the terms of the contract . . . or in the extent or nature of the works . . . and no allowance of time . . . nor any forebearance or forgiveness . . . on the part of the employer or the said engineer shall in any way release the surety from any liability under the above-written bond."

These provisions are designed to overcome the above difficulties. The ICE conditions (clause 10) and tender provide that the contractor may be required to obtain a bond in a specified sum, not exceeding 10 per cent. of the tender total. The JCT form does not provide expressly for a bond, but this may be incorporated into the tender documents. The provision of a bond may be made a condition precedent to the execution of the contract or to the contractor's right to payment.

A bond of the form under discussion is in the nature of a guarantee. The bondsman is not an insurer, and consequently there is no automatic duty of disclosure (see page 131). The terms of the bond may, however, require that notice be given of relevant events. A further matter which should be dealt with in the bond is its intended duration. This may be, for example, until the end of the maintenance period or for some further stipulated period. It is a matter of some difficulty for contractors if bonds do not provide for release, since banks may be unwilling to continue to provide further bonds while those given earlier remain in force. The law relating to guarantee bonds is of some antiquity, and there has been little modern development.

On-demand bonds

Conversely, there has been great development in recent years in a different type of instrument, still called a bond, but having a totally different effect. The on-demand bond usually entitles the holder (the employer) to call for payment by the bondsman (usually a bank) upon giving a particular form of notice. The notice usually requires no more than an assertion of default on behalf of the contractor. The bond money will then be paid irrespective of any disputes that may exist, either in relation to the underlying contract generally, or in relation to the purported reason for calling the bond in particular. The law relating to this type of bond has developed in the English courts through a series of cases in which contractors or sellers have sought injunctions from the court to prevent the bank paying the bond or to prevent the other party to the contract calling for payment. The courts have consistently refused such injunctions, in line with decisions of courts in many other countries. The only material exception to this rule is where the contractor is able to establish (not merely allege) fraud. In *Edward Owen Engineering* v. *Barclays Bank* (1978), the plaintiff, English suppliers to a Libyan customer, gave an on-demand bond. The customer, when himself in default, called the bond and the plaintiff sought an injunction against the bank to restrain payment. Lord Denning explained the procedure: the customer claims from the bank (there may be an intermediary bank involved also), the bank pay "on first demand without proof or conditions," and the bank then claim against the English suppliers. Lord Denning continued:

> "It is obvious that that course of action can be followed not only where there are substantial breaches of contract, but also when the breaches are insubstantial or trivial, in which case they bear the colour of a penalty rather than liquidated damages; or even when the breaches are non-existent. The performance guarantee then bears the colour of a discount on the price of 10 per cent. or five per cent. or as the case may be. The customer can always enforce payment by making a claim on the guarantee and it will then be passed down the line to the English supplier. The possibility is so real that the English supplier, if he is wise, will take it into account when quoting his price for the contract."

The demand for this type of bond has increased as international trade and construction work in particular have grown. Considerable problems remain for a contractor seeking to recover the proceeds of a bond which has been wrongly called, or even claiming credit for the value of the bond in any subsequent dispute. It is a matter of considerable importance that these issues should be dealt with fully in the underlying construction contract, so that they may be brought before arbitrators who may become seized of a dispute under that contract.

Further Reading

Keating, *Building Contracts* (5th ed., 1991).
Hudson, *Building and Civil Engineering Contracts* (10th ed., 1970), Wallace).

CHAPTER 10

STANDARD FORMS OF CONTRACT

THE law of England, subject to very limited exceptions, permits parties to make any commercial arrangements they wish, and enforces those arrangements without regard to their fairness or consequences (for some particular exceptions see page 93). Contracts in the construction industry necessarily involve complex arrangements, with many points of difficulty which have to be anticipated and provided for. This explains why, historically, parties involved in construction work have developed and adopted standard forms of contract covering many types of work. Standard forms go back to the nineteenth century and in some respects even earlier. Many of the standard forms in use today can be traced back to public works contracts drafted by nineteenth century lawyers, and this partly explains their anachronistic appearance.

Since their origin, a number of different trends and influences are discernible leading up to the present day. Thus, the types of standard form currently in use were originally drawn up by public authorities, containing the type of safeguards and sanctions that they wished to impose upon contractors who tendered for the work. Thereafter, professional bodies such as the RIBA and latterly the ICE, and other bodies as well, drafted and put forward their own forms, often based on and containing drafts from these earlier forms. After World War II, concern was expressed about the growing number of these standard forms, and the increasing practice for main contractors to draft their own forms of sub-contract, often containing one-sided provisions. In 1964, the report of the Banwell Committee recommended that a single standard form of contract for the whole construction industry was both desirable and practicable, and that standardisation of sub-contract conditions should follow. This was, however, not to be.

The decades that followed Banwell saw a great upsurge in construction disputes and a parallel increase in the numbers and variety of standard forms; and latterly there has been a great increase in the variety of contractual arrangements for which standard forms are required. The extent to which parties adhere to existing printed forms depends on the economic climate: when work is short, employers tend to amend the forms to their advantage, and vice versa. More recently, with the common availability of word processors, contract forms have proliferated to the point that a substantial amount of construction work is now carried on under ad hoc forms, based on standard or traditional drafts, but tailored to the particular commercial transaction.

Despite this proliferation, there remain a number of forms which can be regarded as standard. The two most frequently encountered are the JCT Standard Form of Building Contract, and the ICE Conditions of Contract. These are each dealt with in more detail in the following two chapters. The purpose of the present chapter is to review other types of standard document likely to be encountered in various types of construction work. For the detailed provisions of these documents and for a full commentary on their contents, reference must be made elsewhere.

FORMS OF MAIN CONTRACT

There are two main contract forms frequently encountered in particular circumstances: the government form GC/Works/1 and the international FIDIC form. These are dealt with further below. In addition, there are now a variety of forms designed for particular types of contract, including management, design-and-build and small works. All of these forms are primarily intended for building or civil construction. Work which contains a substantial element of plant or machinery uses other forms such as the Model Form A and derivatives of it. Finally, the construction of houses and flats is frequently carried out under the NHBC scheme which provides standard forms for this purpose.

Form GC/Works/1

This form is published by H.M. Stationery Office and has the full title General Conditions of Contract for Building and Civil Engineering. It is extensively used by central government departments. The present version is edition 3, issued in December 1989.

Previous editions of the form required the appointment of a "Superintending Officer" (S.O.) who was given wide powers analogous to those of an engineer under an ICE contract. Under edition 3, the S.O. is replaced by the P.M. (Project Manager). It should be noted that, while the powers of the P.M. are somewhat wider than those of the S.O., they did not include management in the normal sense of the word, and his functions do not involve the type of responsibility undertaken by a professional project manager. Edition 3 contains a helpful list of definitions (clause 1). The employer is referred to as "the authority."

Powers of the P.M. include a long list of instructions which he is empowered to give (clause 40). These include ordering variations, giving instructions regarding the order of execution of the works, the hours of working and the extent of overtime or night work to be adopted; suspension of the works and replacement of any persons employed; and a potentially very wide power to give instructions as to "any other matter which the P.M. considers necessary or expedient." The authority itself is given power (clause 65) to execute any other works on the site. The contract also contains a useful procedure for achieving acceleration of the works, not by direct instruction, but by requiring the contractor to submit priced proposals for acceleration, which the authority may then accept (or not).

There are the usual provisions for extensions of time, which, however, include delay due to "any other circumstances (other than weather conditions) which are outside the control of the contractor or his sub-contractors and which could not have been reasonably contemplated under the contract." This is a potentially very wide ground, although it is the "circumstances" and not the delay which are not reasonably to have been contemplated (clause 36). The machinery for assessing extensions contains a useful provision allowing the P.M. to give either an interim or final decision at any stage. In common with previous editions of the contract, there are wide provisions allowing determination. These are now split into three clauses, clause 56 containing general provisions and grounds for determination for default; and clauses 57 and 58 setting out the financial consequences of determination, respectively, for default and at will (the latter entitling the contractor to be paid and compensated for the determination).

The new edition contains more extensive provisions for claiming additional payment. There is an express clause providing for payment for additional work carried out as a result of unforseen ground condition (clause 7). Clause 46 entitles the contractor to claim "any expense which he would not otherwise have incurred" by reason of a variety of matters including "any direction or instruction from the authority or the P.M. regarding the nomination . . . of . . . any person or any instruction . . . of the authority to be given under condition 63(2)." Clause 63 concerns nomination of sub-contractors to carry out prime cost work, clause 63(2) containing the general power of nomination. Clause 63 itself appears designed to limit any additional sums payable as a result of failure of a nominated sub-contractor, to the consequences of insolvency. However, the claim available under clause 46 means that the employer may run the risk of additional claims arising from the use of nomination. This is in sharp contrast to previous editions of the form which simply made the contractor liable for nominated sub-contractors as though they were direct.

Clause 31 (quality) contains an anomaly which may be unintended. The clause requires the contractor to use skill and care to ensure that the works conform to the specification, bill of quantities and drawings. The effect of these words is that the contractor would be liable for non-compliance only if it were shown that there had been a failure to use skill and care, *i.e.* the contractor had been negligent. Clause 31(4) expressly entitles the P.M. to reject goods and materials which do not conform with the specifcation. However, clause 2(1) provides that, in case of discrepancy, the conditions are to prevail over other documents forming part of the contract, *i.e.* the specification.

In the event of disputes arising under the contract, clause 60 provides for arbitration, which, in the absence of agreement, may not be started until after completion. The arbitration is required to be carried out in accordance with a tight programme, not to exceed (without consent) six months from the date of the preliminary meeting to the hearing. As an alternative, disputes arising during the course of the works may be referred to the adjudication of a person to be appointed. The adjudicator, however, is required to be "an officer of the authority or a person acting for the authority who has not been associated with the letting or management of the contract."

A short version of the government form exists for minor works, known as Form GC/Works/2.

International (FIDIC) Conditions of Contract

There has been in existence since 1956 a form of contract based on the ICE conditions, for use in contracts having an international element. The fourth edition of this form was issued in 1987. The conditions are prepared by the International Federation of Consulting Engineers (FIDIC) and are recommended for use both in international and domestic civil engineering contracts. The documents are published in two Parts, Part I containing the general conditions, index, tender and contract agreement; and Part II containing conditions of particular application and guidelines for preparation of particular clauses. Part II may be used, for example, where the type, circumstances or locality of the works necessitates additional clauses. Dredging and reclamation work usually require special clauses to take into account the particuar nature of the work and the plant utilised.

The fourth edition of FIDIC, like its predecessors remains closely related to the ICE conditions of contract, both in terms of its structure and working, and its clause numbering. For example, the disputes clause (clause 66 in the ICE conditions) is numbered 67, most of the earlier clauses (for example adverse physical conditions) having the same numbers as those of the ICE conditions. The following notes relate to part I of the FIDIC conditions.

Clause 1 of the conditions contains a list of definitions, many of which are substantially identical to those under the ICE conditions. Clause 2 deals with the engineer and his representative (E.R.). In recognition of the possibility that the form may be used in countries where the independence of the engineer may not be readily accepted, clause 2.1 provides that if the terms of the engineer's appointment require him to obtain specific approval of the employer before exercising any authority, particulars of this requirement are to be set out in Part II of the conditions. In addition, clause 2.6 expressly requires the engineer, when required to exercise his discretion, to act "impartially within the terms of the contract and having regard to all the circumstances."

Clause 5 deals with the contract documents. This requires there to be stated in Part II the language or languages in which the contract documents are to be drawn up and the national law according to which the contract is to be construed (the proper law). Where there is more than one language Part II is to state the "ruling lanaguage." Clause 5.2, as in the ICE conditions, makes the contract documents mutually explanatory, but goes on to provide that in the event of ambiguity, the documents are to be given the following priority:

(1) the contract agreement;

(2) the letter of acceptance;
(3) the tender;
(4) Part II of the conditions;
(5) Part I of the conditions;
(6) any other documents forming part of the contract.

The latter category (6) will include the technical documents, such as the specification, drawings and bill of quantities.

The contract provides substantially the same structure for claiming additional payment as exists under the ICE conditions, although individual clauses will be found to be differently drafted. Thus, notices and procedure for claim is dealt with in clause 53 (equivalent to the ICE conditions, clause 52(4)). Claims for additional payment are provided in respect of drawings or instructions (clause 6.3), failure to give possession (clause 42.2) and other matters. Clause 12 provides for additional payment in respect of physical obstructions or physical conditions other than climatic conditions, which were not forseeable by an experienced contractor. In respect of any such conditions, clause 11.1 provides that the employer:

"shall have made available to the contractor before the submission by the contractor of the tender, such data on hydrological and subsurface conditions as have been obtained by or on behalf of the employer from investigations undertaken relevant to the works but the contractor shall be responsible for his own interpretation thereof."

This clause goes on to provide that the contractor is deemed to have inspected the site, but also to have based his tender on the data made available by the employer. Clause 53 provides for giving notice and particulars of claims. Where there is a failure to comply with such requirements, clause 53.4 provides that the contractor's entitlement to payment "shall not exceed such amount as the engineer or any arbitrator . . . assessing the claim considers to be verified by contemporary records . . . ." Clause 44 covers extensions of time and provides for interim extensions where appropriate. No final extension may decrease an interim extension.

Clause 51 gives a general power to order variations, including ordering a change to "any specified sequence or timing of construction of any part of the works." Clause 52 provides for the valuation of variations by ascertaining or varying the rates to be applied to the work. Note that the contract, in common with the

ICE conditions, provides no general right to payment of additional expense arising from instructions or variations. The contract does, however, provide a novel type of additional payment where the "effective contract price" (that is, excluding provisional sums and day work allowances) increases by more than 15 per cent. The contractor in such circumstances is entitled to be paid an additional sum to be agreed or fixed by the engineer "having regard to the contractor's site and general overhead costs of the contract." The way in which an appropriate sum would be calculated is, however, quite obscure, and it is not wholly clear whether the adjustment is intended to be by way of addition. Parties entering into this form of contract should seek to clarify what is intended. The contract does not provide, as do the ICE conditions, any claim under clause 13, which is left as a clause simply obliging the contractor to comply with the engineer's instructions on any matter. Similarly, clause 14 provides for the submission of programmes, but not for additional payment.

In regard to sub-contracting, clause 4 contains a general provision requiring consent of the engineer save for the provision of labour and materials and any work for which a sub-contractor is named in the contract. Clauses 58 and 59 contain provisions for nominated sub-contractors, such work being covered by "provisional sums" rather than prime cost sums. In respect of every provisional sum the engineer is given authority to instruct the contractor to carry out the appropriate work as a variation or to use a nominated sub-contractor (clause 58.2). Under clause 59.2 there are stated the minimum terms which the main contractor is entitled to insist on in any nominated sub-contract, including undertaking a "back-to-back" responsibility in respect of the nominated work. Clause 59.3 requires matters of design or specification included in provisional sum work to be expressly stated. These clauses do not attempt to deal expressly with the problems arising from the *Bickerton* case (see page 196). The provisions differ from those under the JCT form of contract in that there is no express requirement for provisional sums to be expended only in favour of sub-contractors (thereby effectively depriving the contractor of the ability to carry out the work himself). It is possible that the *Bickerton* principle could still apply, rendering the employer liable to pay the additional cost arising from failure of a nominated sub-contractor. However, the effect of the clauses will be subject to the proper law of the contract, which in a great number of cases, will not be English law. It will be a matter of some interest if the *Bickerton* principle has to be re-argued under a variety of foreign laws.

Clause 60 covers certificates and payments. The provisions are similar to those under the ICE conditions, but there are likely to be special clauses dealing with foreign currency payments. The contract provides for a final certificate (clause 60.8) covering payment matters only. As regards continuing obligations, the employer is not to be liable for late claims unless they have been included both in the final statement and the statement at completion, to be issued respectively after the defects liability certificate and taking over certificate (clause 60.9). As regards the contractor's liabilities, clause 60.2 provides that the parties are to remain liable for fulfilment of obligations which remain unperformed, but clause 61.1 provides that the defects liability certificate is to constitute approval of the works. Although the position is not clear it is likely that this certificate would be regarded as binding only in regard to matters subject to the engineer's approval.

Clause 67 provides for the settlement of disputes by arbitration, which is to be under the Rules of the International Chamber of Commerce (ICC). Arbitration may be commenced at any time. Such proceedings are, however, subject to two conditions precedent. First, as under the ICE conditions, any dispute must first be referred to the engineer, who is required to give his decision within 84 days after the reference. Thereafter, either party may give notice, within 70 days, of his intention to commence arbitration. In the event that no such notice is given, the engineer's decision is to become final and binding. Under previous editions of the FIDIC form, clause 67 arguably required the service of a request for arbitration in accordance with the ICC Rules, to avoid the finality of the engineer's decision (see I.N. Duncan Wallace: Construction Contracts, Principles and Policies, Chapter 18). The present clause has now clarified the position: only notice of intention to commence arbitration is required.

The second condition precedent to arbitration is the requirement to attempt amicable settlement. Clause 67.2 provides for a notional settlement period of 56 days after the notice of intention to commence arbitration, during which the parties are to attempt settlement. However, on the expiry of this period, the arbitration may commence whether or not any attempt at amicable settlement has in fact been made. This is in effect no more than a "cooling off" period.

It should be noted that the FIDIC conditions, when used in practice, are often heavily amended and supplemented by additional clauses required by particular employers or by the laws or customs of the country in which the works are situated. These additional clauses are often such that the effect of the original conditions is heavily qualified and any such conditions must clearly be read with great care.

House purchaser's agreement

The National Housebuilding Council (NHBC) has been referred to in Chapter 6. In this section the main features of the NHBC system (which operates under the trademark "Buildmark") are reviewed. The system incorporates a variety of contractual obligations involving the house purchaser, the builder or developer and the NHBC, together with relevant insurers. Although the documentation is comparatively brief, it is of considerable economic importance to millions of home owners and potential house purchasers. Its importance is such that it is difficult to obtain a mortgage without the benefit of NHBC protection (since this should ensure that the value of the property, and therefore the security of the lender, is maintained).

The form of contract embodying the NHBC scheme is unusual, and does not provide for formal execution. The way that the scheme works is that, as a condition of registration, a builder (or developer) at the outset applies to the NHBC for inspection on a standard form accompanied by certain particulars. The registration rules provide that by making such an application, the builder authorises the NHBC to issue appropriate Buildmark documents and to offer cover to the first purchaser. The relevant documents are then delivered to the builder, who hands them over to the purchaser. They comprise a contract between the builder, the owner and the NHBC. The terms of this contract are set out in the Buildmark booklet which is periodically revised and reissued. These notes refer to the 1990 edition.

The booklet is divided into a first half, which comprises legally binding conditions applying between the three parties, and a second half consisting of a non-binding home owners' guide. The first half consists of five sections dealing with the meanings of words (Part A) the builder's obligations (Part B), the NHBC's obligations (Part C), claims (Part D), and disputes (Part E). The essential obligation around which the contract centres is the builder's warranty that the home has been or will be built:

(a) in accordance with the NHBC's requirements;
(b) in an efficient and workmanlike manner, with the proper materials, and so as to be fit for habitation.

Part B then proceeds to define the obligations of the builder in regard to defects reported before the end of the "initial guarantee period," which is two years from the date of the 10 year notice, to be issued by the NHBC at completion. Such defects are to be put right by the builder including correcting defects in adjacent property constructed by the same builder if this is causing damage to the subject property. The builder will also bear the cost of removal and alternative accommodation and storage, where necessary (Part B, section 2). After the intitial guarantee period, the owner is covered for a further period of eight years (making a total of 10 years protection), the latter period being referred to as "the structural guarantee period." During this stage, the NHBC undertakes to correct defects, but limited to major damage either:

(a) caused by a defect in the structure; or
(b) caused by subsidence, settlement or heave affecting the structure.

The NHBC also undertakes to pay the cost of putting right any defect in the drainage system, all these obligations applying, however, only to defects which first appeared during the structural guarantee period (Part C, section 3). By a special condition, it is provided that the NHBC will not be liable for a defect of which notice was or could have been given during the initial guarantee period. Part B provides that the builder is not liable during the initial guarantee period, if notice of a defect has not been given. Accordingly, the contract appears to contemplate that the owner could lose his rights in respect of a defect which should be, but which is not notified. However, the warranties referred to above are not stated to be subject to the express provisions obliging the builder to put right the defects, and conversely, are subject to a note stating:

"Your rights for breach of these warranties are in addition to any other rights you may have under the Buildmark."

Accordingly, it would appear that the owner could proceed against the builder for breach of warranty at any time within the limitation period, irrespective of other express obligations as to putting right defects either upon the NHBC or the builder.

The importance of the NHBC's obligations are that they are backed by insurance. Thus, if the builder fails to put right defects in accordance with his obligations under Part B, or fails to honour an arbitration award or judgment, the NHBC will pay the cost of putting right the work. The owner needs to give notice under the contract to acquire these rights, and accordingly will lose the insurance protection if notice is not given. The liability of the NHBC, whether arising because of default of the builder or because the defect arises during the structural guarantee period, is limited to the sum set out in the 10 year notice, subject to increase at 12 per cent. per annum compound. When a claim arises against the builder, Part D of the booklet requires the claim first to be submitted to conciliation by the NHBC. If the owner does not accept the NHBC's recommendation, the matter may then proceed to arbitration (Part E). Where a claim is made against the NHBC, they investigate the matter themselves. If their recommendation is agreed, the owner must nevertheless allow the NHBC themselves to seek compensation, under their right of subrogation. If the matter is not agreed, there may then be an arbitration between the owner and the NHBC.

The NHBC scheme is expressed to benefit subsequent owners (the term "purchaser" includes the first and each subsequent purchaser). The importance of the scheme is that it provides, with the minimum of legal formalities, a route to comparatively rapid compensation in respect of defective work, with the owner being guaranteed in respect of more serious defects for up to 10 years from completion. The scheme is essentially run and financed by and on behalf of the housebuilding industry and can probably claim to have led to material improvements in house-building standards. Because the scheme requires conciliation and arbitration of disputes, the form has rarely been before the courts.

Management contracts

This refers to main contracts in which the contractor offers "management" services in lieu of full responsibility for the performance of the work. The interest in these forms of contract does not centre on the definition of and sanctions regarding the management services to be provided. The question which is of interest, at least to lawyers, is the extent of the main contractor's responsibility for performance by sub-contractors. The usual arrangement is that most if not all of the physical work is to be carried out by sub-contractors. The contractor is usually entitled to be paid the actual cost, so that he is not at risk in this regard. Where default occurs in relation to quality or time, management contracts usually provide, in effect, that the management contractor is liable only if the sub-contractor can also be held liable, so that again the main contractor is not at risk.

Perhaps the best known standard form of management contract is the JCT Standard Form of Management Contract, issued in 1987. In regard to the three elements mentioned (cost, quality and time) this contract provides as follows. The contractor is to be paid prime cost (which, by the second schedule, includes amounts due and payable under sub-contracts) plus the management fee. The major restriction on this indemnity is that the prime cost is to exclude costs incurred as a result of any negligence by the management contractor. As regards default by a sub-contractor (in the contract called a works contractor) the management contractor is to take steps in consultation with the architect to enforce the sub-contract or otherwise secure the satisfactory completion of the project. The employer is required to pay the management contractor all amounts properly incurred by him in fulfilling these obligations. The employer is then given the right to recover amounts so paid or credited, including liquidated damages, from the management contractor, but only to the extent that they have been recovered from the sub-contractor (clause 3.21). The difficulty which arises from such provisions (there are many other variants in other management forms) is that it can be argued that if the management contractors' own liability to the employer is contingent on recovery from the works contractor, he cannot show loss for the purpose of such recovery, with the result that the employer must always bear the loss. No definitive ruling on this point exists: the problem is that all these contracts contain arbitration clauses, and few such disputes will ever come before the courts (see further page 45).

The other point of interest under management contracts is the nature and definition of the services to be provided by the management contractor, in return for the management fee. In the JCT management contract these are defined in clause 1.5 as including the preparation of programmes, entering into works contracts, ensuring the standards of work by supervision, providing site facilities as required, keeping cost records, and ensuring that the project is carried out in an economical and expeditious manner. The third schedule contains a list of specific tasks, which includes the provision of practical advice on all aspects of performance, including the drawings and specification, and specifically to advise on "buildability" (third schedule, item 4).

Forms of Sub-Contract

Many contractors impose their own standard terms on sub-contractors. These often contain one-sided provisions which place the sub-contractors at a disadvantage in a dispute. Conversely some specialists and suppliers impose their own terms on main contractors. A fairer balance may be achieved by using one of the standard forms of sub-contract designed for use with the standard main forms.

JCT nominated sub-contract

A form of sub-contract known as NSC/4 is issued by the Joint Contracts Tribunal for use in nominations under the JCT forms of main contract. By the standard form of tender (NSC/1) the prospective sub-contractor agrees to use form NSC/4. The main contract nomination procedure (clause 35) also contemplates its use. The form contains articles of agreements, including an arbitration clause which is keyed into connected disputes under the main contract (see page 272) and under other forms. The sub-contract incorporates the tender (clause 2.1.1), which includes details of the main contract and particular conditions relating to the sub-contract work, such as programme details.

In the conditions, the sub-contractor undertakes to comply with the main contract so far as it relates to the sub-contract works (clause 5.1.1) and gives wide indemnities to the contractor in respect of liability under the main contract and third party claims (clause 5.1.2). The sub-contractor must comply with the architect's instructions which the contractor issues to the sub-contractor in writing; the contractor may also issue reasonable directions in regard to the sub-contract works (clause 4.2).

The sub-contract tender may be for a lump sum, subject to adjustment in accordance with the conditions (clause 16); or may be subject to complete re-measurement (clause 17). Detailed rules for valuation are provided. The architect is required, by clause 30 of the main contract, to include the value of sub-contract work in certificates. The contractor must pay the sub-contractor (less permitted deductions, including two-and-a-half per cent. discount) within 17 days of the issue of a certificate. This ties in with the 14 days allowed for payment under the main contract (clause 30); but the main contractor must pay the sub-contractor whether he has himself been paid or not.

The sub-contractor undertakes to complete his work within the agreed programme. The contractor may grant extensions of time but only with the architect's consent (clause 11). Under clause 25 of the main contract the contractor is not liable for the sub-contractor's delay. If the sub-contractor fails to complete by the specified or extended date for completion, the contractor may claim any loss caused by the delay. But the contractor's right to claim or set-off such loss is dependent on the architect giving a certificate of delay under the main contract (clause 12). The sub-contractor is given a number or rights to obtain the benefit of, or to pursue disputes under, the main contract (clauses 11.3, 13.1, 21.7 and 22). The extent to which some of these provisions are enforceable or practicable is a matter of doubt.

ICE form of Sub-Contract

This document was issued by the Federation of Civil Engineering Contractors for use in conjunction with the ICE General Conditions of Contract 4th edition (1955). It remains in current use with the ICE conditions, 5th and 6th editions. A revision was issued in September 1984. Being drawn up by one body only, the form is a model of clarity, avoiding the obscurities of the main forms of contract.

The form contains a short recital for the parties' names, and five schedules. These are to contain *inter alia* particulars of the main contract, further documents to be incorporated, a description of the sub-contract works, the contract price and the completion period. The sub-contractor undertakes (save where the sub-contract otherwise requires) to perform the obligations of the contractor under the main contract in relation to the sub-contract works (clause 3(2)), and to indemnify the contractor against liability incurred by reason of any breach of the sub-contract (clause 3(3)).

The sub-contractor's obligations are not tied directly to the operations of the main contract. Thus, extensions of time may be granted without reference to the engineer; save that where the delaying event entitles the contractor to an extension, the sub-contractor's extension is not to exceed the extension under the main contract (clause 6). Instructions and variations ordered under the main contract do not bind the sub-contractor, unless the engineer's order is confirmed in writing by the contractor (clauses 7, 8). The contractor has the same general powers to give instructions under the sub-contract as the engineer has under the main contract, and the sub-contractor has the same rights in relation thereto (clause 7(2)). There is therefore wide scope, both for the exercise of such powers by the contractor and for making claims by the sub-contractors (see clause 13(1), (3), ICE main contract). The sub-contract also provides for vesting of the plant and materials in the contractor, so that these may vest in the employer under the main contract (clause 11: see also clause 53, ICE main contract).

After completion, the sub-contractor is required to maintain his work until completion of the main works and further to maintain them throughout the maintenance period of the main contract (clause 13). The sub-contractor's right to interim payment was, in the original version of the form, dependant upon the contractor having received payment from the employer (clause 15). In the revised form, the right of payment arises automatically after submission of the sub-contractor's statement. The contractor may, however, withhold payment, *inter alia*, where the amounts claimed for the sub-contractor's work are not certified by the engineer or not paid by the employer (clause 15(3)(*b*)). The contractor may determine the sub-contractor's employment if the main contract is determined (clause 16) or if the sub-contractor commits specified defaults corresponding broadly to those under clause 63 of the ICE main contract (clause 17). Disputes are to be referred directly to arbitration without the intervention of the engineer. If there is a dispute under the main contract concerning the sub-contract works, and if an arbitrator has not been appointed under the sub-contract, the contractor may require the sub-contract dispute to be dealt with jointly with the main contract dispute, by the same arbitrator; or if there are proceedings in court under the main contract, the contractor may avoid the arbitration clause and bring the sub-contractor into those proceedings (clause 18).

The form is not specifically designed for use with nominated sub-contractors. It contains provisions broadly in accordance with the minimum requirements for a nominated sub-contract (see clause 59(1), ICE main contract). The form is used both for nominated and direct sub-contracts.

Other Standard Forms

The forms dealt with above, together with the JCT and ICE forms of main contract are those likely to be encountered most often in practice. Mention should also be made of other types of standard form which are in general use.

Design-and-build contracts

As with management contracts, these come in many forms, often being ad hoc drafts. There is good reason for this, as the form of the contract is heavily dependent on the degree of design liability undertaken by the contractor. For example, if the employer wishes to specify the overall design, with the contractor being responsible for details, then the contract will need to contain performance requirements only for the elements that the contractor is to design, and these can be accommodated within a relatively conventional construction contract. However, if the contractor is to undertake the conceptual design as well as the details, then there needs to be a carefully drafted list of employer's requirements, which may go beyond mere technical performance. Further, the contractor, on submitting a tender, will usually put forward detailed proposals, and these will need to be incorporated. Consideration needs also to be given to the submission of details for approval as the work proceeds, and as to what is to happen if the employer is not satisfied or changes his mind.

The latter type of contract is reflected in the JCT Standard Form of Building Contract with Contractor's Design, issued in 1981 and amended on a number of occasions. This form provides for a statement of the employers requirements and the contractor's proposals. Clause 2 of the conditions requires the contractor to carry out and complete the work to these requirements and proposals, and for this purpose to complete the design of the works and carry it out. The contractor is under no further obligation to seek the employer's consent or approval to the details of the design, provided they accord with the requirements and proposals. The employer may make a change in his requirements after the contract has been let, but the contractor has a right of reasonable objection to any such change (if permitted, the change must be treated as a variation). In regard to the contractor's design work, the contract places on the contractor the like liability as would apply in the case of a professional designer, *i.e.* a duty of reasonable professional skill and care. This is to be contrasted with the position in the absence of any such provision, where there would ordinarily be an implied term that the work would be fit for purpose (see page 119).

Smaller works contracts

The JCT issues two forms of contract for smaller works: the minor building works form and the intermediate form. The range of work suitable for these forms is not defined.

The form of contract for minor building works, in keeping with its subject matter, is short. The form of contract was amended in 1980 in line with other JCT documents. The form deals fully with liability for, and insurance against, various risks. This is necessary since the consequential losses which may arise out of building works may bear no relation to the scale of the works. The form contains many of the provisions of the standard JCT contract in an abbreviated form. Thus, provisional sums are provided for, but not prime cost items. The architect may vary the works, including the order or period in which they are to be carried out. The contractor is entitled to interim payments at not less than four-weekly intervals.

In 1984 the JCT issued a new "intermediate" form of building contract known as IFC 84. This form follows closely the format of the minor building works form, while adopting much of the wording of JCT 80. Like the minor works form, IFC 84 contains no provision for prime cost sums or nomination. There is, however, provision for sub-contract work to be placed with a "named person" to be identified in the contract or specified by the architect (clause 3.3). The effect of the contract is to place the "named person" substantially in the same position as a nominated sub-contractor under the main forms, save that the contractor is not entitled to an extension of time for his delay. Where the named person "drops out" there is machinery for recovery of the loss.

More recently, the ICE have issued a form for minor works, which is accompanied by notes for guidance, stating that the form is intended for contracts of value not exceeding £100,000, with the completion period not exceeding six months. This form represents a concise version of the essential elements of the ICE general conditions, re-arranged and expressed in much simpler language. Among features to be noted is the requirement that the engineer is to be a named individual (clause 2.1). The traditional maintenance period is more accurately renamed as the "defects correction period" (clause 5). The contractor is made fully liable for acts or defaults of sub-contractors (clause 8.3). In regard to disputes, the contract provides a novel two-stage procedure, not involving a decision of the engineer. The parties are given an option whether to take their dispute to non-binding conciliation, in accordance with a separate written procedure (the ICE Conciliation Procedure 1988) or to arbitration (in accordance with the ICE Arbitration Procedure 1983, Short Procedure, Part F). Conciliation may be followed by arbitration, unless neither party gives a Notice to Refer within 28 days of receipt of the conciliator's recommendation, in which case it becomes binding on the parties (clause 11.4).

Model Form A

This form is issued by the Institutions of Mechanical and Electrical Engineers and the ACE, for contracts involving substantial elements of plant and machinery. The contract requires the appointment of an independent engineer but, unlike building and civil engineering contracts, there is no general obligation on the engineer to provide drawings and details. Clause 4 provides that the contractor is to submit to the engineer for approval drawings and details as required (clause 4). The engineer is given the usual powers to vary the work (clause 10), but the contractor's consent is required to the issue of variations in aggregate exceeding 15 per cent. of the contract price, any such excess giving rise to a claim. The contract contains elaborate provision for inspection and testing (clauses 14, 27). After final tests, the engineer is required to issue a "taking-over certificate." Thereafter, the contractor's responsibility is limited to defects appearing within 12 months after taking over (clause 30). It is important for users unfamiliar with this form to note that all rights of recourse against the contractor may be terminated at the end of this 12 months period, and it is vital for a thorough inspection to be made within this period. A form loosely based on this contract is issued by FIDIC for international contracts for electrical and mechanical works. This is colloquially known as the "FIDIC M & E" and contains similar excluding provisions regarding defects appearing within 12 months or such other period as may be specified, after taking over. A further domestic variant on this contract is the BEAMA form.

Ground investigation

The ICE, in 1983, issued a version of their conditions of contract amended for use in ground investigation work. The form is substantially the same as the ICE main contract, but with re-definition of the work to be carried out. The form is suitable only for investigation carried out under the control and supervision of an independantly employed engineer. Where, as is frequently the case, a site investigation contractor is employed to use his own expertise in the design and direction of the investigation, other conditions are appropriate. The Construction Industry Research and Information Association (CIRIA) has issued such a form as part of a recent report on methods of procurement in the ground investigation industry (CIRIA Special Publication 45).

Forms of warranty

This refers to a direct warranty to be given by a sub-contractor to the employer, which is discussed above, page 178. The RIBA have for some years published such forms. The form known as the Employer/Nominated Sub-Contractor Agreement is intended for use with nominated sub-contracts under the JCT form of main contract. This form has been re-issued by the JCT in an extended version for use with the 1980 edition of the main and sub-contract. There are two forms available, known as NSC/2 and NSC/2a, depending on whether or not the standard form of tender (NSC/1) is used. In each form the sub-contractor gives warranties of reasonable skill and care in regard to any design work undertaken, and in regard to delay in the sub-contract works. The employer gives warranties as to the operation of the direct payment provisions.

An alternative form of warranty exists for nominated suppliers. The supplier gives a warranty of skill and care in regard to design and a further (unqualified) warranty that goods shall comply with any performance specification. There are further warranties as to delay. The employer gives no cross-warranty. This form has not been re-issued with the 1980 edition of the JCT forms. Each of these forms is expressed to be subject to the employer's nomination. With suitable modification they may be made to operate in respect of any type of sub-contract, and with any form of main contract.

Warranties are now regularly requested and given by a range of parties involved in construction disputes (not limited to sub-contractors). Members of the professional team particularly are frequently asked to give a warranty regarding the design. Although some standard forms exist, there is considerable competition between those interested in narrowing the terms of warranties and those seeking to enlarge them. A list of relevant considerations is given on page 179. A matter of particular importance is the effect of assignment of such warranties, as to which see page 200.

Conditions of engagement

Architects and engineers usually employ standard conditions when they accept engagements. These invariably lay down in precise terms the fee-scale to be payable. This operates usually as a percentage of the value of the work. The conditions may also contain terms defining or limiting the scope of duties to be undertaken, and may therefore become important in a dispute.

The RIBA publish, and periodically revise, Conditions of Engagement for architects. The edition of June 1982 defines the architect's duty as the exercise of "reasonable skill and care in conformity with the normal standards of the architects profession." The conditions provide that where consultants are employed the architect has authority to co-ordinate and integrate their services; but the architect is not to be responsible for the performance of their work. Similarly, the architect is not responsible for design work entrusted to specialists or sub-contractors. In regard to supervision, the architect is required to visit the site at appropriate intervals, but is not to be held responsible for the proper execution of the contractor's work. This provision will not, however, exempt the architect fully from responsibility for supervision of the construction work.

Civil and structural engineers are usually engaged under the Association of Consulting Engineers (ACE) Conditions of Engagement. Engineers are required to work in a wide range of situations, and this is reflected in the provision of alternative forms of engagement. Agreement 1 covers reporting and advisory work; agreement 2 is for work where an architect is not appointed, so that the engineer is in full charge of supervision and administration; agreement 3 is for use where an architect is appointed, where the engineer's role is limited to structural work; agreement 4A covers engineering services in relation to sub-contract works and exists in three versions depending on the services taken on; and agreement 4B covers the provision of engineering services in relation to direct contract works.

Each version of the agreement contains general conditions together with clauses setting out the obligations of the engineer and the client. The standard of care undertaken by the engineer is defined as the exercise of "all reasonable skill care and diligence in the discharge of the services agreed to be performed." Each form of agreement contains a memorandum of agreement defining the services taken on. Both the ACE conditions and the RIBA Conditions of Engagement contain arbitration clauses.

Further Reading

Duncan Wallace, *Building and Civil Engineering Standard Forms* (1969).

CHAPTER 11

THE STANDARD FORM OF BUILDING CONTRACT

THE standard form of building contract is often referred to as the RIBA form because of its long association with that Institute. The form is intended for use with all types of building work. It is issued by the Joint Contracts Tribunal (JCT), whose constituent bodies include the RIBA, the RICS, the Association of Consulting Engineers, the Building Employers Confederation and bodies representing local authorities and sub-contractors. It is more correctly called the JCT form.

A new edition of the form was issued in 1980. It exists in versions for a private employer, or for a local authority; and with or without quantities, giving four combinations. There is also a version with approximate quantities. The different versions contain variations in detail rather than substance. The commentary which follows is based upon the local authorities' edition with quantities, but most of the provisions are common to all the forms. The issuing body makes periodic revisions of the forms which are published either as amendments or as revisions of the complete forms. There were substantial changes in 1987. The Commentary which follows includes amendments up to 1989. In the local authority forms "architect" becomes "architect/Contract Administrator," as it is contemplated that this office may be filled by an employee of the authority who may not be a qualified architect.

The published form contains articles of agreement, which may be executed under seal, an appendix, the conditions of contract, and a supplemental VAT agreement. The conditions create a "lump sum" contract, *i.e.* the contractor undertakes to carry out the work described and measured in the bills, for a stated sum of money. This is subject, however, to many possible alterations, on account, *inter alia*, of variations, price fluctuations and claims.

The conditions contemplate that the work will be carried out under the supervision of the architect/Contract Administrator (for brevity he will be referred to simply as "the architect"). Under the contract the architect is given powers and duties which are wide and important, but which are also limited in their scope. The powers of the architect are considerably less than those of the engineer under the ICE conditions (see Chapter 12), reflecting the less hazardous nature of building work compared to civil engineering construction.

The previous edition of the JCT forms was issued in 1963, and is still used by some clients, being preferred not least for its comparative brevity. The main changes introduced by the 1980 form will therefore be outlined. The cosmetic changes consist of re-numbering and re-grouping of the provisions. Decimal numbering of sub-clauses is adopted throughout; a new definitions clause is added (clause 1); the grounds and procedure for making claims are consolidated into a single clause (26); the clauses are divided into four sections, namely Part 1: General (clauses 1–34), Part 2: Nominated Sub-contractors and suppliers (clauses 35–36); Part 3: Fluctuations (clauses 37–40), and Part 4: Arbitration (clause 41). The principal change in substance is the massive enlargement of terms covering nomination, which (as in the ICE conditions, clauses 58–59) attempts to legislate in detail for the problems arising from defaults. These provisions must now be read with other standardised documents, *viz.* a form of tender (NSC/1), form of employer/sub-contractor agreement (NSC/2) and form of nominated sub-contract (NSC/4). There is also a standard form for nomination (NSC/3).

This commentary does not deal with every aspect of the JCT forms. It is intended as an introduction to the basic working of the contract. The most important clauses or sub-clauses are printed, with notes as to their effect. Other clauses are referred to where appropriate. Some clauses are omitted as being not essential to the basic scheme of the form. These clauses may, of course, be vital to any particular issue or dispute. For a full exposition on the form, reference must be made to the document itself and to one of the standard works noted at the end of the chapter.

THE CONTRACT

The form contemplates that a contract will be made by the parties executing the articles of agreement. This is not essential.

The conditions of contract may be incorporated by reference in any other document of agreement. But the articles provide, in the recitals, for specifying the names of the parties, a brief description of the works and a list of contract drawings.

The articles themselves state:

Now it is hereby agreed as follows

Article 1

For the consideration hereinafter mentioned the Contractor will upon and subject to the Contract Documents carry out and complete the Works shown upon, described by or referred to in those Documents.

Article 2

The employer will pay to the Contractor the sum of .... (hereinafter referred to as 'the Contract Sum') or such other sum as shall become payable hereunder and in the manner specified in the Conditions.

In articles 3A or B and 4 the architect and quantity surveyor are to be named. Article 5 contains the arbitration clause; but the detailed provisions are contained in clause 41. Arbitration remains mandatory.

By clause 2·1 the contractor is required to carry out the work "shown upon the Contract Drawings and described by or referred to in the Contract Bills and in the Articles of Agreement, the Conditions and the Appendix (which Drawings, Bills, Articles of Agreement, Conditions and Appendix are in this Contract referred to collectively as 'the Contract Documents')."

The relative effect of these contract documents is provided for as follows:

14·1 The quality and the quantity of the work included in the Contract Sum shall be deemed to be that which is set out in the Contract Bills.

14·2 .....

2·2 ·1 Nothing contained in the Contract Bills shall override or modify the application or interpretation of that which is contained in the Articles of agreement, the Conditions or the Appendix.

2·2 ·2 Subject always to clause 2·2·1:

·2·1 the Contract Bills, unless otherwise specifically stated therein in respect of any specified item or items, are to have been prepared in accordance with the Standard Method of Measurement of Building Works, 7th Edition published by the Royal Institution of Chartered Surveyors and the Building Employers Confederation;

·2·2 if in the Contract Bills there is any departure from the method of preparation referred to in clause 2·2·2·1 or any error in description or in quantity or omission of items (including any error in or omission of information in any item which is the subject of a provisional sum for defined work) then such departure or error or omission shall not vitiate this Contract but the departure or error or omission shall be corrected; where the description of a provisional sum for defined work does not provide the information required by General Rule 10.3 in the Standard Method of Measurement the correction shall be made by correcting the description so that it does provide such information; and such correction under this clause 2·2·2·2 shall be treated as if it were a Variation required by an instruction of the Architect under clause 13·2.

2·3 ......

The effect of these clauses is that, save for questions of the quality or quantity of the work, the conditions override the contract bills. A provision intended to amend the conditions (such as one for sectional completion) may therefore be ineffective if placed in the bills. But see clauses 13·1 and 25·4·12, which contemplate that the bills or drawings may limit the contractor's access to or use of the site and the order in which the work is to be carried out. See also clause 29, below. The bills will also override the contract drawings so that, while the contractor must perform the work shown on the drawings, any part which is not included in the bills is an extra, to be paid for. In a contract of any size there is likely also to be a specification or descriptive schedule. This, however, is not of itself a contract document and must be incorporated, for example, into the bills. The effect of the articles and conditions is dealt with as follows:

1·2 The Articles of Agreement, the conditions and the Appendix are to be read as a whole and the effect or operation of any article or clause in the Conditions or item in or entry in the Appendix must therefore unless otherwise specifically stated be read subject to any relevant qualification or modification in any other article or any of the clauses in the Conditions or item in or entry in the Appendix.

1·3 .....

The articles and conditions therefore rank equally in the event of an ambiguity, and neither may be overridden by the contract bills or drawings.

The architect is given the power and duty to supply such further details as are necessary.

5·3 ·1 So soon as is possible after the execution of this Contract:

·1 ·1 the Architect without charge to the Contractor shall provide him (unless he shall have been previously so provided) with two copies of any descriptive schedules or other like documents necessary for use in carrying out the Works.....

5·3 ·2 Nothing contained in the descriptive schedules or other like documents referred to in clause 5·3·1·1 . . . shall impose any obligation beyond those imposed by the Contract Documents.

5·4 As and when from time to time may be necessary the Architect without charge to the Contractor shall provide him with two copies of such further drawings or details as are reasonably necessary either to explain and amplify the Contract Drawings or to enable the Contractor to carry out and complete the Works in accordance with the Conditions.

5·5 ......

The architect is further required to provide drawings for setting out the work:

7. The Architect shall determine any levels which may be required for the execution of the Works, and shall provide the Contractor by way of accurately dimensioned drawings with such information as shall enable the Contractor to set out the Works at ground level. The Contractor shall be responsible for, and shall, at no cost to the Employer, amend any errors arising from his own inaccurate setting out. With the consent of the Employer the Architect may instruct that such errors shall not be amended and an appropriate deduction for such errors not required to be amended shall be made from the Contract Sum.

Control of the Work

The conditions envisage that the work will be under the general supervision of the architect. The RIBA conditions of engagement, used by many architects, provide for periodic but not constant supervision. Day-to-day site supervision is therefore left to the contractor and to the employer.

10. The Contractor shall constantly keep upon the Works a competent person-in-charge and any instructions given to him by the Architect or directions given to him by the clerk of works in accordance with clause 12 shall be deemed to have been issued to the Contractor.

11. The Architect and his representatives shall at all reasonable times have access to the Works and to the workshops or other places of the Contractor where work is being prepared for this Contract, and when work is to be so prepared in workshops or other places of a Domestic Sub-Contractor or a Nominated Sub-Contractor the Contractor shall by a term in the sub-contract so far as possible secure a similar right of access to those workshops or places for the Architect and his representatives and shall do all things reasonably necessary to make such right effective. Access in accordance with clause 11 may be subject to such reasonable restrictions of the Contractor or any Domestic Sub-Contractor or any Nominated Sub-Contractor as are necessary to protect any proprietary right of the Contractor or of any Domestic or Nominated Sub-Contractor in the work referred to in clause 11.

12. The Employer shall be entitled to appoint a clerk of works whose duty shall be to act solely as inspector on behalf of the Employer under the directions of the Architect and the Contractor shall afford every reasonable facility for the performance of that duty. If any direction is given to the Contractor by the clerk of works the same shall be of no effect unless given in regard to a matter in respect of which the Architect is expressly empowered by the Conditions to issue instructions and unless confirmed in writing by the Architect within two working days of such direction being given. If any such direction is so given and confirmed then as from the date of issue of that confirmation it shall be deemed to be an Architect's instruction.

On larger projects the architect and employer may agree to employ a resident architect on the works. But he will have no specific power or duty such as those of the Engineers' Representative under the ICE conditions.

GENERAL OBLIGATIONS OF THE CONTRACTOR

The contractor's basic obligations are to comply with the contract documents, which define the work and the time within which it is to be done, and to comply with proper instructions of the architect.

2·1 The Contractor shall upon and subject to the Conditions carry out and complete the Works shown upon the Contract Drawings and described by or referred to in the Contract Bills and in the Articles of Agreement, the Conditions and the Appendix (which Drawings, Bills, Articles of Agreement, Conditions and Appendix are in this Contract referred to collectively as 'the Contract Documents') in compliance therewith, using materials and workmanship of the quality and standards therein specified, provided that where and to the extent that approval of the quality of materials or of the standards of workmanship is a matter for the opinion of the Architect, such quality and standards shall be to the reasonable satisfaction of the Architect.

2·2 .....

The "works" are defined by clause 1·3 as "the works briefly described in the First recital and shown and described in the Contract Drawings and in the Contract Bills." The recital to the articles will not add to the technical description of the work, but may be an aid to construction in case of ambiguity, for example, as to the location or purpose of the work.

Clause 2·3 requires the contractor to give notice of any discrepancy or divergence between the drawings, the bills, and the architect's instructions, and for the architect to issue further instructions in regard thereto.

Clause 2·1 emphasises that, under the conditions, the architect has no general power of approval or control. Where work or materials are required by the bills to be "to the approval of the architect," sub-clause 1 means that the item is required only to meet the architect's reasonable satisfaction (since by clause 2·2 the conditions override the bills). Where there is no stipulation for the architect's approval, his function is to ensure compliance with the contract documents.

4·1 ·1 The Contractor shall forthwith comply with all instructions issued to him by the Architect in regard to any matter in respect of which the Architect is expressly empowered by the Conditions to issue instructions; save that where such instruction is one requiring a Variation within the meaning of clause 13·1·2 the Contractor need not comply to the extent that he makes reasonable objection in writing to the Architect to such compliance.

4·1 ·2 If within seven days after receipt of a written notice from the Architect requiring compliance with an instruction the Contractor does not comply therewith, then the Employer may employ and pay other persons to execute any work whatsoever which may be necessary to give effect to such instruction; and all costs incurred in connection with such employment may be deducted by him from any monies due or to become due to the Contractor under this Contract or may be recoverable from the Contractor by the Employer as a debt.

4·2 ......

This provision makes it clear that the architect's powers are limited to those expressly contained in the contract. The machinery entitling the employer to bring in another contractor in the event of non-compliance with an architect's instruction is a valuable sanction. Clause 4·2 allows the contractor to challenge an instruction by asking under what power it is given. If dissatisfied, the contractor may seek immediate arbitration (clause 41·3·2). Clause 4·3 requires instructions to be given in writing and allows either the contractor or the architect to confirm oral instructions in writing.

Clause 13·1·2 empowers the architect by variation order, to change the specified access to or use of the site or the order in which the work is to be done. It is not clear what limits are to be placed on the grounds of a reasonable objection. Ordinarily, expense would not be a proper ground, it is submitted, since the contract provides for reimbursement (clauses 13 and 26).

The contractor's right to uninterrupted possession of the site may be restricted by the bills or otherwise by agreement.

29·1 Where the Contract Bills, in regard to any work not forming part of this Contract and which is to be carried out by the Employer himself or by persons employed or otherwise engaged by him, provide such information as is necessary to enable the Contractor to carry out and complete the Works in accordance with the Conditions, the Contractor shall permit the execution of such work.

29·2 Where the Contract Bills do not provide the information referred to in clause 29·1 and the Employer requires the execution of work not forming part of this Contract by the Employer himself or by persons employed or otherwise engaged by the Employer, then the Employer may, with the consent of the Contractor (which consent shall not be unreasonably withheld) arrange for the execution of such work.

29·3 Every person employed or otherwise engaged by the Employer as referred to in clauses 29·1 and 29·2 shall for the purpose of clause 20 be deemed to be a person for whom the Employer is responsible and not to be a sub-contractor.

Note that clause 25·4·8·1 (see below) provides for an extension of time, whether or not such work is contemplated by the bills.

Apportionment of various risks arising out of the work and requirements as to insurances are dealt with in clauses 20 to 22.

20·1 The Contractor shall be liable for, and shall indemnify the Employer against, any expense, liability, loss, claim or proceedings whatsoever arising under any statute or at common law in respect of personal injury to or the death of any person whomsoever arising out of or in the course of or caused by the carrying out of the Works, except to the extent that the same is due to any act or neglect of the Employer or of any person for whom the Employer is responsible including the persons employed or otherwise engaged by the Employer to whom clause 29 refers.

20·2 The Contractor shall, subject to clause 20·3 and, where applicable, clause 22C·1, be liable for, and shall indemnify the Employer against, any expense, liability, loss, claim or proceedings in respect of any injury or damage whatsoever to any property real or personal in so far as such injury or damage arises out of or in the course of or by reason of the carrying out of the Works, and to the extent that the same is due to any negligence, breach of statutory duty, omission or default of the Contractor, his servants or agents or of any person employed or engaged upon or in connection with the Works or any part thereof, his servants or agents or of any other person who may properly be on the site upon or in connection with the Works or any part thereof, his servants or agents, other than the Employer or any person employed, engaged or authorised by him or by any local authority or statutory undertaker executing work solely in pursuance of its statutory rights or obligations.

20·3 ·1 Subject to clause 20·3·2 the reference in clause 20·2 to 'property real or personal' does not include the Works, work executed and/or Site Materials up to and including the date of issue of the certificate of Practical Completion or up to and including the date of determination of the employment of the Contractor (whether or not the validity of that determination is disputed) under clause 27 or clause 28 or clause 28A, where clause 22C applies, under clause 27 or clause 28 or clause 28A or clause 22C·4·3, whichever is the earlier.

20·3 ·2 If clause 18 has been operated then, in respect of the relevant part, and as from the relevant date such relevant part shall not be regarded as 'the Works' or 'work executed' for the purpose of clause 20·3·1.

Clause 20·1 renders the contractor liable for third party claims in respect of personal injury, unless due to any act or neglect of the employer. Clause 20·2 renders the contractor liable for third party claims in respect of damage to property only when the contractor is at fault. The words "any property" could include the works themselves, but clause 20·3·1 makes clear that this is not so. However, the effect of clause 20·3·2 is that parts of the Works which have been taken over will qualify as other property for the purpose of clause 20·2. Further, the duty to carry out and complete the works, under clause 2 means that the contractor is generally liable for damage to the works, unless due to the employer's default.

Clause 21·1 requires the contractor to maintain insurance against his own liability under clause 20. Clause 21·2 requires the contractor, where a provisional sum is included in the bills, to take out insurance in the joint names of the employer and the contractor against claims for damage to property other than the works, caused (broadly) by the carrying out of the works. However, this cover is of limited use because of the wide-ranging exceptions provided, namely damage:

21·2·1. . .

·1·1 for which the Contractor is liable under clause 20·2;

·1·2 attributable to errors or omissions in the designing of the Works;

·1·3 which can reasonably be foreseen to be inevitable having regard to the nature of the work to be executed or the manner of its execution;

·1·4 which is the responsibility of the Employer to insure under clause 22C·1 (if applicable);

·1·5 arising from war risks or the Excepted Risks.

21·2·2. . .

The range of cover required is, therefore, very limited, effectively covering unforeseeable accident in the absence of fault. The Excepted Risks are defined in clause 1·3 and cover, broadly, radiation, explosion and like matters.

Clause 22 sets out three alternative provisions (clauses 22A, B and C) by which the main insurance of the Works is to be effected. The cover required is defined in clause 22·2 as "cover against any physical loss or damage to work executed and site materials" but excluding cost under three heads being (broadly) (1) property which is itself defective, (2) defective designs, (3) certain excluded risks, including the Excepted Risks. The three ways in which the main insurance may be placed are described in a note to the form as follows:

> Clause 22A is applicable to the erection of new buildings where the Contractor is required to take out a Joint Names Policy for All Risks Insurance for the Works and clause 22B is applicable where the Employer has elected to take out such Joint Names Policy. Clause 22C is to be used for alterations of or extensions to existing structures under which the Employer is required to take out a Joint Names Policy for All Risks Insurance for the Works and also a Joint Names Policy to insure the existing structures and their contents owned by him or for which he is responsible against loss or damage thereto by the Specified Perils.

The contractor is solely responsible for his method of work and for any temporary works (such as scaffolding) plant and equipment. The architect is given no powers either of approval or control, save for the limited power under clause 13·1·2 (see below).

Workmanship and materials

8·1 ·1 All materials and goods shall, so far as procurable, be of the kinds and standards described in the Contract Bills, provided that materials and goods shall be to the reasonable satisfaction of the Architect where and to the extent that this is required in accordance with clause 2·1.

8·1 ·2 All workmanship shall be of the standards described in the Contract Bills, or, to the extent that no such standards are described in the Contract Bills, shall be of a standard appropriate to the Works, provided that workmanship shall be to the reasonable satisfaction of the Architect where and to the extent that this is required in accordance with clause 2·1.

8·2 ·1 The Contractor shall upon the request of the Architect provide him with vouchers to prove that the materials and goods comply with clause 8·1.

8·2 ·2 In respect of any materials, goods or workmanship, as comprised in executed work, which are to be to the reasonable satisfaction of the Architect in accordance with clause 2·1, the Architect/shall express any dissatisfaction within a reasonable time from the execution of the unsatisfactory work.

8·3 The Architect may issue instructions requiring the Contractor to open up for inspection any work covered up or to arrange for or carry out any test of any materials or goods (whether or not already incorporated in the Works) or of any executed work, and the cost of such opening up or testing (together with the cost of making good in consequence thereof) shall be added to the Contract Sum unless provided for in the Contract Bills or unless the inspection or test shows that the materials, goods or work are not in accordance with this Contract.

8·4 If any work, materials or goods are not in accordance with this Contract the Architect without prejudice to the generality of his powers, may:

8·4 ·1 issue instructions in regard to the removal from the site of all or any of such work, materials or goods; and/or

8·4 ·2 after consultation with the Contractor (who shall immediately consult with any relevant Nominated Sub-Contractor) and with the agreement of the Employer, allow all or any of such work, materials or goods to remain and confirm this in writing to the Contractor (which shall not be construed as a Variation) and where so allowed and confirmed an appropriate deduction shall be made in the adjustment of the Contract Sum; and/or

8·4 ·3 after consultation with the Contractor (who shall immediately consult with any relevant Nominated Sub-Contractor) issue such instructions requiring a Variation as are reasonably necessary as a consequence of such an instruction under clause 8·4·1 or such confirmation under clause 8·4·2 and to the extent that such instructions are so necessary and notwithstanding clauses 13·4, 24 and 26 no addition to the Contract Sum shall be made and no extension of time shall be given; and/or

8·4 ·4 having had due regard to the Code of Practice appended to these Conditions, issue such instructions under clause 8·3 to open up for inspection or to test as are reasonable in all the circumstances to establish to the reasonable satisfaction of the Architect the likelihood or extent, as appropriate to the circumstances, of any further similar non-compliance. To the extent that such instructions are so reasonable, whatever the results of the opening up for inspection or test, and notwithstanding clauses 8·3 and 26 no addition to the Contract Sum shall be made. Clause 25·4·5·2 shall apply unless as stated therein the inspection or test showed that the work, materials or goods were not in accordance with this Contract.

8·5 The Architect may (but not unreasonably or vexatiously) issue instructions requiring the exclusion from the Works of any person employed thereon.

This clause has been substantially expanded to deal with a number of potential difficulties under the original clause contained in JCT 80. The requirement for the architect to express dissatisfaction within a reasonable time (8.2.2) is new. Likewise, the provisions for allowing non-complying work materials or goods to remain with a deduction from the contract sum is new to the contract, although it probably reflects a common practice. Clause 8.4.4 provides a useful mechanism, by use of the Code of Practice, for discovering the extent of defects, without running the risk of having to pay where work is found to comply with the contract. Note that there is no power to order replacement of defective work; this obligation remains on the contractor, however, by virtue of the obligation to complete the works, under clause 2.1. If the contractor fails to comply with an instruction under clause 8.4, the architect may invoke clause 4.1.2. Alternatively, there is a final sanction of determination under clause 27.1.3.

Independent of the contract, the work must, by law, comply with various statutory requirements (see Chapter 14). Difficult questions can arise in the event of conflict between these requirements and the architect's design. This is dealt with as follows:

6·1 ·1 Subject to clause 6·1·5 the Contractor shall comply with, and give all notices required by, any Act of Parliament, any instrument, rule or order made under any Act of Parliament, or any regulation or byelaw of any local authority or of any statutory undertaker which has any jurisdiction with regard to the Works or with whose systems the same are or will be connected (all requirements to be so complied with being referred to in the Conditions as "the Statutory Requirements").

6·1 ·2 If the Contractor shall find any divergence between the Statutory Requirements and all or any of the documents referred to in clause 2·3 or between the Statutory Requirements and any instruction of the Architect requiring a Variation issued in accordance with clause 13·2, he shall immediately give to the Architect a written notice specifying the divergence.

6·1 ·3 If the Contractor gives notice under clause 6·1·2 or if the Architect shall otherwise discover or receive notice of a divergence between the Statutory Requirements and all or any of the documents referred to in clause 2·3 or between the Statutory Requirements and any instructions requiring a Variation issued in accordance with clause 13·2, the Architect shall within 7 days of the discovery or receipt of a notice issue instructions in relation to the divergence. If and insofar as the instructions require the Works to be varied, they shall be treated as if they were Architect's instructions requiring a Variation issued in accordance with clause 13·2.

6·1·4 .....

6·1 ·5 Provided that the Contractor complies with clause 6·1·2 the Contractor shall not be liable to the Employer under this Contract if the Works do not comply with the Statutory Requirements where and to the extent that such non-compliance of the Works results from the Contractor having carried out work in accordance with the documents referred to in clause 2·3 or with any instruction requiring a Variation issued by the Architect in accordance with clause 13·2.

6·2 ......

Provided the contractor adheres to the contract documents, his obligation is limited to giving notice to the architect of any breach of statutory requirements which he in fact discovers. The additional cost of taking down and rebuilding work so as to comply with by-laws is then likely to fall on the architect. Clause 6·1·4 deals with emergency works, carried out before receiving instructions.

Completion and maintenance

The contractor's obligations fall into two separate periods: the period up to the certificate of practical completion, when the work is carried out; and the defects liability period, during which the contractor must make good any defects. These are dealt with as follows:

17·1 When in the opinion of the Architect Practical Completion of the Works is achieved, he shall forthwith issue a certificate to that effect and Practical Completion of the Works shall be deemed for all the purposes of this Contract to have taken place on the day named in such certificate.

17·2 Any defects, shrinkages or other faults which shall appear within the Defects Liability Period and which are due to materials or workmanship not in accordance with this Contract or to frost occurring before Practical Completion of the Works, shall be specified by the Architect in a schedule of defects which he shall deliver to the Contractor as an instruction of the Architect not later than 14 days after the expiration of the said Defects Liability Period, and within a reasonable time after receipt of such schedule the defects, shrinkages and other faults therein specified shall be made good by the Contractor at no cost to the Employer unless the Architect with the consent of the Employer shall otherwise instruct; and if the Architect does so otherwise instruct then an appropriate deduction in respect of any such defects, shrinkages or other faults not made good shall be made from the Contract Sum.

17·3 Notwithstanding clause 17·2 the Architect may whenever he considers it necessary so to do, issue instructions requiring any defect, shrinkage or other fault which shall apppear within the Defects Liability Period and which is due to materials or workmanship not in accordance with this Contract or to frost occurring before Practical Completion of the Works, to be made good, and the Contractor shall within a reasonable time after receipt of such instructions comply with the same and at no cost to the Employer unless the Architect with the consent of the Employer shall otherwise instruct; and if the Architect does so otherwise instruct then an appropriate deduction in respect of any such defects, shrinkages or other faults no made good shall be made from the Contract Sum. Provided that no such instructions shall be issued after delivery of a schedule of defects or after 14 days from the expiration of the Defects Liability Period.

17·4 When in the opinion of the Architect any defects, shrinkages or other faults which he may have required to be made good under clauses 17·2 and 17·3 shall have been made good he shall issue a certificate to that effect, and completion of making good defects shall be deemed for all the purposes of this Contract to have taken place on the day named in such certificate (the "Certificate of Completion of Making Good Defects").

17·5 In no case shall the Contractor be required to make good at his own cost any damage by frost which may appear after Practical Completion, unless the Architect shall certify that such damage is due to injury which took place before Practical Completion.

Clauses 17·2 and 17·3 have been amended so as to provide expressly that, with the employer's consent, there may be a deduction from the contract sum in lien of making good.

The contractor's liability for defects is limited to those which are "due to materials or workmanship not in accordance with the contract or to frost." If defects become manifest due to some other cause, such as unsuitability of the design, the contractor is not obliged to carry out rectification; nor can the architect exercise his power to order a variation after practical completion, it is submitted. The contractor becomes entitled to payment of the retention money, half on the certificate of practical completion and the remainder on the certificate of completion of making good defects (clause 30·4·1).

Clause 18 provides for the consequences of the employer (with the contractor's consent) taking possession of any completed part of the works before completion of the whole. This stipulates for a separate defects liability period in respect of the part, starting when possession is taken; and for proportional reductions in the value of the works to be insured and in liquidated damages. The retention money will be reduced by virtue of clause 30·4·1·2.

Time

The speed with which the contractor carries out the work is likely to be an important element in the performance of the contract. The contract stipulates, in the apendix, for fixed dates of possession and completion, but the period of the work may become extended under the contract.

23·1 ·1 On the Date of Possession possession of the site shall be given to the Contractor who shall thereupon begin the Works, regularly and diligently proceed with the same and shall complete the same on or before the Completion Date.

23·1 ·2 Where clause 23·1·2 is stated in the Appendix to apply the Employer may defer the giving of possession for a period not exceeding six weeks or such lesser period stated in the Appendix calculated from the Date of Possession.

23·2 The Architect may issue instructions in regard to the postponement of any work to be executed under the provisions of this Contract.

23·3 .....

Failure to proceed regularly and diligently may lead to determination under clause 27·1·2. Apart from this sanction and any stipulation in the bills (see note to clause 2·2·1 above), the contractor may proceed at his own pace. The architect is entitled to be provided with a programme, but this does not bind the contractor to perform in accordance with it. The option to defer giving possession under clause 23·1·2 is new; if exercised it qualifies for an extension of time, by clause 25·4·13.

5·3 ·1·2 the Contractor without charge to the Employer shall provide the Architect (unless he shall have been previously so provided) with 2 copies of his master programme for the execution of the Works and within 14 days of any decision by the Architect under clause 25·3·1 or 33·1·3 with 2 copies of any amendments and revisions to take account of that decision.

5·3 ·2 Nothing contained in the . . . (master programme for the execution of the Works or any amendment to that programme or revision therein referred to in clause 5·3·1·2) shall impose any obligation beyond those imposed by the Contract Documents.

5·4 .....

The contractor's programme is of use, however, in giving notice to the architect as to when instructions may be needed (note that clause 26·2·1 still requires written notice); the programme is also some evidence of what constitutes diligent progress.

24·1 If the Contractor fails to complete the Works by the Completion Date then the Architect shall issue a certificate to that effect.

24·2 ·1 Subject to the issue of a certificate under clause 24·1 the Contractor shall, as the Employer may require in writing not later than the date of the Final Certificate, pay or allow to the Employer the whole or such part as may be specified in writing by the Employer of a sum calculated at the rate stated in the Appendix as liquidated and ascertained damages for the period between the Completion Date and the date of Practical Completion and the Employer may deduct the same from any monies due or to become due to the Contractor under this Contract (including any balance stated as due to the Contractor in the Final Certificate) or the Employer may recover the same from the Contractor as a debt.

24·2 ·2 If, under clause 25·3·3 the Architect fixes a later Completion Date the Employer shall pay or repay to the Contractor any amounts recovered allowed or paid under clause 24·2·1 for the period up to such later Completion Date.

The completion date is defined by clause 1·3 as:

The Date for Completion as fixed and stated in the Appendix or any later date fixed under either clause 25 or 33·1·3.

Completion of the works refers to "practical completion" under clause 17·1. The works may be deemed completed although they contain defects which come to light later (see page 188). In this event the employer is not limited to the liquidated damages for delay, but may prove his actual loss. When liquidated damages are recoverable the employer is "empowered" recover part only of the sum due. The reason for introducing this provision is obscure. It may be intended to avoid repayment where a further extension is likely. It is not clear whether election to recover part only operates as waiver of the balance.

The list of grounds entitling the contractor to an extension of time are set out in clause 25. If the work is delayed by a default on the part of the employer which does not permit an extension of time, the liquidated damages clause becomes unenforceable (see page 189).

25·1 In clause 25 any reference to delay, notice or extension of time includes further delay, further notice or further extension of time.

25·2 ·1 ·1 If and whenever it becomes reasonably apparent that the progress of the Works is being or is likely to be delayed the Contractor shall forthwith give written notice to the Architect of the material circumstances including the cause or causes of the delay and identify in such notice any event which in his opinion is a Relevant Event.

·1 ·2 Where the material circumstances of which written notice has been given under clause 25·2·1·1 include reference to a Nominated Sub-Contractor, the Contractor shall forthwith send a copy of such written notice to the Nominated Sub-Contractor concerned.

25·2 ·2 In respect of each and every Relevant Event identified in the notice given in accordance with clause 25·2·1·1 the Contractor shall, if practicable in such notice, or otherwise in writing as soon as possible after such notice:

·2 ·1 give particulars of the expected effects thereof; and

·2 ·2 estimate the extent, if any, of the expected delay in the completion of the Works beyond the Completion Date resulting there-from whether or not concurrently with delay resulting from any other Relevant Event and shall give such particulars and estimate to any Nominated Sub-Contractor to whom a copy of any written notice has been given under clause 25·2·1·2.

25·2 ·3 The Contractor shall give such further written notice to the architect and send a copy to any Nominated Sub-Contractor to whom a copy of any written notice has been given under clause 25·2·1·2, as may be reasonably necessary or as the Architect may reasonably require for keeping up-to-date the particulars and estimate referred to in clauses 25·2·2·1 and 25·2·2·2 including any material change in such particulars or estimate.

25·3 ·1 If, in the opinion of the Architect, upon receipt of any notice, particulars and estimate under clauses 25·2·1·1 and 25·2·2,

·1 ·1 any of the events which are stated by the Contractor to be the cause of the delay is a Relevant Event, and

·1 ·2 the completion of the Works is likely to be delayed thereby beyond the Completion Date

the Architect shall in writing to the Contractor give an extension of time by fixing such later date as the Completion Date as he then estimates to be fair and reasonable. The Architect shall, in fixing such new Completion Date, state:

·1 ·3 which of the Relevant Events he has taken into account, and

·1 ·4 the extent, if any, to which he has had regard to any instruction under clause 13·2 requiring as a Variation the ommission of any work issued since the fixing of the previous Completion Date,

and shall, if reasonably practicable having regard to the sufficiency of the aforesaid notice, particulars and estimates, fix such new Completion Date not later than 12 weeks from receipt of the notice and of reasonably sufficient particulars and estimate, or, where the period between receipt thereof and the Completion Date is less that 12 weeks, not later than the Completion Date.

If, in the opinion of the Architect, upon receipt of any such notice, particulars and estimate it is not fair and reasonable to fix a later date as a new Completion Date, the Architect shall if reasonably practicable having regard to the sufficiency of the aforesaid notice, particulars and estimate so notify the Contractor in writing not later than 12 weeks from receipt of the notice, particulars and estimate, or, where the period between receipt thereof and the Completion Date is less than 12 weeks, not later than the Completion Date.

25·3 ·2 After the first exercise by the Architect of his duty under clause 25·3 ·1 the Architect may in writing fix a Completion Date earlier than that previously fixed under clause 25 if in his opinion the fixing of such earlier Completion Date is fair and reasonable having regard to the omission of any work or obligation instructed or sanctioned by the Architect under clause 13 after the last occasion on which the Architect fixed a new Completion Date.

25·3 ·3 After the Completion Date, if this occurs before the date of Practical Completion, the Architect may, and not later than the expiry of

12 weeks after the date of Practical Completion, shall in writing to the Contractor either

·3 ·1 fix a Completion Date later than that previously fixed if in his opinion the fixing of such later Completion Date is fair and reasonable having regard to any of the Relevant Events, whether upon reviewing a previous decision or otherwise and whether or not the Relevant Event has been specifically notified by the Contractor under clause 25·2·1·1; or

·3 ·2 fix a Completion Date earlier than that previously fixed under clause 25 if in his opinion the fixing of such earlier Completion Date is fair and reasonable having regard to the omission of any work or obligation instructed or sanctioned by the Architect/the Contract Administrator under clause 13 after the last occasion on which the Architect/the Contract Administrator fixed a new Completion Date; or

·3 ·3 confirm to the Contractor the Completion Date previously fixed.

25·3 ·4 Provided always

·4 ·1 the Contractor shall use constantly his best endeavours to prevent delay in the progress of the Works, howsoever caused, and to prevent the completion of the Works being delayed or futher delayed beyond the Completion Date;

·4 ·2 the Contractor shall do all that may reasonably be required to the satisfaction of the Architect to proceed with the Works.

25·3 ·5 The Architect shall notify in writing to every Nominated Sub-Contractor each decision of the Architect under clause 25·3 fixing a Completion Date.

25·3 ·6 No decision of the Architect under clause 25·3 shall fix a Completion Date earlier than the Date for Completion stated in the Appendix.

25·4 The following are the Relevant Events referred to in clause 25:

25·4 ·1 force majeure;

25·4 ·2 exceptionally adverse weather conditions;

25·4 ·3 loss or damage occasioned by any one or more of the Specified Perils;

25·4 ·4 civil commotion, local combination of workmen, strike or lock-out affecting any of the trades employed upon the Works or any of the trades engaged in the preparation, manufacture or transportation of any of the goods or materials required for the Works;

25·4 ·5 compliance with the Architect's instructions

25·4 ·5 ·1 under clause 2·3, 13·2, 13·3 (*except compliance with an Architect's instruction for the expenditure of a provisional sum for defined work*) 23·2, 34, 35 or 36; or

·5 ·2 in regard to the opening up for inspection of any work covered up or the testing of any of the work, materials or goods in accordance with clause 8·3 (including making good in consequence of such opening up or testing) unless the inspection or test showed that the work, materials or goods were not in accordance with this Contract;

25·4 ·6 The Contractor not having received in due time necessary instructions (*including those for or in regard to the expenditure of provisonal sums*), drawings, details or levels from the Architect for which he specifically applied in writing provided that such application was made on a date which having regard to the Completion Date was neither unreasonably distant from nor unreasonably close to the date on which it was necessary for him to receive the same;

25·4 ·7 delay on the part of Nominated Sub-Contractors or Nominated Suppliers which the Contractor has taken all practicable steps to avoid or reduce;

25·4 ·8 ·1 the execution of work not forming part of this Contract by the Employer himself or by persons employed or otherwise engaged by the Employer as referred to in clause 29 or the filure to execute such work;

·8 ·2 the supply by the Employer of materials and goods which the Employer has agreed to provide for the Works or the failure so to supply;

25·4 ·9 the exercise after the Base Date by the United Kingdom Government of any statutory power which directly affects the execution of the Works by restricting the availability or use of labour which is essential to the proper carrying out of the Works or preventing the Contractor from, or delaying the Contractor in, securing such goods or materials or such fuel or energy as are essential to the proper carrying out of the Works;

25·4 ·10 ·1 the Contractor's inability for reasons beyond his control and which he could not reasonably have foreseen at the Base Date to secure such labour as is essential to the proper carrying out of the Works; or

·10 ·2 the Contractor's inability for reasons beyond his control and which he could not reasonably have foreseen at the Base Date to secure such goods or materials as are essential to the proper carrying out of the Works;

25·4 ·11 the carrying out by a local authority or statutory undertaker of work in pursuance of its statutory obligations in relation to the Works, or the failure to carry out such work;

25·4 ·12 failure of the Employer to give in due time ingress to or egress from the site of the Works or any part thereof through or over any land, buildings, way or passage adjoining or connected with the site and in the possession and control of the Employer, in accordance with the Contract Bills and/or the Contract Drawings, after receipt by the Architect of such notice, if any, as the Contractor is required to give, or failure of the Employer to give such ingress or egress as otherwise agreed between the Architect and the Contractor.

25·4 ·13 where clause 23·1·2 is stated in the Appendix to apply, the deferment by the Employer of giving possession of the site under clause 23·1·2.

25·4 ·14 by reason of the execution of work for which an Approximate Quantity is included in the Contract Bills which is not a reasonably accurate forecast of the quantity of work required.

This clause has been substantially enlarged from the 1963 edition, as part of the policy of attempting to legislate for every eventuality. New points to be noted include the requirement for the contractor's notice to specify the relevant event, the expected effects and the delay, and for the notice to be up-dated as necessary.

The architect must make his decision "if reasonably practicable" within 12 weeks or before completion. All extensions are subject to review within 12 weeks of completion. There may be a reduction where omissions are ordered, but only in cases where an extension has initially been allowed, and the date for completion stated in the appendix may not be advanced.

Failure by the contractor to give notice of delay will deprive him of extensions during the currency of the work. But the architect is bound to consider any relevant events, whether notified or not, in his review after completion. Under clause 26·3 the architect is required to specify those extensions relevant to time-dependent loss and expense claims.

Note that under clauses 38 to 40 (see below) the employer's right to "freeze" fluctuation payments at the contractual completion date is dependent on timely exercise of the architect's powers to extend time.

POWERS AND REMEDIES

The limitations of the architect's powers are commented on above. Specific powers already referred to are those under clause 8·3 to order opening up of work; under clause 8·4 to order removal of improper work; under clause 8·5 to order removal of workmen; under clauses 17·2 and 17·3 to require defects to be made good; and under clause 23·2 to order postponement of work.

Instructions must normally be in writing. Clause 4·3 lays down an elaborate provision for dealing with oral instructions.

4·3 ·1 All instructions issued by the Architect shall be issued in writing.

4·3·2 If the Architect purports to issue an instruction otherwise than in writing it shall be of no immediate effect, but shall be confirmed in writing by the Contractor to the Architect within seven days, and if not dissented from in writing by the Architect to the Contractor within seven days from receipt of the Contractor's confirmation shall take effect as from the expiration of the latter said seven days. Provided always:

·2 ·1 that if the Architect within seven days of giving such an instruction otherwise than in writing shall himself confirm the same in writing, then the Contractor shall not be obliged to confirm as aforesaid, and the said instruction shall take effect as from the date of the Architect's confirmation; and

·2 ·2 that if neither the Contractor nor the Architect shall confirm such an instruction in the manner and at the time aforesaid but the Contractor shall nevertheless comply with the same, then the Architect may confirm the same in writing at any time prior to the issue of the Final Certificate, and the said instruction shall thereupon be deemed to have taken effect on the date on which it was issued otherwise than in writing by the Architect.

The widest power given to the architect is to order variations to the works:

13·1 The term "Variation" as used in the Conditions means:

13·1·1 the alteration or modification of the design, quality or quantity of the Works as shown upon the Contract Drawings and described by or referred to in the Contract Bills; including

·1 ·1 the addition, omission or substitution of any work,

·1 ·2 the alteration of the kind or standard of any of the materials or goods to be used in the Works,

·1 ·3 the removal from the site of any work executed or materials or goods brought thereon by the Contractor for the purposes of the Works other than work materials or goods which are not in accordance with this Contract;

13·1 ·2 the imposition by the Employer of any obligations or restrictions in regard to the matters set out in clauses 13·1·2·1 to 13·1·2·4 or the addition to or alteration or omission of any such obligation or restrictions so imposed or imposed by the Employer in the Contract Bills in regard to:

·2 ·1 access to the site or use of any specific parts of the site;

·2 ·2 limitations of working space;

·2 ·3 limitations of working hours;

·2 ·4 the execution or completion of the work in any specific order;

but excludes

13·1 ·3 nomination of a Sub-Contractor to supply and fix materials or goods or to execute work of which the measured quanities have been set out and priced by the Contractor in the Contract Bills for supply and fixing or execution by the Contractor.

13·2 The Architect may, subject to the Contractor's right of reasonable objection set out in clause 4·1·1, issue instructions requiring a Variation and he may sanction in writing any Variation made by the Contractor otherwise than pursuant to an instruction of the Architect. No Variation required by the Architect or subsequently sanctioned by him shall vitiate this Contract.

13·3 The Architect shall issue instructions in regard to:

13·3 ·1 the expenditure of provisional sums included in the Contract Bills; and

13·3 ·2 the expenditure of provisional sums included in a Sub-Contract.

13·4 .....

The employer will be bound by any variation order given by the architect. However, the architect must ensure that he has authority to order the variation, otherwise he may be liable to the employer for its cost. The effect of clause 4·3 is that a variation order must normally be in writing. Although clause 13·1 and 13·2 contemplates that the power to give variations is unlimited, there will be some implied limit, beyond which the contractor may say that the contract has ceased to apply, and that he is entitled to re-price the work. This principle will, in practice, apply only to cases where the work ordered is wholly different to that in the original contract (see page 168).

By clause 4·1·1 the contractor is bound by comply with instructions forthwith. But the contractor may make "reasonable objection" to compliance with an instruction given under clause 13·1·2 (see notes to clause 4 above).

Sub-contractors

It is very rare in practice for the contractor to wish to perform the whole of the work himself. The right to have the work performed by others is restricted as follows:

19·1 Neither the Employer nor the Contractor shall, without the written consent of the other, assign this Contract.

19·1 ·2 Where clause 19·1·2 is stated in the Appendix to apply then, in the event of transfer by the Employer of his freehold or leasehold interest in, or of a grant by the Employer of a leasehold interest in, the whole of the premises comprising the Works, the Employer may at any time after Practical Completion of the Works assign to any such transferee or lessee the right to bring proceedings in the name of the Employer (whether by arbitration or litigation) to enforce any of the terms of this contract made for the benefit of the Employer hereunder. The assignee shall be estopped from disputing any enforceable agreements reached between the Employer and the Contractor and which arise out of and relate to this Contract (whether or not they are or appear to be a derogation from the right assigned) and made prior to the date of any assignment.

19·2 The Contractor shall not without the written consent of the Architect (which consent shall not be unreasonably withheld) sub-let any portion of the Works. A person to whom the Contractor sub-lets any portion of the Works other than a Nominated Sub-Contractor is in this Contract referred to as a "Domestic Sub-Contractor."

19·3 ......

Clause 19·1·2 is a recent addition to JCT 80. Note that it applies only to a transfer of the whole of the premises. The clause does not deal with the question of what damages might be recoverable by the assignee (see further page 200).

Substantial sections of work are frequently intended to be sub-let to particular sub-contractors. Where such work is described in the bills as prime cost or provisional sums, the contract allows the architect to nominate the sub-contractor to perform the work. Under the 1980 edition nomination may also arise in other ways, including naming the sub-contractor in the bills:

35·1 Where

35·1 ·1 in the Contract Bills; or

35·1 ·2 in any instruction of the Architect under clause 13·3 on the expenditure of a provisional sum included in the Contract Bills; or

35·1 ·3 in any instruction of the Architect under clause 13·2 requiring a Variation to the extent, but not further or otherwise,

·3 ·1 that it consists of work additional to that shown upon the Contract Drawings and described by or referred to in the Contract Bills and

·3 ·2 that any supply and fixing of materials or goods or any execution of work by a Nominated Sub-Contractor in connection with such additional work is of a similar kind to any supply and fixing of materials or the execution of work for which the Contract Bills provided that the Architect would nominate a sub-contractor; or

35·1 ·4 by agreement (which agreement shall not be unreasonably withheld) between the Contractor and the Architect on behalf of the Employer

the Architect has, whether by the use of a prime cost sum or by naming a sub-contractor, reserved to himself the final selection and approval of the sub-contractor to the Contractor who shall supply and fix any materials or goods or execute work, the sub-contractor so named or to be selected and approved shall be nominated in accordance with the provisions of clause 35 and a sub-contractor so nominated shall be a Nominated Sub-Contractor for all the purposes of this Contract. The provisions of clause 35·1 shall apply notwithstanding the provisions of Section B·9·1 of the Standard Method of Measurement, 6th Edition.

35·2·1 .....

Clause 35·4 to 35·12 sets out the detailed procedure for nomination. This requires the architect to obtain the sub-contractor's tender and performance warranty on the new standard forms NSC/1 and 2. The contractor is then given a preliminary notice of nomination with instructions to settle with the sub-contractor important terms, including the timing and order of the work. These are matters which often produced dispute under the old procedure. Only when these terms are agreed may the architect make his nomination. Alternatively, by a provision in the bills or an instruction, the architect may opt out of the preliminary procedure, in which case warranty form NSC/2a is to be used.

Provisions dealing with payment to nominated sub-contractors, extensions of time, delay in completion, practical completion and final payment are set out in clause 35·13 to 35·19. In addition to these procedural matters, the clause contains or incorporates the following package of benefits for the main contractor:

(1) the benefit of the standard form of sub-contract NSC/4, including indemnities for non-performance by the sub-contractor;
(2) a discount of two-and-a-half per cent. on the sub-contract price for payment within the period stipulated in the sub-contract;
(3) a right of reasonable objection to any proposed sub-contractor (clause 35·4·1);

   (4) limitation of liability where the sub-contractor's liability is limited (clause 35·22);

   (5) an express right of re-nomination where the sub-contractor defaults (clause 35·24).

By this provision the JCT has finally adopted the construction placed on the 1963 edition by the House of Lords in *N.W. Metropolitan Hospital Board* v. *Bickerton* (1970).

The sub-contractor has the benefit of the right of direct payment, reserved to the employer by clause 35·13·5. The contractor's proof of payment is made mandatory on the contractor by clause 35·13·3. Where the sub-contractor has entered into the direct warranty in forms NSC/2, or 2a, the employer is, by clause 35·13·5·1, bound to operate the direct payment procedure.

Clause 36 covers nominated suppliers, which have traditionally been dealt with separately in the RIBA forms (there is no distinction between sub-contractor and supplier in the ICE form). Nominated suppliers are defined in the following terms:

36·1 ·1 In the Conditions "Nominated Supplier" means a supplier to the Contractor who is nominated by the Architect in one of the following ways to supply materials or goods which are to be fixed by the Contractor:

   ·1 ·1 where a prime cost sum is included in the Contract Bill in respect of those materials or goods and the supplier is either named in the Contract Bills or subsequently named by the Architect in an instruction issued under clause 36·2;

   ·1 ·2 where a provisional sum is included in the Contract Bills and in any instruction by the Architect in regard to the expenditure of such sum the supply of materials or goods is made the subject of a prime cost sum and the supplier is named by the Architect in that instruction or in an instruction issued under clause 36·2;

   ·1 ·3 where a provisional sum is included in the Contract Bills and in any instruction by the Architect in regard to the expenditure of such a sum materials or goods are specified for which there is a sole source of supply in that there is only one supplier from whom the Contractor can obtain them, in which case the supply of materials or goods shall be made the subject of a prime cost sum in the instructions issued by the Architect in regard to the expenditure of the provisional sum and the sole supplier shall be deemed to have been nominated by the Architect;

   ·1 ·4 where the Architect requires under clause 13·2, or subsequently sanctions, a Variation and specifies materials or goods for which there is a sole supplier as referred to in clause 36·1·1·3, in which case the supply of the materials or goods shall be made the subject of a prime cost sum in the instruction or written sanction issued by the Architect under clause 13·2 and the sole supplier shall be deemed to have been nominated by the Architect.

36·1 ·2 In the Conditions the expression "Nominated Supplier" shall not apply to a supplier of materials or goods which are specified in the Contract Bills to be fixed by the Contractor unless such materials or goods are the subject of a prime cost sum in the Contract Bills, notwithstanding that the supplier has been named in the Contract Bills or that there is a sole supplier of such materials or goods as defined in clause 36·1·1·3.

36·2 ......

The contractor is entitled to terms in the contract of sale covering the quality of the goods, rectification of defects and the delivery programme. The supplier must offer five per cent. discount for prompt payment; and ownership of the goods is to pass on delivery to the contractor, whether or not payment has been made (clause 36·4). The latter provision seeks to overcome the effect of so-called *Romalpa* clauses, often inserted by suppliers of goods (see page 122). Where the supplier insists on restricting his liability, the architect must approve the restrictions, whereupon the contractor's liability is to be limited to the same extent (clause 36·5).

An important matter not dealt with is the effect of repudiation by the supplier. Under the 1963 forms it was thought that the *Bickerton* principle applied (see page 196). However, the express provision for re-nomination in clause 35 is a material indication that the procedure is not intended to apply to suppliers. In *Bickerton's* case the House of Lords placed great weight on the words "such sums (Prime Cost) shall be expended in favour of such persons as the architect shall instruct." This is now replaced by a less specific formula:

36·2 The Architect shall issue instructions for the purpose of nominating a supplier for any materials or goods in respect of which a prime cost sum is included in the Contract Bills or arises under clause 36·1.

36·3 .....

The result may be that the contractor must bear the loss caused by the failure of a nominated supplier.

In addition to nominated and ordinary domestic sub-contractors, the bills may place restriction on who may be employed for specific work, thereby creating a new category which may be called a "listed sub-contractor."

19·3 ·1 Where the Contract Bills provide that certain work measured or otherwise described in those Bills and priced by the Contractor must be carried out by persons named in a list in or annexed to the Contract Bills, and selected therefrom by and at the sole discretion of the Contractor the provisions of clause 19·3 shall apply in respect of that list.

19·3 ·2 ·1 The list referred to in clause 19·3·1 must comprise not less than three persons. Either the Employer (or the Architect on his behalf) or the Contractor shall be entitled with the consent of the other, which consent shall not be unreasonably withheld, to add additional persons to the list at any time prior to the execution of a binding sub-contract agreement.

·2 ·2 If at any time prior to the execution of a binding sub-contract agreement and for whatever reason less than three perons named in the list are able and willing to carry out the relevant work then

> either the Employer and the Contractor shall by agreement (which agreement shall not be unreasonably withheld) add the names of other persons so that the list comprises not less than three such persons

> or the work shall be carried out by the Contractor who may sub-let to a Domestic Sub-Contractor in accordance with clause 19·2.

19·3 ·3 A person selected by the Contractor under clause 19·3 from the aforesaid list shall be a Domestic Sub-Contractor.

19·4 .....

In respect both of nominated suppliers and sub-contractors the contractor's liability for the suitability of the work is likely to be excluded by the architect's selection of materials. Further, by virtue of clause 25·4·7, the contractor is not liable for delay by nominated sub-contractors or suppliers. Clause 19·3·3, however, ensures that, in regard to listed sub-contractors, the contractor remains liable to the employer for their default, as though the work had not been sub-let.

Default and determination

In the event of the contractor failing to comply with the contract, the employer has a number of remedies. In respect of defective work or work suspected to be defective, the architect may order the removal of the work or opening up or testing under clause 8 (see above). If the contractor fails to complete by the date for completion the employer is entitled to deduct liquidated damages (clause 24). Note that the work cannot be complete if it contains material patent defects.

If the contractor's default is more serious or if he becomes unable to perform the contract, the employer may become entitled to determine the contractor's employment:

27·1 Without prejudice to any other rights or remedies which the Employer may possess, if the Contractor shall make default in any one or more of the following respects, that is to say:

27·1 ·1 if without reasonable cause he wholly suspends the carrying out of the Works before completion thereof; or

27·1 ·2 if he fails to proceed regularly and diligently with the Works; or

27·1 ·3 if he refuses or persistently neglects to comply with a written notice from the Architect requiring him to remove defective work or improper materials or goods and by such refusal or neglect the Works are materially affected; or

27·1 ·4 if he fails to comply with the provisions of either clause 19 or 19A,

then the Architect may give to him a notice by registered post or recorded delivery specifying the default. If the Contractor either shall continue such default for 14 days after receipt of such notice or shall at any time thereafter repeat such default (whether previously repeated or not), then the Employer may within 10 days after such continuance or repetition by notice by registered post or recorded delivery forthwith determine the employment of the Contractor under this Contract; provided that such notice shall not be given unreasonably or vexatiously.

27·2 In the event of the Contractor becoming bankrupt or making a composition or arrangement with his creditors or having a proposal in respect of his company for a voluntary arrangement for a composition of debts or scheme or arrangement approved in accordance with the Insolvency Act 1986, or having an application made under the Insolvency Act 1986 in respect of his company to the court for the appointment of an administrator, or having a winding up order made or (except for the purposes of amalgamation or reconstruction) a resolution for voluntary winding up passed or having a provisional liquidator, receiver or manager of his business or undertaking duly appointed, or having an administrative receiver, as defined in the Insolvency Act 1986, appointed, or having possession taken, by or on behalf of the holders of any debentures secured by a floating charge, of any property comprised in or subject to the floating charge, the employment of the Contractor under this Contract shall be forthwith automatically determined but the said employment may be reinstated and continued if the Employer and the Contractor, his trustee in bankruptcy, liquidator, provisional liquidator, receiver or manager as the case may be shall so agree.

27·3 .....

The operation of this clause does not terminate the contract; the parties remain bound by its terms. After determination, clause 27·4 entitles the employer to complete the work by other contractors, and to claim from the contractor any additional cost so incurred. Clause 27·3 gives the employer a further right of determination if the contractor or any employee of his gives or offers any gift or consideration as an inducement.

Note that two notices are required to effect a determination under clause 27·1. The grounds may not amount to repudiation by the contractor, so that an incorrect termination may render the employer liable to the contractor for heavy damages (see page 104).

In the case *Central Provident* v. *Ho Bock Kee* (1981) the Court of Appeal of Singapore held invalid a determination under a contract requiring notices to be sent by registered post. The notices were in fact delivered by hand. Receivership, which leads to automatic determination under clause 27·2, does not always indicate an inability to complete. Where the receiver is permitted to continue the work without specific agreement for reinstatement, the employer may waive his rights under this clause.

Note that clause 19A (Fair Wages), referred to in 27·1·4, no longer exists.

Clause 28 gives the contractor rights to determine as follows:

28·1 Without prejudice to any other rights and remedies which the Contractor may possess, if

28·1 ·1 the Employer does not pay the amount properly due to the Contractor on any certificate (otherwise than as a result of the operation of the VAT Agreement) within 14 days from the issue of that certificate and continues such default for seven days after receipt by registered post or recorded delivery of a notice from the Contractor stating that notice of determination under clause 28 will be served if payment is not made within seven days from receipt thereof; or

28·1 ·2 the Employer interfers with or obstructs the issue of any certificate due under this Contract; or

28·1 ·3 the carrying out of the whole or substantially the whole of the uncompleted Works (other than the execution of work required under clause 17) is suspended for a continuous period of the length named in the Appendix by reason of:

·3 ·1 Architect's instructions issued under clause 2·3, 13·2 or 23·2 unless caused by reason of some negligence or default of the Contractor, his servants or agents or of any person employed or engaged upon or in connection with the Works or any part thereof, his servants or agents other than a Nominated Sub-Contractor or the Employer or any person employed, engaged or authorised by the Employer or by any local authority or statutory undertaker executing work solely in pursuance of its statutory obligations; or

·3 ·2 the Contractor not having received in due time necessary instructions, drawings, details or levels from the Architect for which he specifically applied in writing provided that such application was made on a date which having regard to the Completion Date was neither unreasonably distant from nor unreasonably close to the date on which it was necessary for him to receive the same; or

·3 ·3 delay in the execution of work not forming part of this Contract by the Employer himself or by persons employed or otherwise engaged by the Employer as referred to in clause 29 or the failure to execute such work or delay in the supply by the Employer of materials and goods which the Employer has agreed to provide for the Works or the failure so to supply; or

·3 ·4 the opening up for inspection of any work covered up or the testing of any of the work, materials or goods in accordance with clause 8·3 (including making good in consequence of such opening up or testing), unless the inspection or test showed that the work, materials or goods were not in accordance with this Contract; or

·3 ·5 failure of the Employer to give in due time ingress to or egress from the site of the Works or any part thereof through or over any land, buildings, way or passage adjoining or connected with the site and in the possession and control of the Employer, in accordance with the Contract Bills or the Contract Drawings, after receipt by the Architect of such notice, if any, as the Contractor is required to give, or failure of the Employer to give such ingress or egress as otherwise agreed between the Architect and the Contractor.

then the Contractor may thereupon by notice by registered post or recorded delivery to the Employer or Architect forthwith determine the employment of the Contractor under this Contract; provided that such notice shall not be given unreasonably or vexatiously.

28·2 .....

Upon determination, clause 28·2 entitles the contractor to be paid the value of all work done and materials supplied, the cost of removal and any loss caused to him. Note that determination for non-payment requires two notices, while determination on other grounds may be effected by a single notice without prior warning. A note in the appendix suggests the insertion of a period of one month for the period of suspension. The employer may well seek to insert longer periods, since this clause may place him in a vulnerable position, where the suspension is outside his control. As with clause 27, an incorrect determination will have serious consequences: the grounds under clause 28 will rarely amount to repudiation by the employer.

28A·1 Without prejudice to any other rights or remedies which the Employer or the Contractor may possess, if the carrying out of the whole or substantially the whole of the uncompleted Works (other than the execution of work required under clause 17) is suspended for a continuous period of the length named in the Appendix by reason of:

·1 force majeure; or

·2 loss or damage to the Works occasioned by any one or more of the Specified Perils; or

·3 civil commotion;

then the Employer or the Contractor may thereupon by notice by registered post or recorded delivery to the Contractor or to the Employer forthwith determine the employment of the Contractor under this Contract; provided that such notice shall not be given unreasonably or vexatiously.

28A·2 The Contractor shall not be entitled to give notice under clause 28A·1 where the loss or damage to the Works occasioned by the Specified Perils was caused by some negligence or default of the Contractor, his servants or agents or of any person employed or engaged upon or in connection with the Works or any part thereof, his servants or agents other than the Employer or any person employed, engaged or authorised by the Employer or by any local authority or statutory undertaker executing work solely in pursuance of its statutory obligations.

28A·3 Upon such determination under clause 28A·1 the provisions of clause 28·2 shall apply with the exception of clause 28·2·2·6.

This is a new clause which gives both parties the right to determine on grounds which formerly entitled only the contractor to do so. Whoever determines, the contractor is entitled to full payment (by clause 28·2) save that there is no entitlement to loss or damage (clause 28·2·2·6).

CERTIFICATION AND PAYMENT

The sums payable to the contractor may be subject to many alterations, which are discussed below. The contract sum is not, however, to be altered on account of any error:

14·2 The Contract Sum shall not be adjusted or altered in any way whatsoever otherwise than in accordance with the express provisions of the Conditions, and subject to clause 2·2·2·2 any error whether of arithmetic or not in the computation of the Contract Sum shall be deemed to have been accepted by the parties hereto.

The contract contains extensive provisions for payment as the work proceeds, which are vital to the contractor. He will often, during the course of a contract, have a cash turnover exceeding the value of his assets, so that lack of interim payments will create great difficulties. Cash flow has been referred to by the courts as the life-blood of the industry. The issuing of interim certificates is dealt with as follows:

30·1 ·1 ·1 The Architect shall from time to time as provided in clause 30 issue Interim Certificates stating the amount due to the Contractor from the Employer and the Contractor shall be entitled to payment therefor within 14 days from the date of issue of each Interim Certificate.

30·1 ·1 ·2 .....

30·1 ·2 Interim valuations shall be made by the Quantity Surveyor whenever the Architect considers them to be necessary for the purposes of ascertaining the amount to be stated as due in an Interim Certificate.

30·1 ·3 Interim Certificates shall be issued at the Period of Interim Certificates specified in the Appendix up to and including the end of the period during which the Certificate of Practical Completion is issued. Thereafter Interim Certificates shall be issued as and when further amounts are ascertained as payable to the Contractor from the Employer and after the expiration of the Defects Liability Period named in the Appendix or upon the issue of the Certificate of Completion of Making Good Defects (whichever is the later) provided always that the Architect shall not be required to issue an Interim Certificate within one calendar month of having issued a previous Interim Certificate.

30·2 The amount stated as due in an Interim Certificate, subject to any agreement between the parties as to stage payments, shall be the gross valuation as referred to in clause 30·2 less

> any amount which may be deducted and retained by the Employer as provided in clause 30·4 (in the Conditions called "the Retention") and

> the total amount stated as due in Interim Certificates previously issued under the Conditions.

The gross valuation shall be the total of the amounts referred to in clauses 30·2·1 and 30·2·2 less the total of the amounts referred to in clause 30·2·3 and applied up to and including a date not more than seven days before the date of the Interim Certificate:

30·2 ·1 There shall be included the following which are subject to Retention:

·1 ·1 the total value of the work properly executed by the Contractor including any work so executed to which clause 13·5 refers but excluding any restoration, replacement or repair of loss or damage and removal and disposal of debris which in clauses 22B·3·5 and 22C·4·4·2 are treated as if they were a variation, together with, where applicable, any adjustment of that value under clause 40;

·1 ·2 the total value of the materials and goods delivered to or adjacent to the Works for incorporation therein by the Contractor but not so incorporated, provided that the value of such materials and goods shall only be included as and from such times as they are reasonably properly and not prematurely so delivered and are adequately protected against weather and other casualties;

·1 ·3 the total value of any materials or goods other than those to which clause 30·2·1·2 refers where the Architect in the exercise of his discretion under clause 30·3 has decided that such total value shall be included in the amount stated as due in an Interim Certificate;

·1 ·4 the amounts referred to in clause 21·4·1 of Sub-Contract NSC/4 or NSC/4a as applicable in respect of each Nominated Sub-Contractor;

·1 ·5 the profit of the Contractor upon the total of the amounts referred to in clauses 30·2·1·4 and 30·2·2·5 less the total of the amount referred to in clause 30·2·3·2 at the rates included in the Contract Bills, or, in the cases where the nomination arises from an instruction as to the expenditure of a provisional sum, at rates related thereto, or if none, at reasonable rates.

30·2 ·2 There shall be included the following which are not subject to Retention:

·2 ·1 any amounts to be included in Interim Certificates in accordance with clause 3 as a result of payments made or costs incurred by the Contractor under clauses 6·2, 8·3, 9·2 and 21·2·3;

·2 ·2 any amounts ascertained under clause 26·1 or 34·3 or in respect of any restoration, replacement or repair of loss or damage and removal and disposal of debris which in clauses 22B·3·5 and 22C·4·4·2 are treated as if they were a Variation;

·2 ·3 any amount to which clause 35·17 refers;

·2 ·4 any amount payable to the Contractor under clause 38 or 39, whichever is applicable;

·2 ·5 the amounts referred to in clause 21·4·2 of Sub-Contract NSC/4 or NSC/4a as applicable in respect of each Nominated Sub-Contractor.

30·2 ·3 There shall be deducted the following which are not subject to Retention:

·3 ·1 any amount deductible under clause 7 or 8·4·2 or 17·2 or 17·3 or any amount allowable by the Contractor to the Employer under clause 38 or 39, if applicable;

·3 ·2 any amount referred to in clause 21·4·3 of Sub-Contract NSC/4 or NSC/4a as applicable in respect of each Nominated Sub-Contractor.

30·3 ......

The subject-matter of these incorporated clauses is as follows: clause 3, contract sum adjustment; 6, statutory fees; 8, tests; 9, royalties; 13, variations; 17, rectifying defects; 21 and 22, insurance; 26, loss and expense; 30·3, payment for goods off site; 34, antiquities; 35·17, final payment of nominated sub-contractor; 35·18, defects in nominated sub-contractor's work; 35·24, re-nomination; 38 and 39, fluctuations; 40, formula adjustment. NSC/4 or 4a: clause 21·4·1, value of sub-contract work; 21·4·2, additional payments to sub-contractor; 21·4·3, fluctuations repayable.

Clause 16·1 provides that where materials and goods, in accordance with clause 30·2, are included in an interim certificate under which the contractor has received payment, the materials or goods become the property of the employer. Clause 30·3 gives the architect a discretion to include payment for materials or goods before delivery to the site, provided specified conditions are met. Clause 16·2 provides similarly for such materials or goods to become the employer's property when paid for.

Clause 30·4 provides for the employer to hold a retention of five per cent. or any lower agreed rate. The full retention is to be levied on work which has not reached completion, and materials. Work which is certified as practically complete carries half the retention percentage, which is released on the certificate of making good defects. Items which are not subject to retention are set out in clause 30·2·2 above. Interim certificates are required to set out, separately, retentions in respect of nominated sub-contractors.

The procedure for valuing variations is set out in clause 13·5. Where the extra work is of similar character to billed work, such rates are to be used, with allowance for different conditions or significant changes in quantity. Where no similar work is billed, fair rates are to be used. Where extra work cannot be valued by measurement, the contractor is to be paid at daywork rates.

The reference in clause 30·2·2 to amounts under clause 26·1 is to claims for loss and expense which are now consolidated into a single clause:

26·1 If the Contractor makes written application to the Architect stating that he has incurred or is likely to incur direct loss and/or expense in the execution of this Contract for which he would not be reimbursed by a payment under any other provision in this Contract due to deferment of giving possession of the site under clause 23·1·2 where clause 23·1·2 is stated in the Appendix to be applicable or because the regular progress of the Works or of any part thereof has been or is likely to be materially affected by any one or more of the matters referred to in clause 26·2; and if and as soon as the Architect is of the opinion that the direct loss and/or expense has been incurred or is likely to be incurred due to any such deferment of giving possession or that the regular progress of the Works or of any part thereof has been or is likely to be so materially affected as set out in the application of the Contractor then the Architect from time to time thereafter shall ascertain, or shall instruct the Quantity Surveyor to ascertain, the amount of such loss and/or expense which has been or is being incurred by the Contractor; provided always that:

26·1 ·1 the Contractor's application shall be made as soon as it has become, or should reasonably have become, apparent to him that the regular progress of the Works or any part thereof has been or was likely to be affected as aforesaid, and

26·1 ·2 the Contractor shall in support of his application submit to the Architect upon request such information as should reasonably enable the Architect to form an opinion as aforesaid, and

26·1 ·3 the Contractor shall submit to the Architect or to the Quantity Surveyor upon request such details of such loss and/or expense as are reasonably necessary for such ascertainment as aforesaid.

The following are the matters referred to in clause 26·1:

26·2 ·1 The Contractor not having received in due time necessary instructions (*including those for or in regard to the expenditure of provisional sums*), drawings, details or levels from the Architect for which he specifically applied in writing provided that such application was made on a date which having regard to the Completion Date was neither unreasonably distant from nor unreasonably close to the date on which it was necessary for him to receive the same;

26·2 ·2 the opening up for inspection of any work covered up or the testing of any of the work, materials or goods in accordance with clause 8·3 (including making good in consequence of such opening up or testing), unless the inspection or test showed that the work, materials or goods were not in accordance with this Contract;

26·2 ·3 any discrepancy in or divergence between the Contract Drawings and/or the Contract Bills and/or the Numbered Documents;

26·2 ·4 ·1 the execution of work not forming part of this Contract by the Employer himself or by persons employed or otherwise engaged by the Employer as referred to in clause 29 or the failure to execute such work;

·4 ·2 the supply by the Employer of materials and goods which the Employer has agreed to provide for the Works or the failure so to supply;

26·2 ·5 Architect's instructions under clause 23·2 issued in regard to the postponement of any work to be executed under the provisions of this Contract;

26·2 ·6 failure of the Employer to give in due time ingress to or egress from the site of the Works, or any part thereof through or over any land, buildings, way or passage adjoining or connected with the site and in the possession and control of the Employer, in accordance with the Contract Bills and/or the Contract Drawings, after receipt by the Architect of such notice, if any, as the Contractor is required to give, or failure of the Employer to give such ingress or egress as otherwise agreed between the Architect and the Contractor;

26·2 ·7 Architect's instructions issued

under clause 13·2 requiring a Variation or

under clause 13·3 in regard to the expenditure of provisional sums (other than instructions to which clause 13·4·2 refers or an instruction for the expenditure of a provisonal sum for defined work).

26·2 ·8 *the execution of work for which an Approximate Quantity is included in the Contract Bills which is not a reasonably accurate forecast of the quantity of work required.*

26·3 If and to the extent that it is necessary for ascertainment under clause 26·1 of loss and/or expense the Architect shall state in writing to the Contractor what extension of time, if any, has been made under clause 25 in respect of the Relevant Event or Events referred to in clause 25·4·5·1 (so far as that clause refers to clauses 2·3, 13·2, 13·3 and 23·2) and in clauses 25·4·5·2, 25·4·6, 25·4·8 and 25·4·12.

26·4 .....

26·5 Any amount from time to time ascertained under clause 26 shall be added to the Contract Sum.

26·6 The provisions of clause 26 are without prejudice to any other rights and remedies which the Contractor may possess.

Timely notice under clause 26·1 is a condition precedent to the contractor's right to payment. The latest time for such notice is as soon as it should reasonably be apparent that progress *has* been delayed. However, by clause 26·6, these provisions are without prejudice to other rights, which may include a right to sue for damages, for example, for breach of clause 5·4, as an alternative to claiming under clause 26·2·1. In practice, contractual claims are often pleaded with an alternative breach claim to cover any deficiency in notices. An advantage of the claims procedure is that sums ascertained *should* be paid as the work proceeds. Numbered Documents referred to in clause 26·2·3, are those incorporated into a nominated sub-contract:

3. Where in the Conditions it is provided that an amount is to be added to or deducted from the Contract Sum or dealt with by adjustment of the Contract Sum then as soon as such amount is ascertained in whole or in part such amount shall be included in the computation of the next Interim Certificate following such whole or partial ascertainment.

The architect has no power under the contract to deal with claims for breach, which will usually be dealt with after completion. Unfortunately, the same applies often to contractual claims. Clause 26·4 contains provisions similar to the above, in regard to claims by nominated sub-contractors. For the right to add interest to claims see page 26.

Clauses 38 to 40 (now appearing as a separately published Part 3 of the conditions) deal with fluctuation payments. They are alternatives. Clause 37 requires the parties to stipulate in the Appendix which clause is to apply: in default of choice, clause 38 is to apply. This allows tax fluctuations only. Clause 39 allows fluctuations on labour and materials as well. Clause 40 provides for full fluctuations, based on formula adjustments, subject to any non-adjustable elements.

The operation of clauses 38 and 39 depends on the occurrence of increases (or decreases) in rates or prices. It is a condition precedent to the contractor's entitlement that written notice of any such "event" is given within a reasonable time (clauses 38·4 and 39·5). Conversely formula adjustments are independent of the actual constituents of the work, and do not require notice.

In the event of delayed completion of the works, the employer's liability is limited to rates and prices applying up to the contractual completion date, extended as necessary:

39·5 ·7 Subject to the provisions of clause 39·5·8 no amount shall be added or deducted in the computation of the amount stated as due in an Interim Certificate or in the Final Certificate in respect of amounts otherwise payable to or allowable by the Contractor by virtue of clause 39·1 to ·3 or clause 39·4 if the event (as referred to in the provisions listed in clause 39·5·1) in respect of which the payment or allowance would be made occurs after the Completion date.

The rates and prices are therefore frozen at the date for completion required under the contract. Similar provisions appear in clauses 38·4·7 and 40·7·1. This benefit to the employer is conditional, however, on proper exercise of the extension of time clause by the architect.

39·5 ·8 Clause 39·5·7 shall not be applied unless:

·8 ·1 the printed text of clause 25 is unamended and forms part of the Conditions; and

·8 ·2 the Architect has, in respect of every written notification by the Contractor under clause 25, fixed or confirmed in writing such Completion Date as he considers to be in accordance with clause 25.

Note that the architect is required only to give a timely decision on the contractor's applications for extension. If his decision is later revised by an arbitrator the contractor will be entitled to recover further fluctuations *pro tanto*. Similar provisions appear in clause 38·4·8 and 40·7·2.

Final accounting

During the period following practical completion, the architect is required to undertake the final measurement and valuation of the work (clause 30·6). By clause 14·1 (see above) the quantities of work are deemed to be those set out in the contract bills. If there is any error in the bill, either party may ask for re-measurement. The difference in quantity is to be valued as a variation (clause 2·2·2·2). Clause 30·6·2 sets out a list of adjustments required by the conditions to be made to the contract sum. By clause 30·7 the architect is to issue a special interim certificate setting out final adjustments to nominated sub-contractors' accounts. The last certificate, which must be given within specified time limits, is the final certificate.

30·8 The Architect shall issue the Final Certificate (and inform each Nominated Sub-Contractor of the date of its issue) not later than two months after whichever of the following occurs last:
    the end of the Defects Liability Period;
    the date of issue of the Certificate of Completion of Making Good Defects under clause 17·4;
    the date on which the Architect sent a copy to the Contractor of any ascertainment to which clause 30·6·1·2·1 refers and of the statement prepared in compliance with clause 30·6·1·2·2. The Final Certificate shall state:

30·8 ·1 the sum of the amounts already stated as due in Interim Certificates, and

30·8 ·2 the Contract Sum adjusted as necessary in accordance with clause 30·6·2

and the difference (if any) between the two sums shall (without prejudice to the rights of the Contractor in respect of any Interim Certificates which have not been paid by the Employer) be expressed in the said Certificate as a balance due to the Contractor from the Employer or to the Employer from the Contractor as the case may be, and subject to any deductions authorised by the Conditions, the said balance shall as from the 28th day after the date of the said Certificate be a debt payable as the case may be by the Employer to the Contractor or by the Contractor to the Employer.

30·9 ·1 Except as provided in clauses 30·9·2 and 30·9·3 (and save in respect of fraud), the Final Certificate shall have effect in any proceedings arising out of or in connection with this Contract (whether by arbitration under article 5 or otherwise) as

·1 ·1 conclusive evidence that where the quality of materials or the standard of workmanship are to be to the reasonable satisfaction of the Architect the same are to such satisfaction, and

·1 ·2 conclusive evidence that any necessary effect has been given to all the terms of this Contract which require that an amount is to be added to or deducted from the Contract Sum or an adjustment is to be made of the Contract Sum save where there has been any accidental inclusion or exclusion of any work, materials, goods or figure in any computation or any arithmetical error in any computation in which event the Final Certificate shall have effect as conclusive evidence as to all other computations, and

·1 ·3 conclusive evidence that all and only such extensions of time, if any, as are due under clause 25 have been given, and

·1 ·4 conclusive evidence that the reimbursement of direct loss and/ or expense, if any, to the Contractor pursuant to clause 26·1 is in final settlement of all and any claims which the Contractor has or may have arising out of the occurrence of any of the matters referred to in clause 26·2 whether such claim be for breach of contract, duty of care, statutory duty or otherwise.

30·9 ·2 If any arbitration or other proceedings have been commenced by either party before the Final Certificate has been issued the Final Certificate shall have effect as conclusive evidence as provided in clause 30·9·1 after either:

·2 ·1 such proceedings have been concluded, whereupon the Final Certificate shall be subject to the terms of any award or judgment in or settlement of such proceedings or

·2 ·2 a period of 12 months during which neither party has taken any further step in such proceedings, whereupon the Final Certificate shall be subject to any terms agreed in partial settlement,

whichever shall be the earlier.

30·9 ·3 If any arbitration or other proceedings have been commenced by either party within 28 days after the Final Certificate has been issued, the Final Certificate shall have effect as conclusive evidence as provided in clause 30·9·1 save only in respect of all matters to which those proceedings relate.

30·10 Save as aforesaid no certificate of the Architect shall of itself be conclusive evidence that any works, materials or goods to which it relates are in accordance with this Contract.

In versions of the JCT form before 1977 the final certificate was expressed to be conclusive evidence that the work had been properly carried out and completed in accordance with the terms of the contract. This provision was held binding on the courts when the certificate was given *in the course of* litigation about defective works: *Kaye* v. *Hosier & Dickinson* (1972). The final certificate clause often created serious injustice. In the present form, these provisions are almost totally emasculated. The certificate is not evidence of compliance with the terms of the contract save in the very limited areas where the quality is expressly to be to the architect's satisfaction (see clause 2·1). Clause 30·10 confirms that no other certificate is to be evidence of compliance with the contract. The final certificate is also expressed to be conclusive as to the contractor's claims. This is a fairer notion since the contractor ought to be aware of his need to make a claim well before the final certificate (there may be many reasons why the employer is unaware of defects). Note that the conclusive effect covers extensions of time; and that the certificate cannot be avoided by pleading a claim for damages instead of loss or expense (clause 30·9·1·4).

DISPUTES

The contract requires disputes to be settled by arbitration. Note that the right to arbitrate does not arise unless there is a dispute, *i.e.* a claim by one party to the contract which is rejected by the other. Arbitration proceedings may be initiated at any time after completion, within the periods allowed by limitation (see page 112). Some disputes may be arbitrated before completion. The arbitration clause in JCT 80 was contained in article 5. In the current revision, this article contains only the bare obligation to submit to arbitration, the detailed machinery being transferred to the new clause 41.

Article 5

If any dispute or difference as to the construction of this contract or any matter or thing of whatsoever nature arising thereunder or in connection therewith shall arise between the Employer or the Architect on his behalf and the Contractor either during the progress or after the completion or abandonment of the Works or after the determination of the employment of the Contractor, except under clause 31 (*statutory tax deduction scheme*) to the extent provided on clause 31·9 or under clause 3 of the VAT Agreement, it shall be and is hereby referred to arbitration in accordance with clause 41.

41·1 When the Employer or the Contractor require a dispute or difference as referred to in Article 5 including:

> any matter or thing left by this Contract to the discretion of the Architect, or

> the withholding by the Architect of any certificate to which the Contractor may claim to be entitled, or

> the adjustment of the Contract Sum under clause 30·6·2, or

> the rights and liabilities of the parties under clauses 27, 28, 32 or 33, or

> unreasonable withholding of consent or agreement by the Employer or the Architect on his behalf or by the Contractor

to be referred to arbitration then either the Employer or the Contractor shall give written notice to the other to such effect and such dispute or difference shall be referred to the arbitration and final decision of a person to be agreed between the parties as the Arbitrator, or, upon failure so to agree within 14 days after the date of the aforesaid written notice, of a person to be appointed as the Arbitrator on the request of either the Employer or the Contractor by the person named in the Appendix.

41·2 ·1 Provided that if the dispute or difference to be referred to arbitration under this Contract raises issues which are substantially the same as or connected with issues raised in a related dispute between:

> the Employer and Nominated Sub-Contractor under Agreement NSC/2 or NSC/2a as applicable, or

> the Contractor and any Nominated Sub-Contractor under Sub-contract NSC/4 or NSC/4a as applicable, or

> the Contractor and/or the Employer and any Nominated Supplier whose contract of sale with the Contractor provides for the matters referred in clause 36·4·8·2,

and if the related dispute has already been referred for determination to an Arbitrator, the Employer and the Contractor hereby agree:

that the dispute or difference under this Contract shall be referred to the Arbitrator appointed to determine the related dispute;

that the JCT Arbitration Rules applicable to the related dispute shall apply to the dispute under this Contract;

that such Arbitrator shall have power to make such directions and all necessary awards in the same way as if the procedure of the High Court as to joining one or more defendants or joining co-defendants or third parties was available to the parties and to him; and

that the agreement and consent referred to in clause 41·6 on appeals or applications to the High Court on any question of law shall apply to any question of law arising out of the awards of such arbitrator in respect of all related disputes referred to him or arising in the course of the reference of all the related disputes referred to him;

41·2 ·2 save that the Employer or the Contractor may require the dispute or difference under this Contract to be referred to a different Arbitrator (to be appointed under this Contract) if either of them reasonably considers that the Arbitrator appointed to determine the related dispute is not appropriately qualified to determine the dispute or difference under this Contract.

41·2 ·3 Clauses 41·2·1 and 41·2·2 shall apply unless in the Appendix the words 'clauses 41·2·1 and 41·2·2 apply' have been deleted.

41·3 Such reference, except

·1 on article 3 or article 4; or

·2 on the questions:
whether or not the issue of an instruction is empowered by the Conditions; or
whether or not a certificate has been improperly withheld; or
whether a certificate is not in accordance with the Conditions; or
whether a determination under clause 22C·4·3·1 will be just and equitable; or

·3 on any dispute or difference under clause 4·1 in regard to a reasonable objection by the Contractor under clause 8·4, under clause 18·1 or clause 23·3·2 in regard to withholding of consent by the Contractor, and clauses 25, 32 and 33,

shall not be opened until after Practical Completion or alleged Practical Completion of the Works or termination or alleged termination of the Contractor's employment under this Contract or abandonment of the Works, unless with the written consent of the Employer or the Architect on his behalf and the Contractor.

41·4 Subject to the provisions of clauses 4·2, 30·9, 38·4·3, 39·5·3 and 40·5 the Arbitrator shall, without prejudice to the generality of his powers, have power to rectify the contract so that it accurately reflects the true agreement made by the Employer and the Contractor, to direct such measurements and/or valuations as may in his opinion be desirable in order to determine the rights of the parties and to ascertain and award any sum which ought to have been the subject of or included in any certificate and to open up, review and revise any certificate, opinion, decision (except, where clause 8·4 is relevant, a decision of the Architect to issue instructions pursuant to clause 8·4·1), requirement or notice and to determine all matters in dispute which shall be submitted to him in the same manner as if no such certificate, opinion, decision, requirement or notice had been given.

41·5 Subject to clause 41·6 the award of such Arbitrator shall be final and binding on the parties.

41·6 the parties hereby agree and consent pursuant to Section 1(3)(*a*) and 2(1)(*b*) of the Arbitration Act, 1979, that either party

·1 may appeal to the High Court on any question of law arising out of an award made in an arbitration under this Arbitration Agreement; and

·2 may apply to the High Court to determine any question of law arising in the course of the reference;

and the parties agree that the High Court should have jurisdiction to determine any such question of law.

41·7 Whatever the nationality, residence or domicile of the Employer, the Contractor, any sub-contractor or supplier or the Arbitrator, and wherever the Works or any part thereof are situated, the law of England shall be the proper law of this Contract and in particular (but not so as to derogate from the generality of the foregoing) the provisions of the Arbitration Acts 1950 (notwithstanding anything in s.34 thereof) to 1979 shall apply to any arbitration under this Contract wherever the same, or any part of it, shall be conducted.

41·8 If before making his final award the Arbitrator dies or otherwise ceases to act as the Arbitrator, the Employer and the Contractor shall forthwith appoint a further Arbitrator, or, upon failure so to appoint within 14 days of any such death or cessation, then either the Employer or the Contractor may request the person named in the Appendix to appoint such further Arbitrator. Provided that no such further Arbitrator shall be entitled to disregard any direction of the previous Arbitrator or to vary or revise any award of the previous Arbitrator except to the extent that the previous Arbitrator had power so to do under the JCT Arbitration Rules and/or with the agreement of the parties and/or by the operation of law.

41·9 The arbitration shall be conducted in accordance with the "JCT Arbitration Rules" current at the Base Date. Provided that if any amendments to the Rules so current have been issued by the Joint

Contracts Tribunal after the Base Date the Employer and the Contractor may, by a joint notice in writing to the Arbitrator, state that they wish the arbitration to be conducted in accordance with the JCT Arbitration Rules as so amended.

With the limited exceptions mentioned in clause 41.4, any matter of dispute between the parties connected with the contract may be referred to arbitration including, for example, claims in tort. Clause 41.3 prevents the arbitration proceeding before completion, but provides a substantial list of possible exceptions, the widest of which is the ability to challenge any certificate on the grounds that it has been improperly withheld or is not in accordance with the conditions. Thus, virtually any matter of payment may be referred to interim arbitration. Difficulties can arise, however, if a particular and limited dispute, for example, whether a particular instruction is empowered by the conditions, is referred before completion, and the effective resolution of this dispute involves consideration of other issues which may not be arbitrated until completion. Such matters must be anticipated by the parties and by the appointed arbitrator.

In place of the President of the RIBA as the traditional appointor of arbitrators, the appendix (see clause 41.1) allows the parties to choose whether the appointor is to be the President of the RIBA, or the RICS, or the Chartered Institute of Arbitrators.

The provisions of clause 41.2 contain a code for resolving related disputes under the main contract and under a sub-contract and/or warranty. The condition is that the related dispute has already been referred to an arbitrator, the parties here agreeing that the main contract dispute is to be referred to the same arbitrator. If, conversely, the main contract dispute goes to arbitration first, then parallel machinery needs to be found in the related sub-contracts/warranties. While such arrangements are capable of working in theory, they require a degree of co-operation and are in practice susceptible to being overturned by procedural difficulties. One obvious hurdle is the real possibility that several related disputes are referred to different arbitrators. If the ground of objection is the qualifica-tion of the appointed arbitrator (clause 41.2.2), this is a matter which would have to be resolved by a declaration of the High Court, the issue being whether the objecting party can establish that he "reasonably considers" the arbitrator not to be appropri-ately qualified (that is, the court would not be asked to rule on the question itself, but merely to say whether reasonable consideration had been established). There may also be a dispute as to whether the main contract arbitration raises issues which are "substantially the same as or connected with" issues in the related dispute. While this may appear to be a relatively easy test to satisfy, objection may be anticipated where the main contract dispute involves many issues, only a few of which are connected with the sub-contract dispute. Similarly, a sub-contractor who merely wishes to be paid will not readily accept being joined with a much more extensive main contract dispute.

The alternative to multi-party arbitration is litigation in the High Court. Apart from the difficulties of a stay being granted in some of the related disputes, there remains the problem of *Northern Regional Health Authority* v. *Derek Crouch* (1984), which effectively deprived the court of jurisdiction to exercise powers given to the arbitrator (see page 42). The position remains therefore, that multi-party disputes may be fraught with procedural difficulty, in the absence of agreement or co-operation.

One objection to arbitration, at least, in the domestic sphere, has been the restricted right of appeal. This, however, is now fully covered by the giving of advanced consent, either to an appeal after delivery of award, or to taking a point of law to the court during the course of the reference, by clause 41.6. This clause may be deleted should the parties not wish to keep open the right to appeal to the court. The right of appeal is still subject to the requirements of the Arbitration Act 1979, *inter alia*, that the question of law involved could substantially affect the rights of the parties (that is, the court may refuse to entertain a question of law which has a less than substantial effect on the outcome of the dispute).

Note

In the above commentary, the following clauses or parts are not printed; reference must be made to the form of contract; articles 3A, B and 4 (architect and quantity surveyor); clause 1·1 (interpretation), 2·3 (discrepancies), 4·2 (instructions), 5·1, 2, 5–8 (documents), 6·2 (fees), 13·4–7 (variations), 15 (V.A.T.), 16 (materials), 18 (partial possession), 19·4–5 (sub-contracts), 19A (fair wages), 21·1, 3, 22A–C (insurance), 26·4 (claims), 27·3–4, 28·2 (determination), 30·3–7 (payment), 31 (tax deduction), 32, 33 (war), 34 (antiquities), 35·2–26, 36·3–5 (nominated sub-contractors and suppliers), 37–40 (fluctuations).

Of the clauses printed in the text, the following are *not* printed in full: clause 1·3 (definitions), 6·1 (byelaws), 21·2 (insurance of persons and property), 30·1 (interim certificates), 39·5 (fluctuations).

Further Reading

Keating, *Building Contracts* (5th ed., 1991).
Duncan Wallace, *Building and Civil Engineering Standard Forms* (1969).

CHAPTER 12

THE ICE CONDITIONS OF CONTRACT

THE Institution of Civil Engineers' (ICE) form of contract is intended for use in works of civil engineering construction. The form is issued by the ICE, the Association of Consulting Engineers and the Federation of Civil Engineering Contractors. A sixth edition of the form was issued in 1991. The new edition follows the clause numbering and much of the style of previous editions. This accounts for the rather archaic tone of much of the wording. The conditions are published together with forms of tender, agreement and bond. Unlike the JCT forms, the ICE form exists in one version only, for use by private or other employers. The sponsoring bodies have set up a permanent joint committee to keep the conditions under review.

The conditions create a "re-measurement" or "measure and value" contract; *i.e.* the contractor is to be paid at the contract rates (which are themselves subject to variation) for the actual quantities of work executed. This is recognised by omission of any reference to a "contract sum." Instead the conditions refer to the "tender total."

Under the conditions, the work is required to be carried out to the satisfaction of the engineer. He is given powers of control and direction which are both extensive and apparently arbitrary; although as agent of the employer, the engineer must act in the best interest of his principal. The conditions also contain wide-ranging provisions under which the sums payable to the contractor are subject to alteration, usually in favour of the contractor.

As with the chapter dealing with the JCT form, this is not a full commentary on the ICE form. It is an introduction to the basic working provisions of the form. The most important clauses or sub-clauses are printed with notes as to their effect. Other clauses are referred to where appropriate. For a full exposition of the conditions reference must be made to the form itself and to one of the standard works noted at the end of the chapter.

THE CONTRACT

The conditions contemplate that the form of contract will be accompanied by drawings and a specification in which the work is described, and by bills of quantities in which the work is measured and priced. The way in which these documents operate is as follows:

1 (1) (e) "Contract" means the Conditions of Contract Specification Drawings Priced Bill of Quantities the Tender the written acceptance thereof and the Contract Agreement (if completed).

   (f) "Specification" means the specification referred to in the Tender and any modification thereof or addition thereto as may from time to time be furnished or approved in writing by the Engineer.

   (g) "Drawings" means the drawings referred to in the Specification and any modification of such drawings approved in writing by the Engineer and such other drawings as may from time to time be furnished or approved in writing by the Engineer.

The contract itself is thus to be found in the accepted tender, which provides as follows:

GENTLEMEN,

Having examined the Drawings, Conditions of Contract, Specification and Bill of Quantities for the construction of the above-mentioned Works (and the matters set out in the Appendix hereto) we offer to construct and complete the whole of the said Works in conformity with the said Drawings, Conditions of Contract, Specification and Bill of Quantities for such sum as may be ascertained in accordance with the said Conditions of Contract.

We undertake to complete and deliver the whole of the Permanent Works comprised in the Contract within the time stated in the Appendix hereto.

If our tender is accepted we will, if required, provide security for the due performance of the Contract as stipulated in the Conditions of Contract and the Appendix hereto.

Unless and until a formal Agreement is prepared and executed this Tender together with your written acceptance thereof, shall constitute a binding Contract between us.

We understand that you are not bound to accept the lowest or any tender you may receive.

We are, Gentlemen,

Yours faithfully,

Alternatively, by clause 9 of the conditions, the contractor undertakes to execute the contract agreement, which may be under seal. If executed, the agreement becomes the primary contract document. The agreement is in the following form:

WHEREAS the Employer is desirous that certain Works should be constructed, namely the Permanent and Temporary Works in connection with .... and has accepted a Tender by the Contractor for the construction and completion of such Works

NOW THIS AGREEMENT WITNESSES as follows:

1. In this Agreement words and expressions shall have the same meanings as are respectively assigned to them in the Conditions of Contract hereinafter referred to.

2. The following documents shall be deemed to form and be read and construed as part of this Agreement, namely:–
   (*a*) The said Tender and the written acceptance thereof.
   (*b*) The Drawings.
   (*c*) The Conditions of Contract.
   (*d*) The Specification.
   (*e*) The Priced Bill of Quantities.

3. In consideration of the payments to be made by the Employer to the Contractor as hereinafter mentioned the Contractor hereby covenants with the Employer to construct and complete the Works in conformity in all respects with the provisions of the Contract.

4. The Employer hereby covenants to pay to the Contractor in consideration of the construction and completion of the Works the Contract Price at the times and in the manner prescribed by the Contract.

IN WITNESS whereof the parties hereto have caused this Agreement to be executed the day and year first above written.

SIGNED

The sums payable to the contractor by the conditions are defined as follows:

1 (1)(*i*) "Tender Total" means the total of the Bill of Quantities at the date of award of the Contract or in the absence of a Bill of Quantities the agreed estimated total value of the Works at that date.

(*j*) "Contract Price" means the sum to be ascertained and paid in accordance with the provisions hereinafter contained for the construction and completion of the Works in accordance with the Contract.

Clause 5 of the conditions defines the effect of the contract documents:

5 The several documents forming the Contract are to be taken as mutually explanatory of one another and in case of ambiguities or discrepancies the same shall be explained and adjusted by the Engineer who shall thereupon issue to the Contractor appropriate instructions in writing which shall be regarded as instructions issued in accordance with Clause 13.

The engineer's power under this clause is limited to the technical descriptions of the work, it is thought. He is not empowered to re-write the conditions. The Contract documents usually do not contain full working details. The engineer is therefore given both the power and duty to issue such further details as are necessary:

7 (1) The Engineer shall from time to time during the progress of the Works supply to the Contractor such modified or further Drawings Specifications and instructions as shall in the Engineer's opinion be necessary for the purpose of the proper and adequate construction and completion of the Works and the Contractor shall carry out and be bound by the same.

If such Drawings Specifications or instructions require any variation to any part of the Works the same shall be deemed to have been issued pursuant to Clause 51.

(3) The Contractor shall give adequate notice in writing to the Engineer of any further Drawing or Specification that the Contractor may require for the construction and completion of the Works or otherwise under the Contract.

Sub-clause (2) provides for the reverse situation where the contractor is to supply the design details.

Where instructions are issued late clause 7(4) allows the contractor to claim additional payment and an extension of time (see below for these sub-clauses).

Control of the work

The new edition of the conditions deals expressly with the authority and independence of the Engineer, as follows:

2 (1)(a) The Engineer shall carry out the duties specified in or necessarily to be implied from the Contract.

(b) The Engineer may exercise the authority specified in or necessarily to be implied from the Contract. If the Engineer is required under the terms of his appointment by the Employer to obtain the specific approval of the Employer before exercising any such authority particulars of such requirements shall be those set out in the Appendix to the Form of Tender. Any requisite approval shall be deemed to have been given by the Employer for any such authority exercised by the Engineer.

(c) Except as expressly stated in the Contract the Engineer shall have no authority to amend the Terms and Conditions of the Contract nor to relieve the Contractor of any of his obligations under the Contract.

(2) (a) Where the Engineer as defined in Clause 1 (1)(c) is not a single named Chartered Engineer the Engineer shall within seven days of the award of the Contract and in any event before the Works Commencement Date notify to the Contractor in writing the name of the Chartered Engineer who will act on his behalf and assume the full responsibilities of the Engineer under the Contract.

(b) The Engineer shall thereafter in like manner notify the Contractor of any replacement of the named Chartered Engineer.

The conditions envisage that work on site will be given full-time supervision on behalf of the engineer and the contractor.

2 (3)(a) The Engineer's Representative shall be responsible to the Engineer who shall notify his appointment to the Contractor in writing.

(b) The Engineer's Representative shall watch and supervise the construction and completion of the Works. He shall have no authority
   (i) to relieve the Contractor of any of his duties or obligations under the Contract
      nor except as expressly provided hereunder
   (ii) to order any work involving delay or any extra payment by the Employer or
   (iii) to make any variation of or in the Works.

(4) The Engineer may from time to time delegate to the Engineer's Representative or any other person responsible to the Engineer any of the duties and authorities vested in the Engineer and he may at any time revoke such delegation. Any such delegation

(a) shall be in writing and shall not take effect until such time as a copy thereof has been delivered to the Contractor or his agent appointed under Clause 15(2)

(b) shall continue in force until such time as the Engineer shall notify the Contractor in writing that the same has been revoked

(c) shall not be given in respect of any decision to be taken or certificate to be issued under Clauses 12(6), 44, 46(3), 48, 60(4), 61, 63 or 66.

(5) (a) The Engineer or the Engineer's Representative may appoint any number of persons to assist the Engineer's Representative in the carrying out of his duties under sub-clause (3)(b) or (4) of this Clause. He shall notify to the Contractor the names duties and scope of authority of such persons.

(b) Such assistants shall have no authority to issue any instructions to the Contractor save in so far as such instructions may be necessary to enable them to carry out their duties and to secure their acceptance of materials and workmanship as being in accordance with the Contract. Any instructions given by an assistant for these purposes shall where appropriate be in writing and be deemed to have been given by the Engineer's Representative.

(c) If the Contractor is dissatisfied by reason of any instruction of any assistant of the Engineer's Representative appointed under sub-clause (5)(a) of this Clause he shall be entitled to refer the matter to the Engineer's Representative who shall thereupon confirm reverse or vary such instruction.

(6) (a) Instructions given by the Engineer or by the Engineer's Representative exercising delegated duties and authorities under sub-clause (4) of this Clause shall be in writing. Provided that if for any reason it is considered necessary to give any such instruction orally the Contractor shall comply with such instruction.

(b) Any such oral instruction shall be confirmed in writing by the Engineer or the Engineer's Representative as soon as is possible under the circumstances. Provided that if the Contractor shall confirm in writing any such oral instruction and such confirmation is not contradicted in writing by the Engineer or the Engineer's Representative forthwith it shall be deemed to be an instruction in writing by the Engineer.

(c) Upon the written request of the Contractor the Engineer or the Engineer's Representative exercising delegated duties or authorities under sub-clause (4) of this Clause shall specify in writing under which of his duties and authorities any instruction is given.

(7) If the Contractor is dissatisfied by reason of any act or instruction of the Engineer's Representative he shall be entitled to refer the matter to the Engineer for his decision.

(8) The Engineer shall, except in connection with matters requiring the specific approval of the Employer under sub-clause (1)(b) of this Clause, act impartially within the terms of the Contract having regard to all the circumstances.

This clause is over-complicated for the matters dealt with. In substance it requires delegation of powers to the engineer's representative (the E.R.) to be in writing, with notice to the contractor. Such powers may not include giving extensions of time, requesting acceleration, certifying completion, giving the final certificate or the Defects Correction certificate, nor a certificate of default (clauses 44, 46(3), 48, 60(4) 61, 63), nor giving decisions under clause 12 or 66.

The Contractor is also required to supervise the work:

15 (1) The Contractor shall give or provide all necessary superintendence during the construction and completion of the Works and as long thereafter as the Engineer may consider necessary. Such superintendence shall be given by sufficient persons having adequate knowledge of the operations to be carried out (including the methods and techniques required, the hazards likely to be encountered and methods of preventing accidents) as may be requisite for the satisfactory and safe construction of the Works.

(2) The Contractor or a competent and authorised agent or representative approved of in writing by the Engineer (which approval may at any time be withdrawn) is to be constantly on the Works and shall give his whole time to the superintendence of the same. Such authorised agent or representative shall be in full charge of the Works and shall receive on behalf of the Contractor directions and instructions from the Engineer or (subject to the limitations of Clause 2) the Engineer's Representative. The Contractor or such authorised agent or representative shall be responsible for the safety of all operations.

The contractor is required to give the engineer opportunity to inspect the work:

37 The Engineer and any person authorised by him shall at all times have access to the Works and to the Site and to all workshops and places where work is being prepared or whence materials manufactured articles and machinery are being obtained for the Works, and the Contractor shall afford every facility for and every assistance in obtaining such access or the right to such access.

GENERAL OBLIGATIONS OF THE CONTRACTOR

These are contained in a number of clauses, which must be read together.

8 (1) The Contractor shall subject to the provisions of the Contract
  (a) construct and complete the Works; and
  (b) provide all labour materials Contractor's Equipment Temporary Works transport to and from and in or about the Site and everything whether of a temporary or permanent nature

required in and for such construction and completion so far as the necessity for providing the same is specified in or reasonably to be inferred from the Contract.

(2) The Contractor shall not be responsible for the design or specification of the Permanent Works or any part thereof (except as may be expressly provided in the Contract) or of any Temporary Works designed by the Engineer. The Contractor shall exercise all reasonable skill care and diligence in designing any part of the Permanent Works for which he is responsible.

(3) The Contractor shall take full responsibility for the adequacy stability and safety of all site operations and methods of construction.

Sub-clause (1) repeats obligations contained in the tender to "construct and complete the whole of the said works"; and in the form of agreement, to "construct and complete the works." The question of the Contractor's design responsibility is covered also in other clauses:

7 (2) Where sub-clause (6) of this Clause applies the Engineer may require the Contractor to supply such further documents as shall in his opinion be necessary for the purpose of the proper and adequate construction completion and maintenance of the Works and when approved by the Engineer the Contractor shall carry out and be bound by the same.

(6) Where the Contract expressly provides that part of the Permanent Works shall be designed by the Contractor he shall submit to the Engineer for approval:

 (a) such drawings specifications calculations and other information as shall be necessary to satisfy the Engineer as to the suitability and adequacy of the design and

 (b) operation and maintenance manuals together with as completed drawings of that part of the Permanent Works in sufficient detail to enable the Employer to operate maintain dismantle reassemble and adjust the Permanent Works incorporating that design. No certificate under Clause 48 covering any part of the Permanent Works designed by the Contractor shall be issued until manuals and drawings in such detail have been submitted to and approved by the Engineer.

(7) Approval by the Engineer in accordance with sub-clause (6) of this Clause shall not relieve the Contractor of any of his responsibilities under the Contract. The Engineer shall be responsible for the integration and co-ordination of the Contractor's design with the rest of the Works.

See clause 58(3) for design responsibility where a nominated sub-contractor is involved. Clause 20 makes the contractor generally responsible for the works with exceptions (the "Excepted

Risks") which include the Engineer's design. The Contractor's design responsibility may therefore not be limited to reasonable skill as stated in clause 8(2). The meaning of "Temporary" and "Permanent" work is as follows:

1 (1)   (n) "Permanent Works" means the permanent works to be constructed and completed in accordance with the Contract.
   (o) "Temporary Works" means all temporary works of every kind required in or about the construction and completion of the Works.
   (p) "Works" means the Permanent Works together with the Temporary Works.

These definitions are not at all precise. It is often difficult to decide whether work is permanent or temporary, for example, a cofferdam which is intended to be left in position, after temporary use to facilitate excavation. Temporary works are not mentioned in the JCT contract. They are dealt with in these conditions because such works are often very costly and are frequently designed by the contractor, who assumes responsibility therefor.

The Contractor's responsibility for methods of construction is dealt with further below. In addition to his responsibility for the site operations and methods of construction and for the works themselves (clause 20(2), see below), the contractor is required to take the risk of the site and the sub-soil:

11 (1) The Employer shall be deemed to have made available to the Contractor before the submission of the Tender all information on the nature of the ground and sub-soil including hydrological conditions obtained by or on behalf of the Employer from investigations undertaken relevant to the Works.

The Contractor shall be responsible for the interpretation of all such information for the purposes of constructing the Works and for any design which is the Contractor's responsibility under the Contract.

(2) The Contractor shall be deemed to have inspected and examined the Site and its surroundings and information available in connection therewith and to have satisfied himself so far as is practicable and reasonable before submitting his tender as to
   (a) the form and nature thereof including the ground and sub-soil
   (b) the extent and nature of work and materials necessary for constructing and completing the Works and
   (c) the means of communication with and access to the Site and the accommodation he may require
and in general to have obtained for himself all necessary information as to risks contingencies and all other circumstances which may influence or affect his tender.

(3) The Contractor shall be deemed to have
  (a) based his tender on the information made available by the Employer and on his own inspection and examination all as aforementioned and
  (b) satisfied himself before submitting his tender as to the correctness and sufficiency of the rates and prices stated by him in the Bill of Quantities which shall (unless otherwise provided in the Contract) cover all his obligations under the Contract.

The contractor's liability is subject to two exceptions. First, clause 11(2) expressly permits the contractor to take account of any sub-soil information provided, *i.e.* any site investigation data. The effect of this provision is obscure, but it may permit the contractor to bring proceedings under the Misrepresentation Act 1967, if the data is misleading. Secondly, clause 12 may entitle the contractor to additional payment if unforeseeable physical conditions or artificial obstructions are encountered in the subsoil (see below). There will be a further exception where the Employer has failed to disclose relevant sub-soil information. Since the tender is deemed to be based on the information made available (clause 11(3)(*a*)) there may be a claim for re-pricing. Other clauses which bear on the contractor's general responsibility are as follows:

13 (1) Save in so far as it is legally or physically impossible the Contractor shall construct and complete the Works in strict accordance with the Contract to the satisfaction of the Engineer and shall comply with and adhere strictly to the Engineer's instructions on any matter connected therewith (whether mentioned in the Contract or not). The Contractor shall take instructions only from the Engineer or (subject to the limitations referred to in Clause 2) from the Engineer's Representative.

This clause gives the Engineer very wide powers to give instructions. This is important in regard to claims, as to which see clause 13(3), referred to below. The contractor is not obliged to carry out the work to the extent it is legally or physically impossible nor is the employer obliged to pay for work omitted on this ground. The degree of impossibility required to absolve the contractor from further performance was considered in the case of *Turriff* v. *Welsh Water Authority* (1979), where it was held sufficient that the work was commercially impossible in a practical sense. The contractor was attempting to join pre-cast sections of culvert, whose design tolerances prevented a seal being achieved. It was held the contractor was not under a duty to re-design the work to render it capable of being constructed.

Subject to specified exceptions the contractor is required to assume responsibility for the works, irrespective of fault:

20 (1)(*a*) The Contractor shall save as in paragraph (*b*) hereof and subject to sub-clause (2) of this Clause take full responsibility for the care of the Works and materials plant and equipment for incorporation therein from the Works Commencement Date until the date of issue of a Certificate of Substantial Completion for the whole of the Works when the responsibility for the said care shall pass to the Employer.

   (*b*) If the Engineer issues a Certificate of Substantial Completion for any Section or part of the Permanent Works the Contractor shall cease to be responsible for the care of that Section or part from the date of issue of such Certificate of Substantial Completion when the responsibility for the care of that Section or part shall pass to the Employer.

   (*c*) The Contractor shall take full responsibility for the care of any outstanding work and materials plant and equipment for incorporation therein which he undertakes to finish during the Defects Correction Period until such outstanding work has been completed.

   (2) The Excepted Risks for which the Contractor is not liable are loss or damage to the extent that it is due to

   (*a*) the use or occupation by the Employer his agents servants or other contractors (not being employed by the Contractor) of any part of the Permanent Works

   (*b*) any fault defect error or omission in the design of the Works (other than a design provided by the Contractor pursuant to his obligations under the Contract)

   (*c*) riot war invasion act of foreign enemies or hostilities (whether war be declared or not)

   (*d*) civil war rebellion revolution insurrection or military or usurped power

   (*e*) ionising radiations or contamination by radio-activity from any nuclear fuel or from any nuclear waste from the combustion of nuclear fuel radio-active toxic explosive or other hazardous properties of any explosive nuclear assembly or nuclear component thereof and

   (*f*) pressure waves caused by aircraft or other aerial devices travelling at sonic or supersonic speeds.

   (3)(*a*) In the event of any loss or damage to
      (i) the Works or any Section or part thereof or
      (ii) materials plant or equipment for incorporation therein
      while the Contractor is responsible for the care thereof (except as provided in sub-clause (2) of this Clause) the Contractor shall at his own cost rectify such loss or damage so that the Permanent Works conform in every respect with the provisions of the Contract and the Engineer's

instructions. The Contractor shall also be liable for any loss or damage to the Works occasioned by him in the course of any operations carried out by him for the purpose of complying with his obligations under Clauses 49 and 50.

(b) Should any such loss or damage arise from any of the Excepted Risks defined in sub-clause (2) of this Clause the Contractor shall if and to the extent required by the Engineer rectify the loss or damage at the expense of the Employer.

(c) In the event of loss or damage as a result of an Excepted Risk and a risk for which the Contractor is responsible under sub-clause (1)(a) of this Clause then the Engineer shall when determining the expense to be borne by the Employer under the Contract apportion the cost of rectification into that part caused by the Excepted Risk and that part which is the responsibility of the Contractor.

This is a most important clause, which can override other specific responsibilities. The Contractor must make good loss to the works occurring before completion, subject to the right to payment if the loss is due to an "Excepted Risk."

Clauses 21 to 25 contain important requirements as to insurance and liability for losses. Clause 21 requires the contractor to insure the works and his materials and plant against loss, from any cause other than the excepted risks, so as to cover his liability under clause 20. This insurance is required to be in the joint names of employer and contractor. It is important for the employer to note that the works are therefore not insured against damage caused by any fault in the engineer's design. The employer's ability to recover for such loss will depend on the limit of the engineer's professional indemnity policy (see page 135).

Clause 22 apportions liability for third party claims which arise out of or in consequence of the work; and clause 23 requires the contractor to insure his own liability. Clause 24 deals with injuries to workmen. Clause 25 gives the employer the right to effect any insurance which the contractor fails to take out.

The Contractor's methods of work

Prima facie, the contractor's methods of carrying out the work are his responsibility and his choice. The contractor is responsible for the works and for their safety (clauses 20 and 8(3)). There is an exception if the contract designates the method of construction and that method becomes impossible: see *McAlpine* v.

Yorkshire Water Authority and discussion above at page 161. Other clauses which bear on the choice and responsibility for the method are as follows:

13 (2) The whole of the materials plant and labour to be provided by the Contractor under Clause 8 and the mode manner and speed of construction of the Works are to be of a kind and conducted in a manner acceptable to the Engineer.

14 (1)(*a*) Within 21 days after the award of the Contract the Contractor shall submit to the Engineer for his acceptance a programme showing the order in which he proposes to carry out the Works having regard to the provisions of Clause 42(1).

(*b*) At the same time the Contractor shall also provide in writing for the information of the Engineer a general description of the arrangements and methods of construction which the Contractor proposes to adopt for the carrying out of the Works.

(*c*) Should the Engineer reject any programme under sub-clause (2)(*b*) of this Clause the Contractor shall within 21 days of such rejection submit a revised programme.

(2) The Engineer shall within 21 days after receipt of the Contractor's programme

(*a*) accept the programme in writing or

(*b*) reject the programme in writing with reasons or

(*c*) request the Contractor to supply further information to clarify or substantiate the programme or to satisfy the Engineer as to its reasonableness having regard to the Contractor's obligations under the Contract.

Provided that if none of the above actions is taken within the said period of 21 days the Engineer shall be deemed to have accepted the programme as submitted.

(3) The Contractor shall within 21 days after receiving from the Engineer any request under sub-clause (2)(*c*) of this Clause or within such further period as the Engineer may allow provide the further information requested failing which the relevant programme shall be deemed to be rejected.

Upon receipt of such further information the Engineer shall within a further 21 days accept or reject the programme in accordance with sub-clauses (2)(*a*) or (2)(*b*) of this Clause.

(4) Should it appear to the Engineer at any time that the actual progress of the work does not comform with the accepted programme referred to in sub-clause (1) of this Clause, the Engineer shall be entitled to require the Contractor to produce a revised programme showing such modifications to the original programme as may be necessary to ensure completion of the Works or any Section within the time for completion as defined in Clause 43 or extended time granted pursuant to Clause 44(3).

In such event the Contractor shall submit his revised programme within 21 days or within such further period as the Engineer shall allow.

Thereafter the provisions of sub-clauses (2) and (3) of this Clause shall apply.

(5) The Engineer shall provide to the Contractor such design criteria relevant to the Permanent Works or any Temporary Works design supplied by the Engineer as may be necessary to enable the Contractor to comply with sub-clauses (6) and (7) of this Clause.

(6) If requested by the Engineer the Contractor shall submit at such times and in such further detail as the Engineer may reasonably require information pertaining to the methods of construction (including Temporary Works and the use of Contractor's Equipment) which the Contractor proposes to adopt or use and calculations of stresses strains and deflections that will arise in the Permanent Works or any parts thereof during construction so as to enable the Engineer to decide whether, if these methods are adhered to the Works can be constructed and completed in accordance with the Contract and without detriment to the Permanent Works when completed.

(7) The Engineer shall inform the Contractor in writing within 21 days after receipt of the information submitted in accordance with sub-clauses (1)(*b*) and (6) of this Clause either

> (*a*) that the Contractor's proposed methods have the consent of the Engineer or
>
> (*b*) in what respects in the opinion of the Engineer they fail to meet the requirements of the Contract or will be detrimental to the Permanent Works.

In the latter event the Contractor shall take such steps or make such changes in the said methods as may be necessary to meet the Engineer's requirements and to obtain his consent. The Contractor shall not change the methods which have received the Engineer's consent without the further consent in writing of the Engineer which shall not be unreasonably withheld.

(8) If the Contractor unavoidably incurs delay or cost because

> (*a*) the Engineer's consent to the proposed methods of construction is unreasonably delayed or
>
> (*b*) the Engineer's requirements pursuant to sub-clause (7) of this clause or any limitations imposed by any of the design criteria supplied by the Engineer pursuant to sub-clause (5) of this Clause could not reasonably have been foreseen by an experienced contractor at the time of tender

the Engineer shall take such delay into account in determining any extension of time to which the Contractor is entitled under Clause 44 and the Contractor shall subject to Clause 52(4) be paid in accordance with Clause 60 such sum in respect of the cost incurred as the Engineer considers fair in all the circumstances. Profit shall be added thereto in respect of any additional permanent or temporary work.

(9) Acceptance by the Engineer of the Contractor's programme in accordance with sub-clauses (2) (3) or (4) of this Clause and the consent of the Engineer to the Contractor's proposed methods of construction in accordance with sub-clause (7) of this Clause shall not relieve the Contractor of any of his duties or responsibilities under the Contract.

Clause 14 deals both with programme and method. By sub-clause (7) the engineer is required to respond to the contractor's method information. In most circumstances the contractor will remain responsible for the method, but it is to be noted that clause 51(1) includes a method change within the definition of a variation.

In addition to the general obligation as to safety under clause 8(3), the contractor is specifically required to have regard to the safety of persons on the site:

19 (1) The Contractor shall throughout the progress of the Works have full regard for the safety of all persons entitled to be upon the Site and shall keep the Site (so far as the same is under his control) and the Works (so far as the same are not completed or occupied by the Employer) in an orderly state appropriate to the avoidance of danger to such persons, and shall *inter alia* in connection with the Works provide and maintain at his own cost all lights, guards, fencing, warning signs and watching when and where necessary or required by the Engineer, or the Engineer's Representative, or by any competent statutory or other authority for the protection of the Works or for the safety and convenience of the public or others.

(2) If under Clause 31 the Employer shall carry out work on the Site with his own workmen he shall in respect of such work
    (*a*) have full regard to the safety of all persons entitled to be upon the Site and
    (*b*) keep the Site in an orderly state appropriate to the avoidance of danger to such persons.

If under Clause 31 the Employer shall employ other contractors on the Site he shall require them to have the same regard for safety and avoidance of danger.

Clause 22 provides for indemnities in respect of personal injury or damage to property. Every contractor must also comply with regulations as to site safety, under the Health and Safety at Work Act (see Chapter 15).

Workmanship and materials

The following clauses should be read in the light of the general obligations to comply with the contract (clause 13(1), tender and form of agreement):

36 (1) All materials and workmanship shall be of the respective kinds described in the Contract and in accordance with the Engineer's instructions and shall be subjected from time to time to such tests as the

Engineer may direct at the place of manufacture or fabrication or on the Site or such other place or places as may be specified in the Contract. The Contractor shall provide such assistance instruments machines labour and materials as are normally required for examining measuring and testing any work and the quality weight or quantity of any materials used and shall supply samples of materials before incorporation in the Works for testing as may be selected and required by the Engineer.

The "instructions" referred to must arise under some express power in the contract: this clause does not empower the engineer to change the specification without an order to do so, which must be paid for, *e.g.* under clauses 51(1) or 13(1). Clause 36(2) and (3) stipulates how the cost of tests and samples is to be borne.

38 (1) No work shall be covered up or put out of view without the consent of the Engineer and the Contractor shall afford full opportunity for the Engineer to examine and measure any work which is about to be covered up or put out of view and to examine foundations before permanent work is placed thereon. The Contractor shall give due notice to the Engineer whenever any such work or foundations is or are ready or about to be ready for examination and the Engineer shall without unreasonable delay unless he considers it unnecessary and advises the Contractor accordingly attend for the purpose of examining and measuring such work or of examining such foundations.

Clause 38(2) permits the engineer to order uncovering of work and provides for apportioning the cost.

39 (1) The Engineer shall during the progress of the Works have power to instruct in writing the
    (*a*) removal from the Site within such time or times specified in the instruction of any materials which in the opinion of the Engineer are not in accordance with the Contract
    (*b*) substitution with materials in accordance with the Contracts and
    (*c*) removal and proper re-execution, notwithstanding any previous test thereof or interim payment therefor, of any work which in respect of
    (i) material or workmanship or
    (ii) design by the Contractor or for which he is responsible
is not in the opinion of the Engineer in accordance with the Contract.

(2) In case of default on the part of the Contractor in carrying out such instruction the Employer shall be entitled to employ and pay other persons to carry out the same and all costs consequent thereon or incidental thereto as determined by the Engineer shall be recoverable from the Contractor by the Employer and may be deducted by the

Employer from any monies due or to become due to him and the Engineer shall notify the Contractor accordingly with a copy to the Employer.

(3) Failure of the Engineer or any person acting under him pursuant to Clause 2 to disapprove any work or materials shall not prejudice the power of the Engineer or any such person subsequently to take action under this Clause.

This clause is of importance. Without it the engineer's only remedy for defective work would be determination (under clause 63) or refusal to certify payment on completion, the latter carrying the sanction of liquidated damages. Note that work is not in accordance with the contract if it does not comply with the drawings or the specification (clause 1(1)(e)).

The Contractor is responsible for setting-out errors, unless based on incorrect data supplied:

17 (1) The Contractor shall be responsible for the true and proper setting-out of the Works and for the correctness of the position levels dimensions and alignment of all parts of the Works and for the provision of all necessary instruments appliances and labour in connection therewith.

(2) If at any time during the progress of the Works any error shall appear or arise in the position levels dimensions or alignment of any part of the Works the Contractor on being required so to do by the Engineer shall at his own costs rectify such error to the satisfaction of the Engineer unless such error is based on incorrect data supplied in writing by the Engineer or the Engineer's Representative in which case the cost of rectifying the same shall be borne by the Employer.

(3) The checking of any setting-out or of any line or level by the Engineer or the Engineer's Representative shall not in any way relieve the Contractor of his responsibility for the correctness thereof and the Contractor shall carefully protect and preserve all bench-marks sight rails pegs and other things used in setting out the Works.

Independent of the contract, the work must, by law, comply with various statutory requirements (see Chapter 14). Difficult questions can arise in the event of conflict between these require-ments and the engineer's design. This is dealt with as follows:

26 (1) The Contractor shall save as provided in Clause 27 give all notices and pay all fees required to be given or paid by any Act of Parliament or any Regulation or By-law of any local or other statutory authority in relation to the construction and completion of the Works and by the rules and regulations of all public bodies and companies

whose property or rights are or may be affected in any way by the Works.

(2) The Employer shall repay or allow to the Contractor all such sums as the Engineer shall certify to have been properly payable and paid by the Contractor in respect of such fees and also all rates and taxes paid by the Contractor in respect of the Site or any part thereof, or anything constructed or erected thereon, or on any part thereof or any temporary structure situated elsewhere but used exclusively for the purposes of the Works or any structures used temporarily and exclusively for the purposes of the Works.

(3) The Contractor shall ascertain and conform in all respects with the provisions of any general or local Act of Parliament and the Regulations and By-laws of any local or other statutory authority which may be applicable to the Works and with such rules and regulations of public bodies and companies as aforesaid and shall keep the Employer indemnified against all penalties and liability of every kind for breach of any such Act Regulation or By-Law. Provided always that

(a) the Contractor shall not be required to indemnify the Employer against the consequences of any such breach which is the unavoidable result of complying with the Contract or instructions of the Engineer

(b) if the Contract or instructions of the Engineer shall at any time be found not to be in conformity with any such Act Regulation or By-law the Engineer shall issue such instructions including the ordering of a variation under Clause 51 as may be necessary to ensure conformity with such Act Regulation or By-law

(c) the Contractor shall not be responsible for obtaining any planning permission which may be necessary in respect of the Permanent Works or any Temporary Works design supplied by the Engineer and the Employer hereby warrants that all the said permissions have been or will in due time be obtained.

If the contractor, in following the engineer's design, contravenes any statute or by-law, etc., the employer is not entitled to indemnity because of proviso (a). But the contractor may not be entitled to payment for work carried out contrary to by-laws, etc., since the work is in breach of contract by virtue of sub-clause (2).

Clause 27 requires the employer to give notices under the Public Utilities Street Works Act 1950. There has been an extensive review of the workings of this Act and amending legislation is likely, which will lead to changes in clause 27.

Completion and defects correction

The contractor's obligations fall into two separate periods: the period up to the completion certificate, when the work is carried out; and the period during which the contractor must repair any defects. These are dealt with in the following provisions. It is important to note that these clauses do not limit the Contractor's continuing liability for any failure to comply with the contract.

48 (1) When the Contractor considers that
   (a) the whole of the Works or
   (b) any Section in respect of which a separate time for completion is provided in the Appendix to the Form of Tender
has been substantially completed and has satisfactorily passed any final test that may be prescribed by the Contract he may give notice in writing to that effect to the Engineer or to the Engineer's Representative. Such notice shall be accompanied by an undertaking to finish any outstanding work in accordance with the provisions of Clause 49(1).

(2) The Engineer shall within 21 days of the date of delivery of such notice either
   (a) issue to the Contractor (with a copy to the Employer) a Certificate of Substantial Completion stating the date on which in his opinion the Works were or the Section was substantially completed in accordance with the Contract or
   (b) give instructions in writing to the Contractor specifying all the work which in the Engineer's opinion requires to be done by the Contractor before the issue of such certificate.
If the Engineer gives such instructions the Contractor shall be entitled to receive a Certificate of Substantial Completion within 21 days of completion to the satisfaction of the Engineer of the work specified in the said instructions.

(3) If any substantial part of the Works has been occupied or used by the Employer other than as provided in the Contract the Contractor may request in writing and the Engineer shall issue a Certificate of Substantial Completion in respect thereof. Such certificate shall take effect from the date of delivery of the Contractor's request and upon the issue of such certificate the Contractor shall be deemed to have undertaken to complete any outstanding work in that part of the Works during the Defects Correction Period.

(4) If the Engineer considers that any part of the Works has been substantially completed and has passed any final test that may be prescribed by the Contract he may issue a Certificate of Substantial Completion in respect of that part of the Works before completion of the whole of the Works and upon the issue of such certificate the Contractor shall be deemed to have undertaken to complete any outstanding work in that part of the Works during the Defects Correction Period.

(5) A Certificate of Substantial Completion given in respect of any Section or part of the Works before completion of the whole shall not be deemed to certify completion of any ground or surfaces requiring reinstatement unless such certificate shall expressly so state.

Note the engineer's useful power to certify completion despite outstanding works. These must be such that the employer may still take over and use the works, it is submitted; otherwise the engineer should certify in respect of completed parts. The employer must take over any parts which are useable in order to mitigate any damages for delay. The later discovery of hidden defects does not invalidate the completion certificate (see page 188).

49 (1) The undertaking to be given under Clause 48(1) may after agreement between the Engineer and the Contractor specify a time or times within which the outstanding work shall be completed. If no such times are specified any outstanding work shall be completed as soon as practicable during the Defects Correction Period.

(2) The Contractor shall deliver up to the Employer the Works and each Section and part thereof at or as soon as practicable after the expiry of the relevant Defects Correction Period in the condition required by the Contract (fair wear and tear excepted) to the satisfaction of the Engineer. To this end the Contractor shall as soon as practicable execute all work of repair amendment reconstruction rectification and making good of defects of whatever nature as may be required of him in writing by the Engineer during the relevant Defects Correction Period or within 14 days after its expiry as a result of an inspection made by or on behalf of the Engineer prior to its expiry.

(3) All work required under sub-clause (2) of this Clause shall be carried out by the Contractor at his own expense if in the Engineer's opinion it is necessary due to the use of materials or workmanship not in accordance with the Contract or to neglect or failure by the Contractor to comply with any of his obligations under the Contract. In any other event the value of such work shall be ascertained and paid for as if it were additional work.

(4) If the Contractor fails to do any such work as aforesaid the Employer shall be entitled to carry out such work by his own workpeople or by other contractors and if such work is work which the Contractor should have carried out at his own expense the Employer shall be entitled to recover the cost thereof from the Contractor and may deduct the same from any monies that are or may become due to the Contractor.

The term "Maintenance Period" appearing in previous editions of the form is now replaced by "Defects Correction Period," which more accurately reflects the effect of the clause. Note that the contractor is obliged to put right any defects, whether or not they are due to his failure to comply with the contract. Clause 49(3) entitles the contractor to payment if the defect is not due to his default. The engineer has specific power to order tests. This may be exercised after completion, and is not, apparently, limited to the maintenance period:

50 The Contractor shall if required by the Engineer in writing carry out such searches tests or trials as may be necessary to determine the

cause of any defect imperfection or fault under the directions of the Engineer. Unless such defect imperfection or fault shall be one for which the Contractor is liable under the Contract the cost of the work carried out by the Contractor as aforesaid shall be borne by the Employer. But if such defect imperfection or fault shall be one for which the Contractor is liable the cost of the work carried out as aforesaid shall be borne by the Contractor and he shall in such case repair rectify and make good such defect imperfection or fault at his own expense in accordance with Clause 49.

If defects are discovered after the defects correction period the contractor remains liable (within the period of limitation) and is not entitled to insist on carrying out remedial work himself. But, in practice, it is often to the advantage of both parties to agree upon remedial works to be carried out by the contractor.

Upon completion the contractor must clear the site:

33 On the completion of the Works the Contractor shall clear away and remove from the Site all Contractor's Equipment surplus material rubbish and Temporary Works of every kind and leave the whole of the Site and Permanent Works clean and in a workmanlike condition to the satisfaction of the Engineer.

Time

The speed with which the contractor carries out the work is an important element in the performance of the contract. The appendix specifies the time for completion, but the contract contains extensive provisions under which the engineer may extend the completion date.

41 (1) The Works Commencement Date shall be
    (a) the date specified in the Appendix to the Form of Tender or if no date is specified
    (b) a date within 28 days of the award of the Contract to be notified by the Engineer in writing or
    (c) such other date as may be agreed between the parties.
(2) The Contractor shall start the Works on or as soon as is reasonably practicable after the Works Commencement Date. Thereafter the Contractor shall proceed with the Works with due expedition and without delay in accordance with the Contract.

By clause 42 the contractor must be given possession of the site so far as necessary. Sub-clause (3) deals with the consequences of failure to give possession:

42 (1) The Contract may prescribe

(a) the extent of portions of the Site of which the Contractor is to be given possession from time to time

(b) the order in which such portions of the Site shall be made available to the Contractor

(c) the availability and the nature of the access which is to be provided by the Employer

(d) the order in which the Works shall be constructed.

(2) (a) Subject to sub-clause (1) of this Clause the Employer shall give to the Contractor on the Works Commencement Date possession of so much of the Site and access thereto as may be required to enable the Contractor to commence and proceed with the construction of the works.

(b) Thereafter the Employer shall during the course of the Works give to the Contractor possession of such further portions of the Site as may be required in accordance with the programme which the Engineer has accepted under Clause 14 and such further access as is necessary to enable the Contractor to proceed with the construction of the Works with due despatch.

(3) If the Contractor suffers delay and/or incurs additional cost from failure on the part of the Employer to give possession in accordance with the terms of this Clause the Engineer shall determine

(a) any extension of time to which the Contractor is entitled under Clause 44 and

(b) subject to Clause 52(4) the amount of any additional cost to which the Contractor may be entitled. Profit shall be added thereto in respect of any additional permanent or temporary works.

The Engineer shall notify the Contractor accordingly with a copy to the Employer.

(4) The Contractor shall bear all costs and charges for any access required by him additional to those provided by the Employer. The Contractor shall also provide at his own cost any additional facilities outside the Site required by him for the purposes of the Works.

Except where the contract lays down the parties' intention, the contractor's right to possession depends on the provisions of the programme under clause 14 (see below), which requires the engineer's approval. The definition of the site, under clause 1(1), is imprecise:

(v) "Site" means the lands and other places on under in or through which the Works are to be executed and any other lands or places provided by the Employer for the purposes of the Contract together with such other places as may be designated in the Contract or subsequently agreed by the Engineer as forming part of the Site.

It is advisable, therefore, to define in the contract both the extent of the site and the times at which it will be released to the contractor.

During the course of the work the engineer has powers to require expedition of progress under clause 14(4) (see above) and clause 46 (see below), where the contractor is in default. Repeated failure to proceed at an adequate rate may lead to determination under clause 63. Conversely the engineer may, at the employer's cost, order suspension of the work:

40 (1) The Contractor shall on the written order of the Engineer suspend the progress of the Works or any part thereof for such time or times and in such manner as the Engineer may consider necessary and shall during such suspension properly protect and secure the work so far as is necessary in the opinion of the Engineer. Subject to Clause 52(4) the Contractor shall be paid in accordance with Clause 60 the extra cost (if any) incurred in giving effect to the Engineer's instructions under this Clause except to the extent that such suspension is

    (a) otherwise provided for in the Contract or

    (b) necessary by reason of weather conditions or by some default on the part of the Contractor or

    (c) necessary for the proper execution or for the safety of the Works or any part thereof in as much as such necessity does not arise from any act or default of the Engineer or the Employer or from any of the Excepted Risks defined in Clause 20(2).

Profit shall be added thereto in respect of any additional permanent or temporary work.

The Engineer shall take any delay occasioned by a suspension ordered under this Clause (including that arising from any act or default of the Engineer or the Employer) into account in determining any extension of time to which the Contractor is entitled under Clause 44 except when such suspension is otherwise provided for in the Contract or is necessary by reason of some default on the part of the Contractor.

(2) If the progress of the Works or any part thereof is suspended on the written order of the Engineer and if permission to resume work is not given by the Engineer within a period of three months from the date of suspension then the Contractor may unless such suspension is otherwise provided for in the Contract or continues to be necessary by reason of some default on the part of the Contractor serve a written notice on the Engineer requiring permission within 28 days from the receipt of such notice to proceed with the Works or that part thereof in regard to which progress is suspended. If within the said 28 days the Engineer does not grant such permission the Contractor by a further written notice so served may (but is not bound to) elect to treat the suspension where it affects part only of the Works as an omission of such part under Clause 51 or where it affects the whole Works as an abandonment of the Contract by the Employer.

This is the only power given to the contractor to determine the contract (*c.f.* clause 28 JCT form), outside common law rights (see page 104).

43 The whole of the Works and any Section required to be completed within a particular time as stated in the Appendix to the Form of Tender shall be substantially completed within the time so stated (or such extended time as may be allowed under Clause 44) calculated from the Works Commencement Date notified under Clause 41.

44 (1) Should the Contractor consider that
      (*a*) any variation ordered under Clause 51(1) or
      (*b*) increased quantities referred to in Clause 51(3) or
      (*c*) any cause of delay referred to in these Conditions or
      (*d*) exceptional adverse weather conditions or
      (*e*) other special circumstances of any kind whatsoever which may occur
be such as to entitle him to an extension of time for the substantial completion of the Works or any Section thereof he shall within 28 days after the cause of any delay has arisen or as soon thereafter as is reasonable deliver to the Engineer full and detailed particulars in justification of the period of extension claimed in order that the claim may be investigated at the time.

(2) (*a*) The Engineer shall upon receipt of such particulars consider all the circumstances known to him at that time and make an assessment of the delay (if any) that has been suffered by the Contractor as a result of the alleged cause and shall so notify the Contractor in writing.

     (*b*) The Engineer may in the absence of any claim make an assessment of the delay that he considers has been suffered by the Contractor as a result of any of the circumstances listed in sub-clause (1) of this Clause and shall so notify the Contractor in writing.

(3) Should the Engineer consider that the delay suffered fairly entitles the Contractor to an extension of the time for the substantial completion of the Works or any Section thereof such interim extension shall be granted forthwith and be notified to the Contractor in writing. In the event that the Contractor has made a claim for an extension of time but the Engineer does not consider the Contractor entitled to an extension of time he shall so inform the Contractor without delay.

(4) The Engineer shall not later than 14 days after the due date or extended date for completion of the Works or any Section thereof (and whether or not the Contractor shall have made any claim for an extension of time) consider all the circumstances known to him at that time and take action similar to that provided for in sub-clause (3) of this Clause. Should the Engineer consider that the Contractor is not entitled to an extension of time he shall so notify the Employer and the Contractor.

(5) The Engineer shall within 14 days of the issue of the Certificate of Substantial Completion for the Works or for any Section thereof review

all the circumstances of the kind referred to in sub-clause (1) of this Clause, and shall finally determine and certify to the Contractor with a copy to the Employer the overall extension of time (if any) to which he considers the Contractor entitled in respect of the Works or the relevant Section. No such final review of the circumstances shall result in a decrease in any extension of time already granted by the Engineer pursuant to sub-clauses (3) or (4) of this Clause.

An interim extension under clause 44(3) may be allowed where the contractor has not given notice under sub-clause (1). The engineer is bound to review the grounds for extension, under sub-clauses (4) and (5), at the contractual date for completion and the actual date, whether or not extensions have been requested. This allows the engineer to grant extensions on what he considers the true grounds of delay, when the contractor may have applied on other grounds. The grounds which entitle the contractor to extensions, other than those mentioned in clause 44(1), are, principally: late instructions (clause 7), adverse conditions (clause 12), instructions under clauses 5 or 13, delayed or unforeseen requirements (clause 14), other contractors (clause 31), suspension of work (clause 40), and non-possession (clause 42).

The contractor's failure to complete the work by the date or extended date for completion entitles the employer to deduct liquidated damages specified in the appendix. Clause 47 contains extensive provisions governing the deduction of liquidated damages for the whole or for specified sections of the work. In the event of the work being delayed by a default on the part of the employer which does not permit an extension to be granted, the liquidated damages clause becomes unenforceable. In this regard, the general words of clause 44 "other special circumstances" may not be applicable (see page 189).

POWERS AND REMEDIES OF THE ENGINEER AND EMPLOYER

Many of these have already been dealt with. The engineer has a sweeping power under clause 13(1) to give instructions and directions on any matter connected with the works. Under clauses 13(2) and 14 the engineer has powers to control the contractor's methods of work. Clause 14 also deals with the question of programming the works. Sub-clauses (1) to (4) require the contractor to provide a programme acceptable to the engineer, and empowers the engineer to require a revision should the work fall into delay.

Note that the programme is not a contract document and does not strictly bind either party. It is intended to monitor performance of other obligations required to be carried out timeously. As an additional remedy for slow progress, the engineer may require the contractor to specify steps to expedite the work under clause 46, which also contains provisions for agreed acceleration:

46 (1) If for any reason which does not entitle the Contractor to an extension of time the rate of progress of the Works or any Section is at any time in the opinion of the Engineer too slow to ensure substantial completion by the time or extended time for completion prescribed by Clauses 43 and 44 as appropriate, the Engineer shall notify the Contractor in writing and the Contractor shall thereupon take such steps as are necessary and to which the Engineer may consent to expedite the progress so as substantially to complete the Works or such Section by that prescribed time or extended time. The Contractor shall not be entitled to any additional payment for taking such steps.

(2) If as a result of any notice given by the Engineer under sub-clause (1) of this Clause the Contractor shall seek the Engineer's permission to do any work on Site at night or on Sundays such permission shall not be unreasonably refused.

(3) If the Contractor is requested by the Employer or the Engineer to complete the Works or any Section within a revised time being less than the time or extended time for completion prescribed by Clauses 43 and 44 as appropriate and the Contractor agrees so to do then any special terms and conditions of payment shall be agreed between the Contractor and the Employer before any such action is taken.

In default of compliance by the contractor the employer's positive powers are limited to deduction of liquidated damages or determination (clauses 47, 63).

The engineer's most important express power under the contract is to vary the works:

51 (1) The Engineer
    (a) shall order any variation to any part of the Works that is in his opinion necessary for the completion of the Works and
    (b) may order any variation that for any other reason shall in his opinion be desirable for the completion and/or improved functioning of the Works.

Such variations may include additions omissions substitutions alterations changes in quality form character kind position dimension level or line and changes in any specified sequence method or timing of construction required by the Contract and may be ordered during the Defects Correction Period.

(2) All variations shall be ordered in writing but the provisions of Clause 2(6) in respect of oral instructions shall apply.

(3) No variation ordered in accordance with sub-clauses (1) and (2) of this Clause shall in any way vitiate or invalidate the Contract but the value (if any) of all such variations shall be taken into account in ascertaining the amount of the Contract Price except to the extent that such variation is necessitated by the Contractor's default.

(4) No order in writing shall be required for increase or decrease in the quantity of any work where such increase or decrease is not the result of an order given under this Clause but is the result of the quantities exceeding or being less than those stated in the Bill of Quantities.

The exception at the end of sub-clause (3) is new to the 6th edition and is intended to prevent a contractor who is in default taking advantage of a chance instruction which could be construed as a variation order. Note that the engineer's powers include varying the works and also ordering changes in the specified sequence, method or timing of construction required by the contract. The *obligation* to order a variation under sub-clause (1)(*a*) is of limited ambit, and will normally apply where the work becomes impossible to carry out in accordance with express requirements of the contract, such as an incorporated method of working (see above, page 161). Valuation of variations and of changes in quantities of the work are dealt with in clauses 52 and 56(2).

Sub-contractors

Clauses 3 and 4 deal with the question of vicarious performance. Clause 3 prevents assignment (by either party) without consent. Clause 4 permits sub-contracting of any parts of the work.

3 Neither the Employer nor the Contractor shall assign the Contract or any part thereof or any benefit or interest therein or thereunder without the prior written consent of the other party which consent shall not unreasonably be withheld.

4 (1) The Contractor shall not sub-contract the whole of the Works without the prior written consent of the Employer.

(2) Except where otherwise provided the Contractor may sub-contract any part of the Works or their design. The extent of the work to be sub-contracted and the name and address of the sub-contractor must be notified in writing to the Engineer prior to the sub-contractor's entry on to the Site or in the case of design on appointment.

(3) The employment of labour only sub-contractors does not require notification to the Engineer under sub-clause (2) of this Clause.

(4) The Contractor shall be and remain liable under the Contract for all work sub-contracted under this Clause and for acts defaults or neglects of any sub-contractor his agents servants or workpeople.

(5) The Engineer shall be at liberty after due warning in writing to require the Contractor to remove from the Works any sub-contractor who mis-conducts himself or is incompetent or negligent in the performance of his duties or fails to conform with any particular provisions with regard to safety which may be set out in the Contract or persists in any conduct which is prejudicial to safety or health and such sub-contractor shall not be again employed upon the Works without the permission of the Engineer.

The contractor is to remain fully liable for the sub-contractors of his own choosing. Where the contract provides for specific work to be carried out by a nominated sub-contractor, clauses 58 and 59 lay down extensive provisions governing the parties' rights, particularly in regard to default by the sub-contractor. Such work will be designated as either a provisional sum or a prime cost item. In regard to these the engineer's powers are as follows.

58 (1) In respect of every Provisional Sum the Engineer may order either or both of the following
> (a) work to be executed or goods materials or services to be supplied by the Contractor the value thereof being determined in accordance with Clause 52 and included in the Contract Price
> (b) work to be executed or goods materials or services to be supplied by a Nominated Sub-contractor in accordance with Clause 59.

(2) In respect of every Prime Cost Item the Engineer may order either or both of the following
> (a) subject to Clause 59 that the Contractor employ a sub-contractor nominated by the Engineer for the execution of any work or the supply of any goods materials or services included therein
> (b) with the consent of the Contractor that the Contractor himself execute any such work or supply any such goods, materials or services in which event the Contractor shall be paid in accordance with the terms of a quotation submitted by him and accepted by the Engineer or in the absence thereof the value shall be determined in accordance with Clause 52 and included in the Contract Price.

(3) If in connection with any Provisional Sum or Prime Cost Item the services to be provided include any matter of design or specification of any part of the Permanent Works or of any equipment or plant to be incorporated therein such requirement shall be expressly stated in the

Contract and shall be included in any Nominated Sub-contract. The
obligation of the Contractor in respect thereof shall be only that which
has been expressly stated in accordance with this sub-clause.

In regard to design, the contract must contain an express
provision to make the contractor liable for the design of the
permanent works (clause 8(2)). It frequently happens that sub-
contractors are chosen for nomination because they can carry out
specialist designs. Clause 58(3) requires this obligation to appear
also in the sub-contract before the main contractor can be made
liable. The employer should, in such a case, also consider taking
a direct warranty from the sub-contractor (see page 178).

Clauses 59 contains extensive provisions in regard to nominated sub-contractors, covering the following matters:

> terms which the contractor is entitled to have in any nomi-
> nated sub-contract;
> powers available to the engineer if the parties to the sub-
> contract cannot agree terms;
> payments in respect of nominated sub-contract work,
> including the power to make direct payment to the sub-
> contractor;
> consequences of termination of a nominated sub-contract;
> limitation of the contractor's liability in the event of default
> by a nominated sub-contractor.

The last two of these matters are of great concern to the
employer, and comfort to the contractor. Clause 59 provides
that, where a nominated sub-contract is terminated, the Engineer
must either make a re-nomination or order a variation, in the first
instance at the employer's expense. Where the termination was
with the Engineer's consent, clause 59(4) provides for the contractor to attempt recovery of the employer's loss, subject to the
employer reimbursing any unrecovered expenses. These provisions are based on clauses in the JCT management contract
(particularly clause 3.21). It is questionable whether they provide
any real benefit to the employer.

In regard to default by a nominated sub-contractor which does
not lead to termination, the main contractor is fully liable:

59 (3) Except as otherwise provided in Clause 58(3) the Contractor
shall be as responsible for the work executed or goods materials or
services supplied by a Nominated Sub-Contractor employed by him as if
he had himself executed such work or supplied such goods materials or
services.

There is, however, a restriction on withholding sums on account of default by a nominated sub-contractor:

60 (8) The Engineer shall have power to omit from any certificate the value of any work done goods or materials supplied or services rendered with which he may for the time being be dissatisfied and for that purpose or for any other reason which to him may seem proper may by any certificate delete correct or modify any sum previously certified by him. Provided that

> (a) the Engineer shall not in any interim certificate delete or reduce any sum previously certified in respect of work done goods or materials supplied or services rendered by a Nominated Sub-contractor if the Contractor shall have already paid or be bound to pay that sum to the Nominated Sub-contractor;
>
> (b) if the Engineer in the final certificate shall delete or reduce any sum previously certified in respect of work done goods or materials supplied or services rendered by a Nominated Sub-contractor which sum shall have been already paid by the Contractor to the Nominated Sub-contractor the Employer shall reimburse to the Contractor the amount of any sum overpaid by the Contractor to the Sub-contractor in accordance with the certificates issued under sub-clause (2) of this Clause which the Contractor shall be unable to recover from the Nominated Sub-contractor together with interest thereon at the rate stated in sub-clause (7) of this Clause from 28 days after the date of the final certificate issued under sub-clause (4) of this Clause until the date of such reimbursement.

Clause 60(1) to (4) is set out below. Clause 60(7) (not printed) provides for interest on unpaid sums at two per cent. above base lending rate.

Default by the contractor

In the event that the contractor fails to comply with the contract, the employer has (in addition to the sanctions discussed below) some degree of security against loss. As to the work done and materials supplied, the employer withholds a percentage of the contract value until completion (see under "Payment" below). The employer also has valuable rights over the contractor's plant and materials on the site.

53 (1) All Contractor's Equipment Temporary Works materials for Temporary Works or other goods or materials owned by the Contractor shall when on Site be deemed to be the property of the Employer and

shall not be removed therefrom without the written consent of the Engineer which consent shall not unreasonably be withheld where the items in question are no longer immediately required for the purposes of the completion of the Works.

(2) The Employer shall not at any time be liable save as mentioned in Clauses 22 and 65 for the loss of or damage to any Contractor's Equipment Temporary Works goods or materials.

(3) If the Contractor fails to remove any of the said Contractor's Equipment Temporary Works goods or materials as required by Clause 33 within such reasonable time after completion of the Works as the Engineer may allow then the Employer may sell or otherwise dispose of such items. From the proceeds of the sale of any such items the Employer shall be entitled to retain any costs or expenses incurred in connection with their sale and disposal before paying the balance (if any) to the Contractor.

The deemed vesting of the contractor's plant and materials gives the employer the right, in the event of forfeiture, to take physical possession, as security. Note that the plant, etc. remains vested until removed from the site by consent. As to the effect of insolvency see page 201.

Some of the sanctions exercisable on the default of the contractor are discussed above. If the contractor does not make adequate progress the engineer may require steps to be taken to expedite progress under clause 46, and require a revised programme under clause 14. If the works are not completed by the date or extended date for completion the employer may deduct liquidated damages. Where defective work is done the engineer has important powers under clause 39 to order its removal and proper replacement. In respect of all these powers, the choice remains with the contractor to obey the engineer's instructions or pay for his default.

Where the contractor's default is more serious, or when he becomes unable to perform the contract, the employer may become entitled to determine the contractor's employment.

63 (1) If
    (*a*) the Contractor shall be in default in that he
        (i) becomes bankrupt or has a receiving order or administration order made against him or presents his petition in bankruptcy or makes an arrangement with or assignment in favour of his creditors or agrees to carry out the Contract under a committee of inspection of his creditors or (being a corporation) goes into liquidation (other than a voluntary liquidation for the purposes of amalgamation or reconstruction) or

        (ii) assigns the Contract without the consent in writing of the
            Employer first obtained or
       (iii) has an execution levied on his goods which is not stayed or
            discharged within 28 days or

(b) the Engineer certifies in writing to the Employer with a copy
    to the Contractor that in his opinion the Contractor
      (i) has abandoned the Contract or
     (ii) without reasonable excuse has failed to commence the
        Works in accordance with Clause 41 or has suspended the
        progress of the Works for 14 days after receiving from the
        Engineer written notice to proceed or
     (iii) has failed to remove goods or materials from the Site or to
        pull down and replace work for 14 days after receiving
        from the Engineer written notice that the said goods
        materials or work have been condemned and rejected by
        the Engineer or
     (iv) despite previous warnings by the Engineer in writing is
        failing to proceed with the Works with due diligence or is
        otherwise persistently or fundamentally in breach of his
        obligations under Contract

then the Employer may after giving seven days' notice in writing to the
Contractor specifying the default enter upon the Site and the Works and
expel the Contractor therefrom without thereby avoiding the Contract or
releasing the Contractor from any of his obligations or liabilities under
the Contract. Provided that the Employer may extend the period of
notice to give the Contractor opportunity to remedy the default.

    Where a notice of determination is given pursuant to this sub-clause it
shall be given as soon as is reasonably possible after receipt of the
Engineer's certificate.

    (2) Where the Employer has entered upon the Site and the Works as
hereinbefore provided he may himself complete the Works or may
employ any other contractor to complete the Works and the Employer
or such other contractor may use for such completion so much of the
Contractor's Equipment Temporary Works goods and materials which
have been deemed to become the property of the Employer under
Clauses 53 and 54 as he or they may think proper and the Employer may
at any time sell any of the said Contractor's Equipment Temporary
Works and unused goods and materials and apply the proceeds of sale in
or towards the satisfaction of any sums due or which may become due to
him from the contractor under the Contract.

    Note that the operation of this clause does not determine the
contract. Clause 63(4), which remains binding on the contractor,
entitles the employer to be paid the additional costs of completing the work by another contractor. Sub-clause (3) requires the
contractor to assign sub-contracts to the employer after determination.

    This clause is, in practice, difficult to operate. If the employer
expels the contractor from the site without complying precisely

with sub-clause (1), he is likely to have repudiated the contract, rendering himself liable to the contractor in damages (see page 104). The clause is an example of the unnecessary obscurity which pervades much of the contract. It is not clear to what extent these remedies supersede other remedies based on the same grounds; for example, if the engineer exercises the power under clause 39(2) to bring in another contractor to re-execute defective work (see above) can notice also be given under clause 63(1)(*b*)(iii)?

CERTIFICATION AND PAYMENT

These provisions are vital to the contractor, who will often, during the course of the work, lay out sums of money or incur liabilities greatly exceeding the value of his assets. The provisions for interim payment make this possible. Cash flow has been referred to by the courts as the life-blood of the industry.

Clause 60 lays down the basic monthly accounting procedure:

60 (1) The Contractor shall submit to the Engineer at monthly intervals a statement (in such form if any as may be prescribed in the Specification) showing
> (*a*) the estimated contract value of the Permanent Works executed up to the end of that month
> (*b*) a list of any goods or materials delivered to the Site for but not yet incorporated in the Permanent Works and their value
> (*c*) a list of any of those goods or materials identified in the Appendix to the Form of Tender which have not yet been delivered to the Site but of which the property has vested in the Employer pursuant to Clause 54 and their value
> (*d*) the estimated amounts to which the Contractor considers himself entitled in connection with all other matters for which provision is made under the Contract including any Temporary Works or Contractor's Equipment for which separate amounts are included in the Bill of Quantities

unless in the opinion of the Contractor such values and amounts together will not justify the issue of an interim certificate.

Amounts payable in respect of Nominated Sub-contracts are to be listed separately.

(2) Within 28 days of the date of delivery to the Engineer or Engineer's Representative in accordance with sub-clause (1) of this Clause of the Contractor's monthly statement the Engineer shall certify and the Employer shall pay to the Contractor (after deducting any previous payments on account)

(*a*) the amount which in the opinion of the Engineer on the basis of the monthly statement is due to the Contractor on account of sub-clauses (1)(*a*) and (1)(*d*) of this Clause less a retention as provided in sub-clause (5) of this Clause

(*b*) such amounts (if any) as the Engineer may consider proper (but in no case exceeding the percentage of the value stated in the Appendix to the Form of Tender) in respect of sub-clauses (1)(*b*) and (1)(*c*) of this Clause.

The amounts certified in respect of Nominated Sub-Contracts shall be shown separately in the certificate.

Note that retention is not deducted on the value of unfixed goods. The contractor is entitled only to the percentage of their value specified in the appendix. Clause 54 lays down conditions to be satisfied if the contractor wishes to obtain payment for materials (to be specified in the appendix) before delivery to the site. Such goods must become the property of the employer.

Clause 60(3) provides for a minimum amount for certificates. Clause 60(4) deals with the final account. Clause 60(5) regulates the deduction of retention, which is recommended not to exceed five per cent. Clause 60(6) provides for payment of the retention. Subject to reductions for sectional completion, the money is to be paid to the contractor as to half on the certificate of completion of the whole of the works, and half on expiry of the period of maintenance, subject to deduction for outstanding work.

Clause 60(7) provides for payment of interest on certificates withheld or unpaid at a rate of two per cent. over base lending rate.

The measurement of the work is dealt with in the following group of clauses:

55 (1) The quantities set out in the Bill of Quantities are the estimated quantities of the work but they are not to be taken as the actual and correct quantities of the Works to be executed by the Contractor in fulfilment of his obligations under the Contract.

(2) Any error in description in the Bill of Quantities or omission therefrom shall not vitiate the Contract nor release the Contractor from the execution of the whole or any part of the Works according to the Drawings and Specification or from any of his obligations or liabilities under the Contract. Any such error or omission shall be corrected by the Engineer and the value of the work actually carried out shall be ascertained in accordance with Clause 52. Provided that there shall be no rectification of any errors omissions or wrong estimates in the descriptions rates and prices inserted by the Contractor in the Bill of Quantities.

56 (1) The Engineer shall except as otherwise stated ascertain and determine by admeasurement the value in accordance with the Contract of the work done in accordance with the Contract.

(2) Should the actual quantities executed in respect of any item be greater or less than those stated in the Bill of Quantities and if in the opinion of the Engineer such increase or decrease of itself shall so warrant the Engineer shall after consultation with the Contractor determine an appropriate increase or decrease of any rates or prices rendered unreasonable or inapplicable in consequence thereof and shall notify the Contractor accordingly.

(3) The Engineer shall when he requires any part or parts of the work to be measured give reasonable notice to the Contractor who shall attend or send a qualified agent to assist the Engineer or the Engineer's Representative in making such measurement and shall furnish all particulars required by either of them. Should the Contractor not attend or neglect or omit to send such agent then the measurement made by the Engineer or approved by him shall be taken to be the correct measurement of the work.

Sub-clause (4) deals with dayworks.

57 Unless otherwise provided in the Contract or unless general or detailed description of the work in the Bill of Quantities or any other statement clearly shows to the contrary the Bill of Quantities shall be deemed to have been prepared and measurements shall be made according to the procedure set out in the "Civil Engineering Standard Method of Measurement Second Edition 1985" approved by the Institution of Civil Engineers and the Federation of Civil Engineering Contractors in association with the Association of Consulting Engineers or such later or amended edition thereof as may be stated in the Appendix to the Form of Tender to have been adopted in its preparation.

These clauses mean that the contract is subject to re-measurement; *i.e.* the contractor is to be paid for the actual quantities of work executed at the contract rates, which may themselves be varied under clause 56(2). The effect of clauses 57 and 55(2) is that work shown on the drawings or in the specification but omitted from the bill, contrary to the Standard Method, is to be paid for as an extra.

The amounts to which the contractor is entitled under clause 66(1)(*d*) "in connection with all other matters for which provision is made under the contract" depend on many clauses including 7(3), 12(3), 13(3), 14(6), 31(2), 40(1), 42(2) and 52. The most important is the provision for valuing variations.

52 (1) The value of all variations ordered by the Engineer in accordance with Clause 51 shall be ascertained by the Engineer after consultation with the Contractor in accordance with the following principles

(*a*) where work is of similar character and executed under similar conditions to work priced in the Bill of Quantities it shall be valued at such rates and prices contained therein as may be applicable

(*b*) where work is not of a similar character or is not executed under similar conditions or is ordered during the Defects Correction Period the rates and prices in the Bill of Quantities shall be used as the basis for valuation so far as may be reasonable failing which a fair valuation shall be made.

Failing agreement between the Engineer and the Contractor as to any rate or price to be applied in the valuation of any variation the Engineer shall determine the rate or price in accordance with the foregoing principles and he shall notify the Contractor accordingly.

(2) If the nature or amount of any variation relative to the nature or amount of the whole of the contract work or to any part thereof shall be such that in the opinion of the Engineer or the Contractor any rate or price contained in the Contract for any item of work is by reason of such variation rendered unreasonable or inapplicable either the Engineer shall give to the Contractor or the Contractor shall give to the Engineer notice before the varied work is commenced or as soon thereafter as is reasonable in all the circumstances that such rate or price should be varied and the Engineer shall fix such rate or price as in the circumstances he shall think reasonable and proper.

Note that the engineer's power to vary the contract rates under sub-clause (2) applies "to any rate or price contained in the contract for any item of work" and is not limited to the work which is varied. A claim under clause 52(2) is the nearest equivalent to a claim for loss and/or expense under clause 26 of the JCT form.

Clause 52(3) enables the engineer to order additional or substituted work to be executed on a daywork basis. Clause 52(4) provides for notices to be given of claims under any clause of the contract (see below).

In addition to sums due for varied work, there are many other provisions which may entitle the contractor to claim further payment. In addition to payment at the rates and prices fixed under the contract, there may be incorporated optional fluctuations clauses. Separate clauses are available for use where the contract consists primarily of civil engineering work (the CE clause) or of fabricated structural steelwork (the FSS clause). Both may be used, together with a regulating clause referred to as CE/FSS.

These clauses operate exclusively on formula adjustments. The amounts payable therefore depend only on the net value of works executed and index changes, and are independent of the actual constituents of the work. The current index figures, from which payments are calculated, are defined as:

> (2)(c) "Current Index Figure" shall mean the appropriate Final Index Figure to be applied in respect of any certificate issued or due to be issued by the Engineer pursuant to Clause 60 and shall be the appropriate Final Index Figure applicable to the date 42 days prior to
>> (i) the due date (or extended date) for completion or
>> (ii) the date certified pursuant to Clause 48 of completion of the whole of the Works or
>> (iii) the last day of the period to which the certificate relates; whichever is the earliest.

Payments are thus frozen at the prices applying when the work should be completed. There are no requirements such as those incorporated into the JCT form: see clause 39.5.8 (page 270 above).

Claims

Additional payments which may be due to the contractor under provisions other than those covering valuation of the work done are often referred to as "claims." The term may also include damages for breach of contract; but this section is limited to consideration of sums due under the contract.

The principal claims available to the contractor are set out below. Clause 7(4) entitles the contractor to payment in respect of the late issue of drawings or instructions:

> 7 (4)(a) If by reason of any failure or inability of the Engineer to issue at a time reasonable in all the circumstances Drawings Specifications or instructions requested by the Contractor and considered necessary by the Engineer in accordance with sub-clause (1) of this Clause the Contractor suffers delay or incurs cost then the Engineer shall take such delay into account in determining any extension of time to which the Contractor is entitled under Clause 44 and the Contractor shall subject to Clause 52(4) be paid in accordance with Clause 60 the amount of such cost as may be reasonable.
>
> (b) If the failure of the Engineer to issue any Drawing Specification or instruction is caused in whole or in part by the failure of the Contractor after due notice in writing to submit drawings specifications or other documents which he is required to submit under the Contract the Engineer shall take

into account such failure by the Contractor in taking any action under sub-clause (4)(*a*) of this Clause.

Clause 12 allows the contractor to claim additional payment for work to overcome unforeseen physical conditions or artificial obstructions:

12 (1) If during the execution of the Works the Contractor shall encounter physical conditions (other than weather condition or conditions due to weather conditions) or artificial obstructions which conditions or obstructions could not in his opinion reasonably have been foreseen by an experienced contractor the Contractor shall as early as practicable give written notice thereof to the Engineer.

(2) If in addition the Contractor intends to make any claim for additional payment or extension of time arising from such condition or obstruction he shall at the same time or as soon thereafter as may be reasonable inform the Engineer in writing pursuant to Clause 52(4) and/ or Clause 44(1) as may be appropriate specifying the condition or obstruction to which the claim relates.

(3) When giving notification in accordance with sub-clauses (1) and (2) of this Clause or as soon as practicable thereafter the Contractor shall give details of any anticipated effects of the condition or obstruction the measures he has taken is taking or is proposing to take their estimated cost and the extent of the anticipated delay in or interference with the execution of the Works.

(4) Following receipt of any notification under sub-clauses (1) (2) or (3) of this Clause the Engineer may if he thinks fit *inter alia*

    (*a*) require the Contractor to investigate and report upon the practicality cost and timing of alternative measures which may be available

    (*b*) give written consent to measures notified under sub-clause (3) of this Clause with or without modification

    (*c*) give written instructions as to how the physical conditions or artifical obstructions are to be dealt with

    (*d*) order a suspension under Clause 40 or a variation under Clause 51.

(5) If the engineer shall decide that the physical conditions or artificial obstructions could in whole or in part have been reasonably foreseen by an experienced contractor he shall so inform the Contractor in writing as soon as he shall have reached that decision but the value of any variation previously ordered by him pursuant to sub-clause (4)(*d*) of this Clause shall be ascertained in accordance with Clause 52 and included in the Contract Price.

(6) Where an extension of time or additional payment is claimed pursuant to sub-clause (2) of this Clause the Engineer shall if in his opinion such conditions or obstructions could not reasonably have been foreseen by an experienced contractor determine the amount of any costs which may reasonably have been incurred by the Contractor by

reason of such conditions or obstructions together with a reasonable percentage addition thereto in respect of profit and any extension of time to which the Contractor may be entitled and shall notify the Contractor accordingly with a copy to the Employer.

Clause 12 is widely used as a vehicle for presenting claims for additional cost. Claims usually relate to sub-soil conditions, but the terms of sub-clause (1) are not limited to any particular sort of condition or obstruction. A further claim provision of general application is clause 13(3):

13 (3) If in pursuance of Clause 5 or sub-clause (1) of this Clause the Engineer shall issue instructions which involve the Contractor in delay or disrupt his arrangements or methods of construction so as to cause him to incur cost beyond that reasonably to have been foreseen by an experienced contractor at the time of tender then the Engineer shall take such delay into account in determining any extension of time to which the Contractor is entitled under Clause 44 and the Contractor shall subject to Clause 52(4) be paid in accordance with Clause 60 the amount of such cost as may be reasonable except to the extent that such delay and extra cost result from the Contractor's default. Profit shall be added thereto in respect of any additional permanent or temporary work. If such instructions require any variation to any part of the Works the same shall be deemed to have been given pursuant to Clause 51.

An instruction under clause 5 is one given to explain and adjust an ambiguity in the contract. Clause 13(1) refers to instructions on any matter connected with the works (whether mentioned in the contract or not). In practice, instructions are often given without specifying any clause. It is thought that an instruction is given in pursuance of clause 13(1) only if it cannot be given under any other clause. But the contrary is arguable, *i.e.* that *any* instruction gives rise to a claim under clause 13(3).

Clause 14(8) allows claims in respect of the engineer's requirements in regard to the methods of construction (printed above).

Clause 31 requires the contractor to give facilities for other contractors and provides for payment of unforeseen cost:

31 (1) The Contractor shall in accordance with the requirements of the Engineer or Engineer's Representative afford all reasonable facilities for any other contractors employed by the Employer and their workmen and for the workmen of the Employer and of any other properly authorised authorities or statutory bodies who may be employed in the execution on or near the Site of any work not in the Contract or of any contract which the Employer may enter into in connection with or ancillary to the Works.

(2) If compliance with sub-clause (1) of this Clause shall involve the Contractor in delay or cost beyond that reasonably to be foreseen by an experienced contractor at the time of tender then the Engineer shall take such delay into account in determining any extension of time to which the Contractor is entitled under Clause 44 and the Contractor shall subject to Clause 52(4) be paid in accordance with Clause 60 the amount of such cost as may be reasonable. Profit shall be added thereto in respect of any additional permanent or temporary work.

Claims for extra cost arising from suspension of the works or non-possession are provided by clauses 40(1) and 42(1), set out above.

In respect of all such claims, the cost recoverable may include overheads and interest incurred:

1 (5) The word "cost" when used in the Conditions of Contract means all expenditure properly incurred or to be incurred whether on or off the Site including overhead finance and other charges properly allocatable thereto but does not include any allowance for profit.

The addition of profit is dealt with in individual clauses: see, e.g., clauses 12(6), 13(3) and 31(2) above.

All the above claims (and others) are subject to clause 52(4) which requires the contractor to give notice in writing "as soon as reasonably possible" (note that stricter notices are required for claims under clauses 52 and 56). The contractor's right to final and interim payments in respect of claims are governed by paragraphs (e) and (f):

(4) (a) If the Contractor intends to claim a higher rate or price than the one notified to him by the Engineer pursuant to sub-clauses (1) and (2) of this Clause or Clause 56(2) the Contractor shall within 28 days after such notification give notice in writing of his intention to the Engineer.

(b) If the Contractor intends to claim any additional payment pursuant to any Clause of these Conditions other than sub-clauses (1) and (2) of this Clause or Clause 56(2) he shall give notice in writing of his intention to the Engineer as soon as may be reasonable and in any event within 28 days after the happening of the events giving rise to the claim. Upon the happening of such events the Contractor shall keep such contemporary records as may reasonably be necessary to support any claim he may subsequently wish to make.

(c) Without necessarily admitting the Employer's liability the Engineer may upon receipt of a notice under this Clause instruct the Contractor to keep such contemporary records or further contemporary records as the case may be as are reasonable and may be material to the claim of which notice has been given and the Contractor shall keep such records. The Contractor shall permit the Engineer to inspect all records kept pursuant to this Clause and shall supply him with copies thereof as and when the Engineer shall so instruct.

(*d*) After the giving of a notice to the Engineer under this Clause the Contractor shall as soon as is reasonable in all the circumstances send to the Engineer a first interim account giving full and detailed particulars of the amount claimed to that date and of the grounds upon which the claim is based. Thereafter at such intervals as the Engineer may reasonably require the Contractor shall send to the Engineer further up to date accounts giving the accumulated total of the claim and any further grounds upon which it is based.

(*e*) If the Contractor fails to comply with any of the provisions of this Clause in respect of any claim which he shall seek to make then the Contractor shall be entitled to payment in respect thereof only to the extent that the Engineer has not been prevented from or substantially prejudiced by such failure in investigating the said claim.

(*f*) The Contractor shall be entitled to have included in any interim payment certified by the Engineer pursuant to Clause 60 such amount in respect of any claim as the Engineer may consider due to the Contractor provided that the Contractor shall have supplied sufficient particulars to enable the Engineer to determine the amount due.

If such particulars are insufficient to substantiate the whole of the claim the Contractor shall be entitled to payment in respect of such part of the claim as the particulars may substantiate to the satisfaction of the Engineer.

Note that paragraph (*e*) sets no time limit on the engineer's investigation. The contractor may re-submit his claim if further information comes to light.

Final Accounting

After the completion of the work and correction of notified defects and omissions, the engineer is required to issue the Defects Correction Certificate. This is followed by vetting the contractor's accounts and issuing a final certificate.

61 (1) Upon the expiry of the Defects Correction Period or where there is more than one such period upon the expiration of the last of such periods and when all outstanding work referred to under Clause 48 and all work of repair amendment reconstruction rectification and

making good of defects imperfections shrinkages and other faults referred to under Clauses 49 and 50 shall have been completed the Engineer shall issue to the Employer (with a copy to the Contractor) a Defects Correction Certificate stating the date on which the Contractor shall have completed his obligations to construct and complete the Works to the Engineer's satisfaction.

(2) The issue of the Defects Correction Certificate shall not be taken as relieving either the Contractor or the Employer from any liability the one towards the other arising out of or in any way connected with the performance of their respective obligations under the Contract.

60 (4) Not later than three months after the date of the Defects Correction Certificate the Contractor shall submit to the Engineer a statement of final account and supporting documentation showing in detail the value in accordance with the Contract of the Works executed together with all further sums which the Contractor considers to be due to him under the Contract up to the date of the Defects Correction Certificate.

Within three months after receipt of this final account and of all information reasonably required for its verification the Engineer shall issue a certificate stating the amount which in his opinion is finally due under the Contract from the Employer to the Contractor or from the Contractor to the Employer as the case may be up to the date of the Defects Correction Certificate and after giving credit to the Employer for all amounts previously paid by the Employer and for all sums to which the Employer is entitled under the Contract.

Such amount shall subject to Clause 47 be paid to or by the Contractor as the case may require within 28 days of the date of the certificate.

Neither the Defects Correction certificate nor the final certificate constitutes a binding approval of the work. This should be compared to the final certificate under clause 30·8 of the JCT form.

DISPUTES

When a dispute exists clause 66 provides for settlement by a two-tier system. When the dispute concerns a claim by the contractor, the system has three tiers: the claim must be referred to and rejected by the engineer under the relevant clause before a dispute exists; the dispute must then be referred back to the engineer under clause 66; and the engineer's decision may then be the subject of arbitration. In addition, the 6th edition includes an optional provision for conciliation, which may precede or even replace arbitration. Both arbitration and conciliation are subject to a mandatory procedure which vests the arbitrator or conciliator with particular powers (see Chapter 3 for further notes on ICE Arbitration Procedure (1983)).

66 (1) Except as otherwise provided in these Conditions if a dispute of any kind whatsoever arises between the Employer and the Contractor in connection with or arising out of the Contract or the carrying out of the Works including any dispute as to any decision opinion instruction direction certificate or valuation of the Engineer (whether during the progress of the Works or after their completion and whether before or after the determination abandonment or breach of the Contract) it shall be settled in accordance with the following provisions.

(2) For the purpose of sub-clauses (2) to (6) inclusive of this Clause a dispute shall be deemed to arise when one party serves on the Engineer a notice in writing (hereinafter called the Notice of Dispute) stating the nature of the dispute. Provided that no Notice of Dispute may be served unless the party wishing to do so has first taken any steps or invoked any procedure available elsewhere in the Contract in connection with the subject matter of such dispute and the other party or the Engineer as the case may be has

    (a) taken such step as may be required or

    (b) been allowed a reasonable time to take any such action.

(3) Every dispute notified under sub-clause (2) of this Clause shall be settled by the Engineer who shall state his decision in writing and give notice of the same to the Employer and the Contractor within the time limits set out in sub-clause (6) of this Clause.

(4) Unless the Contract has already been determined or abandoned the Contractor shall in every case continue to proceed with the Works with all due diligence and the Contractor and the Employer shall both give effect forthwith to every such decision of the Engineer. Such decisions shall be final and binding upon the Contractor and the Employer unless and until as hereinafter provided either

    (a) the recommendation of a conciliator has been accepted by both parties or

    (b) the decision of the Engineer is revised by an arbitrator and an award made and published.

(5) In relation to any dispute notified under sub-clause (2) of this Clause and in respect of which

    (a) the Engineer has given his decision or

    (b) the time for giving an Engineer's decision as set out in sub-clause (3) of this Clause has expired

and no Notice to Refer under sub-clause (6) of this Clause has been served either party may give notice in writing requiring the dispute to be considered under the Institution of Civil Engineer's Conciliation Procedure (1988) or any amendment or modification thereof being in force at the date of such notice and the dispute shall thereafter be referred and considered in accordance with the said Procedure. The recommendation of the conciliator shall be deemed to have been accepted in settlement of the dispute unless a written Notice to Refer under sub-clause (6) of this Clause is served within one calendar month of its receipt.

(6) (*a*) Where a Certificate of Substantial Completion of the whole of the Works has not been issued and either

    (i) the Employer or the Contractor is dissatisfied with any decision of the Engineer given under sub-clause (3) of this Clause or

    (ii) the Engineer fails to give such decision for a period of one calendar month after the service of the Notice of Dispute or

    (iii) the Employer or the Contractor is dissatisfied with any recommendation of a conciliator appointed under sub-clause (5) of this Clause

then either the Employer or the Contractor may within three calendar months after receiving notice of such decision or within three calendar months after the expiry of the said period of one month or within one calendar month of receipt of the conciliator's recommendation (as the case may be) refer the dispute to the arbitration of a person to be agreed upon by the parties by serving on the other party a written Notice to Refer.

(*b*) Where a Certificate of Substantial Completion of the whole of the Works has been issued the foregoing provisions shall apply save that the said periods of one calendar month referred to in (*a*) above shall be read as three calendar months.

(7) (*a*) If the parties fail to appoint an arbitrator within one calendar month of either party serving on the other party written Notice to Concur in the appointment of an arbitrator the dispute or difference shall be referred to a person to be appointed on the application of either party by the President for the time being of the Institution of Civil Engineers.

(*b*) If an arbitrator declines the appointment or after appointment is removed by order of a competent court, or is incapable of acting or dies and the parties do not within one calendar month of the vacancy arising fill the vacancy then either party may apply to the President for the time being of the Institution of Civil Engineers to appoint another arbitrator to fill the vacancy.

(*c*) In any case where the President for the time being of the Institution of Civil Engineers is not able to exercise the functions conferred on him by this Clause the said functions shall be exercised on his behalf by a Vice-President for the time being of the said Institution.

(8) (*a*) Any reference to arbitration under this Clause shall be deemed to be a submission to arbitration within the meaning of the Arbitration Acts 1950 to 1979 or any statutory re-enactment or amendment thereof for the time being in force. The reference shall be conducted in accordance with the Institution of Civil Engineers Arbitration Procedure (1983) or any amendment or modification thereof being in force at the time of the appointment of the arbitrator. Such arbitrator

shall have full power to open up review and revise any decision opinion instruction direction certificate or valuation of the Engineer.

(b) Neither party shall be limited in the proceedings before such arbitrator to the evidence or arguments put before the Engineer for the purpose of obtaining his decision under subclause (3) of this Clause.

(c) The award of the arbitrator shall be binding on all parties.

(d) Unless the parties otherwise agree in writing any reference to arbitration may proceed notwithstanding that the Works are not then complete or alleged to be complete.

(9) No decision given by the Engineer in accordance with the foregoing provisions shall disqualify him from being called as witness and giving evidence before the arbitrator on any matter whatsoever relevant to the dispute or difference so referred to the arbitrator.

The clause places no bar on the time at which a dispute may be referred to arbitration. If the work is not complete, the engineer must give his decision in one month, as opposed to three months after completion.

The formula "any dispute or difference" includes claims in breach of contract. These must be referred direct to the engineer under this clause since he has no power to deal with them as claims (nor any power to include the sums due in certificates). If the engineer's decision is not challenged as provided, it becomes binding both on the parties and on the courts.

In view of the possible binding effect of the engineer's decision under clause 66, the contractor should make it plain whether a claim for payment is being re-submitted under the appropriate clause of the contract or being submitted as a dispute. Further, the engineer should make it quite clear that he is giving a decision under clause 66, if this is the case.

The existence of an arbitration agreement does not prevent either party from issuing proceedings in the courts. But the court will not be vested with the power of an arbitrator to review decisions of the engineer, unless by agreement (see page 42).

Scotland

The form is intended for use either side of the border. When used in Scotland, the following clause applies:

67 (1) If the Works are situated in Scotland the Contract shall in all respects be construed and operate as a Scottish contract and shall be

interpreted in accordance with Scots Law and the provisions of this Clause shall apply.

(2) In the application of these Conditions and in particular Clause 66 thereof

 (i) the word "arbiter" shall be substituted for the word "arbitrator"

 (ii) for any reference to the "Arbitration Acts" there shall be substituted reference to the "Arbitration (Scotland) Act 1894"

 (iii) for any reference to the Institution of Civil Engineers Arbitration Procedure (1983) there shall be substituted a reference to the Institution of Civil Engineers Arbitration Procedure (Scotland) (1983) and

 (iv) notwithstanding any of the other provisions of these Conditions nothing therein shall be construed as excluding or otherwise affecting the right of a party to arbitration to call in terms of Section 3 of the Administration of Justice (Scotland) Act 1972 for the arbiter to state a case.

The ICE Arbitration Procedure (Scotland) is published as a separate document, and takes into account the substantial differences which exist between English and Scottish law relating to arbitration.

Note

In the above commentary the following clauses or parts are not printed; reference must be made to the form of contract: clause 1(2)–(4) and (6) (interpretation), 6, 7(5) (documents), 9 (agreement), 10 (sureties), 16 (removal of employees), 18 (boreholes), 20(3) (excepted risks), 21–25 (insurance and risks), 27 (public utilities), 28 (patents), 29 (royalties), 30 (highways), 32 (fossils), 35 (labour), 36(2), (3) (cost of tests), 38(2) (uncovering), 45 (night work), 47 (liquidated damages), 52(3) (daywork), 54 (goods off site), 56(4) (daywork), 60(3), (5)–(7), (9), (10) (certificates), 62 (urgent repairs), 63(3)–(5) (determination), 64 (frustration), 65 (war), 68 (notices), 69 (tax), 70 (V.A.T.).

Of the clauses printed in the text the following appear in part only: clause 1(1) (definitions), 59 (nominated sub-contractors); also un-numbered fluctuation clauses.

Further Reading

Keating, *Law and Practice of Building Contracts* (5th ed., 1991).

Duncan Wallace, *The ICE Conditions of Contract* (5th ed., 1979).

Abrahamson, *Engineering Law and ICE Contracts* (4th ed., 1979).

CHAPTER 13

TORT

THE law of tort is mostly to be found in the common law, but there are some important statutes. It is not easy to give a satisfactory definition of a tort. It can be defined as a civil wrong independent of contract, or as liability arising from breach of a legal duty owed to persons generally. The practical consequences of the law of tort are concerned with the adjustment of losses. Where the elements of fault and damage exist, the law determines who should bear the resulting financial loss.

There is no complete body of general principles which applies to all torts, in the way that all contracts are governed by the same general principles. Some jurists view torts as a series of separate civil wrongs. For more practical reasons the torts discussed in this chapter are set out in separate sections. There are, however, some principles common to all or most torts, and these are discussed by way of introduction.

There are, naturally, qualifications to the definitions given above. For example, there are torts which are actionable where there is fault, whether or not the plaintiff suffered damage, such as libel. There may also be an action for damages where there is no fault, but where liability is strict, such as under the rule in *Rylands* v. *Fletcher* (see page 346). Further, unless an act is recognised as unlawful, no amount of intention, malice or damage can make it actionable.

This chapter covers those specific torts which are most relevant to the construction industry and to those professionally involved in it. Inevitably there are some torts not included which may be of relevance, such as trespass, and others which can be of importance in any sphere of activity, such as defamation. Mention should also be made of a group of torts which, although insignificant in terms of the number of actions brought, is of great importance in the field of industrial relations. These include interference with contractual relations, intimidation and conspiracy. For the law on these and other torts, reference should be made to one of the works noted at the end of the chapter.

Tort, crime and contract

The same act may be both a tort and a crime. When this is so the "tortfeasor" is liable to prosecution as well as to a civil action for damages. For example, a motor accident may result in proceedings in tort between the parties, as well as in prosecution of one or more of them. There has been much discussion in the cases about the relationship between tort and contract. This may arise in a number of ways. First, where two parties contract with each other, it was once the law that this precluded a parallel duty in tort. Then, following the rapid developments in other areas of tort, it was held that duties in tort could exist irrespective of what the parties had agreed. An example of this is the case of *Batty* v. *Metropolitan Realisations Limited* (1978), where a developer was held liable in breach of contract for having sold to the plaintiff a house which was not fit for habitation because it had been built at the top of a potentially unstable slope. When the question arose whether the plaintiffs were entitled also to have judgment entered in tort Megaw L.J. held:

> "In my judgment the plaintiffs were entitled here to have judgment entered in their favour on the basis of tortious liability as well as on the basis of breach of contract, assuming that the plaintiffs had established a breach by the first defendant of the common law duty of care owed to the plaintiffs. I have no doubt that it was the duty of the first defendants, in the circumstances of this case, apart altogether from the contractual warranty, to examine with reasonable care the land, which in this case would include adjoining land, in order to see whether the site was one on which a house fit for habitation could safely be built. It was a duty owed to prospective buyers of the house."

This case was subsequently doubted by the House of Lords in the *D. & F.* case and in *Murphy* v. *Brentwood*, because the plaintiffs in *Batty* had suffered no physical damage; but the decision as regards parallel duties in contract and in tort remains applicable. The existence of parallel duties has been considered in other situations, widely different from that of building developer and purchaser. In the leading case of *Lister* v. *Romford Ice & Cold Storage* (1957) the House of Lords had to consider the following strange set of facts. A lorry driver employed by the defendant company took along his father to act as mate. While negligently driving the lorry, the son injured his own father who succeeded in recovering damages against the company for the son's negligence. The company claimed indemnity against the son, and because of the complicated rules about contribution the court had to consider whether the potential liability of the son arose in contract or in tort. The majority opted for contract and held the son liable to the company and not entitled to be indemnified by them or their insurer (so that in the result the family recovered nothing). In a strong dissenting judgment, Lord Radcliffe said:

> "Since in any event the duty in question is one which exists by imputation or implication of law and not by virtue of any express negotiation between the parties, I should be inclined to say that there is no real distinction between the two possible sources of obligation. But it is certainly, I think, as much contractual as tortious."

This case was considered more recently in *Tai Hing* v. *Liu Chong Hing Bank* (1986), where the Privy Council had to consider the position of a bank customer where a bank clerk had fraudulently drawn and cashed cheques against the customer's accounts, and the customer had failed to detect or notify the bank about the losses. It was argued that, apart from the terms of contract between the customer and the bank, the customer owed a duty in tort to prevent such losses to the bank (on the footing they were otherwise liable to repay the money). The Privy Council decided the case in contract, holding that the bank's terms were not sufficient to impose liability on the customer for the loss. In regard to the tort claim, it was said:

> "Their Lordships do not, therefore, embark on an investigation as to whether in the relationship of banker and customer it is possible to identify tort as well as contract as a source of the obligations owed by the one to the other. Their Lordships do not, however, accept that the parties' mutual obligations in tort can be any greater than those to be found expressly or by necessary implication in their contract . . . the bank cannot rely on the law of tort to provide them with greater protection than that which they have contracted."

This observation is in line with a number of other cases, including *Junior Books* v. *Veitchi* (1982)—a case much criticised for its decision, but interesting in having raised the question of the possible impact on tort of terms in another contract. In that case, Lord Roskill made the following observation:

> "During the argument it was asked what the position would be in a case where there was a relevant exclusion clause in the main contract. My Lords, that question does not arise for decision in the instant appeal, but in principle I would venture the view that such a clause according to the manner in which it was worded might in some circumstances limit the duty of care just as in the *Hedley Byrne* case the plaintiffs were ultimately defeated by the defendants' disclaimer of responsibility."

Two other construction cases have touched on the important question of the contract—tort relationship. In *Greater Nottingham Co-op* v. *Cementation* (1988) a piling sub-contractor had caused damage to an adjoining property, and this had resulted in losses and claims as between the main contractor and the employer. The question arose whether the employer could claim these losses against the sub-contractor in tort, where the sub-contractor had been required to enter into the usual direct warranty covering design but not the execution of the work. The Court of Appeal held that the fact that these parties had deliberately made a contract (the warranty) which excluded the work in relation to which the tortious duty was alleged, was sufficient to exclude the existence of a duty in tort to fill the gap. Conversely, in the case of *Warwick University* v. *McAlpine*, a similar point was resolved the other way. The unusual facts of this case were that McAlpine were carrying out remedial work arising from an earlier contract. During the course of the work it was decided to bring in Cementation Chemicals Limited (C.C.L.) to carry out specialist work. The university had the opportunity of employing C.C.L. direct, but instead requested McAlpine to employ them, without taking a warranty. The tortious duty alleged was "failing to warn the plaintiffs or the defendants of the damage that would result from the use of such materials and services." Garland J. held as follows:

> "If this is the duty, then the university are not seeking to establish an essentially contractual one, fitness for purpose, but a normal tortious one—to take reasonable care to avoid reasonably foreseeable damage to a sufficiently proximate plaintiff. The fact that the university might have created a contractual duty by an express warranty is not something which in my view should negative the existence of any duty. Where there is a direct warranty which omits to provide for a particular category of damage, the omission may lead to the conclusion that any duty in tort or the consequences of a breach should be correspondingly restricted—*Greater Nottingham Co-op* v. *Cementation* . . . in my view there was a duty in the terms I have set out."

The decision in this case has been reversed by the Court of Appeal on the facts but the original judgment remains of interest.

General exemptions

There are some exemptions from liability which apply to torts generally. Thus, there can be no redress for damage which is a necessary consequence of something done under statutory authority (unless the statute provides for compensation). The question in issue is then likely to be whether the damage was a necessary consequence or whether it could have been avoided. Further, where a person consents to run the risk of suffering harm, he may have no remedy for the harm he suffers. This principle used to afford a defence to employers against workmen who suffered injury due to the employer's negligence. But this is no longer the law, and in practice the defence of consent to the risk is always difficult to establish. Even where liability is strict there may be certain defences, such as that the damage was caused by the plaintiff's default, or by act of God. This latter expression, which is often found in insurance policies, means an occurence which man has no power to foresee or prevent, such as a violent storm.

There is normally no duty to act postively for another's benefit, so that if a man is drowning an onlooker is under no duty to rescue him. But if someone does attempt a rescue, and is so careless as to cause injury, the rescuer may then be liable in negligence.

NEGLIGENCE

Negligence is by far the most important of torts, for several reasons. It forms the cause of action in the majority of cases brought in tort; its scope is very wide; and it may also be an element in liability for other torts such as nuisance. The term negligence is also found in the context of breach of contract, for example, where an architect is alleged to have carried out negligent design or supervision. A typical and common type of action in negligence heard in the courts is that between two or more drivers involved in a road accident. In such cases it is not infrequent for all parties to be held to be negligent in some degree.

Element of liability

The plaintiff in an action for negligence must show three things: that the defendant owed him a duty of care; that there was a breach of that duty; and that recoverable damage was thereby caused. Considering the first of these elements, it is necessary to decide whether in the particular circumstances one person (the defendant) owed a duty of care to the other (the plaintiff).

The classic test as to when a duty of care might arise was stated in the leading case of *Donoghue* v. *Stevenson* (1932). In this case a manufacturer of ginger beer was held to owe a duty to the ultimate consumer, who found a decomposing snail in the empty bottle and thereby suffered damage. The consumer could not sue in contract because the ginger beer had been purchased by a friend, and in any event the default was that of the manufacturer, not the seller.

In a celebrated judgment Lord Atkin held as follows:

> "The rule that you are to love your neighbour becomes in law, you must not injure your neighbour; and the lawyer's question who is my neighbour? receives a restricted reply. You must take reasonable care to avoid acts or omissions which you can reasonably foresee would be likely to injure your neighbour. Who, then, in law is my neighbour? The answer seems to be—persons who are so closely and directly affected by my act that I ought reasonably to have them in contemplation as being so affected when I am directing my mind to the acts or omissions which are called in question."

The list of cases where one person owes the duty of care to another is long and being added to continually. A few common examples are the duty owed between road users, between employer and employee and between a manufacturer and the consumer of his products.

Tort in construction: the expansion

The question of liability in tort of persons in the construction industry was considered in the leading case of *Dutton* v. *Bognor Regis U.D.C.* (1971). As is now well known, this case led to a rapid expansion in the law of tort generally, much of this relating to construction activities.

Whenever a change in the law is argued for, allowing new claims to be brought, the "floodgates" argument is raised, *i.e.* if you allow this claim, it will be followed by a flood of other claims. *Donoghue* v. *Stevenson* was not followed by any rapid development in the law of tort. But *Dutton* v. *Bognor Regis*

Urban District Council (1971) was quite otherwise. That case produced not merely a flood of litigation but also an almost unprecedented upheaval in the common law, which ultimately led to the House of Lords deciding to disapprove its own previous decisions. A brief account of this exciting piece of legal history is necessary, not least because there will undoubtedly be more development before this branch of the law can be said to be settled. This episode also illustrates the perils of expansion and contraction of the common law: during the expansion period many claims will be brought, which, if still outstanding during the contraction, will be found unsustainable with disastrous consequences for the unfortunate plaintiff, who may have to withdraw his claim and pay costs. Thus, although in theory the common law does not "change" but is restated, the practical effect is not only that the law does change, but that it changes retrospectively, which is regarded as constitutionally improper in regard to changes in statute law.

The first case in the saga, already mentioned, is *Dutton's* case, in which the plaintiff, a second purchaser of a house built on a rubbish tip, was unable to sue in contract. Proceedings were brought in tort against the original builder and against the local authority who had approved the plans and inspected the work on site. The case against the builder was settled but Mrs. Dutton proceeded against the local authority. In the Court of Appeal it was argued that the council owed no duty and that there was no physical damage to found an action in tort. It was further pointed out that the council should not be held liable because the builder was not liable in tort. Lord Denning M.R. rejected all these arguments holding not only that the council was liable but, incidentally, the builder would also have been liable in tort. *Dutton's* case had two important consequences. First, claims in tort were potentially available against parties not hitherto thought liable; and secondly, claims in tort could be brought as an alternative to claims in contract. The importance of the second point is that claims in contract become statute barred within (usually) six years of the date of the breach, whereas claims in tort do not arise until damage is suffered. In addition to more claims being available, *Dutton* created the possibility of bringing claims which hitherto would have been long barred by limitation. Thus, the flood produced by *Dutton* was two-fold. A rush of cases was brought in tort against local authorities, contractors and professionals of all sorts; and compounding this flood, many of the claims were extremely stale. Plaintiffs alleged that, although a house was built many years before, damage had occurred only within the period of six years before issuing the writ. This development led to yet another series of cases on the question when the cause of action in tort arose. In regard to latent defects in buildings, the doctrine was developed that the plaintiff was under no duty to bring his action until he ought reasonably to have been aware of the existence of the damage. Thus, there could be not merely a latent defect, but latent damage existing for many years, and only upon the damage becoming reasonably discoverable did the limitation period begin to run. The courts had, therefore, to consider many stale claims involving defendants and witnesses who had died, retired or (often in the case of building inspectors) emigrated.

One of the difficulties with development of the law through judicial decision is that the court can only decide the issues in the case before it. The court cannot decide hypothetical questions, nor resolve issues which do not arise in the particular case. Thus, change or development is dependent upon the accidents of litigation. Thus, it was not until 1977 that the opportunity arose for the House of Lords to reconsider the *Dutton* decision. This they did in the case of *Anns* v. *The London Borough of Merton*. The case concerned allegations of negligence against the local authority's building inspectors, the primary issue being whether the claim was statute-barred. However, the appellant council also argued that *Dutton's* case, which was the foundation of the cause of action, was wrongly decided. The opportunity therefore presented itself for the House of Lords to restate this whole area of law. The case resulted in the House of Lords approving, with some modification, the decision in *Dutton* so that the flood of litigation was bound to continue. The judgment of the House of Lords in *Anns* in fact appeared to widen the grounds in which a duty of care would arise, Lord Wilberforce suggesting a two-stage test:

> "First, one has to ask whether as between the alleged wrongdoer and the person who has suffered damage there is a sufficient relationship of proximity or neighbourhood such that, in the reasonable contemplation of the former, carelessness on his part may be likely to cause damage to the latter—in which case a *prima facie* duty of care arises. Secondly, if the first question is answered affirmatively, it is necessary to consider whether there are any considerations which ought to negative or reduce or limit the scope of the duty or the class of person to whom it is owed or the damages to which a breach of it may give rise."

Significantly, the *Anns* case did hold that the cause of action arose only when the state of the building was such that there was present or imminent danger to health or safety of occupiers. This point was subsequently developed in a number of other cases.

The next step which could be regarded as the zenith in the development of the law of tort is the case of *Junior Books* v. *Veitchi*, decided in July 1982. This was a Scottish case (the Scots law of delict was for the purpose of the appeal regarded as identical with the English law of tort), in which the plaintiff owners of a factory brought a claim in tort for economic loss against a nominated sub-contractor who was alleged negligently to have installed flooring, the loss representing the financial consequences of having to replace the defective floor. The House of Lords allowed the claim, holding that there was no good reason to restrict the loss recoverable to the cost of making good physical damage. Lord Brandon delivered a strong dissenting judgment which has subsequently achieved greater currency than the case itself.

The retrenchment period

The position after *Junior Books* seemed to be that you were better off relying on tort than contract. Much more generous limitation periods were available, tort claims were generally free from limitation or exclusion clauses, and there was no difficulty about recovering damages. However, all this was to change. Within months of *Junior Books*, the House of Lords had to consider again the effect on limitation of the law of tort. In the leading case of *Pirelli* v. *Oscar Faber*, decided in December 1982, the House held that the cause of action against consulting engineers for negligent design which had resulted in cracks in a chimney arose when that damage came into existence and not at the later date when the cracks were or should with reasonable diligence have been discovered. The case was complicated because the report of the Law Reform Committee which subsequently led to the Latent Damage Act 1986, was then available, and indicated that if the House decided that the claim was statute-barred (as it did) the law would then be changed back by the new Act. The House was not deterred by this argument (see further page 356).

The next opportunity to reconsider the law came in a number of cases dealing with local authorities. In *Peabody* v. *Parkinson and London Borough of Lambeth* (1985) the Court of Appeal reversed the findings of an official referee that the local authority had been negligent in permitting the installation of drainage not complying with the relevant by-laws. The House of Lords, in dismissing the appeal, held that the local authority owed no duty to the plaintiff owners, and that the appropriate test as to whether there was such a duty, given the existence of proximity, was whether it was just and reasonable. Thereafter, in *Investors in Industry Limited* v. *South Beds District Council* (1986) the Court of Appeal, following *Peabody*, held that it would not normally be just and reasonable to impose a duty on a local authority where the building owner relied on other professional advisers, and that the duty owed by the local authority would ordinarily be limited to a duty to subsequent owners. Thus, at two strokes, the flood of cases against local authorities was stopped. This left, however, the enlargement in the law of tort against other parties. There rapidly followed a series of cases in which the *Junior Books* case was heavily criticised by the Court of Appeal and, is now to be regarded as a case where there was a special relationship between the parties. A number of cases also held that the right to sue for damages in tort was available only where the plaintiff had a proprietary or possessory right in the property damaged: it was not sufficient for the plaintiff to have a mere contractual right: *Candelwood Corp.* v. *Mitsui Limited* (1986). This Privy Council decision concerned damage to a ship, where the time charterer was held not entitled to recover damages in tort for loss of profit and other economic loss occasioned by damage negligently caused by the defendant's ship.

The most far-reaching decision in this period of retrenchment was the case of *D. & F. Estates* v. *Church Commissioners and Others* (1988). Here, the owners of a flat brought a claim in tort, *inter alia*, against Wates, who were main contractors when the block of flats was constructed, in respect of alleged negligence by their plastering sub-contractor (who was not a party to the action). The plaster was found to be cracked and unsound, and the plaintiffs claimed the cost of renewing it. The House of Lords held that Wates were not under the duty alleged, but went on to consider the claim that would have been available had they been under such a duty. The House referred to and approved the dissenting judgment of Lord Brandon in *Junior Books* (see above) in which he said:

> "It is, however, of fundamental importance to observe that the duty of care laid down in *Donoghue* v. *Stevenson* was based on the existence of a danger of physical injury to persons or their property . . . the relevant property for the purpose of the wider principle on which the decision . . . was based was property other than the very

property which gave rise to the danger of physical damage concerned."

"It has always been either stated expressly or taken for granted that an essential ingredient in the cause of action relied on was the existence of danger or the threat of danger, of physical damage to persons or their property excluding for this purpose the very piece of property from the defective condition of which such danger, or threat of danger, arises."

Lord Bridge went on to say that if the principle of *Donoghue* v. *Stevenson* is applied to the liability of the builder of a structure which is dangerously defective:

"Liability can only arise if the defect remains hidden until the defective structure causes personal injury or damage to property other than the structure itself. If the defect is discovered before any damage is done, the loss sustained by the owner of the structure, who has to repair or demolish it to avoid a potential source of danger to third parties, would seem to be purely economic. Thus, if I acquire a property with a dangerously defective garden wall which is attributable to the workmanship of the original builder, it is difficult to see any basis in principle on which I can sustain an action in tort against the builder for the cost of either repairing or demolishing the wall."

The question of the existence of a duty of care, considered in relation to local authorities in the *Peabody* and *Investors* cases (see above), arose again in the case of *Caparo Industries* v. *Dickman* (1990). The plaintiff had purchased shares in a public company. After publication of statutory accounts prepared by the defendant, the plaintiff, relying on the report, decided to purchase more shares and eventually launched a successful takeover of the company. Subsequently errors were found in the accounts, and the plaintiff claimed damages in tort from the accountants. The case of *Hedley Byrne* v. *Heller* (1964) established that such an action was maintainable, but the particular issue in the *Caparo* case was whether a duty was owed by accountants to shareholders and to investors. The Court of Appeal held that a duty was owed to shareholders only. The House of Lords allowed the defendant's appeal, holding that no duty at all was owed. Lord Bridge described the test as follows:

"What emerges is that, in addition to the foreseeability of damage, necessary ingredients in any situation giving rise to a duty of care are that there should exist between the party owing the duty and the party to whom it is owed a relationship characterised by the law as one of 'proximity' or 'neighbourhood' and that the situation should be one in which the court considers it fair, just and reasonable that the law should impose a duty of a given scope upon the one party for the benefit of the other.''

The latest and seemingly final stage in the retrenchment of the Law of Tort in regard to buildings occurred in the case of *Murphy* v. *Brentwood District Council* (1990). In that case, the Court of Appeal had upheld the decision of the Official Referee, allowing recovery by a plaintiff houseowner who discovered cracks which were attributable to the negligent passing of plans by the local authority. Instead of carrying out repairs, Mr. Murphy sold his defective house and recovered the loss as against what the value would have been without the defects. Although the House of Lords in *D. & F.* expressed doubt about the decision in *Anns*, they did not disapprove the decision, one difficulty being that the local authority was not a party to *D. & F.* In *Murphy*, the House of Lords did have the opportunity to reconsider *Anns*, and did so in an unusual court of seven Law Lords, including the Lord Chancellor. The decision, which is of far-reaching importance, established, or re-established, the following principles:

(1) A builder owed duty of care within the principle of *Donoghue* v. *Stevenson*, to persons likely to suffer injury as a result of his negligence;
(2) This extended, however, only to injury caused by latent, *i.e.* undiscovered defects in the building;
(3) Where a defect came to light, whether through the existence of cracks or through a survey, expenditure on remedial work was to be regarded as pure economic loss, not recoverable in tort;
(4) Contrary to *Dutton* and *Anns*, cracks representing the manifestation of underlying defects were not to be regarded as material damage;
(5) The House of Lords left open the question whether a local authority exercising powers to secure compliance with building regulations owed any duty to owners or occupiers of the relevant building.

Ordinarily, such liability in tort will be limited to injury to persons or other property, excluding the property which gave rise to the injury (*i.e.* the building itself). Lord Bridge, in the Murphy case, recognised two possible exceptions. The first was expressed in the following passage, which also summarises the general extent of the builder's liability:

"If a builder erects a structure containing a latent defect which renders it dangerous to persons or property, he will be liable in tort for injury to persons or damage to property resulting from that dangerous defect. But if the defect becomes apparent before any injury or damage has been caused, the loss sustained by the building owner is purely economic. If the defect can be repaired at economic cost, that is the measure of the loss. If the building cannot be repaired, it may have to be abandoned as unfit for occupation and therefore valueless. These economic losses are recoverable if they flow from breach of a relevant contractual duty, but, here again, in the absence of a special relationship of proximity they are not recoverable in tort. The only qualification I would make to this is that, if a building stands so close to the boundary of the building owner's land that after discovery of the dangerous defect it remains a potential source of injury to persons or property on neighbouring land or on the highway, the building owner ought in principle to be entitled to recover in tort from the negligent builder the cost of obviating the danger, whether by repair or demolition, so far as that cost is necessarily incurred in order to protect himself from potential liability to third parties."

The second exception arises from the possibility of damage to "other property." What is the position if the other property is part of the defective building itself? This was considered in the *D. and F.* case and dubbed the "complex structure theory." Despite wide and searching academic criticism, the House of Lords in *Murphy* appear to regard the theory as still sound. Lord Bridge re-stated his view of the theory as follows:

"A critical distinction must be drawn here between some part of a complex structure which is said to be a 'danger' only because it does not perform its proper function in sustaining the other parts and some distinct item incorporated in the structure which positively malfunctions so as to inflict positive damage on the structure in which it is incorporated. Thus, if a defective central heating boiler explodes and damages a house or a defective electrical installation malfunctions and sets the house on fire, I see no reason to doubt that the owner of the house, if he can prove that the damage was due to the negligence of the boiler manufacturer in the one case, or the electrical contractor in the other, can recover damages in tort on the *Donaghue* v. *Stevenson* principles but the position in law is entirely different where, by reason of the inadequacy of the foundations of the building to support the weight of the superstructure, differential settlement and consequent cracking occurs. Here, once the first cracks appear, the structure as a whole is seen to be defective, and the nature of the defect is known."

Losses recoverable in negligence

The result of the recent House of Lords decisions, particularly *Murphy* is that the law of negligence is no longer to be regarded as concerned with danger to health or safety, so that discussion in the cases concerning when such causes of action arise is no longer relevant, the law of negligence is now to be regarded as concerned with actual damage in the form, usually, of physical injury to persons or property, necessarily caused by latent defects. Ordinarily, the property must be something distinct from that which the negligent defendant has supplied or constructed. The question whether a local authority will ever be liable for the negligent exercise of its powers in accordance with these principles, remains to be decided. However, it is to be noted that in all the flood of local authority litigation, there appear to be no cases in which a plaintiff suffered loss or injury of a type that would now be regarded as recoverable.

The *Murphy* case may also be regarded as having settled, for practical purposes, the debate as to when damage to a building is to be regarded as "purely economic loss" and therefore unrecoverable. In both *Dutton* and *Anns*, it was held that the cracks to the building themselves constituted physical damage. This analysis has been decisively rejected by the House of Lords in *Murphy*. In the result, expenditure on repairing damaged or defective parts of buildings will not normally be recoverable, unless falling within one of the exceptions referred to above. A further exception arises if there is a "special relationship" between the parties within the principle of *Hedley Byrne* v. *Heller* (see below). In some tort cases complex factual questions arise as to which losses are properly to be regarded as economic, and where the line is to be drawn. An example of this is the case of *Spartan Steel* v. *Martin* (1973), where the Court of Appeal grappled with problems arising from the negligent cutting off of the electricity supply to a factory. This caused physical "damage" to certain products which were being manufactured in the plaintiffs' machinery at the time of the power cut. The plaintiffs recovered the value of the material damaged and also loss of profit on this material as consequential (economic) loss. The Court of Appeal refused to allow recovery in respect of other material which the plaintiffs were unable to process during the power cut, regarding this as purely economic. The case has been much discussed, particularly as to whether these distinctions were matters of law or policy. Lord Oliver, in his judgment in the *Murphy* case commented on *Spartan Steel* as follows:

> "The solution to such borderline cases has so far been achieved pragmatically, not by the application of logic but by the perceived necessity as a matter of policy to place some limits—perhaps arbitrary limits— to what would otherwise be an endless cumulative causative chain bounded only by theoretical foreseeability."

No doubt the debate as to when and on what legal basis certain losses are irrecoverable, will continue. However, the general rule that losses in tort must arise from physical damage is now firmly re-established.

Breach and damage

If a duty of care exists, it is necessary to establish a breach of that duty. The standard of care required is that of a "reasonable man." This is a legal abstraction which represents a person who weighs up the circumstances, considers the characteristics of the persons endangered, takes greater care when there is greater danger, and never loses his temper. He is sometimes epitomised as the man on the Clapham omnibus. The duty is to guard against probabilities, not bare possibilities. But where the risk is greater, such as where children are involved, reasonable possibilities must be guarded against. The required standard of care thus depends on the circumstances, but in any particular case there is one appropriate standard below which a person is legally negligent. The term "gross negligence" is sometimes used, but the adjective has no legal significance. There is only one appropriate standard of care, any breach of which, gross or slight, incurs liability in law.

Finally, the injury to the plaintiff must have been caused by the defendant's act, and the damage must not be too remote (see page 253). If the plaintiff succeeds in his action in negligence but the loss was caused partly by his own default, the court will reduce the damages recovered in accordance with the Law Reform (Contributory Negligence) Act 1945. Section 1 of this Act provides:

> "Where any person suffers damage as a result partly of his own fault and partly of the fault of any other person or persons, a claim in respect of that damage shall not be defeated by reason of the fault

of the person suffering the damage, but the damages recoverable in respect thereof shall be reduced to such extent as the Court thinks just and equitable having regard to the claimant's share in the responsibility for the damage."

Contributory negligence applies also to breaches of statutory duty, but not ordinarily to a claim brought in contract alone (see page 111).

Negligent mis-statement

Liability for statements has developed, historically, along different lines from liability for acts or omissions. The leading case is *Hedley Byrne* v. *Heller* (1963), where a bank gave a gratuitous reference for a customer in respect of a company with whom they proposed to do business. The reference was favourable but was given "without responsibility." The reference was given negligently, and the customer lost money. The House of Lords held that the bank owed a duty of care and would have been liable, but was protected by the express disclaimer of responsibility. In giving judgment, the House considered the circumstances in which liability might arise for statements. Lord Devlin expressed the matter thus:

"Wherever there is a relationship equivalent to contract, there is a duty of care. Such a relationship may be either general or particular. Examples of a general relationship are those of solicitor and client and of banker and customer. . . . Where, as in the present case, what is relied on is a particular relationship created ad hoc, it will be necessary to examine the particular facts to see whether there is an express or implied undertaking of responsibility."

Thus, persons such as engineers and architects must be on their guard when making statements to their clients, even concerning matters in which they are not directly instructed. And a duty of care may equally arise when giving gratuitous advice to strangers if the circumstances are such that there is an implied undertaking of responsibility.

This branch of the law was further developed in the case of *Esso Petroleum* v. *Mardon* (1976). The defendant had taken a lease of a garage after representations were made by the plaintiffs as to the likely throughput of petrol. Their figures were based on the original design for the garage, but planning permission was refused and the garage was in fact built fronting away from the main road. In the result, the volume of trade was considerably reduced and the defendant lost money. The question arose whether the plaintiff's statements could be relied on when they were followed by a contract. Lord Denning held that the defendant was entitled to succeed in his counterclaim:

> "If a man who has or professes to have special knowledge or skill makes a representation by virtue thereof to another (be it advice, information or opinion) with the intention of inducing him to enter into a contract with him, he is under a duty to use reasonable care to see that the representation is correct, and that the advice, information or opinion is reliable. If he negligently gives unsound advice or misleading information or expresses any erroneous opinion, and thereby induces the other side to enter into a contract with him, he is liable in damages."

In both of these cases, the defendant had made a relatively simple statement upon which the plaintiff had relied, in the second case the statement being followed by a contract. What is less clear, is the precise ambit of this principle. Before the recent developments in the law of tort this question was of limited importance, but since the retrenchment elsewhere, the *Hedley Byrne* principle may be the only avenue by which pure economic loss can be recovered in tort. It is therefore to be anticipated that there will be further attempts to bring cases within this principle. In *I.B.A.* v. *E.M.I.* (see page 187) the designing sub-contractor responded to a request from the employer concerning the performance of the television mast, stating "we are well satisfied that the structure will not oscillate dangerously." The Court of Appeal treated this as contractually binding, but the House of Lords regarded it as falling within the principles of *Hedley Byrne.* It is indeed difficult to see any logical dividing line between the provision of a design, upon which the building owner will invariably place reliance, and the simple provision of information, particularly if a statement that "our design is adequate" is regarded as sufficient.

A further, unsuccessful, attempt to apply the *Hedley Byrne* principle occurred in *Pacific Associates* v. *Halcrow* (1988). In this case the defendant was appointed engineer under a FIDIC contract. As a result of rejecting claims brought by the contractor, arbitration proceedings had to be pursued against the employer, which resulted in a partially successful settlement. The plaintiff contractor then attempted to sue the engineer in tort to recover the remainder of his loss. The engineer responded by an application to strike out the claim. The application succeeded both before the Official Referee and the Court of Appeal, the latter holding that there was no voluntary assumption of responsibility. The case was complicated by argument based on a clause in the main contract providing that the engineer was not to be liable, but the case assists in defining the limits of the *Hedley Byrne* principle.

OTHER ASPECTS OF NEGLIGENCE

Liability of occupiers

Under the Occupiers' Liability Act 1957 an occupier of premises owes a duty of care to all visitors lawfully on the premises. Unless the occupier can and does modify or exclude his obligations by agreement, he owes to any visitor a duty to take reasonable care so that the visitor will be reasonably safe in using the premises for the purposes for which he is permitted to be there. The occupier may escape liability by giving adequate warning of existing dangers, and he may also expect persons such as workmen entering to carry out a job to guard against special dangers of their trade. Thus, where two chimney sweeps were warned of the danger of fumes and, disregarding the warning were asphyxiated, the occupier was not liable: *Roles* v. *Nathan* (1963). An occupier is not liable for the faulty work of an independent contractor (see page 351) unless he is himself in some way to blame. An occupier may avoid such liability if he has taken reasonable steps to ensure that the contractor was competent and the work properly done.

The statute applies to those who occupy land and buildings (including building and construction sites) and any fixed or movable structure such as a vehicle, vessel, lift or scaffolding. An "occupier" need not be the owner of the premises but is merely a person having some degree of control. There may therefore be more than one occupier of the same premises. On a construction site, the contractor or the employer may be an occupier. In *A.M.F.* v. *Magnet Bowling* (1968) both the general contractor and the employer were held to be occupiers with respect to a specialist direct contractor. A sub-contractor may also be an occupier of the whole or part of the site.

The Occupiers' Liability Act does not apply to persons who are not visitors, whether they come onto the land lawfully, such as for the purposes of using a right of way, or unlawfully as trespassers. In the past, this has created great difficulty, particularly in the case of children who may stray into dangerous areas. Construction sites are a particular case where children and others may be at risk. The common law extended the principle of the Occupiers' Liability Act to provide that an occupier might, in such circumstances, owe a limited duty. This has now been superseded by the Occupiers' Liability Act 1984, which deals expressly with these difficulties.

The new Act provides that an occupier owes a duty to a person who is not a visitor if he is aware, or has reasonable grounds to believe that a danger exists and also knows or has reasonable grounds to believe that the other person is or may come into the vicinity of the danger, and further if the risk is one against which the occupier may be expected to offer some protection. Where such a duty exists, the occupier must take reasonable care to avoid injury, but this duty may be discharged in an appropriate case by giving appropriate warning or discouraging persons from incurring the risk.

The Unfair Contract Terms Act 1977 provides, in respect of a business occupier, that liability as an occupier cannot be excluded by a contract term or notice, in respect of death or personal injury resulting from negligence, and in respect of other loss, liability can be excluded or restricted only so far as fair and reasonable. The 1984 Act restricts the operation of this provision to persons who are granted access for the purpose of the business of the occupier, so that, for example, owners of quarries who allow access for rock climbing may now exclude liability for the dangerous state of the premises.

Employers' liability

An employer may be liable for injury caused to his employee in three ways. First, if the injury is caused by the negligence of a fellow employee acting in the course of his employment (see page 351); secondly, if it is caused by the employer's breach of a statutory duty (see page 391); and thirdly, if it is caused by the employer's negligence. The third possibility is discussed here.

There is no doubt that an employer owes his employees a duty of care. The problem for the common law has been to trace its extent. It has been defined as a three-fold duty: the provision of a competent staff of men, adequate material, and a proper system and effective supervision. However, the duty can be viewed as a single duty to take reasonable care for the safety of employees in all the circumstances. Thus the duty is not absolute, and an employer is only liable for injury caused by his failure to take sufficient care.

The standard of care that is required varies with the circumstances so that where potentially dangerous plant is being used the employer may have to provide safety devices or protective equipment. The employer remains liable for breach of his duty even though he may delegate its performance. This was held in *Wilsons and Clyde Coal* v. *English* (1937), where the owners of a coal mine were unaware of the system of working which was in operation or of any defect in it, having delegated to their managers the provision of a system of working. Lord Macmillan answered the point thus:

> "Now I take it to be settled law that the provision of a safe system of working in a colliery is an obligation of the owner of the colliery. He cannot divest himself of this duty, though he may—and if it involves technical management and he is not himself technically qualified, must—perform it through the agency of an employee. It remains the owner's obligation and the agent whom the owner appoints to perform it performs it on the owner's behalf. The owner remains vicariously responsible for the negligence of the person whom he has appointed to perform his obligation for him, and cannot escape liability by merely proving that he has appointed a competent agent. If the owner's duty has not been performed, no matter how competent the agent selected by the owner to perform it for him, the owner is responsible."

However, where an employee is experienced and the danger apparent, the duty upon the employer may be a limited one, particularly where the employer is not in control of the premises. Thus, in the case *Wilson* v. *Tyneside Window Cleaning* (1958) the plaintiff, an experienced window cleaner, was injured when a handle came away from a window, causing him to lose his balance. He had never received any instructions regarding safety, except that if he found a window which presented unusual difficulty or risk he was to report for further instructions. It was held that there was no breach of duty by the employer. Pearce L.J. observed:

> "The master's own premises are under his control: if they are dangerously in need of repair he can and must rectify the fault at once if he is to escape the censure of negligence. But if a master sends a plumber to mend a leak in a respectable private house, no one could hold him negligent for not visiting the house himself to

see if the carpet in the hall creates a trap. Between these extremes are countless possible examples in which the court may have to decide the question of fact: did the master take reasonable care so to carry out his operations as not to subject those employed by him to unnecessary risk. Precautions dictated by reasonable care when the servant works on the master's premises may be wholly prevented or greatly circumscribed by the fact that the place of work is under the control of a stranger. Additional safeguards intended to reinforce the man's own knowledge and skill in surmounting difficulties or dangers may be reasonable in the former case but impracticable and unreasonable in the latter."

Thus, the duty of employers of men working on construction projects may vary considerably according to the degree of control exercised by the employer.

In addition to the duties laid on the employer, the employee must show regard for his own safety, and if he is injured as a result of his own negligence this may reduce or extinguish the employer's liability. The employee also owes the employer a duty to exercise reasonable skill and care at his work and may be liable to his employer for causing injury in breach of this duty.

Rylands v. Fletcher liability

When a person keeps on his land some potentially dangerous object or carries on a dangerous operation, the ordinary law of negligence may not afford adequate protection. Instead of stretching the duty of care to its limit, the common law has set apart certain things for which liability is strict, without regard to lack of care. A person who deals in such things does so at his peril.

This special liability is known by the name of the celebrated case in which it was first formulated. In *Rylands* v. *Fletcher* (1868) the defendant had a reservoir built on his land by reputable engineers and with the necessary permission. But when the reservoir was filled, the water escaped down through a disused mine shaft and flooded the plaintiff's coal mines on adjoining land. Although the defendant's actions were without any fault, he was held liable for the plaintiff's loss. In giving judgment Lord Cairns held:

"On the other hand if the defendants, not stopping at the natural use of their close, had desired to use it for any purpose which I may term a non-natural use, for the purpose of introducing into the close that which in its natural condition was not in or upon it, for the purpose of introducing water either above or below ground in quantities and in a manner not the result of any work or operation upon or under the land—and if in consequence of their doing so, or in consequence of any imperfection in the mode of their doing so, the water came to escape and to pass off into the close of the plaintiff, then it appears to me that that which the defendants were doing they were doing at their own peril; and if in the course of their doing it, the evil arose to which I have referred, the evil, namely the escape of water and its passing away into the close of the plaintiff and injuring the plaintiff, then for the consequence of that, in my opinion, the defendant would be liable."

In addition to reservoirs, strict liability has been attached to colliery spoil heaps, inflammable goods, and vibrations from pile driving. Thus, where a contractor drove a large number of piles into soil and, due to the vibrations produced, caused damage to an old house belonging to the plaintiff, the contractor was held liable, without proof of negligence: *Hoare* v. *McAlpine* (1923). Although vibrations may also constitute a nuisance (see below) it may be a defence to nuisance that the property damaged was unusually frail. Liability in *Rylands* v. *Fletcher* is, however, strict.

To incur liability the object or operation must be non-natural, so that while there is strict liability for a reservoir, the owner of a natural lake can be liable only under the ordinary principles of tort, such as in negligence or nuisance. To establish strict liability there must also be an "escape" from the plaintiff's land which causes the damage, such as a slide of material from a spoil heap. Thus, where an explosion in a munitions factory injured a person on the premises there was no such strict liability since the dangerous thing had not escaped from the defendant's land: *Read* v. *Lyons* (1946). In this case, Lord Macmillan observed:

"The two prerequisites of the doctrine (of *Rylands* v. *Fletcher*) are that there must be the escape of something from one man's close to another man's close and that that which escapes must have been brought upon the land from which it escapes in consequence of some non-natural use of that land, whatever precisely that may mean. Neither of these features exists in the present case. I have already pointed out that nothing escaped from the defendant's premises and were it necessary to decide the point I should hesitate to rule that in these days and in an industrial community, it was an non-natural use of land to build a factory on it and conduct there the manufacture of explosives."

Although *Rylands* v. *Fletcher* liability is strict, it is not absolute. The defendant may escape liability if the escape was due to the plaintiff's default or due to an act of God. However, where these defences preclude strict liability, there may still be liability for ordinary negligence or nuisance, or for other torts.

PRODUCT LIABILITY

Claims based on negligence or the Defective Premises Act require proof of fault. An alternative claim may now be available under the Consumer Protection Act 1987, based on the European Community Directive on Product Liability. Subject to very limited defences, the Act imposes strict liability for personal injury and also for damage to property, other than the defective product itself. The Act provides special limitation periods of three years from discoverability of the damage with a longstop period of 10 years from the time of supply of the product (rather than 15 years from the negligent act as under the Latent Damage Act).

NUISANCE

Private nuisance may be defined as an unlawful interference with the use or enjoyment of another person's land. The interference may result in damage to property, such as by flooding or vibrations, or it may be only an annoyance, such as excessive noise or dust. There must be a substantial interference. A nuisance is often a continuing state of affairs, although an isolated happening may support an action in nuisance. Neighbours must exercise give and take, but deliberate acts intended to annoy neighbours can create an actionable nuisance. Persons who live in noisy or industrial neighbourhoods must usually put up with the attendant discomforts, although actual damage to property will be actionable.

Usually the only person who can sue for nuisance is the occupier of the land, although other persons may be able to sue on the same facts, for instance in negligence. The person liable is usually the occupier of the land or premises where the nuisance exists, but the person who created the nuisance may be liable. Thus, *prima facie* a building or engineering contractor will be liable for interference with adjoining land caused by the construction operations, but the employer may also be liable (see page 350).

Unlike negligence, liability for nuisance does not depend primarily on the standard of conduct of the defendant. Thus, it is not necessarily a defence to nuisance that reasonable care was taken to avoid it. But in the context of building and construction operations, those carrying out such work are under a duty to take proper precautions to see that nuisance is reduced to a minimum. Thus, where no steps were taken by a demolition contractor to minimise noise and dust near to the plaintiff's hotel, an actionable nuisance was created for which the employer was liable: *Andreae* v. *Selfridge* (1938). Sir Wilfred Green M.R. held, in the Court of Appeal:

> "Those who say that their interference with the comfort of their neighbours is justified because their operations are normal and usual and conducted with proper care and skill are under a specific duty, if they wish to make good that defence, to use that reasonable and proper care and skill. It is not a correct attitude to take to say: 'We will go on and do what we like until someone complains.' That is not their duty to their neighbours. Their duty is to take proper precautions, to see that the nuisance is reduced to a minimum. It is no answer for them to say: 'But this would mean that we should have to do the work more slowly than we would like to do it or it would involve putting us to some extra expense.' All those questions are matters of common sense and degree and quite clearly it would be unreasonable to expect people to conduct their work so slowly or so expensively, for the purpose of preventing a transient inconvenience, that the cost and trouble would be prohibitive. It is all a question of fact and degree and must necessarily be so."

A nuisance may also be controlled by the relevant local authority under the Public Health Act 1936. Sections 92 and 93 empower the authority to serve an abatement notice where there is a "Statutory Nuisance" as defined by the Act. This includes:

> (a) Any premises in such a state as to be prejudicial to health or a nuisance. . . .
> (c) Any accumulation or deposit which is prejudicial to health or a nuisance. . . .
> (d) Any dust or effluvia caused by any trade, business, manufacture or process and being prejudicial to the health of or a nuisance to the inhabitants of the neighbourhood. . . .

Where a statutory nuisance is not abated, the authority may acquire powers to carry out necessary work. These provisions are, however, not intended to be used by over-fastidious neighbours, who must exercise reasonable restraint. Under the Control of Pollution Act 1974 a local authority has powers to control noise on construction sites. They may serve a notice restricting the use of specified plant, restricting hours of work and limiting the level of noise. The act also permits the contractor to obtain the prior consent of the authority to the methods of work proposed (sections 60, 61).

Other nuisances

In addition to interference with land, a nuisance may be committed by interference with certain rights over land, such as a right of support. There is a natural right of support for unweighted land, and a nuisance is committed if subsidence is caused either by removing the lateral support by excavation, or by undermining. Generally it is unimportant how the withdrawal of support occurs, but as an important exception there is no liability for causing subsidence by withdrawal of subterranean percolating water. Thus, where pumping was carried out to keep excavations dry and resulted in lowering of the water table and settlement of buildings on adjacent land, the adjoining owner had no redress: *Langbrook* v. *Surrey C.C.* (1969). In this case, Plowman J. after reviewing the authorities, concluded that a landowner was entitled to abstract water under his land which percolates in undefined channels, notwithstanding that this may cause neighbouring land to subside. The Judge went on to consider whether there could, in such circumstances, be liability for nuisance or negligence, and held:

> "Since it is not actionable to cause damage by the abstraction of underground water, even where this is done maliciously, it would seem illogical that it should be actionable if it were done carelessly. Where there is no duty not to injure for the sake of inflicting injury, there cannot, in my judgment, be a duty to take care not to inflict the same injury."

The right of support for a building, as opposed to the land on which it stands, is not a natural right and must be acquired as an easement by grant or by usage (see page 367). Once acquired, the right is usually a right of support both from adjacent land and from adjoining buildings. Other rights which may give rise to an action in nuisance for interference include rights of light and air, water rights and rights of way.

Where an interference is caused to a wider group of persons than the occupier of neighbouring land, such conduct may constitute a public nuisance. This is primarily a crime, but a civil action may be brought in respect of a public nuisance by an individual who has suffered special damage different from that suffered by the public at large. Common examples of public nuisance are obstruction of the highway, and creating dangers upon or near the highway.

VICARIOUS LIABILITY

Vicarious liability in this context means liability for the torts of others. In the construction industry this may arise in two ways. First, the employer may be liable for the torts of the contractor or the contractor may be liable for the torts of his sub-contractors; secondly, any of the parties involved in the work may be liable for the torts of their own individual employees.

As to the first type of vicarious liability, it is a general rule that a person is not liable for torts committed by his independent contractors. However, there are substantial exceptions to the general rule, whereby the employer may be liable for the torts of his contractor. The circumstances in which such liability may arise include: where the liability is strict, such as under the rule in *Rylands* v. *Fletcher*; where work involves danger on or near a highway; and where work will involve danger to other property unless proper care is taken (see above). Even where *prima facie* the employer is not responsible he may still be liable for his own negligence in employing an incompetent contractor or for failing to give adequate directions to avoid damage to another. The employer will also be liable under the law of agency if he authorises or ratifies his contractor's unlawful act.

Master and servant

As a general rule a master is vicariously liable for the unauthorised tort of his servant if it is committed within the course of his employment. The master is liable for torts which he authorises or ratifies. The terms "master" and "servant" have acquired a special meaning in law which is rather wider than employer and employee. A precise definition is difficult to give; but a servant may be said to be a person employed to carry out work not as an independent contractor. The work of the servant is an integral part of the master's business, while an independent contractor undertakes only to produce a given result. The distinction can be of great importance since, as discussed above, the employer is generally not liable for the torts of his independent contractor. Persons are frequently found on construction sites who are technically self-employed, but who may be difficult to categorise as servants or independent contractors.

In addition to deciding who is a servant, it may be necessary to decide who is the master, for instance, where a servant is hired by his employer to another employer. It is presumed that the original employer remains liable as the master, unless the right to control the way in which the work was done passes to the temporary employer. Thus, where an employer hired a crane together with its driver to carry out unloading work and the hirer supervised the work but not the management of the crane, the original employer was held to be responsible for the driver's negligence: *Mersey Docks* v. *Coggins & Griffiths* (1947). In this case Lord Porter, in the House of Lords, observed:

> "Amongst the many tests suggested I think the most satisfactory, by which to ascertain who is the employer at any particular time, is to ask who was entitled to tell the employee the way in which he is to do the work upon which he is engaged. If someone other than his general employer is authorised to do this he will, as a rule, be the person liable for the employee's negligence. But it is not enough that the task to be performed should be under his control, he must also control the method of performing it."

The master will be liable for the tort of his servant only if the tort is committed during the course of his employment; that is, it must be a wrongful way of doing that which he is employed to do. Thus, an employer will be liable if the employee carries out his duties negligently or fraudulently. The employer may even be liable if the employee does something which he has expressly been forbidden to do, provided it is within the scope of his employment. But where a driver, employed on a building site to carry only fellow-employees, carried an employee of another firm on the site, this was held to be an act which he was not employed to perform. The employer was therefore not liable for the driver's negligence: *Conway* v. *Wimpey* (1951). In giving judgment in the Court of Appeal, Asquith L.J. held:

> "I should hold that taking men not employed by the defendants on to the vehicle was not merely a wrongful mode of performing the act of the class this driver was employed to perform, but was the performance of an act of a class which he was not employed to perform at all. In other words, the act was outside the scope of his employment."

Whether or not the master is liable, the servant is generally liable for his own tort and may be sued jointly with the master, or separately. Similarly where an employer is liable for his independent contractor, the contractor may also be sued jointly or separately. The practical importance to a plaintiff of vicarious liability is that one defendant may have more money than another. The damages may only be recovered once, but it is important to ensure that those sued are able to satisfy a judgment.

REMEDIES

The remedy claimed in most tort actions is damages. The successful plaintiff in an action for damages will generally be awarded a sum which is intended to compensate for the real loss suffered. The sum awarded must take into account future loss since usually only one action may be brought. Damages may be proportionally reduced if contributory negligence is found against the plaintiff. In certain extreme cases the damages recovered may vary greatly from the actual loss. Thus, in an action where the plaintiff has succeeded in law, the law court may show its disapproval of his conduct by awarding contemptuous damages of perhaps 1p and may deprive the plaintiff of his costs. At the other end of the scale the court may, in very limited circumstances, show its disapproval of the defendant's conduct by awarding exemplary damages to penalise the defendant.

Remoteness and causation

Once liability is established, the question may arise whether the damage claimed is too remote to be recoverable. The general test is that compensation may be recovered for damage which is of a reasonably foreseeable kind. If this is so it does not matter if damage occurred in an unforeseeable manner or to an unforeseeable extent; the defendant will be liable for the whole loss. The rules of remoteness in contract and in tort are not identical. The tortfeasor is liable for loss which is foreseeable as the possible result of his conduct and therefore may bear a heavier burden than the contract breaker, who is liable only for the probable result of his actions (see page 106).

The test of foreseeability was established in the leading case of *Overseas Tankship* v. *Morts Dock & Engineering Co.* (*The Wagon*

Mound) (1961), in which the Privy Council had to consider the following facts. A large quantity of furnace oil was discharged through the negligence of the defendants from their ship while moored. The oil spread to a wharf belonging to the plaintiffs who were engaged in refitting work, including welding. Believing there to be no danger, the plaintiffs continued the welding. The oil ignited and caused serious damage. The Privy Council held the defendants not liable. Lord Simonds, after reviewing the extensive authorities said:

> "The essential factor in determining liability is whether the damage is of such a kind as the reasonable man should have foreseen. This accords with the general view thus stated by Lord Atkin in *Donoghue* v. *Stevenson*: 'The liability for negligence . . . is no doubt based on a general public sentiment of moral wrong-doing for which the offender must pay.' It is not a departure from this sovereign principle if liability is made to depend solely on the damage being the direct or natural consequence of the precedent act. Who knows or can be assumed to know all the processes of nature? But if it would be wrong that a man should be held liable for damage unpredictable by a reasonable man because it was direct or natural, equally it would be wrong that he should escape liability however indirect the damage, if he foresaw or could reasonably foresee the intervening events which lead to it being done. . . . Thus forceability becomes the effective test."

The question of causation, rejected in *The Wagon Mound* may still be of relevance. In *Barnett* v. *Chelsea Hospital Committee* (1969) a nightwatchman presented himself at the hospital casualty department complaining of vomiting after drinking tea. He was told to go home to bed, where he later died of arsenic poisoning. In an action by the widow for negligence, it was held that the plaintiff had failed to establish that the defendant's negligence had caused the death. Coversely in the case of *Baker* v. *Willoughby* (1970) the plaintiff sued for injury to his leg caused by the defendant's negligent driving. But before the claim was heard, he was involved in an armed robbery in which the injured leg was shot and had to be amputated. The House of Lords refused to reduce the damages on this account, holding the second injury a mere concurrent cause. The questions of remoteness and causation, both in tort and contract, will continue to produce many complex legal problems.

Contribution

Where there are two or more defendants responsible for the same loss the plaintiff is entitled to recover judgment against each to the full amount of their individual liability. The plaintiff is then entitled to enforce the judgment obtained against either, provided that he does not recover more than the total damages proved. To mitigate this, the court has power under the Civil Liability (Contribution) Act 1978 (which amends provisions formerly in the Law Reform (Married Women and Tortfeasors) Act 1935) to apportion liability between defendants. The apportionment is dealt with by the judge after deciding upon the liability of the defendants to the plaintiff. The effect is to give any defendant entitled to contribution the right to recover from another defendant the amount of that defendant's liability. If, therefore, one or more of the defendants is without the means to pay, the remaining defendants must bear the whole loss. In many construction cases, this has operated to the disadvantage of professionals who have insurance available, when contractors or sub-contractors may be insolvent. For an example of the law of contribution see *Eckersley* v. *Binnie* (page 111).

The rules as to contribution apply whether or not the other persons liable have been sued by the plaintiff. A defendant may bring into an action as a third party anyone whom he considers should contribute to the plaintiff's loss as a joint tortfeasor. Or the defendant may bring separate proceedings claiming contribution after the plaintiff has obtained judgment. Thus a builder sued in negligence by the subsequent owner of a house may recover contributions from the negligent architect and others involved.

Injunction

An alternative remedy to damages, which may be appropriate particularly in cases of nuisance, is an injunction, either to restrain the defendant from doing some act or to compel the performance of an act. An injunction is an equitable remedy and therefore lies in the court's discretion. It will usually be refused where damages would be an adequate remedy, or where to grant it would be in vain. One very valuable feature of this remedy is the power of the courts to issue an interlocutory injunction (until trial) in a proper case. Thus, a temporary relief may sometimes be obtained within days or even hours of a cause of complaint arising. The power to grant an injunction extends to a threatened but unperformed act.

Limitation

A final consideration in any action must be the period during which the action may be brought. The Limitation Act 1980

provides that an action founded on tort shall not be brought after
the expiration of six years from the date on which the cause of
action accrued (section 2). There is a further limitation where the
claim is for damages in respect of personal injuries arising from
negligence, nuisance or breach of duty. Here, the action must
normally be brought within three years from the date on which
the cause of action accrued (section 11) subject to certain
extensions.

The main difference between limitation in a contract action and
in tort is that in the former case, the cause of action accrues at the
date of the breach (see page 112). In tort, however, the cause of
action accrues only when damage is suffered, so that the cause of
action may not arise until long after the relevant work was carried
out. Thus, if a builder negligently erects a chimney stack, a cause of
action in contract arises in favour of the employer when the work is
done, or when the builder purports to finish it. If the work remains
in place and no complaint is made, the right of action in contract
will be lost after six years. If, after 10 years, the chimney falls, to
injure a passer-by, a right of action in tort then immediately vests in
the injured person.

There has been great development in the law of limitation
relating to defects in building work in recent years. The impetus
came from those cases (see above) which held that a right of
action in tort was available, and this led to a series of cases in
which local authorities, builders, designers and other professionals were held liable long after the relevant work was carried
out. In a number of cases it was held that the cause of action
accrued only when the building owner became aware, or ought
reasonably to have become aware, of the existence of the defect.
Six years were then available to issue proceedings. However, this
was contrary to the law of limitation as applied in personal injury
cases. Here, the House of Lords held in *Cartledge* v. *Jopling*
(1963) that the plaintiff's action was statute-barred before the
damage (contraction of pneumoconiosis) could reasonably have
been known. As a result of this case, an amendment to the
Limitation Act was passed, now contained in sections 11 to 14 of
the Limitation Act 1980, allowing a further three years to bring
an action from the date when the plaintiff knew or ought to have
known that he had a cause of action. No such change was then
made regarding damage to buildings or other property. After the
advent of new claims in tort (now seen to be temporary)
regarding damage to buildings, the question of limitation of such
claims was referred to the Law Reform Committee. But before
any change in statute law occurred, a case came before the courts

which directly raised the question whether the *Cartledge* v. *Jopling* principle applied to buildings.

This case was *Pirelli* v. *Oscar Faber* (1983), which concerned the design of a chimney, built in 1969. Not later than 1970, cracks developed near the top of the chimney, but this was not discovered until 1977. A writ was issued in 1978. The House of Lords, while agreeing that the law was unsatisfactory, held that the cause of action arose in 1970 and was therefore statute-barred. *Cartledge* v. *Jopling* applied equally to damage to property and the previous contrary decisions of the Court of Appeal were wrong.

The effect of this case was subsequently changed by the Latent Damage Act 1986. This Act introduced new sections 14A and 14B into the Limitation Act 1980. The material effect of these provisions is, first, that an action for damages for negligence may be brought within three years of the date upon which a reasonable person would conclude that proceedings could and should be instituted (section 14A). Secondly, a long stop period of 15 years is applied to the bringing of any such action, this period running from the date of the last alleged act of negligence (section 14B). The wording of the act is long and complicated and needs to be considered carefully. The act also introduces a change to the law where a person buys a house which has a defect such that a cause of action has already arisen. In the case of *Perry* v. *Tendring District Council* (1984) the Official Referee held, in such circumstances, that the cause of action vested in the original owner and could not ordinarily be transferred to a purchaser. Section 3 of the Latent Damage Act 1968 reverses this decision by providing that a fresh cause of action is to accrue to the purchaser on the date that he acquires an interest in the property, that cause of action being treated as having accrued on the same date as the original cause of action of the previous owner (so that, the defendant is not to be placed in any worse position). These cases must all be reconsidered in the light of the *Murphy* case (see above).

It is ironic that, even while the Latent Damage Act was going through Parliament, the courts were embarking on the series of tort cases already referred to which, by 1990 finally established that tortious liability would normally be limited to cases of actual physical injury. Thus, the resolution of doubt over the law of limitation in tort has coincided with emasculation of the rights of action.

A further important development, overshadowed at the time by changes in the law of tort, was the passing of the Defective

Premises Act 1972 (see page 138). This Act creates a general duty on persons to see that work is done in a workmanlike or professional manner, with proper materials and so that the dwelling will be fit for habitation (section 1). For the purpose of limitation, the Act provides that any cause of action in respect of a breach of these duties:

> "shall be deemed . . . to have accrued at the time that the dwelling was completed, but if after that time a person who has done work for or in connection with the provision of the dwelling does further work to rectify the work he has already done, any such cause of action in respect of that further work shall be deemed for those purposes to have accrued at the time when the further work was finished."

The Act, therefore, creates in clear terms, a statutory duty similar (although rather wider) to that which the courts had sought to impose under the law of tort, and also provides what may be regarded as a fair limitation rule, which has no need of a longstop provision. Since the *D. & F.* and *Murphy* cases the Defective Premises Act represents the principal remedy outside contract in respect of damaged buildings.

Section 32 of the Limitation Act 1980 (see page 112) also applies to claims based on tort or breach of statutory duty. This section postpones the limitation period in a case where facts relevant to the plaintiff's right of action have been deliberately concealed from him by the defendant. Section 32 of the 1980 Act is amended by the Latent Damage Act 1986 with the effect that sections 14A and 14B (see above) do not apply in the case of deliberate concealment, where the normal period of limitation will apply after the plaintiff has discovered or could reasonably have discovered the concealment. Normal limitation provisions will also be overriden where a claim for contribution is brought under the Civil Liability (Contribution) Act 1978. Here, by section 10 of the Limitation Act 1980, an action to recover contributions may be brought within two years of the judgment, award or settlement which establishes the liability of the person claiming contribution.

INTERNATIONAL CASES

In Chapter 2 (page 36) the effect of a foreign element upon the procedure in a case is considered. In this section it is assumed that the English courts are proceeding to hear a case in tort containing a foreign element. The question then arising is which national law should the court apply.

If a tort is committed in England by or to a foreign party, then any action brought here is tried by English law as an ordinary domestic case. The conflict of law arises only where torts are committed abroad. Despite acceptance in other common law countries, the concept of a "proper law" of tort is not accepted in English courts (see page 113).

The rule as to which law applies in a tort action is a compromise between the law of the place of commission and English law. The general rule is that in order to found a suit in England for a tort committed abroad, it must be actionable under English law and also actionable as a civil wrong at the place of commission. The defendant's conduct is therefore to be judged by both laws. It seems that such matters as the amount of damages claimable may be determined by English law, while the law of the place of commission may affect the defences available to the defendant.

An incidental problem may be to decide where a tort is committed. This may arise if a fire is negligently started in England and spreads across the border to do damage in Scotland. Although there are at least two possible views on this point, the English rule is generally that a tort is committed where the wrongful act takes place; in this example, in England.

Further Reading

Salmond on Torts (19th ed., 1987), Heuston and Buckley.
Winfield and Jolowicz on Tort (13th ed., 1989), Rogers.
Baker, *Tort* (4th ed., 1991), (Concise College Texts).

CHAPTER 14

LAW RELATING TO LAND

In England the law relating to land has always been different and distinct from law relating to other property. There are many reasons for this. Perhaps the most obvious is that a piece of land is indestructible and unique. No other land is quite the same. On a practical level, it is common for two or more persons to hold simultaneously different interests in the same land, and this is one of the reasons why a sale of land is more complicated and lengthy than a sale of other property.

Although the expression "land owner" is often encountered it requires some qualification in legal terms. It is not possible to "own" land in the absolute way that other property (such as a motor car) may be owned. Instead, the law speaks of owning an estate or interest in land, which gives the owner certain rights over that land. The largest estate which may be owned is called a fee simple absolute in possession. This is what is commonly known as "freehold" and for convenience it is so called in this section, although in legal terms an estate lasting only for the life of the holder may be a type of freehold.

Another type of estate in land is a tenancy. This may be created out of the estate of the freeholder or of a superior tenant. The word "tenancy" refers to a right to possession of land for a limited period. This may be for a fixed term of years (when the tenancy must normally be created by a lease) but also includes periodic tenancies such as a weekly or quarterly tenancy. In practice a building owner is likely to be concerned only with long tenancies created by lease.

Interests in land generally indicate something less than an estate; they may be of many kinds. Two of the most important are easements and restrictive covenants, and these are mentioned further below. Another very common interest in land is a mortgage, where the land is used as a security.

Two further provisions may illustrate the special legal status of land. First, an infant, (*i.e.* a person under 18 years) cannot own an estate in land. Secondly, a contract for the sale of land or any interest in land is unenforceable unless in writing and signed by or on behalf of each party, or in the case of contracts which are exchanged, unless each counterpart is signed (Law of Property (Miscellaneous Provisions) Act 1989, section 2).

Throughout its history land law has been profoundly affected by the principles of equity (see page 9). The result is that interests in land are for some purposes classified as being either legal or equitable. The practical importance of this distinction is that a legal interest attaches to the land itself and is enforceable against any person. An equitable interest binds only certain persons, and is not enforceable against a bona fide purchaser of the land who has no notice (actual or constructive) of such interest. An equitable interest is, therefore, less secure. An example of an equitable interest is an agreement for a lease. Practically, this is as good as an actual lease but if another person purchases the land without notice of the agreement, it becomes unenforceable against that person.

RIGHTS OF THE OWNER OR OCCUPIER OF LAND

When a person wishes to build on land there are many factors to be considered. He must obtain a sufficient interest to give him a right of possession. He must consider what restrictions there are as to what may be done with the land. He will also wish to know who is entitled to ownership or use of things on or in the land. These points are considered below. Another factor, which may be of great importance, is the question of rights which other persons hold concurrently over the land. Such rights are considered in the following section.

Leases

The most common legal device for obtaining possession of premises for business use is by a lease. There is no fixed definition of the term, but it is usually taken to mean a formal tenancy granted by deed. For most purposes a simple written tenancy agreement will have the same legal effect. The process is also colloquially referred to as "letting." Whatever term is used, the process has two separate elements. First, there is conveyance of the property as defined for the period stated (which may be periodic and renewable); secondly, there are terms (sometimes called covenants) which operate as a contract enforceable between the parties. But because the transaction relates to land, the terms or covenants may be enforceable directly by or against other parties who take over the interest of either landlord or tenant (see page 366) and there are also statutory restrictions on enforcement.

Leases and tenancy agreements are in many ways more convenient than buying a freehold interest. Commercial buildings are erected as investments, and the letting, subletting, and assignment of such premises are part of the commercial activity of any business community. It is now comparatively rare for commercial companies, at least in inner city areas, to own the freehold of their own premises. The mobility afforded by letting arrangements has allowed the substantial re-development of commercial areas which has been carried out over the last decades. Business leases are subject to security of tenure under the Landlord and Tenant Act 1954. At the end of a lease, the tenant may apply to the court for a new tenancy. However, the need to demolish and reconstruct the premises or to carry out substantial reconstruction work is a ground upon which the court can refuse a new lease, the tenant receiving compensation instead; and it is possible to contract out of the provisions for security in the Act.

The detailed operation of leases and their covenants is beyond the scope of this book. However, mention should be made of two classes of construction dispute which frequently arise out of lettings. Leases invariably contain repairing covenants of some variety. These require the tenant to carry out certain works, usually defined in terms of the intended result, such as to keep the premises in "good and tenantable repair." Leases usually require the premises to be yielded up in a repaired state, and when the end of the tenancy arrives, there may be a dispute as to its state. This is referred to as a "dilapidations" claim, which often consists of long schedules and counterschedules settled by surveyors for each party. Such a dispute is concerned only with the assessment and valuation of wants of repair in accordance with the covenants. Sometimes disputes of this sort arise during the term of a tenancy. Here, the position is more complex because, if there are a number of years of tenancy still to run, the landlord usually suffers no damage. Accordingly, the Leasehold Property (Repairs) Act 1938 provides that, where there are three years or more of the term remaining, the landlord must obtain leave of the court before proceeding with any action for breach of a repairing covenant, and the court will grant such leave only on exceptional grounds, such as where it is shown that immediate remedying of the breach is necessary.

In addition to specific covenants covering repairs, payment of rent and other matters, leases usually contain a "forfeiture" clause permitting the landlord to take back the lease, or "re-enter" for breach of covenant. For the protection of tenants, the law has evolved a series of protective measures. First, under the Law of Property Act 1925, section 146, no such right of forfeiture may be enforced (except in the case of non-payment of rent) unless the landlord has first served a notice specifying the breach and requiring remedy and compensation. When such a notice has been served, and not complied with (perhaps because the tenant disputes that repairs are necessary), the landlord must seek an order from the court for forfeiture, and the tenant can then apply for the equitable remedy of relief (now embodied also in statute) which may be granted on such terms as the court thinks fit. The result of the dispute is, in effect, to decide the rights of the parties under the contractual terms or covenants of the lease, and to enforce them. Only in exceptional circumstances will leases be declared forfeit. Indeed, there is little purpose in the tenant allowing the lease to be forfeited, because he will remain liable for the financial consequences of previous breaches of covenant.

Another type of construction dispute that may arise out of a lease is one relating to the nature of the repairs that the tenant is responsible for. What is the tenant's position under a normal repairing covenant if the premises become defective due to design defects in the original construction? In the case of *Ravenseft Properties* v. *Davstone* (1980) a tenant undertook covenants which included an obligation "well and sufficiently to repair, renew, rebuild, uphold, support, sustain, maintain" the premises. The building had been constructed in concrete with external stone cladding, but with no expansion joints to allow differential movement between the stone and concrete. The cladding bowed and needed substantial repair as a result of this inherent defect. It was held that it was a question of degree whether the remedying of an inherent defect was work of repair, and where (as in this case) the work of inserting expansion joints was a comparatively trivial part of the whole building, so as not to involve giving back to the landlord a wholly different building, the tenant was liable for the repairs. In answer to a further argument that the tenant should not be liable for repair necessary to remedy an inherent defect Forbes J. said:

> "It was proper engineering practice to see that such expansion joints were included, and it would have been dangerous not to include them. In no realistic sense, therefore, could it be said that there was

any other possible way of reinstating the cladding than by providing the expansion joints which were in fact provided."

Thus, the tenant was held liable for the whole cost of repair, in the only way that it could realistically be done.

The effect of this, and other cases to like effect, has been to cause tenants to bring claims for their own loss (including loss of use or loss of profit) against contractors and designers. The fact that such claims are now not generally maintainable in tort (see page 335) has meant that tenants in particular have sought direct contractual warranties from those responsible for the work (see page 178).

Rights of occupation

A right to occupation of land which is not sufficient to create a true tenancy is said to create a licence. This is essentially a right to do some act which would otherwise be a trespass. Examples of the operation of licences are a person occupying a cinema seat or an hotel room, and a contractor in possession of a building site. Essentially a licence is a personal arrangement between grantor and grantee which does not bind third parties. There may, however, be circumstances where an interest in the land affecting third parties is created. Thus, where a man allowed his son to build a bungalow on his (the father's) land and then died leaving the land to others, it was held that the son should be allowed to remain in the bungalow as long as he desired: *Inwards* v. *Baker* (1965). Lord Denning, in the Court of Appeal, held:

"All that is necessary is that the licensee should, at the request or with the encouragement of the landlord, have spent the money in the expectation of being allowed to stay there. If so, the court will not allow that expectation to be defeated where it would be inequitable so to do. In this case it is quite plain that the father allowed an expectation to be created in the son's mind that this bungalow was to be his home. It was to be his home for his life, or at all events, his home as long as he wished it to remain his home. It seems to me, in the light of that equity, that the father could not in 1932 have turned to his son and said: 'You are to go. It is my land and my house.' Nor could he at any time thereafter so long as the son wanted it as his home."

It is not to be recommended, however, that building developers should proceed upon such a tenuous interest in the land.

A gratuitous licence merely to enter land may be revoked at any time; while a licence coupled with an interest in the property (such as a right to dig gravel) cannot be revoked. A more usual type of licence in business transactions is one given under a contract. Such a licence will be regarded as part of the contract creating it and its revocation in breach of contract may in some circumstances be resisted by injunction. In a case in the Chancery Division, a contractor's employment under a building contract had been terminated by the employer. But the contractor, contending the termination was invalid, refused to leave the site. The employer claimed an injunction to remove him. The injunction was refused. The employer was held to be under an implied obligation not to revoke the contractor's licence except in accordance with the contract: *Hounslow L.B.C.* v. *Twickenham* (1971). In this case Megarry J. observed:

> "Now in this case the contract is one for the execution of specified works on the site during a specified period which is still running. The contract confers on each party specified rights on specified events to determine the employment of the contractor under the contract. In those circumstances I think that there must be at least an implied negative obligation on the Borough not to revoke any licence (otherwise than in accordance with the contract) while the period is still running."

Having decided that the Borough had not conclusively established the validity of its determination notices, the Judge went on to say:

> "I fully accept the importance to the Borough on social grounds as well as others of securing the due completion of the contract, and the unsatisfactory nature of damages as an alternative. But the contract was made, and the contractors are not to be stripped of their rights under it, however desirable that may be for the Borough. A contract remains a contract, even if (or perhaps especially if) it turns out badly."

This case, however, has been criticised and may not be followed, should similar circumstances arise.

Rights over the land

The question of what the owner or occupier is entitled to do with the land depends upon many factors. It is subject to numerous statutory provisions, such as the Housing Acts and Public Health Acts. Building work itself is closely controlled by regulations and by-laws (see Chapter 15). The occupier of land may become liable to his neighbours in tort, for example, by committing a nuisance (see page 348). Perhaps the most fundamental restriction upon the user of land arises through statutory planning controls (see below). Rather than to say that land is owned subject to restrictions, it is probably more accurate to say that land is held for the benefit both of the owner or occupier and of the community.

As to ownership of things on or in the land (as opposed to "ownership" of the space occupied by the land), it is presumed that the owner of the freehold owns everything upon or below the land. He is generally entitled to everything which is attached to the land. Such items are commonly called fixtures (as opposed to mere fittings) and they will belong to the freeholder as against a tenant. The question of what attachment is sufficient to make an object a fixture is a matter of degree and purpose. Thus a corrugated iron building bolted to, but not embedded in, a concrete floor was held not to be a fixture: *Webb* v. *Bevis* (1940). In this case, Scott L.J. in the Court of Appeal, held:

> "That the concrete floor was so affixed to the ground as to become part of the soil is obvious. It was completely and permanently attached to the ground and, secondly, it could not be detached except by being broken up and ceasing to exist either as a concrete floor or as the cement and rubble of which it had been made. Does that fact of itself prevent the superstructure from being a tenant's fixture? I do not think so. If it had been erected on concrete blocks, one under each post, the top level with the surface of the ground and the attachment of post to block had been plainly removeable at ground level, 'the object and purpose' of the attachment would have been obvious—namely to erect a mere tenant's fixture. In my opinion it was equally so in the actual construction adopted for holding the posts in position on their concrete supports."

Building materials will become the property of the freeholder as soon as they are (like the concrete floor in the above case) attached to the land or to the permanent works, whether paid for by the employer or not. As between landlord and tenant there are certain exceptions to the rule, which relate, particularly to trade and agricultural fixtures.

RIGHTS OVER LAND OF OTHERS

Of the many types of interest over land belonging to or in the possession of other persons, the most important so far as a building developer is concerned are easements and restrictive covenants. In this context the building developer is seen as the "other person" over whose land rights exist which may affect its use or development. The short account given below describes the nature of these interests; for the much wider topic of their creation, transmission and extinguishment, reference should be made to one of the standard works on the subject.

Easements

An *easement* is a right which allows the holder to use, or restrict the use of, the land of another person in some way. Common examples are private rights of way, rights of light and rights of support. An easement can exist only in relation to other land which is nearby, which is said to "benefit" from the easement. A "quasi-easement" (which is referred to in clause 22 of the ICE conditions) is a term used to describe an habitual right exercised by a person over a part of his own land, which would be an easement if the two parts were in different occupation, such as a right of support between adjoining buildings. A quasi-easement may become a real easement upon a sale of one or both parts of the land.

Rights of light often restrict development on sites adjoining the land of the "dominant tenement." An action to preserve a right of light lies in nuisance. But even where the right has been acquired by long usage, the holder cannot demand unlimited light. The courts have held that the right is to have enough light adequately to light a room "according to the ordinary notions of mankind": *Colls* v. *Home and Colonial Stores* (1904).

It is not always appreciated by building owners that it is not the function of a planning authority to guard or preserve rights of light or other easements. Thus, the fact that a right of light is enjoyed does not prevent a developer obtaining planning permission for a building which will block the right; nor does the grant of planning permission guarantee that the developer will not be prevented from erecting the building in breach of the rights of neighbours.

There are a number of other rights which are similar to, but which do not comprise easements. For example, a profit (or *profit à prendre*) is a right to take something from the land of another person, such as grass or sand; a licence is a private right to go upon another's land (see page 364). Either of these rights may exist without the holder owning land which is benefitted. An easement of support relates only to a building and is distinct from the natural right to have unweighted land supported by adjoining land (see page 349).

Covenants

A contractual provision which seeks to constrain the way in which the holder of land may use it is termed a *restrictive covenant*. An example of the type of covenant which might be relevant to a building developer is one not to build on certain land. As between the original parties a covenant is binding, for instance, when the covenantee and covenantor are respectively landlord and tenant. It will also be binding on successors if it constitutes an easement (see above). Otherwise, only in limited circumstances will a restrictive covenant be enforceable by and against successors in title. A plaintiff who wishes to enforce a restrictive covenant must show that he has acquired what is known as the "benefit" of the covenant and that the defendant has acquired the "burden."

An example of the operation of restrictive covenants occurs where an estate is laid out in lots to be sold or leased for building and each purchaser or lessee agrees to restrictive covenants. It is necessary that the area be clearly defined and that restrictions are imposed by the common vendor or lessor which are consistent with the general scheme of the development. The covenants must be for the benefit of all the lots and the sale or leasing must be transacted with this intention. Provided these conditions are satisfied, the covenants will be enforceable by and against the owners or lessees for the time being of any plot on the estate. The covenants therefore constitute a local law for the estate

Party walls

Problems frequently occur in heavily built-up areas over the rights possessed by adjoining owners in a party wall. There is no absolute definition of the term, but it is used where the boundary line between two premises is built on, or where one adjoining owner has acquired rights in a wall built up to the boundary on neighbouring land. The problem is frequently to define where the boundary lies, and this is often an intractable problem where there have been alterations and extensions over the years. Having identified the position of the boundary, it is often found that walls vary in line and in thickness, and foundations usually extend out beyond the wall itself, so that there is often no simple answer to the question of ownership.

Assuming that ownership can be established, there are rights at common law to carry out work to a party wall, notwithstanding that part of the wall is not owned by the party wishing to carry out the work. In London, where the problem is most acute, the rights are codified in the London Building Acts. These provisions set out the rights of adjoining owners and provide a code for exercise of such rights. An essential requirement is for the party wishing to carry out the work to serve notice on the other party. If there is any objection or dispute, there is machinery for this to be rapidly resolved by each party appointing a surveyor and for the two surveyors (with the assistance of a third surveyor if necessary) to settle a "party wall award." Such an award sets out the work agreed to be carried out and provides for the payment of all costs and compensation if necessary. The system works well in practice and demonstrates how short technical disputes can be resolved quickly and cheaply.

PLANNING LAW

Planning law is substantially a creature of the twentieth century. The first attempts at systematic town planning were introduced in 1909, and since then the scope and complexity of planning law have widened enormously. The destruction brought about by the Second World War with its consequent opportunities for replanning has been responsible for much of this development. The principal enactment is now the Town and Country Planning Act 1990, which consolidates the previous statute law relating to planning. There are also other important Acts together with regulations, rules and orders made under statutory powers. Recent developments have shown increasing emphasis on conservation in all forms.

The practical effect of modern planning law is that the owner's rights to use his land are to a large extent subordinated to the good of the community. In general, a land owner has no right to use his land for any purpose other than its present use unless he obtains permission. Further, he may be dispossessed of even its present use by authorities exercising powers of compulsory acquisition. The economic importance of planning law to the individual is demonstrated by the direct effect which planning consent has upon the value of land.

In origin, planning law is entirely statutory, that is to say, it is all contained in Acts of Parliament and the delegated legislation made under the Acts. Most statutes are periodically considered and interpreted by the courts and this usually makes them easier to understand. But planning law is brought before the courts on comparatively rare occasions. The usual procedure is that planning decisions are made initially in a purely administrative way, by the local authority or government department. An appeal is usually allowed to the Minister, and his function is sometimes described as quasi-judicial. But in either case the decision is not of legal rights (as in the case of a decision in the courts) but of the proper administration of planning policy. Thus, in a case which arose under the New Towns Act 1946, the Minister stated publicly that Stevenage would be the first new town. He made a draft order to this effect and an inquiry was held into objections. The Minister then confirmed his order. The court held that there was no judicial duty upon the Minister, but only a duty to consider the objections: *Franklin* v. *Minister of Town and Country Planning* (1948). In this case, Lord Thankerton, in the House of Lords, held:

> "In my opinion, no judicial or quasi-judicial duty was imposed on the (Minister) and any reference to judicial duty, or bias, is irrelevant to the present case. . . . The (Minister) was required to satisfy himself that it was a sound scheme before he took the serious step of issuing a draft order. It seems clear also, that the purpose of inviting objections and, where they are not withdrawn, having a public inquiry, to be held by someone other than the (Minister) to whom that person reports, was for the further information of the (Minister). . . . I am of the opinion that no judicial duty is laid on the (Minister) in discharge of those statutory duties and that the only question is whether he has complied with the statutory directions to appoint a person to hold the public inquiry and to consider that person's report."

There may be an application to the High Court for judicial review if a point of law is disclosed in the manner or form of the action taken by a local planning authority. It is only through such decisions of the court that case law is created. Otherwise, decisions made by planning authorities or by the minister are administrative decisions only which do not create any precedent. While such decisions may serve as a guide to enable applicants to assess the likelihood of planning consent being granted, each decision is a matter of discretion.

Planning authorities and their functions

The administration of planning law at local levels is carried out by the local planning authority. This body will be either a county council or a district council or, in London, the relevant Borough Council. The authority responsible for central administration is referred to in the Acts as the Secretary of State.

In addition to these authorities, there are other bodies which have specific functions in relation to planning administration. In particular, the Lands Tribunal, among its various functions, has powers to settle disputes over the valuation of land arising out of planning decisions.

Development plan

A primary creative duty of the planning authority is periodically to produce plans for future development. The development plan has two parts. First, the structure plan formulates policy and general proposals for development and use of land, relating this to relevant proposals for neighbouring areas. The structure plan is prepared by the county planning authority, and must indicate any "action areas" which are selected for imminent development. Secondly, local plans may be prepared by district planning authorities to show development proposals in any part of the area. Local plans must be provided for action areas, but different plans may cover the same area for different purposes. Both the structure plan and local plans must be given adequate publicity and inquiries may be held. The structure plan must be approved by the Secretary of State; and a local plan must be adopted by the local planning authority, but the Secretary of State may direct that his approval is required. A local authority, when considering a planning application is required to "have regard" to the provisions of the development plan. The courts have held that this does not impose an obligation to adhere slavishly to the plan: *Niarchos (London) Ltd.* v. *Secretary of State for the Environment* (1977).

The ultimate objective of a planning authority is to see that its development plan is carried out. Where this can be achieved by planning restrictions the problem is reduced to one of enforcement, but positive development may require more than mere control. One of the most important powers of local authorities in this respect is the power to acquire land compulsorily for planning purposes, with the authorisation of the Secretary of

State. The measure of compensation which is payable upon compulsory acquisition is basically the market value, but subject to some statutory modifications. There are also provisions for additional compensation for such matters as disturbance and severance of lands. Local authorities may compulsorily acquire land within their own areas and also in other areas. They may also acquire land by agreement, when the consent of the Secretary of State is generally not required.

Where land has been acquired or appropriated by a local authority for planning purposes, the local authority itself may carry out building or work upon the land; or instead of carrying out development itself the authority may make arrangements with an authorised association to carry out such operations. Alternatively the local authority may dispose of land so as to secure the use or development of the land needed for the proper planning of the area. This latter method has been used to secure the re-development of war-damaged land. Where land which was acquired compulsorily is to be disposed of the previous occupants must, so far as is practicable, be afforded an opportunity to return to their land.

Requirement of planning consent

In general any development of land requires a formal application for planning consent to be made to the local planning authority and the development may not be carried out unless such consent is granted. "Development" is defined by the Town and Country Planning Act 1990 as meaning *the carrying out of building, engineering, mining or other operations in, on, over or under land, or the making of any material change in the use of any buildings or other land* (section 55). The Act contains further definitions of many of its terms, such as "building," "land" and "use" (section 336). There are, however, some classes of exceptions under which things may be done to or with land without the necessity of obtaining planning consent.

The first exception is that no planning permission is required if the project is not within the meaning of "development." The Act states that certain operations or uses of land are not to be taken to involve development. These include most works which do not materially affect the external appearance of a building, and highway maintenance. But the division of a dwelling-house into two or more separate units requires planning permission, as does also the extension of a refuse tip, in area or in height, so as to exceed the level of adjoining land (section 55).

Where land is being used for a purpose specified in an order (the Town and Country Planning (Use Classes) Order 1987), the change to another use of the same class does not constitute development. Thus, the change from a grocery shop to a tobacconist does not require planning permission; but the change to a fried-fish shop or to an office is a development and requires permission. If there is uncertainty as to whether any project constitutes a development within the meaning of the Act, it may be resolved by application to the local planning authority (section 64) with an appeal to the Secretary of State and a further appeal to the High Court.

Secondly, the Secretary of State has power to make orders known as development orders which may permit either a particular development or some class of development. An order may itself grant planning permission or provide for permission to be granted by the local planning authority. An order may be limited in its area of application and may be subject to conditions. The general order applicable to all land in England and Wales is the Town and Country Planning General Development Order 1977, which has been amended a number of times. The Order sets out classes of permitted development for which the order itself constitutes planning permission. The classes include limited additions to a house, fences and walls of limited size, and specified classes of development by local authorities and statutory undertakers. There are also local development orders.

The third exception is that planning permission is not required in some specified cases relating to the resumption of a former use of land, such as after the expiry of planning permission granted for a limited period (section 57). A fourth exception applies to local authorities and statutory undertakers. Where authorisation is required from a government department for a development, the department may itself grant deemed planning permission (section 90).

Applications for planning consent

If a project requires planning permission to be obtained then the usual course is to make application to the local planning authority. An application must be made in such a manner as is prescribed by regulations, and must be accompanied by plans and other particulars of the project. In some cases the applicant is required to certify that he has given certain notices. For example, where the applicant is not the freeholder or leaseholder of all the land in question, he must take steps to notify the owner of the land of the application. Also, applications relating to certain classes of development must arrange for the local advertisement of the application (sections 65–69). Planning applications require payment of a fee.

An application may be made for "outline planning permission," in accordance with the provision of a development order (section 92). Such permission will be subject to subsequent approval of "reserved matters" not particularised in the application. Local authorities will, however, rarely grant outline planning permission if the site of the application lies within a conservation area. Outline planning permission will only be granted subject to application for approval of reserved matters, and commencement of the development, being made within specified periods. The procedure for outline planning applications may be useful for a prospective developer who does not own the land in question.

The local planning authority must generally give its decision within two months of an application for planning permission. In coming to a decision the authority must have regard to the development plan, and to other material matters. There are provisions requiring various persons and bodies to be consulted. Where applications require local advertisement, the planning authority must take into account representations received. Where the applicant is not the freeholder or leaseholder the representations of owners of the land must be considered (section 71). In particular, works to buildings listed as being of historic or architectural importance are given special consideration, and require an additional application. Such applications, however, do not require a further fee to be paid.

Effect of planning consent

Planning permission may be granted or refused or granted subject to conditions, and unless it is granted unconditionally reasons must be given for the decision. The conditions imposed may be permanent or of limited duration, although they must relate to the development. For example, a condition that payment should be made to the local authority does not relate to the development, and is invalid. The planning permission may itself be granted for a limited period, requiring the land to be reinstated at the end of such period (section 72). As an alternative to planning applications being determined by the local planning authority, the Secretary of State may "call in" particular applications or classes of application and himself determine them (section 77). Such applications may also be referred to an ad hoc Planning Inquiry Commission for special inquiry and report (section 101).

Once planning permission is obtained it attaches to the land for the benefit of subsequent owners. However, there is generally an implied condition that the development will be begun within five years unless other express time limits are laid down (section 91). The local planning authority is also given powers to promote timely completion of developments. Thus, the authority may serve a "completion notice" (to be confirmed by the Secretary of State), whereby planning permission will cease to have effect after a specified period in respect of uncompleted work (section 94). The authority also has powers to modify or revoke planning permission, with the confirmation of the Secretary of State (section 97).

Appeals

An appeal against the local planning authority's decision may be made to the Secretary of State, generally within six months. He will reconsider the whole application, so that an appeal against the conditions imposed with a consent may result in a refusal of consent. If any party wishes to make representations there will be a private hearing before an inspector, or the Secretary of State may direct that a public local inquiry be held (section 78). There is a final appeal from the Minister's decision to the High Court on a point of law. As an alternative, there is provision for an appeal from a decision of the local planning authority relating to the design or external appearance of a building to be heard by an independent tribunal. A Planning Inquiry Commission may hear appeals if a central government department or statutory undertaker seeks permission, or if there are considerations of regional or national importance involved.

Powers of control

If a development is carried out without planning consent, or contrary to conditions imposed with such consent, the local planning authority may enforce their control by serving an enforcement notice (section 172). This must specify the matters of complaint, the steps required for their rectification and the period for compliance. The steps required to be taken may include demolition or alteration of buildings or works. Such a notice must be served generally within four years of the offence. A copy must be served on the owner and on the occupier of the land and on any other persons having a sufficient interest. The period for compliance must be reasonable, but development may be stopped on three days' notice by an interim "stop notice" (section 183). An appeal against a notice may be made to the Secretary of State and the appeal is deemed also to be an application for planning permission in respect of the offending building or works (section 174). There is a further appeal to the High Court on a point of law. If the enforcement notice takes effect and the required steps are not taken then the local planning authority may itself carry out the work and recover the cost from the land owner. The owner is also liable to a fine. The wrongful exercise of enforcement controls or stop orders will entitle the injured developer to compensation.

Compensation

Since permission to develop land has such a direct influence on its value it is obviously right that a measure of redress should be provided for those who suffer loss through planning restrictions. Redress may be available in one of two ways. First, if planning restrictions prevent or hamper development or cause depreciation in the value of the land, compensation may be payable in a limited number of cases. Such restrictions may take the form of a refusal of planning consent or may arise from the exercise of powers, such as those to revoke or modify an existing consent or to order removal of an existing building (sections 97, 102). Compensation may also be payable where land value drops as a result of the future possibility of compulsory purchase.

Secondly, when planning permission is refused, or granted subject to conditions, the owner may in some cases require his land to be purchased by the local authority. But this is possible only if the land is virtually useless in its existing state.

The discussion above has been concerned principally with building and construction works. The 1990 Act also contains provisions relating to trees, waste land and advertisements. Buildings of special architectural or historic interest are covered by the Planning (Listed Buildings and Conservation Areas) Act 1990.

New town development

The concept of building new towns dates from the end of the Second World War when the policy of rebuilding devastated city centres produced an excess of population which needed to be rehoused. New towns were seen as the only alternative to continued urban sprawl. The main Act currently in force is the New Towns Act 1981.

The first step in creating a new town is the designation of the area by the Minister. In some cases this has been virgin land but more usually an existing small town is chosen as a nucleus. Before designating a site the Minister will consult local authorities in the area, and if any person or body objects to the site chosen a public local inquiry must be held. However, after considering the objections, the Minister may properly override them and make his decision on the grounds of policy: see *Franklin's* case above.

The development of a new town will be undertaken by an ad hoc authority called a development corporation. This is a corporate body consisting of a number of persons selected by the Minister, and having statutory objects and powers. The purpose of the corporation is to prepare proposals for the development of the new town and to secure their implementation. The corporation does not displace the local planning authority, but is absolved from the normal requirements for obtaining planning consents.

To achieve their purposes, development corporations are invested with wide powers. These include acquisition of land (by compulsory purchase if necessary), carrying out building or other operations, provision of services, and carrying on any business or undertaking for the purposes of the new town. However, the Minister retains a general power of control over any of the powers of the development corporation. Further, a corporation may not undertake, *inter alia*, the supply of water, electricity or gas without first obtaining specific powers to do so.

A new town development corporation is intended to have a limited life. When the laying out and development of a new town has been substantially achieved the corporation will be wound up and its property transferred to the Commission for New Towns, although since 1976 the Secretary of State has had powers to transfer dwellings and associated property to the district council for the area.

ENVIRONMENT LAW

This term applies to a group of topics formerly existing under titles such as public health. In some areas, the law existed solely as private rights between individuals, for example, under the law of nuisance. There has been a growing trend towards the creation of wider powers and controls over the use of land and the environment, and increasingly this has taken the form of administrative powers exercisable by public authorities. This has naturally relegated the role of the individual to that of requesting public authorities to exercise their powers, and in appropriate cases of seeking public law remedies where the individual is affected (see further page 33).

Much of the modern structure of environment law goes back to the Public Health Acts enacted over the last hundred years and particularly to the massive Act of 1936 (much of which is still in force). This Act dealt with matters such as domestic water supply and sewerage, collection of refuse, provision of recreation grounds and many other topics. Substantial amendments were made in the Public Health Act 1961, which contains provisions dealing with sanitation and trade effluent. A major environmental impact resulted from the Clean Air Act 1956, which controls the omission of smoke and other effluent from both industrial and domestic premises. This Act had a dramatic effect on pollution in all urban communities. The other major piece of legislation on the topic is the Control of Pollution Act 1974.

Because environment law is a comparatively new concept, there is, as yet, little case law. The following section concentrates on two topics: the control of noise on building sites and the available enforcement procedure; and the use and abuse of water. In each area, the courts have made some progress in considering the relevant legislation.

At the time of writing, there is before Parliament a new Environment Protection Bill which is intended to make far-reaching changes in the field of environment law. The bill seeks to establish a new integrated approach to pollution control, to be operated by the Inspectorate of Pollution. In regard to less serious pollution, new functions are placed on local authorities; and in regard to waste disposal, local authorities are given new powers and duties. In some areas, including Greater London, new waste authorities are created.

The bill provides for amendment and replacement of Part I of the Control of Pollution Act 1974 with extended controls over waste. There are other provisions for dealing with statutory nuisances and new measures to deal with litter.

Control of noise

The Control of Pollution Act has specific application to noise on construction sites. Under section 60 of the Act the relevant local authority is empowered to serve a notice imposing requirements as to the way in which the works are to be carried out. The Act makes the following provisions about notice:

"60(3) The notice may in particular—

(a) specify the plant or machinery which is or is not to be used;

(b) specify the hours during which the works may be carried out;

(c) specify the level of noise which may be omitted from the premises in question or at any specified point on those premises or which may be so omitted during specified hours; and

(d) provide for any change of circumstances."

Section 60(5) requires the notice to be served on the person who appears to be carrying out or going to carry out the works and on others who appear to be responsible for or have control over the works. The recipient may appeal the notice to a magistrates' court; otherwise, it becomes an offence to contravene any requirement of the notice "without reasonable excuse." Section 61 of the Act makes provision for obtaining prior consent of the local authority to work which is to be carried out. This is a useful device if the contractor needs to know whether he will be permitted to use particular plant and machinery, and if so during what hours. Although the Act uses only the term "noise," this is defined as including vibration.

Enforcement proceedings

Where contravention of a notice occurs, the local authority may prosecute the contractor who, in the event of conviction, will be liable to a fine, currently being a maximum of £2,000, together with a further fine of £50 for each day the offence continues after conviction. If the offences are serious or repeated, consideration may need to be given to other action. This is particularly so where the contractor is under financial or other pressure to continue with the work in contravention of the notice. In such a case, the local authority may invoke the civil jurisdiction of the court to grant an injunction to restrain further contravention of the notice. If granted, any further contravention of the injunction would be punishable by all the means available to the court, including imprisonment. The circumstances in which the local authority can take this step is, therefore, of general interest, because it applies in many other areas where a local authority is charged with the proper administration of the law. One example is the proper administration of planning law, which has given rise to a number of cases where there have been flagrant breaches of the law relating to caravan sites, tree preservation orders, and the like. If the relevant enforcement notices have been issued and are being ignored, despite criminal proceedings and the imposition of (modest) fines, the local authority may need to take sterner action. Another example is Sunday trading, where fines which can be imposed even for persistent and intentional breaches of the law, are trivial compared to the profits made from illegal trading.

The legal basis for action in these circumstances by the local authority is section 222 of the Local Government Act 1972, which empowers the local authority to take action in their own name where this is expedient "for the promotion or protection of the interests of the inhabitants of their area." In resolving to take such action, the local authority is exercising a public law power, and as such is liable to control through judicial review if it acts improperly (see page 33). Further, in deciding whether or not to grant an injunction, the court has to consider whether it is appropriate to grant this civil remedy in aid of enforcement of the criminal law, which provides its own remedy. Thus, over a number of cases, the courts have evolved principles upon which an injunction will be granted. These matters were considered by the Court of Appeal in *City of London* v. *Bovis* (1988), where the City were seeking an injunction to restrain further breaches of a notice served under section 60 of the Control of Pollution Act. Bingham L.J. stated that the guiding principles were:

1. that the jurisdiction was to be invoked and exercised exceptionally and with great caution;
2. there must be something more than mere infringement of the criminal law; and
3. the court must conclude that the defendants' unlawful operations would continue unless restrained by injunction.

Bingham L.J. also summarised the alternative courses of action that might have been open:

> "Any individual resident of Petticoat Square could have sued in private nuisance. The Attorney General could have sued in public nuisance either *ex officio* or on the relation of the local authority or a resident of Petticoat Square. The local authority could have sued in their own name for a public nuisance by virtue on section 222 of the Local Government Act 1972 if they considered it expedient for the protection of the interests of the inhabitants of their area. . . . As it was none of these procedures was invoked. Instead, the local authority decided . . . to issue summonses under section 60(8) alleging contraventions of the section 60 notice."

A point argued in the *Bovis* case was whether a Construction Manager under a form of contract providing for work to be carried out by trade contractors, should be regarded as the appropriate person for service and enforcement of a notice under section 60. Sub-section (5) provides:

> "A notice under this section shall be served on the person who appears to the local authority to be carrying out or going to carry out the works and on such other persons appearing to the local authority to be responsible for or to have control over the carrying out of the works as the local authority thinks fit."

The Court of Appeal had no doubt that a Construction Manager came within the section and was properly to be held accountable for breaches of the notice. The categories under section 60(5) were not mutually exclusive, and it was sufficient that Bovis under their contract (and under parallel provisions in the trade contracts) were given control of the building operations. Where there is any doubt about the person responsible, the local authority has power under section 93 of the Act to serve notice requiring information. This may allow the authority, for example, to obtain copies of relevant commercial documents which will establish who is in control for the purpose of noise abatement.

Water, use and abuse

Water-borne pollution may be seen as one of the most serious problems which environment law has to tackle. Off-shore and deep-sea pollution are matters for international law and treaty;

but inland and coastal waters are subject to close statutory control of their use.

A land owner who borders a watercourse is known as a "riparian owner" and he normally owns the land up to the middle of the stream. At common law the riparian owner is entitled to the use of flowing water for ordinary purposes such as domestic use. He may also use the water for an extraordinary purpose such as manufacturing or irrigation, provided the water is returned in the same volume and character to the stream. However, there are very stringent statutory controls on the right to abstract water from any source of supply, whether it be a watercourse or a well or bore-hole, for other than domestic purposes: see Water Resources Act 1963, Part IV.

The question as to what persons are entitled to put into water is strictly controlled by the Control of Pollution Act 1974, Part II, re-enacting earlier statutes. Under this Act it is an offence, punishable by fines or imprisonment, to cause or knowingly to permit pollution of a river or coastal waters. Where the offender is a corporate body an officer of that body (such as a director or manager) may also be liable. A manufacturer was held liable for causing pollution of a river, even though he had taken elaborate precautions to prevent it and accidental spillage occurred only because of a defect in the apparatus: *Alphacell Ltd.* v. *Woodward* (1972). In this case, the House of Lords considered whether an offence under the Act was committed by a person who had no knowlege of the fact that pollution was occurring and had not been negligent. Lord Dilhorne held:

> "Here, the acts done by the appellants were intentional. They were acts calculated to lead to the river being polluted if the acts done by the appellants, the installation and operation of the pumps, were ineffective to prevent it. Where a person intentionally does certain things which produce a certain result, then it can truly be said that he has caused that result, and here in my opinion the acts done intentionally by the appellants caused the pollution."

Further Reading

Encyclopedia of Planning Law and Practice, Heap.
Heap, *An Outline of Planning Law* (10th ed., 1991).
Megarry, *Manual of the Law of Real Property* (6th ed., 1982).

CHAPTER 15

CONSTRUCTION STATUTES

CONTRACTS under which work is carried out in the construction industry are affected directly by few statutory provisions. However, matters such as the design of the works and the mode of carrying out operations are likely to be subject to many statutory controls. These may impose obligations on one or more of the parties involved. A breach of such an obligation may give rise to statutory penal sanctions and also to consequences at civil law, in tort or for breach of contract (see JCT, clause 6 and ICE, clause 26).

The more directly relevant statutes which affect the construction industry include the Public Health Acts 1936 and 1961, the Health and Safety at Work Act 1974, the various planning Acts and the Building Act 1984. There are also a number of statutes which apply only to London, which include the three Acts known as the London Building Acts. Many of the Acts referred to contain powers for the creation of further delegated legislation in the form of regulations or by-laws, which lay down detailed provisions.

In this chapter three types of statutory provision are discussed, which are of importance to construction work. First, the Building Regulations, which govern the design and construction of building works. Secondly, a brief account is given of the law relating to highways, which is primarily governed by statute. Thirdly, statutory provisions relating to health and safety are described.

BUILDING REGULATIONS

Statutory provisions relating to building regulations are now consolidated into the Building Act 1984, which applies throughout England and Wales, including the Inner London

Area. Before 1965 the design and construction of buildings was regulated by by-laws made under the Public Health Acts by individual local authorities. There were variations between different authorities, but latterly provisions became based on model by-laws issued by central government. In 1965 the first set of Building Regulations applying throughout England and Wales was issued. These have been amended periodically. The provisions now in force are the Building Regulations 1985.

The current regulations are shorter than previous Building Regulations, and are so expressed that rigid enforcement is discouraged. The intentions are that the new regulations will be interpreted so as to achieve reasonable standards of health or safety. A particular innovation in the Building Act 1984 is the use of "approved documents" under section 6. The effect of such documents is defined by section 7 as follows:

> "(1) A failure on the part of a person to comply with an approved document does not of itself render him liable to any civil or criminal proceedings; but if, in any proceedings whether civil or criminal, it is alleged that a person has at any time contravened a provision of building regulations—
>
> (a) a failure to comply with a document that at that time was approved for the purposes of that provision may be relied upon as tending to establish liability, and
>
> (b) proof of compliance with such a document may be relied on as tending to negative liability."

Powers and duties of the local authority in regard to passing or rejection of plans are set out in section 16 of the Building Act 1984. In addition, the new regulations contain detailed provisions as to notices and forms. There are, however, provisions by which Building Regulation compliance or approval may be secured other than by a decision of the local authority. These are:

(i) Under section 17 of the Building Act 1984, "approved persons" may be designated to give a certificate of compliance with Building Regulations. Such a person must also provide evidence of insurance arrangements complying with regulations; alternatively there may be an "approved scheme" to provide insurance.

(ii) Under sections 12 and 13 of the Building Act 1984, there may be approvals of any type of "building matter," i.e. any matter to which the Building Regulations are applicable. Such approvals may be made with or without specific application (note that this provision is yet to be brought into effect).

Content and application of new regulations

As well as being comparatively short, the new regulations are differently arranged from previous Building Regulations, and are as follows: A, Structure; B, Fire; C, Site preparation and resistance to moisture; D, Toxic substances; E, Resistance to the passage of sound; F, Ventilation; G, Hygiene; H, Drainage and waste disposal; J, Heat producing appliances; K, Stairways, ramps and guards; L, Conservation of fuel and power. These matters are set out in schedule 1 of the regulations and are referred to as "Requirements." This is followed by schedule 2: Facilities for disabled people; and schedule 3: Exempt buildings and work.

These technical requirements are preceded by numbered regulations which set out the application of the technical provisions. Thus, regulation 4 requires that the building work should be carried out so that it complies with the relevant requirements of schedules 1 and 2. As regards extension to or alteration of an existing building, regulation 4(2) requires that it shall not be adversely affected in relation to compliance with schedule 1 (that is, there is no obligation to bring the whole building up to current regulations).

The regulations apply, *inter alia*, to the erection or extension of a building or to a material alteration (regulation 3). Control is also imposed on a material change of use, defined by regulation 5 as including changing to use as a dwelling, the creation of a flat within a building or changing a building for use as an hotel or public building. Regulation 6 sets out requirements that apply to a material change of use.

In addition to the technical requirements, regulation 7 makes a general requirement that any building work shall be carried out "with proper materials and in a workmanlike manner," thus reflecting similar obligations which would arise by implied terms in a construction contract, or by statute, for example, the Defective Premises Act 1972, or the Supply of Goods and Services Act 1982. However, there is a general limitation on application of the technical requirements in that regulation 8 provides that no obligation imposed by Parts A to K of schedule 1, or by regulation 7 is to require anything to be done "beyond what is necessary to secure reasonable standards of health and safety for persons in or about the building or others who may be affected. . . ."

The regulations do not apply in a number of circumstances. Schedule 3 lists buildings and works which are exempt from the regulations, including buildings not frequented by people, temporary buildings, greenhouses and agricultural buildings. The technical requirements set out in schedule 1 are accompanied by notes stating the limits beyond which the requirements are not applicable.

Notices and compliance with new regulations

A person who intends to carry out building work must submit to the local authority either a "building notice" containing the particulars specified in regulation 12, or he may at his option submit "full plans" complying with regulation 13. Alternatively, there may be compliance instead with the "approved persons" procedure (see above). Full plans are required where the work concerns means of escape, and the Fire Precautions Act 1971 applies (regulation 11(2)). By section 16 of the Building Act 1984, the authority must pass or reject the submitted plans within a period of five weeks, which may be extended by agreement to two months. Where plans are defective or show a contravention the authority may, as an alternative to rejection, pass the plans subject to conditions requiring modification and further deposit of plans.

In addition to obtaining approval under the regulations, a person intending to carry out building work must give notice at various stages of the work. These include notice 48 hours before commencement of the works, 24 hours before covering up a foundation or damp-proof course, etc., 24 hours before covering a drain and seven days after completing drain work (regulation 14(1)). In addition, notice must be given within seven days of completion of building work (regulation 14(5)). During the course of work, the local authority may exercise a right to make tests on drains (regulation 15), or to take samples of materials (regulation 16), to establish compliance with the requirements of the regulations.

Building regulations in London

Historically, London has had its own statutes and building control system, with features differing materially from those applying to the rest of England and Wales. For this purpose, London means the 12 inner London boroughs. Powers to introduce a uniform system throughout England and Wales, including London, were contained in the Building Act 1984. Shortly after issuing the new Building Regulations in 1985, a statutory instrument known as the Building (Inner London) Regulations 1985 applied these building regulations to the inner London area, with comparatively minor provisions where the application of regulations in London differs. The former building control system in London was contained partly in three statutes known as the London Building Acts, being the Acts of 1930 and 1935 and the London Building Acts (Amendment) Act 1939. Parts of these Acts still remain in force, applying only to the inner London area. These parts relate primarily to precautions against fire, dangerous structures and party walls.

CIVIL LIABILITY

The Public Health Acts, the Building Act and Building Regulations are enforced primarily through the criminal law. But the regulations are frequently incorporated into building contracts so that failure to comply will be a breach by the builder. The JCT and ICE forms of contract contain general obligations to comply with statutory provisions (see clauses 6 and 26 respectively) which include the regulations. A provision for imposing general civil liability for breach of a duty imposed by Building Regulations was contained in section 71 of the Health and Safety at Work Act (1974), now section 38 of the Building Act 1984. Neither provision has been brought into effect.

During the 1970s and 1980s there were many cases before the courts where local authorities and builders were held liable for failing to ensure compliance with Building Regulations, under the law of tort. These decisions were all based on the case of *Anns* v. *London Borough of Merton* (1977), which has now been overruled in *Murphy* v. *Brentwood D.C.* (1990) (see page 335 and Chapter 13 generally). In regard to the liability of local authorities, the leading cases of *Peabody* v. *Sir Lindsay Parkinson* (1985) and *Investors in Industry Ltd.* v. *South Beds D.C.* (1986), established limitations on the circumstances in which a local authority would be held to owe a duty of care to a subsequent owner or occupier of a building for the purpose of bringing an action against the local authority. Now, the *Murphy* case has ruled that liability in tort is, with a few exceptions, limited to cases where the plaintiff has suffered actual injury or damage to person or property. Where a building is found to be defective, but has not yet caused injury to person or property, money spent in repairing the building must be regarded as purely economic loss, not normally recoverable under the law of tort. In the

Murphy case the House of Lords left open the question whether the local authority owed any duty at all. In the result, it is unlikely that circumstances will arise in which a local authority is liable for permitting work to be carried out in breach of Building Regulations, in the absence of actual physical injury. As regards builders, there is less difficulty in establishing a duty of care to future owners or occupiers. But here again, there will be no general liability for economic loss. Effectively a whole chapter of litigation has been closed by the *Murphy* decision and the principal right of redress outside the field of contract, will be under the Defective Premises Act 1972 (see above page 138).

HIGHWAYS

This section illustrates the operation of statute law in a particular area, which is of importance both to those involved in highway construction and in other fields of construction, such as housing development. The principal governing legislation is now the Highways Act 1980, which consolidates and amends a number of previous Acts. The Act does not attempt to define the term "highway," this being a term of some antiquity and of importance under the common law, for example in relation to the acquisition of rights of passage. Generally, a highway is a defined way over land which is exercisable by the public in general, although the right of use may be limited to particular classes of traffic. Highways thus range from country footpaths and suburban culs-de-sac to motorways. The 1980 Act provides that a bridge or tunnel over or through which a highway passes is to be taken as part of the highway (section 328(2)).

Rights and duties

Questions that arise in relation to construction projects are: who owns or is responsible for a highway? In particular, who is responsible for maintenance? What rights and duties exist in regard to services or apparatus under a highway? The first question raises interesting issues about rights and easements (see page 367) as opposed to legal ownership. There are many possibilities which depend on the way in which the highway was created. There is a general presumption that the owner of land adjoining a highway also owns the soil, and all other rights that go with ownership, up to the middle line of the road. The highway built over the land is in law no more than a right of passage, together with such rights and obligations as are necessary for maintenance and operation as a highway. These rights and obligations are vested by statute in a "highway authority" who will usually be either a county council or central government, acting through the relevant Minister of State. Some minor highway functions are vested in district councils and there are other exceptions.

A highway authority is generally responsible for the construction, maintenance and improvement of highways. A local highway authority may undertake work on behalf of the Minister, either pursuant to an agency agreement or by the provision of services. Different local highway authorities may make agreements between themselves for the carrying out of their functions.

The creation and designation of major roads falls into two categories. Trunk roads, as defined under section 10 of the Highways Act 1980, are intended to form a network of routes for through traffic, relieved of local traffic. This was the main national road network up to the 1950s. Section 16 of the Act deals with a category known as Special Roads, which include motorways. The creation of a Special Road requires a scheme to be drawn up by the proposed authority, being either the Minister or the local highway authority, and the Act lays down detailed provisions for publication and enquiry before confirmation of the scheme.

Adoption of highways

Builders and developers of housing and industrial estates often construct road systems to serve the new buildings. When the buildings have been sold or leased off, the question arises who is to undertake responsibility for continuing maintenance of the new roads? This may go beyond mere resurfacing, as the new highways may include earthworks and structures, including bridges. The same question arises in relation to new sewers constructed to serve an estate.

There is no reason why the developer or the purchasers of the building should not keep the road in their own private ownership and at their own expense. However, a convenient alternative is provided by the Highways Act 1980. Section 38 provides that the highway authority may enter into an agreement with the person responsible for maintenance. The terms of the agreement (colloquially known as a "section 38 agreement") usually provide for the road to be constructed and completed to the highway authority's standard specification or satisfaction, and for the highway then to become a public highway maintained at the expense of the authority. Similar provisions apply to new sewers, which may become vested in the relevant water authority under section 18 of the Public Health Act 1936.

Street works

Many highways, particularly in urban areas, carry services belonging to public utilities, such as gas, electricity, water, sewerage, telephones and others. This gives rise to many potential problems when the services are installed or need repair. Excavations give rise to questions of reinstatement and repair of the carriageway, as well as the possibility of damage to other services. These matters are dealt with in the Public Utilities Streetworks Act 1950. The workings of the Act have given rise to certain problems which were the subject of a review chaired by Professor M. R. Horne "Roads and the Utilities," produced in 1985. Although the report made a substantial number of recommendations, these have not yet been implemented.

The 1950 Act (PUSWA) is in four parts. Part I together with schedules 1–3 contain "the streetworks code" which makes uniform provision for works in streets by public utilities. Part II provides a similar code to govern relations between utilities and authorities promoting road works which affect services of the utilities. Part III contains procedures to be applied when works of one utility affect the services of another; and Part IV contains provision for enforcement and the arbitration of disputes arising under the Act. Section 31 provides that in any such arbitration, in default of agreement, the arbitrator is to be appointed by the President of the Institution of Civil Engineers.

PUSWA is dealt with expressly under the ICE conditions, clause 27. This requires the employer, before commencement of the works, to notify the contractor whether the works are such that the Act will apply. The employer is generally required to serve notices (and to obtain relevant approvals). The contractor is required only to give notice to the employer before commencing work. However, in relation to the carrying out of the work, the contractor is required by clause 27(7) to comply with obligations under PUSWA and to indemnify the employer against any failure. Reinstatement and making good after execution of works is dealt with in detail in the third schedule of PUSWA, and these obligations are reflected in clause 49(5) of the ICE conditions.

HEALTH AND SAFETY

This section deals with operations on construction sites, and the safety of those engaged on the work. Construction is notoriously dangerous, not through the callous attitude of employers, but usually because workmen take unnecessary risks. This may be seen as a failure by those in control to impose safety requirements on those working on sites. Statistics show that in 1988, 157 workers were killed in construction accidents, and over 20,000 injured.

As between employer and employee, there is a clear duty of care (see page 344), and it is of little importance whether this is regarded as arising in tort or in contract, since the damages for personal injury will be recoverable either way. However, historically there has been considerable statutory intervention aimed at providing positive protection for workers, formerly through the Factories Acts and currently through the Health and Safety at Work Act 1974. The 1974 Act created the new Health and Safety Executive, whose inspectors administer the Act and its detailed regulations. These provisions apply throughout industry, but there are particular regulations applying to construction work.

Health and Safety at Work Act 1974

The Health and Safety Executive operates under the direction of the Health and Safety Commission, which is itself charged with the overall duty of achieving the purposes of Part I of the Act, which are to secure the health, safety and welfare of persons at work (section 1(1)). The Commission may order investigations or enquiries into accidents, which may be carried out by the Executive itself or by others. Enforcement of the Act and its regulations is carried out through inspectors.

The Act creates general duties on employers to ensure, so far as is reasonably practicable, the health, safety and welfare at work of employees (section 2). A similar duty is placed on employers and self-employed persons to ensure, so far as reasonably practicable, that other persons are not exposed to risks to health or safety (section 3). Persons having control of premises must ensure, so far as is reasonably practicable, that the premises are safe and without risk to health (section 4).

Powers available to inspectors include the right to enter premises to make examination and investigation, to take samples, and to require the production of documents and information (section 20). Where there is a contravention, the inspector may serve an "Improvement Notice" (section 21); and where the contravention involves the risks of serious personal injury, he may give a "Prohibition Notice," which may have immediate effect (section 22). The Act provides penalties for breach of its provisions and for other offences.

Civil liability

The Health and Safety at Work Act does not itself confer any civil right of action (section 47(1)). However, a breach of safety regulations may give rise to civil liability, and there are many cases in which the courts have held employers liable on this basis, either in addition to or as an alternative to liability in tort (see page 344).

To succeed in a civil action for breach of a regulation it must be shown that: (i) the regulation was intended to protect a class of which the plaintiff was a member; (ii) the regulation was broken; (iii) he has suffered damage of a kind against which the regulation was intended to protect; and (iv) the damage was caused by the breach.

These requirements may appear self-evident, but their effect in practice may be less than obvious. Thus, in a number of cases it has been held that self-employed workmen were not entitled to the protection of the Construction Regulations. Instead of having a right of action in respect of their injuries, self-employed men may themselves be liable to prosecution for breach of the regulations. However, the Court of Appeal has now laid down that the question whether a man is employed or self-employed is to be approached broadly. The fact that he pays his own income tax is not decisive: *Ferguson* v. *John Dawson & Partners* (1976). In this case a roofing worker was employed expressly as a "self-employed labour only sub-contractor." Despite this, the court found that the reality of the relationship created was that of employer and employee. Megaw L.J. observed:

> "The parties cannot transfer a statute-imposed duty of care for safety of workmen from an employer to the workman himself merely because the parties agree, in effect, that the workman shall be deemed to be self-employed, where the true essence of the contract is, otherwise, of a contract of service."

The kinds of damage against which the Construction Regulations are intended to protect include personal injuries, but not, for example, loss of earnings due to unsafe scaffolding preventing work. The damage must also be caused by the breach. Thus, where a workman was killed in a fall because he did not wear a safety belt, it was found that the contractor, in breach of regulations, failed to provide belts for the men. But the contractor showed that the deceased would not have worn a belt even if it had been provided, and consequently was held not liable in civil law for damages: *Cummings* v. *Arrol* (1962). Viscount Kilmuir observed, in this case, that:

> "The necessity, in actions by employees against their employers on the grounds of negligence, of establishing not only the breach of duty but also the causal connection between the breach and the injury complained of is, in my view, part of the law of both England and Scotland."

Safety regulations

Detailed regulation governing day-to-day activities on construction sites have been issued and amended periodically. The principal regulations presently in force were issued before the Health and Safety at Work Act, although they now take effect under it. These are the Construction (General Provisions) Regulations and the Construction (Lifting Operations) Regulations, both of 1961; and the Construction (Working Places) Regulations and the Construction (Health and Welfare) Regulations, both of 1966. In more recent years there has been considerable discussion about placing increased responsibility upon contractors through contract terms. The latest proposals made by the Health and Safety Commission are for employers to be required to appoint a safety adviser on practically all construction sites, and for designers to be required to design with a view to the work being carried out safely, including maintenance and repair, and to provide information about design aspects relevant to safety. In addition, the European Commission has issued a Directive on construction site safety which may lead to further safety measures being required in the UK.

Further Reading

Building Regulations, *Encyclopedia of Environmental Health Law and Practice*, Cross.
Health and Safety Act and Construction Regulations, *Redgrave's Health and Safety in Factories* (1980), Fife and Machin.

GLOSSARY OF LEGAL TERMS

ADJOURN: To put off the hearing of a case or matter to a later date.

AFFIDAVIT: A written statement sworn on oath which may be used in certain cases as evidence.

AGENT: A person with authority to act for another (the principal).

APPELLANT: The party who brings an appeal to a higher court.

APPEARANCE: Acknowledgment, by the *defendant* in a civil action, of the *writ* or *summons*.

ARBITRATION: Proceedings before a private tribunal to which the parties agree to submit disputes.

ASSETS: Property which is available for paying debts.

ASSIGNMENT: The transmission by agreement of a right or interest to another person.

ATTESTATION: Authentication of a document by the signatures of witnesses.

AWARD: The decision given by an arbitrator.

BAILMENT: Delivery of goods into the possession of a person who is not their owner.

BANKRUPT: A person who cannot pay his debts and who is adjudicated a *bankrupt*.

BAR: The profession of barristers from which practically all judges are recruited.

BREACH: Non-fulfilment of some contractual (or other) obligation.

BY-LAWS: Rules, usually made under statutory authority and having full force of law.

CASE STATED: A statement of facts prepared by a court or arbitrator for the decision of a higher court on a point of law.

CAVEAT EMPTOR: "Let the buyer beware"; a maxim indicating that any risk is upon the buyer and not the seller.

CHANCERY: One of the three divisions of the *High Court*.

CHARGE: An interest, usually over land, given as security.

CHATTELS: Personal property.

CHOSE IN ACTION: An intangible right which can be enforced by action; such as a debt.

CLAIMANT: The party who initiates *arbitration* proceedings.

COMMERCIAL COURT: A special court in the *Queen's Bench* Division for dealing with commercial actions.

COMMON LAW: Law embodied in case precedent as opposed to *Statute* law or *Equity*.

CONDITION: An important term of a *contract*.

CONSIDERATION: The bargain or inducement provided by a party to a *contract*.

CONSOLIDATION: Joining of two separate actions so that they may be tried together.

CONTRACT: An agreement which is binding in law.

CONVEYANCE: A written instrument which transfers property (especially land) from one person to another.

COUNTERCLAIM: A cross action brought by the *defendant* against the *plaintiff*, or by the *respondent* against the *claimant*.

COUNTY COURTS: Local courts which deal with smaller civil claims.

COURT OF APPEAL: The court which hears appeals from (*inter alia*) the *High Court* and *county courts*.

COVENANT: An undertaking contained in a document, especially in a *deed* or *lease*.

CROWN COURT: The branch of the *Supreme Court* which deals with criminal trials (and also some civil cases).

DAMAGES: The money award made to a successful party in a civil action.

DEED: A written instrument, signed, *sealed* and delivered.

DEFENCE: A pleading from the *defendant* in answer to the *Statement of Claim*.

DEFENDANT: The person sued in an ordinary civil action.

DETINUE: An action in *tort* for recovery of a specific *chattel*.

DISCOVERY: Disclosure of all the documents relating to a case, before the trial.

DOMICILE: The country or state with which a person or company is most closely connected.

EASEMENT: A right enjoyed over land belonging to another person.

EQUITY: Law based upon discretion and conscience, derived from the old Court of Chancery.

ESTATE: General term for an interest in land.

EX PARTE: By one side only, for example, an application *ex parte* for an *injunction*.

EXECUTION: Methods of enforcement of a *judgment* in an action.

EXHIBIT: A document used in evidence, especially when annexed to an *affidavit*.

FI FA: Abbreviation of *Fieri Facias*; *execution* of a *judgment* by seizing and selling the debtor's goods.

FORCE MAJEURE: Irresistible compulsion; especially such as to cause breach of *contract*, such as war or Act of God.

FORFEITURE: A provision, especially in a *contract* or *lease*, enabling one party to strip the other of his whole interest in certain events; for example, determination of a building contract.

FRUSTRATION: Determination of a *contract* by some intervening event, such as destruction of the subject matter.

GARNISHEE: A person against whom a *judgment* debt is enforced by ordering him to pay a debt owed to the debtor to the judgment creditor instead.

GENERAL DAMAGES: Unascertained *damages*, to be assessed by the judge.

GENERAL INDORSEMENT: A brief description of the plaintiff's claim *indorsed* on the *writ*; a full *statement of claim* must then be served separately.

HEARSAY: Testimony by a witness as to a matter not within his personal knowledge.

HIGH COURT: The principal court in which civil actions are heard at first instance.

HOUSE OF LORDS: The highest court of England and Scotland.

INCORPOREAL: Rights and interests which are intangible are said to be incorporeal, such as debts or shares in a company.

INDORSEMENT: Something written on the back of a document, such as the claim indorsed on a *writ*.

INJUNCTION: An order of the court which commands a person to do or refrain from doing some act.

INNS OF COURT: The four societies of Inner and Middle Temple, Lincoln's Inn and Gray's Inn. Every barrister must be a member of one of the Inns.

INTERIM: Provisional, until further direction, for example, an *interim* order.

INTERLOCUTORY: A matter dealt with before the trial of an action; such as an *interlocutory injunction*.

INTERROGATORIES: Questions formally put in writing by one party to another, before the trial of a civil action.

JOINT: Where two or more persons share some right or obligation such that their interest is not severed, each having an interest in the whole, for example, a *joint* tenancy or account.

JUDGMENT: The order given by a court after hearing a case.

JURISDICTION: Authority of a court or arbitrator to hear and determine causes, thus, the *county court jurisdiction* is limited financially and geographically.

KING'S BENCH: A division of the *High Court*, called *Queen's Bench* when the sovereign is female.

LAW REPORTS: Authenticated reports of decided cases in the superior courts.

LAW SOCIETY: The governing body of English solicitors.

LEASE: A letting or demise of land; also the instrument containing the demise and its covenants.

LEGAL AID: A system for providing free or assisted legal advice or representation, for persons of slender means.

LICENCE: An authority, especially to enter land without having exclusive possession.

LIEN: A right to retain possession of some article until a claim by the holder is satisfied.

LIMITATION: Statutory periods within which actions must be commenced.

LIQUIDATED DAMAGES: Ascertained or calculated monetary loss claimed in an action. *Also* a sum provided by a *contract* as payable in the event of breach, which is not deemed to be a *penalty*.

LIQUIDATION: Winding up of a company.

LORD JUSTICE OF APPEAL: Title of a judge of the *Court of Appeal*.

LORD OF APPEAL IN ORDINARY: Title of a judge in the *House of Lords* or *Privy Council*; commonly called a "Law Lord."

MASTER: An official of the *High Court* who decides many *interlocutory* matters.

MITIGATION: Abatement of loss or damage.

MORTGAGE: A *conveyance*, *assignment* or *lease* of property as security for a loan.

MUTATIS MUTANDIS: With the necessary changes.

NEGLIGENCE: Conduct falling short of the duty of care owed to persons generally.

NUISANCE: Unlawful interference with the use or enjoyment of another person's land.

OBITER DICTUM: Statement of a judge on a point not directly relevant to his decision and therefore not strictly of authority.

OFFICIAL REFEREE: A judge who tries technical cases in the *Queen's Bench* Division of the *High Court*.

OFFICIAL SOLICITOR: An officer of the *Supreme Court* who acts for persons under a disability.

PARI PASSU: In proportion; on an equal footing.

PARTICULARS: Details of some allegation pleaded in an action. If a pleading is insufficient the opponent may ask for further and better *Particulars*.

PARTNERSHIP: An unincorporated association of persons in business with a view to profit.

PENALTY: A sum provided by a *contract* as payable in the event of breach, which sum is not deemed to be *liquidated damages*.

PETITION: A document used to begin certain civil actions such as a divorce or a winding up.

PLAINTIFF: The party who begins an ordinary civil action.

PLEADING: A written statement of a party's case in a civil action.

POINTS OF CLAIM, DEFENCE: The title of pleadings in an *arbitration*.

PRESCRIPTION: A claim to some right, based upon long user.

PRIVY COUNCIL: The judicial committee of the *Privy Council* is the final court of appeal for some Commonwealth countries.

PROFIT À PRENDRE: A right to take something from another person's land.

PUISNE JUDGE: A judge of one of the divisions of the *High Court*, who should be referred to as Mr. Justice—.

QUEEN'S BENCH: One of the three divisions of the *High Court*.

QUEEN'S COUNSEL: A senior barrister, appointed by the Lord Chancellor. Q.C.'s are known coloquially as "silks" because they wear silk gowns.

QUANTUM MERUIT: An action claiming a reasonable price for work or goods.

RATIFICATION: Confirmation, for example, of a *contract*, so as to make it binding.

RATIO DECIDENDI: The relevant part of a judge's decision in a case, which is authoritative.

REAL PROPERTY: Certain interests and rights in land; as opposed to personal property.

RECTIFICATION: Correction by the court of a document so as to express the parties' true intention.

REPLY: A *pleading* from a *plaintiff* in answer to a *defendant's defence*.

REPUDIATION: An express or implied refusal by one party to perform his obligation under a *contract*.

RESPONDENT: The *defendant* in certain types of action, including an *arbitration*.

RIPARIAN OWNER: An owner of land bordering on a watercourse.

SEAL: An impressed piece of wax attached to a document so as to make it "under seal."

SEQUESTRATION: Order of the *High Court* to seize goods and lands of a *defendant* who is in contempt of court.

SET-OFF: Diminution or extinction of the *plaintiff's* claim in an action by deducting the *defendant's counterclaim*.

SEVERAL: Where two or more persons share an obligation so that it may be enforced in full against any one of them, independently.

SHERIFF: A local office of great antiquity. The present-day duties of a *Sheriff* in civil cases are principally the *execution* of *judgments*.

SIMPLE CONTRACT: A *contract* not under *seal*, whether oral or in writing.

SPECIAL DAMAGES: Ascertained or calculated monetary loss; as opposed to unascertained or *general damages*.

SPECIAL INDORSEMENT: A full *statement of claim indorsed* on a *writ*; as opposed to a *general indorsement*.

SPECIFIC PERFORMANCE: An equitable remedy whereby a person may be compelled to perform his obligation under a *contract*.

STATEMENT OF CLAIM: The plaintiff's initial *pleading* in an ordinary civil action in the *High Court* (followed by the *defence* and *reply*).

STATUTE: An Act of Parliament.

STATUTORY INSTRUMENT: A form of delegated legislation, which has full force of law.

SUBPOENA: An order requiring a person to appear in court and give evidence or produce documents.

SUBROGATION: The right to bring an action in the name of another person.

SUE: To take legal proceedings for a civil remedy.

SUMMONS: An order to appear before a judge or magistrate. Some civil actions are begun by an originating *summons*.

SUPREME COURT: The *High Court*, the *Court of Appeal* and the *Crown Court* are collectively known as the *Supreme Court* of Judicature.

TAXATION: Settlement by the Taxing *Master* (or in the *County Court*, the Registrar) of the amount payable by one party to the other as costs.

THIRD PARTY: A person not originally a party to an action, but who may be brought in by a *defendant*.

TORT: A civil wrong, independent of *contract* or breach of trust.

TRESPASS: A tortious injury to the person or goods of another, or an unwarrantable entry upon his land.

TRUST: A disposition of property to be held by trustees for the benefit of beneficiaries.

UBERRIMA FIDES: The utmost good faith, required in certain transactions, such as insurance contracts.

ULTRA VIRES: Beyond their powers; especially of a limited company or statutory body. The opposite of *intra vires*.

UNLIQUIDATED DAMAGES: Damages which cannot be calculated as a monetary loss, and which are assessed by the judge; such as damages for personal injury.

VACATION: The periods between legal terms, when the superior courts do not sit. There are four vacations in the year.

WARRANTY: A term of a *contract* which is not a *condition*; especially a statement by the vendor as to the quality of goods.

WITHOUT PREJUDICE: Correspondence in connection with a dispute, thus headed, is privileged and cannot be taken as implying any admission by the writer.

WRIT: A document used to begin an ordinary civil action. It must bear a *special* or a *general indorsement* of the *plaintiff's* claim.

INDEX